Portable Australian Authors

HAL PORTER

PORTABLE AUSTRALIAN AUTHORS

This series provides carefully selected volumes introducing major Australian writers and movements. The format is designed for compactness and for pleasurable reading. Each volume is intended to meet a need not hitherto met by any single book. Each is edited by an authority distinguished in his field, who adds an introductory essay and other helpful material.

General Editor: L.T. Hergenhan

Also in this Series:

Marcus Clarke edited by Michael Wilding
Henry Lawson edited by Brian Kiernan
Five Plays for Stage, Radio, and Television edited by Alrene Sykes
The 1890s: Stories, Verse, and Essays edited by Leon Cantrell
Rolf Boldrewood edited by Alan Brissenden
The Jindyworobaks edited by Brian Elliott
Barbara Baynton edited by Sally Krimmer and Alan Lawson

In Preparation:

Joseph Furphy edited by John Barnes
Henry Kingsley edited by Stan Mellick

*Portable
Australian Authors*

Hal Porter

*Selected and edited with an
Introduction and Bibliography by*

Mary Lord

University of Queensland Press

Published by University of Queensland Press, St Lucia, Queensland,
1980

©Hal Porter, 1958, 1980
Introduction ©Mary Lord, 1980

Phototypeset by Press Etching Pty. Ltd., Brisbane.
Printed and bound by Southwood Press Pty. Ltd., Sydney

Distributed in the United Kingdom, Europe, the Middle East, Africa,
and the Caribbean by Prentice-Hall International, International Book
Distributors Ltd, 66 Wood Lane End, Hemel Hempstead, Herts.,
England

National Library of Australia
Cataloguing-in-Publication data

Porter, Hal, 1911-
   Hal Porter.

   (Portable Australian authors)
   Bibliography
   ISBN 0 7022 1465 5
   ISBN 0 7022 1466 3 Paperback
   I. Lord, Mary. II. Title. (Series)

A828'.3

For Mollie and Herb Godbehear

Contents

Illustrations by Hal Porter

Acknowledgments

Almost all the material selected for this book, including *A Handful of Pennies,* was written with the support of the Literature Board of the Australia Council, or the earlier Commonwealth Literary Fund.

Acknowledgments are due to Faber and Faber Ltd for permission to reprint an extract from *The Watcher on the Cast-Iron Balcony*, to Macmillan (London and Basingstoke) and St Martin's Press (New York) for permission to include Porter's piece on Thomas Keneally from *Contemporary Novelists* (1972), to *Overland* where "The Jetty" and "The Author's Afterthoughts" first appeared, and to Hal Porter himself not only for permission to reprint the rest of the material here but for his help and advice in making the selection and for his unfailing patience.

My particular thanks are due to Mimi Colligan and Gail Ward of the Department of English, Monash University, who cheerfully helped in the often tedious and always unrewarding task of preparing the materials used in this collection.

Mary Lord

Introduction

Hal Porter is the "odd man out" of Australian letters. His career as a writer is in so many ways untypical of his generation that it is only possible to discuss him in terms of his own special strengths and weaknesses and not to place or rank him amongst his peers. He was born in the Melbourne suburb of Albert Park in 1911. His family moved to Bairnsdale in Gippsland when he was six and it was there that he went to school and spent his formative years. It was there that he formed his deep affection for the lush countryside about which he has frequently written and which he has sometimes drawn, and it was there, one suspects, that he developed the deep conservatism which most often emerges as satire in his writing. Hal Porter's stories, novels and plays generally attack what he sees as the complicated deceits of urban Australians, whether at home or abroad: these are opposed, by implication, against the simplicities of country life or childhood or irrecoverable past. What is certain is that the element of nostalgia in Porter's writing is not merely part of his frequently boasted "lack of fictional imagination", but an essential element in his talent as writer. He is an historian, in the finest sense of that word, of time, place, scene and event. He records us as he sees us — we may not like it, but that is not his business. He has never denied his fundamental provincialism but this is one of the things that sets him apart from most other Australian writers. Henry Lawson, for example, spent most of his life in the city (though he was born and grew up in the country) and wrote stories and ballads of the "bush" while living in Sydney.

Although Porter has travelled widely and has lived for

varying periods of time in different parts of Australia, it is the Victorian countryside to which he is most deeply attached and where he feels most at home. Since 1961, at the comparatively late age of fifty, when Porter decided to devote himself to full-time writing, he has lived and worked quietly in the country with occasional forays into the cities of Australia or trips overseas. At this stage in his career he had published little. A volume simply entitled *Short Stories* had been privately published in Adelaide in 1941 or 1942 in a limited edition, and a slim volume of poetry, *The Hexagon*, appeared in 1956. In 1957 he edited the anthology, *Australian Poetry 1957*, but his growing reputation as a writer rested mainly on his short stories which had begun to appear in the *Bulletin* during the 1950s. At the end of 1956 he received a grant from the Commonwealth Literary Fund to write his first novel, *A Handful of Pennies,* which is the major text in this volume. This was based on the two years Porter spent in Japan as a schoolmaster teaching the children of the Australian Occupation Forces, living as a civilian in an Officers' Mess, and getting to know the Japanese, their country, their customs, and something of their ancient culture and its traditions.

A Handful of Pennies received a mixed critical reception when it first appeared. It has not previously been reprinted, and has fallen into undeserved neglect. A number of reasons might be suggested for this, the most obvious being that reviewers of the time found its surface brilliance and verbal density baffling, if not impenetrable; in its stylistic uniqueness and degree of formal experimentation it could not be further removed from the mainstream of the Australian novel or, for that matter, from the modern novel generally. It does not have a central character in the usual sense but a group of characters who act out their separate dramas in occupied Japan immediately after the Second World War. Porter's central focus is reserved for his theme which is announced in the novel's opening sentences:

> Peace is his apparent twin but he is not Peace nor his twin. Nor is he War pale with truce and painted with smiles: his smiles are his own brushed on the eggshell of a face believed to be candid.

Name?
Name: Occupation-Democracy.
He is Delusion's son, the weak uncle, the sponsor of no
Christ but of guilds of Pontius Pilates.

It is not coincidental that "Occupation-Democracy" is personified in these sentences: Porter intentionally raises his
theme to the status of chief protagonist, masculine, and dangerous because deceived and deceiving. Although the novel
is set in occupied Japan, the setting does not so much provide the background as dominate the characters and the
action. In particular, the characters — a handful of pennies
— are victims of the delusion that "Occupation-
Democracy" means the introduction of democratic ideals
and attitudes into a feudal system which has been defeated
in war.

Porter's attitude to his theme and his satirical intention is
inescapable in these opening sentences. The use of "apparent" in "Peace is his apparent twin" implies that the
peace is not real or, at best, only a superficial peace; that
below the surface the hostility still exists between the recent
antagonists. This "Peace" is associated with "Delusion",
"weak uncle" suggesting childlessness and impotence, and
"Pontius Pilate" suggesting cowardice and hypocrisy. The
characters in *A Handful of Pennies*, although for the most
part they are carefully observed and meticulously recorded,
are in one sense puppets manipulated by the author to show
the futility and the shallowness of "Occupation-Democracy"
Both the Australians and the Japanese are victims of
the effects of the Australian Occupation Forces on the post-
war Japanese, the clashes between "victor and vanquished,
male and female . . . unorthodox and pagan, virgin and
sated, godless and god-ridden, adult and child, Western and
Oriental . . ." The central focus is on "Occupation-Democracy", especially its self-indulgences, weaknesses, sentimen-
talities, blindnesses, and barbarities, viewed with a mixture
of cynicism and pity. But the Australians fare worse than
the Japanese in Porter's *exposé* of the clash of cultures — a
view which could hardly be expected to be received with
much enthusiasm in Australia twenty years ago.

The author has extensively revised *A Handful of Pennies*
for this edition. The plot has been tightened and the verbal
exuberance has now been pared to what he sees as an essen-

tial minimum. For example, chapter 18 of the first version
has been deleted from the revised novel except for the first
three paragraphs. This is an extreme example of Porter's
pruning. More characteristic is his cutting of descriptive
words he now sees as superfluous. In chapter 17, for example, the following two sentences originally appeared as one
sentence joined by a semi-colon, and included the words
italicized here:

> Of the three *bastard* brothers, War is Wisdom's child, is the
> *wisest*, most outspoken, the austere and formal eldest. He is less
> pennywise with the gifts of death.

On the other hand, where Porter has detected an occasional flatness in his prose he has elaborated to intensify his
point, to make it more pungently, or to lift the prose to the
poetic level which pervades the whole. In the original text
chapter 20 closed with the coldly practical Paula Groot
pursuing her Japanese lover, with whom she has irrevocably
quarrelled, to repossess an expensive raincoat she had given
him. She is halted at her gate

> . . . when someone said, "Good night, Miss Groot."
> It was Maxie Glenn.
> "A pleasant evening," she said, and was pleased to hear her
> voice as a soft one.
> The lights kept on swinging; Kazuo moved out of her sight,
> out of her physical life.
> The two spoiled and corruptible beings chatted for a moment
> or two; the Oriental air flowed between them and they seemed
> pleasant to each other.

In the process of revision Porter has achieved all these aims
with some deft additions, deletions and substitutions. This
passage, which now closes chapter 19, reads

> . . . when someone said, "Good night, Miss Groot."
> It was Maxie Glenn, decorative, loitering, thwarting.
> "A pleasant evening," she said, and was pleased to hear her
> voice as a soft one, though she felt like screaming.
> The lights kept on swinging; Kazuo moved out of her sight,
> out of her physical life.
> The two spoiled, corruptible and corrupting beings chatted
> for a while; Oriental air flowed between them as they enacted
> civility with whatever Western clichés came to mind.

Coming, as it does, towards the close of the novel, this passage is given the overall effect of added concentration by the revisions. Paula Groot has been exposed as having been corrupted by her own sexuality and she has corrupted her lover, Kazuo, who hoped for "Edification" from her but found only crassness and, to his eyes, a failure of intelligence. He has corrupted her physically by transmitting a venereal disease to her. For this she abuses and dismisses him and is herself automatically repatriated to Australia. To him venereal disease is the expected corollary of incontinence. Maxie Glenn also has been revealed as "corruptible and corrupting"; he has been discovered "performing well" for the pederastic Padre Hamilton at something other than the Latin and Greek the padre was supposedly coaching him in. This passage does more than carry the plot forward; it encapsulates the main thrust of Porter's satire. The Westerners in occupation not only corrupt the vanquished Japanese, each corrupts the other and himself.

Porter's fascination with Japan has continued over the years although his views on the Japanese themselves have undergone some modification. He has written a travel book on Japan, *The Actors: An Image of the New Japan* (1968), a play with a Japanese setting, *The Professor* (1966) and, most recently, a collection of short stories with Japanese settings, *Mr Butterfry and Other Tales of New Japan* (1970). The story "Mr Butterfry" is included here both for its intrinsic merit and for the contrast it offers with the view of the relations between the Australians and the Japanese in *A Handful of Pennies*.

The Mr Butterfry of the title is unremittingly centre stage in this story of Japan revisited after eighteen years. Unlike *A Handful of Pennies* this is essentially a character study of a member of the Occupation Forces who made a fortune on the black market, married a Japanese housegirl by whom he had two daughters, has somehow managed to stay on in Japan but yearns to return to the Australian fishing village of his childhood. The story is both funny and savage. It emerges that "the foul-mouthed, uncouth, embittered, loathed Mr Butterfry" was once the "vivaciously boring Blue" recalled with difficulty by the narrator in whose past he seems to have played a role of no significance whatever. Now he is a social leper, beyond insult, "and per-petually steeped, even at his gayest and bawdiest, in a rage against something he has not, although he never stops talk-ing of himself, got to the point of directly revealing". Mr Butterfry, con-man and spiv, has conned himself and, as "a dupe of nature" been conned into fathering two daughters who, "in appearance...are unsulliedly Japanese, racially un-tainted" and successful models. The "oh-so-sweet-and-cute housegirl" he married has become a "gluttonously ambitious Japanese mother" who has squandered his spuriously gained riches on "bribes to buy continuing prominence for Lana and Shirley". She hates her husband with an implacable malice, a hatred he returns. Mr Butterfry is doomed never to escape from Japan or from his wife because, being "a dupe of nature" he "deeply loves his daughters", and because, ultimately, he has nowhere to go. He is beyond pity and contempt.

The character of Mr Butterfry comes under Porter's at-tack in part because he exhibits much the same social and moral crudeness as do some of the Australian characters in *A Handful of Pennies*, where the Japanese, even in defeat, have the advantage as inheritors of an ancient culture and transcending philosophy.

> The Oriental past with its elegant ferocity, its tragedies with the sensibilities and neuroses of flame, its sword-hacked generalissimos writing minute verses about snow and the moon, could not stir the Westerner; he failed to recognize nobility in disguised shape, a discipline sublimer than his own.

In "Mr Butterfry" the Japanese are coarser grained. The night-places in Tokyo are "alive with hostesses of a coquet-tishness so defined as to be nearly bellicose albeit nauseatingly saccharine". They are "simian" and govern their social behaviour by "the Japanese rules of duplicity". Mr Butterfry's wife is "charged with power and evil, with all the glib treachery and rancorous lunacy of her race". The contrast in authorial attitudes here is as marked as it is pro-found.

Porter's second major publication was another novel, *The Tilted Cross*, published in the year he decided to make writing his sole occupation. Set in colonial Hobart of the convict era this work enjoyed and continues to enjoy a popular success which it certainly deserves, but it is debatable whether it is a better novel than *A Handful of Pennies*, even in the original version. *The Tilted Cross* is more straightforward in its structure, more obviously attractive to Australians interested in the early history of their country, and less controversial in its views. In addition, it appeared at a time when Porter's reputation as a writer was becoming firmly established.

In 1962, Hal Porter produced a volume of short stories [1] which contained revised versions of almost all the stories which had appeared in the privately printed *Short Stories* twenty years earlier. These stories had been published during the fifties, mainly by the *Bulletin* and contained, as the author stated in his prefatory note, all "I care to pickle of what might be called my First Period". At last literary fashions or editorial preferences had caught up with Porter. A.D. Hope described him as "the most distinctive and perhaps the most distinguished writer of short stories"[2] in Australia at the time, a view that has been confirmed by Porter's three later collections of short stories and by Leonie Kramer's *Hal Porter: Selected Stories* (1971).

In spite of his late blossoming, Porter's literary output has been astonishing both in its quantity and its range. In all he has published to date three novels, four volumes of short stories (not counting the early limited edition of *Short Stories*), three volumes of autobiography, three volumes of poetry, three plays, one travel book, one biographical reference book, one book of local history, as well as a number of smaller pieces, uncollected stories, travel articles, and so on, and edited one volume of poetry and two of short stories. For some of his works of non-fiction he has drawn extensive illustrations, two of which are included here not merely to demonstrate that his drawing skills are impressive in their own right, but also to show that his eye for detail and his passion for exactitude and appropriate ornateness are essential to his perceptions of the world around him; these qualities are, in fact, as characteristic of his prose as of his drawings.

The task of an anthologist is never easy and it is particularly difficult in the case of a writer as prolific and as various

in the literary forms he has attempted as Porter. The problem of selection has been arbitrarily narrowed by excluding
from consideration those works of what we might call
"general interest", such as his travel book and articles, his
history of Bairnsdale and his biographical work, *Australian
Stars of Stage and Screen*. This is in no way intended to
minimize these works as contributions to our literature or
cultural history, or to suggest that they are less worthy of
our attention than his works in the recognized *genres* of im-
aginative literature — his short stories, poems and so on.
Rather, I have concentrated on gathering a representative
selection of Porter's works which have indisputable claims
to be regarded as literature in the strictest sense. This selection includes autobiography, a form attempted with considerable success by a number of Australian writers and one
in which Hal Porter is widely agreed to excel. Porter's first
volume of autobiography, *The Watcher on the Cast-Iron
Balcony* (1963), is regarded by many to be his masterpiece
and a major contribution to Australian letters. It has been
the subject of critical discussion in several important literary
journals, has remained constantly in print since its first
publication in 1963, although it remains unmentioned in
the text of the *Penguin Literature of Australia*3 on the
doubtful grounds that autobiography, biography and some
other prose forms cannot truly be thought of as literature in
the highest sense. Nevertheless, an extract from *The
Watcher* is included here because no selection claiming to
represent Porter at his best would be complete without it.
Unfortunately the extract is necessarily brief.

In the writing of his autobiography, Porter has raised the
straightforward recording of a personal history to an art
form in which many of the techniques of fictional prose,
especially the short story, and some methods of poetic con-
densation have been used to produce a work that is multi-
faceted, highly complex, and interweaves a number of
themes, giving it a unity quite distinct from the simple
chronological relating of events most commonly found in
biography and autobiography. As well, the themes and
characters are presented from several perspectives, sometimes simultaneously. *The Watcher on the Cast-Iron Balcony*
deals with the writer's life from birth until the death of his

mother when he was eighteen. It was first published in
1963 when Hal Porter was fifty-two. It is part of its charm
and its complexity that the experiences related are told from
two points of view — that of the child who is uncritically
engaged in them, and that of the man the child became, a
writer, detached, shrewd, clinically observant. The extract
included in this volume demonstrates the value of *The
Watcher* as social history; it records the kind of social
occasion and reflects social attitudes typical of Australian
country life in the early years of this century. It is also, of
course, a meticulous recording of the first years in the life of
a born writer, one "egged on by my nature to listen and
watch". The easy oscillation between child and man is a
structural principle in *The Watcher* which is written in that
rarely used tense, the historic present, so that both past and
present, boy and writer, may be comfortably fused:

> . . .at the age of ten, I am so in love with the hubbub and
> braggadocio and seeming confidence of the family that I see
> them as a skylarking herd to whom nothing is ever a problem,
> to whom a problem has never presented itself and never will.
> Knowing all this now, I am nevertheless able to see them all,
> still not found out by Life or me, on that Show Day forty years
> ago, loud-mouthed and showing-off, over-hearty and
> carelessly high-spirited, and yet keeping meticulously to the
> hidden rules.

The Watcher on the Cast-Iron Balcony is a very tightly
structured work from which it is impossible to extract without, to some degree, misleading the reader. While the extract included here may give the impression that it is self-
contained, its full richness can only truly be appreciated by
reading the work as a whole. Porter's second volume of
autobiography, *The Paper Chase* (1966) shares the virtues of
The Watcher on the Cast-Iron Balcony. As well, it has particular interest for readers of *A Handful of Pennies*, because
many of the characters and situations described in this
remarkable first novel reappear in *The Paper Chase* stripped
of their fictional names and disguises. Students of Porter's
work might well find it profitable to compare the different
ways Porter handles the same material, particularly as these
seem to involve not merely changes in style, but changes in
attitude; the characteristic Porterian detachment from his

characters and situations in his fictions remains, but paradoxically this is mixed with a degree of personal involvement which makes the writer the butt of satirical comedy as often as not, and the other characters are shown in a much more sympathetic, at times affectionate, light.

I have not included any of Porter's plays or extracts from them for several reasons. To include the full text of a play would inevitably result in the exclusion of other, and in my view, more valuable material; it would be difficult to include a scene or other extract from any of the plays which would do more than give an impression of Porter's skill in handling dialogue and this is apparent in *A Handful of Pennies*, the short stories and the extract from *The Watcher on the Cast-Iron Balcony*. Porter himself considers his plays to be little more than potboilers, spin-offs from, or substitutes for, more substantial works.

> My attitude towards theatre nowadays is *dégagé* to a degree . . . Any play I write is, largely, based on an idea for a novel there's no time (and no *strong* inclination to make time) to work on. A novel takes five or six months, a play two or three weeks.[4]

On the other hand I have included Porter's outline for a composite film which was planned in four segments, each to be written by a leading Australian writer. Porter's sequence, which he called "The Jetty", was later changed by Tim Burstall, the producer, to "The Child" to fit in with the overall theme of the film which was titled *Libido*. "The Jetty" is not a work Porter would consider publishable as a short story, at least in its present form, but is included here to show something of what he believes can be conveyed in a medium which is more visual than verbal and shows, in a subtler way than his plays do, Porter's ability to convey gradations of mood, to build up atmosphere especially through contrasts, and to suggest the sinister without descending to the melodramatic. The outline for "The Jetty" contains very little dialogue and depends quite heavily on the visual potentialities of film to convey its delicate perceptions.

Porter was overseas when the film was being made and a number of changes were made to the story which gave it a fairly explicit Freudian interpretation, added some obvious symbolism and, in Hal Porter's view, coarsened the fine distinctions he was hoping to make in the relationships between the various characters. For example, the lonely ten-year-old boy in "The Jetty" falls innocently in love with a young and beautiful friend of his rather giddy, widowed mother. The young lady is gentle and affectionate with him; he is no longer lonely. He discovers that she is engaged to be married and regards her fiancé as an unwanted interloper in an idyllic relationship; his dream world becomes sinister, nightmarish. Seeing the lovers kissing passionately in the moonlit rose-garden and knowing that the fiancé cannot swim, he offers next day to teach him rowing but, quite deliberately, pulls the rowing boat away as the man is stepping into it. The man drowns as the boy has intended he should. He returns, once again radiantly happy, to the house carrying a perfect rose from the garden as a gift for his beloved who receives it with a smile, sings and plays the piano for him as she did before. The idyll has, from the boy's point of view, merely been interrupted and is now restored.

In the filmed version, "The Child", the beautiful young lady becomes a surrogate mother, the boy catches the engaged couple half-naked and making love and, at the end of the film, the young man falls into the water accidentally from the rowboat, the boy ignores his pleas for help and continues rowing away while the beautiful young lady who has heard her fiancé's cries for help watches from the jetty.

These brief outlines which do justice neither to Porter's original outline nor to Burstall's film, may help to explain the writer's sense of outrage in "Afterthoughts", an outrage one hopes is now assuaged: Porter has subsequently written "The Jetty" as a short story which was his original intention. It is now published here for the first time, titled, perhaps ironically, "The End of the Jetty". The story is faithful to the film outline and a comparison between the two reveals Porter's exceptional talent for creating powerful visual impressions in his writing. It is a distinctive and inescapable quality in his work, especially in his short stories and autobiographies. When the short story is compared to the film outline the inadequacy of the camera to convey the

subtleties of Porter's perceptions — and judgments — is
abundantly clear. Compare this passage from the film outline:

> He says nothing. He touches, and makes tinkle, the lustres at
> his end of the mantel-piece. She reads a little more, puts a
> fringed book-mark in its place, closes the book, reaches for the
> palm-leaf fan, and agitates it with the artful gesture of one of
> the figurines, her arm curved like a porcelain one, her fingers as
> curled as porcelain fingers. Still not looking at him she blows
> smoke towards the ceiling.

with its counterpart in "The End of the Jetty":

> He says nothing.
> Can he, can one, say: at such-and-such an hour, of this thrust
> in the heart or that thrust or the other, love found itself at last
> dead? Can one? Dead, and answerless for ever? Can he?
> Two lustres of crystal, one each end of the mantel-shelf,
> flank the posturing gala, the waspish faces and tiny cold breasts,
> the brittle wrists and sightless eyes. A moment has arrived for
> him to do something. He touches the lustres at the end of the
> mantel-piece, and makes them tinkle — not gently, not at all
> gently.
> The transparent shade which passes — oh, swiftly! — across
> her face is perhaps the wraith of an unpleasing emotion. It is
> gone. He has not yet spoken. She reads, or affects to read,
> another page of the yellow-back. She has not looked at him.
> She closes the book, and drops it to the carpet. She reaches
> for the palm-leaf fan, and agitates it with the artful gesture of
> one of the figurines, her arm curved like a porcelain one, her
> fingers as curled as porcelain fingers. Her profile a cameo, she
> blows smoke towards the ceiling . . .

It is fruitless to speculate just how much of the woman's
artful chilliness and the boy's calculated hostility could be
conveyed by sensitive direction and consummate acting in
this scene. Even so it seems unlikely that the camera could
record this as the moment when the boy recognizes that he
can no longer love his mother.

The four poems included are taken from Porter's two
latest collections. "The Moon is Round, the Snow is White
. . ." and "Elijah's Ravens" both appeared in *Elijah's Ravens*
(1968) and "Alexandra Tea-room" and "The Married
Couple" with its companion drawing were collected in *In*

an Australian Country Graveyard (1974). These poems are among the author's favourites and also, I believe, among his best. Porter's maturation as a poet has been slow but steady. Generally speaking, the poems in his first collection, *The Hexagon* (1956) were characterized by a brilliant but almost impenetrable surface, and were largely responsible for his earning a reputation as one of Australia's most conscious stylists — a reputation he has never quite lived down. His later poems show a developing eloquence, a keen sense of observation and a dry, if sometimes acerbic, wit. The best of them are vignettes in verse, the poetic form being a mode of communication rather than, as seemed often the case in his earlier poems, an end in itself. Porter has not been a prolific poet but his growing mastery in this field suggests that any future contributions he might make in this genre may well place him in the front rank of Australia's satiric poets. "The Married Couple", for example, treats a difficult subject with tactfully controlled irony and while the style is inimitably Porter's it is never obtrusive; it has become the servant of the poet's vision of his subject, of life experienced or observed.

In contrast to his gradual development as a poet, Porter seems to have emerged from the juvenilian chrysalis as a fully formed short story writer, with a sure talent, a highly individual way of looking at himself and the world around him, and a quite individual style to match it. The stories collected here cover Porter's career as a short story writer to date. The first story, "The Room", was written in 1936, and the last, "The End of the Jetty", in 1979. The stories included in this volume show not only Porter's versatility in the form, but also something of the range of material he finds worthy of recording. They also show some of the variety of settings Porter the writer finds stimulating: the Victorian countryside, country town and city, Tasmania, Italy, and, of course, Japan. Although he writes from a point of view that is unquestionably Australian and most frequently *about* Australians, he quite often sets them against foreign or, at least, unusual backgrounds. In Porter's best stories, background is at least as important as plot, often more so, and serves as a key to character which is the central focus in most of his fictional writings.

Hal Porter's customary authorial stance is satiric though the satire is most frequently softened by comedy. He has been described as treating his characters with "pitiless pity", a view with which he agrees.[5] It is not unreasonable to suggest that it was his essentially satiric stance, one of the basic ingredients of his style, which restrained him from publishing much during the 1930s and 1940s. His style was at the polar extreme from the social realists who dominated and to some extent determined literary fashion during those years and, unlike them, he was an apolitical writer. During the 1950s the literary climate changed, Porter fished out old manuscripts, was "discovered", became fashionable among the literary connoisseurs, and began a period of intense productivity which shows no sign of abating. In his novels, stories, plays and poems, he remains more or less invisible, except for his distinctive style. His first-person narrators are not to be trusted and are no more to be thought of as the author's personal voice expressing his personal views than we would think of equating Gulliver with Swift. They are, as Porter readily admits, merely narrative devices.[6]

This, of course, is not true of Porter in his autobiographies where his honesty is as startling as his opinions are unfashionable. It is something of a contradiction that a writer, who has been so adventurous and experimental in his writing that the bulk of his early writings went unpublished until he was in his late forties, should, as a man rather than a writer, hold very traditional, conservative views. Nowhere do these appear more clearly than in his third volume of autobiography, *The Extra* (1975), where, for example, he makes clear his complete distaste for the changes wrought on Australian society as a result of the influx of migrants after the Second World War.

> Foreigners are only truly entertaining in their natural habitat, and preferably in national costume making horrible local delicacies or hideous local knick-knacks, and giving picturesque imitations of themselves. The effect of these refugees from the Old World and a seedy way of life on the tone of Australian society is, you observe, already in the mid-1950s, regrettable and standard-lowering. The dishes of poverty are sidling into Australian menus, and the customs and habits of migrant riff-raff (escapees from their own culture, discontented, go-getting,

venal, often criminal, and very often near-moronic) into the conduct of the native lower element.[7]

Unlikely too are his views on censorship:

> I've never been censored in Australia. I have, however, in England, been censored several times — by the Chapel of Printers, by the Lord Chamberlain. Why protest? Who cares? Not I. And if I *were* censored in Australia, who'd care? Again, not I.

and on unionism, especially writers' unions:

> . . .why should I also belong to an élite union, some Fellowship of This or Association of That? As well join a fraternity of such legendary creatures as the barber's cat, the pox-doctor's clerk, and the daring young man on the flying trapeze . . .
>
> Since I earn far less than bricklayers, navvies, slaughtermen, truck-drivers, any member of the wealthy working class, having written, I'm too needy not to have to chaffer in the market-place. No place this to put a union price on what I, for grim and inexplicable self-satisfaction, have tried to express. How, anyway, draw up a scale of charges? What fee for a bad lyric? Same as for a good one? How much for a perfect sentence, a new cliché? Writing, like virtue, is its own reward.[8]

This aggressive conservatism in Porter, the man, does not emerge *directly* in his writings (other than the auto-biographies), but certainly forms part of the satirical stance from which he views the world in his novels, short stories and plays. He most frequently attacks vulgarity, trendiness, pretentiousness and social change. What his writing celebrates (or mourns?) is the irrecoverable past. Some of his most successful works have captured on paper a way of life that no longer exists, recollected with affectionate nostalgia.

The Extra, which brings Porter more or less up-to-date as an autobiographer, is of particular interest to students of contemporary literary history for the pen-portraits of other Australian writers Porter has known, and sometimes for the vignettes — almost short stories in themselves, of some writers who have provoked his unique brand of percipience. His accounts of meetings with Kenneth Slessor, Katharine Susannah Prichard and Eve Langley are characteristic of Porter at his best — and his best is very good indeed. They exhibit his concern with thematic unity and artistic shapeliness, his ruthless honesty even when it concerns those he loves, and his special genius for raising simple autobiography from the realm of *reportage* to a major art form. Where the writer of *The Watcher on the Cast-Iron Balcony* is equally involved and detached, participant and observer, the narrator in *The Extra* is the author unabashed, sometimes involved but always the observer. It is here that his "pitiless pity" is most clearly apparent and it is here that his intrepid honesty has left him open to censure from those who would have their literary idols enshrined without blemishes. Hal Porter, like Hogarth, records them with affection, but as he saw them, "warts and all".

It could be argued that Porter's most recent major work, *Bairnsdale: Portrait of an Australian Country Town*, although presented as a local history, is also a contribution to his autobiographical writings. In many ways, it covers much of the material and period dealt with in *The Watcher on the Cast-Iron Balcony*, but the authorial stance in this work is purely objective. Nevertheless, while I do not wish to detract from its intrinsic merits, I would like to suggest that it makes a fascinating companion piece to *The Watcher on the Cast-Iron Balcony*, and the student or scholar who is interested in *The Watcher* ignores Porter's *Bairnsdale* at his own peril. Although no extract from this work is included here, part of its special charm lies in the author's copious illustrations. One is reproduced on page 366.

The most obvious characteristics of this and, indeed, of all Porter's writings are his deep and abiding affection for Australia and Australians (however acidly he might deal with some of Australia's less attractive aspects or however satirically he might display patterns of behaviour in some Australians at home or abroad) and his intense nostalgia for the kind of Australia and Australians he knew as a child and young man. With his customary honesty but rather uncharacteristic direct address to the reader in the closing pages of *The Extra* he confides:

> By this time, the end of the book in sight, the reader must've come to conclusions about the colour of the spectacles through which I view the world, and noted some quirks of infatuation or rejection. All's not stated, but, to sum up, I love Australia beyond all other places even though, over the years, and before my eyes, many of its unique and most estimable aspects have

been needlessly tampered with, altered, or destroyed. A passion for destruction's not exclusively Australian. What puts Australian passion in the record class, and side by side with its outstanding score of annual road deaths, is the adolescence of it, the imitative pointless quality. However, this watcher's no reformer — *che sarà sarà*! My love of Australia's incurable even if much of it's for what used to be rather than for what is and will be.9

In spite of the uncharacteristic and slightly colloquial directness here and the firm assertion that the writer/ watcher is no reformer, one suspects that satire is merely the other side of the reformer's coin, that Hal Porter would halt the march of so-called "progress" if he could, and turn back the hands of time if that were possible.

Notes

1. *A Bachelor's Children* (Sydney: Angus & Robertson, 1962).
2. *Australian Literature 1950-1962* (Melbourne: Melbourne University Press, 1963), p.15.
3. Ed. Geoffrey Dutton (Ringwood: Penguin 1964, rev. ed., 1976). See especially Introduction, pp.7-9, in either edition.
4. See "Answers to the Kind, Funny Man", p.379.
5. *Ibid.*
6. "Hal Porter" in *Contemporary Novelists*, ed. James Vinson (London: St James Press 1972), p.994.
7. *The Extra*, p.34.
8. *Ibid.*, pp.196-97.
9. *Ibid.*, p.237.

A Note on the Texts

The major work in this volume is the novel, *A Handful of Pennies*, originally published in 1958 and never reprinted. Hal Porter has substantially revised the text for this edition. Many of Porter's short stories and poems have been published several times, often in revised versions, before being collected into volumes by the author, sometimes with additional, if minor, revisions. With two exceptions the versions published here have been taken from the collections listed below and may be considered to incorporate Porter's final revisions. "At McGarrigle's Inn" was published in *Quadrant* in 1977 and remains so far uncollected. "The Jetty", in its short story form, "The End of the Jetty", appears here for the first time. Discussions by Porter, Tim Burstall and others of Porter's film outline, "The Jetty", plus the text of the outline, appear in *Overland* 74 (1978).

The stories "The Room", "Everleigh's Accent" and "Uncle Foss and Big Bogga" are from *A Bachelor's Children* (1962); "Boy Meets Girl" and "First Love" are from *The Cats of Venice* (1965); "Mr Butterfry" and "They're Funny People" are from *Mr Butterfry and Other Tales of New Japan* (1970); "Brett" and "The Sale" are from *Fredo Fuss Love Life* (1974). The poems "The Moon is Round, the Snow is White . . ." and "Elijah's Ravens" are from *Elijah's Ravens* (1968); "Alexandra Tea-room" and "The Married Couple" with its companion drawing are from *In an Australian Country Graveyard* (1974). The illustration accompanying the poem, "The Married Couple", was drawn as a companion piece for this poem and is inseparable from it.

The extract from Porter's first volume of autobiography

has been taken from the original edition which, although it has been reprinted a number of times, has never been revised. Porter's criticism of Thomas Keneally as novelist has been extracted from a longer essay in *Contemporary Novelists,* a bio-bibliographical reference work published in London in 1972. Porter contributed critical essays on several major Australian novelists for this work.

The article, "Interview with Hal Porter", has been revised slightly by Hal Porter since its original publication in *Australian Literary Studies.*

Porter has drawn his own illustrations for several of his books and for a number of travel articles. Two are included here from works not otherwise represented partly because they seem to me to have some appropriateness to the context in which I have placed them, but mainly because they demonstrate a remarkable correspondence in style between his writing and pictorial skills; in both he shows a unique concern with exact yet decorative detail. The drawing of "An important cultural property, Aizen-myo-o (God of Love in the Inner Heart), in the Museum of the Atami Paradise of the Church of World Messianity (Sekai Kyn-seikyo)" is from *The Actors: An Image of the New Japan* (1968) and "Evening School" is from *Bairnsdale: Portrait of an Australian Country Town* (1977).

Full documentation for the works included in this volume or mentioned in the introduction are listed along with other material in the select bibliography.

A Handful of Pennies

A New, Revised Edition

An important cultural property, Aizen-myo-o (God of Love in the Inner Heart), in the Museum of the Atami Paradise of the Church of World Messianity (Sekai Kynseikyo). Drawing by Hal Porter.

1

Peace is his apparent twin but he is not Peace nor his twin.

Nor is he War pale with truce and painted with smiles: his smiles are his own brushed on the eggshell of a face believed to be candid.

Name?

Name: Occupation-Democracy.

He is Delusion's son, the weak uncle, the sponsor of no Christ but of guilds of Pontius Pilates.

In the Year of the Tiger, 2614, twenty-fourth year of the Era of Radiant Peace, 1950 Anno Domini — call it what you will, it was a moment of the immutable past and therefore permanent — the weak uncle's feast was at its height.

Victor and vanquished, male and female, black and white and brown and yellow and brindled, Roman Catholic and Buddhist, orthodox and pagan, virgin and sated, godless and god-ridden, adult and child, Western and Oriental, gorged and gulped in a mischievous and enclosed weather while outside, outside, cyclones, clouds and hours swam through days like vast wounds in the hide of reality, swam over generations of islands balanced on earthquake, admonished by typhoons and taboos, and over-freighted by the hermaphrodite souls of millions resignedly multiplying themselves in a mid-light of East and West.

It was a country in which, while one adored, the exquisite air could in a twink transform itself to a fatal winnowing fan, or the modest water erect itself to an Everest of annihilation; it was a landscape not naturally beneficent but tamed and trained, shackled, shaved and humanized; it was a landscape of secular and sacred vegetation, of mountains holy as Zion, and gods numerous as fleas; it was a landscape in which the celluloid kewpie still existed, and Betty Boop clocks marked off foreign minutes with an aluminium tittering; it was a landscape above all never without figures.

Enclosing it were skies in which there seemed no refreshment, only the tints of bygone dooms, the stains of inerasable humiliations. Towards these, countless mountains and roofs, pine-trees and cryptomerias, countless bronze mandorlas and hydro-electric eiffels triangled up . . . ancient cities, too . . . and one imperial and ephemeral city no older than its latest cataclysm.

A chimera almost, this city run by a tradition of chivalrous gangsterdom, a city of wattle-and-daub, of pine and paper, of neon and stucco, of colossal department stores bombed to Grünewalds in which lattice-laths bore above rubble mistletoe-like hangings. Here the unbombed wood warped and split; the stairs of inferior concrete mimicked in miniature the earthquake crevasses into which at any second they might be toppled.

Makeshift all: the synthetic marble of Ionic pillars seemed already to feel Samson's hand, the smudged carbon copies of Belgian Gothic awaited a titanic epilepsy of Earth to disintegrate to scree, bearing with them in their fall the roof-top shrines, the tourist-inspired atrocities, the silks more articulate than the bodies they parcelled.

Lawns and lantern-lit lanes exhaling memories of past seasons of feud, passion, and fiesta, were perpetually littered with debris of the defiling Present: Peace, Player's, and Lucky Strike cigarette packets, chopstick papers, Pabst beer tins, loquat seeds and Coca-Cola straws.

Meanwhile, the wind massaging the rice-fields took a census of some dubious future; Buddha with nothing in his hands except his own fingers sat by; Christ, His oleograph heart aflame like a cannibal's altar, showed palms split by His murder.

The opposite odours of excrement and daphne, of decline and patience, of charm and desolation, swept a land whose mythology was as entrancing and brutal as that of the Old Testament, whose eight million gods nourished and nestled in rock and road, larch, hemlock, looking-glass and the exosphere.

In their gods Grecian, but short-legged as the Welsh and with a calculated ambiguity, a wary equivocation between fact and vision, the Conquered played at the game of Occupation with those hairy poachers, those loud-mouthed *bravi*, larrikins, and hill-billies, their Conquerors.

Neither Conqueror nor Conquered had experience in this

game. They disconcerted, fascinated and disappointed each other.

The Oriental past with its elegant ferocity, its tragedies with the sensibilities and neuroses of flame, its sword-hacked generalissimos writing minute verses about snow and the moon, could not stir the Westerner; he failed to recognize nobility in disguised shape, a discipline sublimer than his own.

For Orientals — grave but touchy in a world rightly pitted with cores of pain — heroism that proclaims itself, victory that let its tongue perpetrate orotund bunkum, were to be derided behind the fan. Feeling all they failed to conceal betrayed them, they believed everything they put into words diminished them.

Yet, with the compass set in one and no direction, and each knowing a single fact only about each other — that one dies of one's body — East and West walked hand in hand.

Nothing these adults of two races could do to each other could surpass the violations already done to them as children by other children of their own race, yet they attempted to transcend old anguishes or ecstasies for, along with the Occupationnaires, had arrived Mara the King of Passions, with his three sons Gaiety, Caprice, and Wantonness, his three daughters Thirst, Sensuality, and Discontent.

2

A children's song and sorcery behind a bamboo fence — no
more — that was yesterday.

Yesterday, Paula Groot had heard some Oriental little
girls whom she could not see and would not ever see, whose
language she could not understand, singing a song she
would not hear again, singing a *rain-rain-go-away* to the
cut-out-paper priest swinging on a branch Grinling
Gibbons might have carved:

> *Shiny priest, shiny priest, tomorrow make*
> *fine as it was only other day:*
> *I'll give you silver-silver bell to shake.*

> *But if you sulk till your tears are shed*
> *and make tomorrow rainy-rainy rain,*
> *I'll chippy-chippy-choppy-chop your head.*

The charm had worked.

The festival day arrived rainless and remained rainless to
please little girls and other Orientals. It was therefore also
rainless for the Westerners who had a coinciding holiday.

Holiday can make a present of solitude in which one sees
far too clearly for truth. One keeps to the tower; one is a
Lady of Shalott; one is alone immortal and safe; those who
venture, those scrambling elsewhere, seem dressed for
doom.

Not Paula G., thought Paula Groot, as she sprawled
naked, a Venus coolly and soullessly sustaining her ardour
on arrangements of lettuce on the official green plush of the
bed-cover in her Y.W.C.A. Hostel room, an electric fan
bandying a tepid and invisible searchlight from plaster wall
to plaster wall, all of them flaking primrose. A bowl of gar-
denias grew older and more jaundiced; a clock in the hall
outside spoke *Two!* and bounded zealously towards three
and four and danger.

Yet, hearing no more than *Two*, she rose and dressed,
swindled by her imagined invulnerability, also because she
had an appointment. She felt alone, and in error continued
certain of protection from jeopardy, among sixty empty

rooms furnished exactly as hers was: green quilt, electric fan, arm-chair, brown linoleum, floral mat, bedside table, wardrobe of wood grained with nightmare, Doré chasms.

She was certainly the only human being. The other school-teachers, the canteen salesgirls, army typists, Red Cross women, off-duty nurses and Dew Drop Inn manageresses bounded ostentatiously in jeeps through the sweet-potato fields, clambered with pimply teetotal sergeants to scene-viewing eminences, haggled about cultured pearls and scarves deliberately-inartistically printed for their admiration, spent their black-market rake-offs, or took photographs of the constrained and picturesque poverty-stricken by temple gates and under maple-trees.

Miss Groot, the schoolmistress, had a different, more time-honoured thing to do. At vainglorious thirty, why not?

God-houses, waterfalls, snowy glimpses, mineral springs and fields of arrowroot she had already seen without deep interest, and she possessed cultured pearls. To visit weather then?

In her native Tasmania she had submitted to visits from all kinds of weather; snow that an Oriental West-south rearranged on woodcut thatches and rush-prickled marshes might well have been dusted willy-nilly from Mount Wellington; sunset, reflection, wave, and shrub did not strike her as novel.

Dressed, dark-spectacled against the sun, she left her safety and began to stroll for she thought she knew where she was going. Alas, not this time.

At the end of these exposed and gently firm progressions the one sort of thing always waited: what did it matter if her independence led through Dickensian sleet, by plots of auricula and convict-hewn stone or through heat, as now, and down an earth-and-bamboo street tinkling with wind-bells and officered by squat policemen in blue spectacles?

Yes, hot: lower-class women fanned their revealed and bubble breasts; there was a smell of oiled sunshades frying in hotel porches; already some cannas were out, and the loofah vines before pinball dens and mah-jongg parlours had begun to climb their spindly ladders; some displayed first flowers.

Concealing their bandiness beneath loose blue-and-white

cotton robes patterned with wintry undulations of reeds,
eddies, wings, wave-crests and ripples, younger women
minced pigeon-toed in rice-white faun-hoof-cloven booties
and wooden clogs, bobbed along beneath parasols of cyclamen, cineraria, fuchsia, Parma violet, all the gradations of
Firbank- and homo-mauve. Paula Groot, also, was in blue-
and-white, a Kodak girl of the twenties. Eleanor Boardman,
was it?

Side-stepping a man who wore in his buttonhole a red
feather to show that he had paid his rates, she inescapably
faced a sombre and uncomely young woman.

*The mirror cracked from side to side; the curse is come upon
me . . . .*

It was Hoshi, her housegirl, who quickly pretended excitement and, on a whim which immediately irked her so
much that her squint became worse, said, "I will be very
joy if you come my ed-if-ice for green tea. Pliss? Pliss?"
And she bowed and bowed and bowed.

Women of Paula Groot's kind, tropical in manner and
dashing on the surface, but at core antarctic and vulgar, advance on rapture or downfall, on the first meeting with the
unknown who is to be bliss or disaster, less by paths
crooked as Labyrinth's than by those mordantly straight as
bayonets. She had convinced herself that being good-looking enough, and fearless enough, formed a document of safe
conduct; she neglected to consider those fluctuations or set-
backs some call divinities. She left the loom, she took three
paces, she accepted her housegirl's invitation — once over,
she thought, the visit will be over.

Hoshi, annoyed, successfully simulated *very joy*, gave an
exhibition of delight.

Just as tall as Hoshi, who was taller than is usual for her
race, with eyes as dark as Hoshi's but with pale instead of
black hair, she walked towards her unpleasant fate chattering coldly-cordially to the broad-faced servant who washed
her clothing and wore it when discarded, polished her
linoleum with Dark Tan Kiwi, was nauseated by the smell
of Bonox, and sustained an affection for her shot through
with permanent envy and weathercock hatred.

Black dragonflies flew geometrically about stalls of backscratchers, dried squid, popguns, and water-melons in wooden tubs of ice; locusts were vibratingly fluent.

Controlling an ague of nervousness, Hoshi brightly led the Tasmanian, expensively dressed and scentless, past tap-rooms, tea-shops, and the sago-palms of inns, to her mother's house.

Here, Hoshi immediately perceived that, though her mother was out as she had expected, her brother was home, a thing she had not foreseen: his clogs of pawlonia wood lay by the shoe-removing step where she also left hers and Paula Groot her sandals. Concealing horror and a fear she could not classify, for she loved her intelligent brother and felt he honoured her, Hoshi chirruped with giggling but rigid formality.

Thus to Scene Three.

Already, the brother, Kazuo, twenty-two years old, had discarded his student's uniform and the peaked mortar-board of his college for a gull-grey kimono. He was reading, seated cross-legged on the padded floor, and, although this was the first white woman he had met, knew enough to rise.

He knew more; he said, "How do you do? My name Kazuo Tabuchi."

Paula Groot noticed his legs — nice.

"We are to drink green tea," said his sister.

He detected her fear but did not understand it; he understood, however, why she was kicking herself under her graciousness and thought it improper. Women!

His mind was as astringent as the art and architecture of his race; he saw no health in ethics or metaphysics, he desired not Truth, for that and Sin and Forgiveness are no more than Christian symbols, but Edification. He had merely a Doric severity and simplicity, and eyes like Bambi's. Under their accidentally galvanizing gaze sat a graceful white woman to whom he would talk; she would be Edification, he hoped.

He had not hoped this of the Australian and American women he had seen striding like athletes in Eastern Capital, women with bony legs, green eyes, hairy ankles, and voices more intolerable than politicians'.

Edification could not come from them; from ugly men perhaps, but not from ugly women.

"Tea, please, sister," he ordered.

Hoshi left Kazuo and Paula Groot together.

Scene Four.

The curtain rose.

He cleared his throat.

"I am university student," he said. "It is vacation era. Today vacation era is commencing. This afternoon I closely read in my mother's edifice."

Paula Groot smiled at the word: Hoshi's model smiled at the smile.

Young? Not young? Hard to tell, but he was surprised that she was so feminine; her bare legs were smooth as an Oriental's; her skin was pale and unflawed; her eyes as dark and oily as his own. Moreover, he was comfortingly taller than she.

Suddenly, in a pause, the unavoidable pause before the pistol-shot, a rabid emotion possessed both these good-looking creatures and showed in their eyes.

Edification was to take a form he could not have foretold, she was to course a field it would not have seemed to her worth the coursing. Each, while half uncertain of certainty, desired the other and knew the other knew it.

Urbanity was necessary.

"What are you reading . . . Kazuo?" she said. *Kazuo* meant *I am interested in Kazuo.* Her bland voice was another amenity he required and would not have expected.

"I read Jean-Paul Sartre." His French accent was impeccable.

Writers, French or otherwise, were in the abstract not her line, therefore: "Oh!" she said, which meant nothing to him.

He laid his hand on — on the wretched, silly book.

"What is your opinion of —" he now spoke with laborious indifference so that he could pronounce the "l" — "ex-istention-a-lism?"

On the stupid book, uselessly, his hand.

"I'm afraid my views are not worth discussion."

Hand.

What was worth discussion was a mutual future she foresaw without seeing the organization to bring it about. Her housegirl's brother! . . . that did not matter. What mattered was *where*, was *when*.

For a while, he meantime pedantically delivering views, she toyed with the conceit of commanding Hoshi to the Y.W.C.A. on some errand; she was sure this ascetic house held no more than the three of them. Lust has an extra ear.

"We must," she said, "meet again and talk about all this."

"Oh yes, yes," he said, and went on minutely analyzing in a voice resonant enough to violate her.

She needed neither to fret nor calculate for, though he was prone to lionize subjects esoteric and antique as well as the fashionable and Gallic, he had no indecision in matters of lust. It would happen — so! They were male and female, mutually wounded by Nature, kleptomaniacs of each other's weaknesses under the confusing paraselene of a dictated Renaissance. A dark cave for two would be found.

His world of extravagantly involved ways of killing time, of flowers arranged canonically, of flowerless gardens representing placid moods, of unending glossaries, of grave faces at incense-smelling or tea ceremonies, would never appear to her through the fog of over-lapping customs.

Her football matches were of the present and therefore primitive; his were of the past, played by stately men in golden brocade who bore fans and paper handkerchiefs, with goal-posts of pine and maple, willow and cherry, and quarters marked by the smouldering away of incense sticks. Her immature world was more immature and uncouth than he could have believed.

She who was provincial saw, correctly, no difference between the provincialites of Hobart and the occupied zones: the latter's were less complex and more loopholed than the ones she had lived among, and eluded or used for her own clear-cut purposes.

Bodies were everywhere; bodies alone were in the final count understandable, their demands eternally the same, their appeasement predictable. An Adonis or two occurred, but more Angelos and plenty of Claudios.

Hoshi's return to show off with frothed-up tea and

seaweed-speckled biscuits made no track across Paula Groot's *how? when? where?*: those unlit fields with their ravishing grasses.

Kazuo went on didactically, "I am so firmly of opinion that, as famed English poet, T.S. Eliot, is saying . . ."

Etiquette required him to act thus; as well he misguidedly thought he demanded not admiration but appreciation of his presence. Eliot, Auden, Spender therefore, the Boys of the Old Brigade.

Tea — and the drinking of it. Biscuits — and their eating. Tea-and-biscuit conversation, the scene drawing to its end.

Curtain.

And good-bye, good-bye, *when? where?*

Paula Groot was obliged to bear her questions away along the streets and on through a bombed dockland where, from tumuli of rust-red boilers, turbine casings and grounded buoys, upreared a fretwork of girders, a jagged crossword of rust, a filigree of iron weeds from which the blood-coloured sap had crusted and dyed the mould and stones seen in section from famous waters, under the seeming jewel-scattered surface of which the presence of battleships, submarines, bodies, and the relics of innumerable ancient vendettas did not at all deplete the abundance of fluke-ridden fishes esteemed raw by the Orientals.

Her second-last lover in this country awaited her, a Major Bruce with a hypnotist's goatee concealing a chin-infection. He smelt of whisky and Aqua-Velva.

As he entered her she was thinking of Kazuo and unfairly continued to do so throughout.

In time it was night.

Houses had been decorated for the Star Festival; by the wooden pail of water reflecting years-off planets and suns leaned the bamboo branch bearing odes on green, red, yellow, white, and purple paper-slips.

Elsewhere strip-tease girls postured with flagrant clumsiness, rolling Goya eyes in tangles of false eyelashes; touts bawdy as Juliet's nurse wheedled in misformed English; *après-guerre* and stomach girls loitered under stuttering fluorescents.

Now and then, a wind, the very breath of concupiscence,

floundered peacockishly along streets where aroused wind-bells, like the succeeding flushes of shadow on a millet crop, overflowed glassy elegies one upon the other.

Phallic Hermae of an Oriental kind stood along remote night roads.

One superannuated ex-harlot was prone by a seal-maker's, her hands clinging in the substance of a kimono so rotten it seemed the objectified aura of her own age and disease. Kazuo passed her, stepping vigorously towards what she was when young. He was naturally not to recognize a Cassandra saved from the knife, a pertinent omen of a portion of his future, even of his near future.

As well, on his way to a brothel which he thought had never received Westerners, he circumspectly did not recognize as Australians and Americans the Calibans smelling of metal, red-eyed, raucous, also hunting flesh.

Kazuo was spotless and lusty. His plans for Paula Groot were well laid.

He did not know everything or what he was to be.

3

Captain Truscott, temporarily of "X" Officers' Mess, had arrived two days before with a Manila hang-over and was scarcely settled in. He did not go to Thursday Bingo at the Officers' Club, but he needed a nightcap.

Consequently, at half past eight, when he entered the Mess bar he was in the company of the few who were not Bingo-addicts.

There was . . . who was it? Wilkinson? of the Finance Department? . . . someone with an erased-looking group-face, the face at the back of the hall, who was working in a corner at a *Bulletin* crossword.

In another corner was an Army Padre, Captain Hamilton, and a handsome adolescent; the Padre murmured Socratically; they murmured together at their table over drinks venial to glance at, but one or both could have been gin-squashes or double gin-squashes. Softly lit, they seemed the wrong people to be so. Captain Truscott was surprised at the schoolboy in his sandals, shorts, and too-green shirt. What went on?

At the bar counter sat Major Everard-Hopkins, whose tall body was abraded and burnt down to hollows, its juices depleted of richness, so that he seemed wonderfully sick and had a clinically clean gaze. Too young his gaze at fifty.

"Ah," said the Major, "not a Bingo-man, dear boy? What do you drink?"

"Whisky," said Truscott, young, countrified and unguilty. "What is Bingo?"

"A form of housey-housey in which one can suffer the humiliation of winning a bottle of Australian *crème de menthe*, a smoker's stand of plastic and nickel, a musical cigarette box . . . you know the sort of thing."

"But isn't housey-housey illegal . . .?"

"Not in this tabernacle," said Everard-Hopkins.

Truscott, spare-time and inferior poet, was to find the other man an unpacific intellectual with an eye like a jeweller's lupe in a face resembling the Tollund man's — that oldest face in the world — and kippered by the fumes of his denunciations.

Ascetic fanatic? Prolix crank? Insolvent idealist?

Truscott could not know; he was too laxly intelligent to surmise; he was artless, sensual, virgin and lenient — at least lenient enough to hide distaste. Now and again he submerged, fakir-like, to an underneath-life's-megaphoning of milky vision. This rarely: usually he was in view, twenty-three years old, sandy, a dimpled chin, teeth parted in the middle; everyone who found people charming found him charming.

Everard-Hopkins?

Perhaps he, too, was attracted for, fuelling himself with whiskies, he gave a display of himself and denounced, at ironic length, the weekly Bingo party which rebuked his ostracism with occasional outbursts of applause, from the Club which flared richly just downhill from the Mess.

Past the Mess, past the Club, down to the sea, the oyster-gardens and the mislaid torpedoes, gravitated a stream spluttering lines by Sappho; sometimes a train called out smartly as a banshee — the hill echo-answered like a wife.

Wilkinson rustled; the Padre and the boy murmured on; the ceiling-fans revolved like roulette wheels; Major Everard-Hopkins declaimed: Sardonic Oldster entertains Pleasant Youngster!

"What," Truscott at last found himself able to ask as conspiratorially as the Second Murderer, "is that kid doing here?"

Everard-Hopkins did not look round.

"He," said Everard-Hopkins, emptying his glass, "is the Captain of the Dependants' School at Rainbow Village. His name quite eludes me. The . . . the Padre has been tutoring him in the . . . the Padre's room. Latin, I hear, dear boy."

He signed to one of the bar-boys and, the glasses being filled, said to no one, "Latin, I *hear*. It may be Greek. Or some other . . . lingo." His face was expressionless.

It is time, Truscott thought, for me to be Young Man Seeking Knowledge.

He asked several questions about the district and the Orientals; the Major's voice, sooted by the smoke of half a million cigarettes, jaded by whiskies and oblique ironies, answered these, and then, of its own self, began to flow.

"The Orientals, my boy, *I* believe to be Poverty's most delightful offspring; they live with scrupulous taste, and are fully aware of the value of restraint unsullied by tolerance, because their aim for centuries has been to create ruthlessly a society less ruthless than nature. Taboo and ritual are the means. Their taboos differ from ours, their rituals, too, and their tendernesses, inhumanities, chivalry, repugnances, and fervours. That means just that, and no more than *different*. Savvy? They possess their special consolations, mysterious virtues, urbanities, spleen, and perverse rectitude. At the moment, and for several years, you'll not see them at their best, for defeat is incoherence, and on this we have planked down . . . what did I say before? . . . our *tabernacle*. Yes. We have thought up for them an unfitting ritual which we are incapable of unthinking. Democracy! More whisky, boy."

What *have* I started, thought Truscott.

One of the bar-boys was nicknamed Brigadier; he was deft and ladylike. As Brigadier he impassively overheard denigration of his race by the ignorant, and rhapsodizing by the deluded. As Yoshiharo Minato, he carefully went on, between serving drinks, with the truth of studying trigonometry.

"Democracy," continued Everard-Hopkins and his whisky, "is a Western foible . . . ideas, you know, based on a defiant conceit we imagine is freedom — politics based on, of all sands, religion! How naive of the West to disprove an Oriental divinity without proving a Western one, particularly here where a series of cataclysms has turned cynical even the most unworldly."

"Surely —" and Truscott modified his protest with a pseudo-boyish smile "— we have done some good."

The Major closed his eyes, drank again, then with motherly dispassion: "I cannot answer that, dear boy. Good? I do not know; though I have *my* convictions. I, for example, admire and . . . dear me . . . love these Orientals. No, I cannot answer. But I am intensely, oh, *intensely*, interested in observing the results of a vanity which suggests by its purgings and reformations that the Seven Deadly Sins are better than the Eight Dusts of Anger, Selfishness, Covetousness, et cetera. Is thirteen a better unlucky number than the Oriental four, is it wiser to beckon palm-up as we do or palm-down as they do, is hanging more aesthetic than beheading? We are unable to prove, even to ourselves, that what we consider important is important to us, let alone these . . . foreigners."

Truscott found the Major just less than boring and was himself trite.

"Surely," he said, "we are the foreigners."

"Indeed, indeed."

"But the . . . victorious ones. Doesn't that give us a sort of right to impose our own standards?" Does it? Why don't I just go to bed?

"My dear Truscott! Can those who do not even subscribe to the table etiquette of their own race set an example, here, in moral etiquette? We lead in this place an agitated and flamboyant existence, filled with bickerings and barbarities."

"What about human relationships?" Truscott's eyes shone. He had had several drinks.

"There are many varieties, dear boy. Buyer and seller, servant and boss, man and woman . . . and sex *decidedly*. Ah!" The Major raised his hand like a marble senator in a forum of lath. Brigadier filled the glasses under the impulse of this, and returned to his trigonometry.

"Do you think that I, anyone else in this Mess, this Area, or the whole Occupation Force, takes this people's complete humanity for granted? After all, a nation is a creature; and this one creature has a justified national pride. We have outraged that too, too competently."

Thereupon, as though piqued by something they could not have heard from within the cocoon of their intimate murmurings, the Padre and the schoolboy left the room.

By his elbow Truscott was surprised to see a drained glass which had not been there before and was not his. The other person — Wilkins? Tomlinson? — had invisibly drunk by his elbow and had gone, too. Upon a fearful summons?

Brigadier did trigonometry; Butch, the assistant bar-boy, finished his work with violence; with chimpanzee swagger then went off to learn English expressions he had noted down during the day; *fresh out of coffin nails, too bloody right, eager beaver, I'm jack of the great galah*. Butch was a recent employee, and intended to become fluent with the idiom of the powerful.

Everard-Hopkin's voice was becoming more smudged but showed no signs of fading.

"And, my dear Truscott, they hanker to have their complete humanity taken for granted. Admittedly it titillates to be regarded as wily, as impenetrable, as this or that. All humans prefer misconception to indifference, though both may lead to revolt or slaughter. But, even . . . I repeat *even* . . . from our point of view the total must be assessed — the butchery *plus* the martyrdom, the persisting feudality *plus* the incipient futurity. Otherwise —" and he selected words with the tipsy neatness of Bacchus picking grape by grape like lice from his curls —"otherwise the . . . bonfires of their souls smoke peevishly . . .."

"Back again! Back again!"

It was the Padre, I-am-Fortune's-steward-ing, back again behind his Falstaff's belly as though from some bracing snow-storm. With spurious forcefulness he strutted straight to the Major and Truscott: yo-ho, chaps, yo-ho! He was sound without fury, the Army Man's priest not strong enough for bigotry, brave enough for wisdom nor sage enough for honesty; freed from the obligation to knock on doors, he was the hail-murderer-well-met, the bluff trampler-under of nuances.

"A grog, a grog! Leap to it, Brigadier, boy. Come you toss-pots, Truscott, Major, have one!"

"Thanks, no," said the Major, said Everard-Hopkins, said the Lord Chief Justice, *Have you your wits? Know you what 'tis you speak?*

The Padre's *was* gin squash; clamping his glass daintily in coarse fingers, becoming the stage uncle, he said, "The child's keen as mustard — keen as Keen's, ho, ho, ho! He deserved his squashes; he performed well tonight."

"Child?" said Everard-Hopkins. Vaguely, was it?

An insolent vagueness, thought Truscott, who sensed some barely audible signal backstage, some message chalked on the brick wall. From behind his semblance of vagueness Everard-Hopkins now looked accurately at the Padre, who dabbed his chin with a khaki handkerchief and said, "Glenn, Maxie Glenn."

"He . . . performed well?" The four syllables settled pharisaically under the ceiling fans like those plump doves on the *No More Atom Bomb* posters ornamenting the cities now Hausmannizedly replacing bombed ones — those gorged messenger doves of the patron god of warriors.

"Nice chap, Maxie," said the Padre. "Drink?" Yo-ho!

"I'm off to bed before the Bingo crowd returns," said the Major, and, "You were wise to choose tonight, Padre."

Then, immediately, he turned and left, desiccated, fatigued, and indicting. Truscott followed him.

They stood beneath a gingko-tree and looked downhill.

Sprinkled between the sea and the base of the slope on which the Westerners' settlement was arranged, like shoe-boxes with kindergarten-sketched windows, was the Oriental town in which the Major lovingly conceived mild old men to play elaborate draughts, dainty maidens to shuffle flower-cards, and motherly mothers to throw purifying salt on braziers defiled by the stewing of quadruped meat. Actually, there, and there, and there, such things were going on; but at the same time many slender fingers paper-folded tiny ballerinas to represent a fashionable idol whose death was adored, Moira Shearer in *Red Shoes*; Francis Xavier's mummified forearm, which had been shrining around among Roman Catholic Orientals, rested lizard-like for the night; people vilified, mollified, and enticed people.

"Why does it sparkle so?" asked Truscott.

"Opened shutters and shadeless light bulbs," the Major said.

Then his voice coarsened, became more elemental, "Opened shutters, of course. Naked lights on domestic wrangling and shrewd innocence. That's all. But, look at us, the saviours and exemplars! On the hilltop, our crown!"

Above them, higher than the Western messes, hostels, hospitals and barracks, higher than temple, shrine, chapel or church, tangling with stars, a barbaric crown of barbed wire and arc-lights, effulgent and garish as a chandelier, sentry-and-bayonet guarded, topped all.

"That is our most prudent self-indictment: the House that Jack Built."

Truscott did not understand.

"Jack is the euphemism," said the Major, "for venereal disease. Good night, Truscott."

As Truscott got into bed he heard two delicate barks from the next room where Captain Dugald drank gin after gin, and mumbled to his cocker spaniel. It answered, apparently as delighted this Thursday as on all other nights.

Thursday night went on.

In the bar Yoshiharo Minato, who was called Brigadier, alone with the Padre, listened to him assessingly, trying to translate the impulse behind the murmured words, for the Padre had dropped heartiness. No yo-ho now.

As the first jeeps of the Bingo-players returning from the Club entered the Mess compound, Brigadier finally promised to show the Padre, some time, the scars of moxa-burning on his back.

As the Padre left, the bar-boy's face held the look of one who had been bought, as he was to be.

Next, he combed his camellia-oiled hair, braced his eyes, and acquired a smile, not too cerebral or servile, rather winning and with a ghost of gold in it, to greet the officers with machine-gun voices, the brood of Potiphar's wives with chlorinated hair, and eyeballs filigreed with brandy veins, the gay spinsters on the ran-tan, the fillers-in.

Above this, all this and error, dimly shone the Pleiades, stars of Shakespeare and Crippen.

On the faces of gods whose eyes and mouths of stone were sealed with lichen the moon also shone.

No Man in the Moon, but the Hare in the Moon, perfunctorily pestling in a rice-mortar, ascended perfunctorily. It was the Hour of the Wild Boar and would soon be the Hour of the Rat.

Uproar increased in "X" Mess bar.

At the piano Major Bruce again and again played "Some Enchanted Evening" in a key no one could divinely sing to; the closing paragraphs of the dismal prospectus of enjoyment were being reached. Paula Groot, who drank little, remembered to return moltenly the pianist's molten gaze and thought of Kazuo, who was meanwhile reading a poster:

Picture and Nude Carnival.
East Capital Eccentric Strip Show
organized with
Young Virgins Only
Pink Rose in a Special Act
the Fully Numerous Flowers of Nude Beauties
&
with above, Republic present
Angel on the Amazon
Could it be up along the Amazon where the
ferocious beasts are roaring?
Dead Beautiful Woman Shedding the Smell of Riddle.

Near by, a peroxided Laurence Olivier and bewigged Jean Simmons, their eyes Orientalized, agonized together in vertical columns of Oriental calligraphy.

Shakespeare's moon, and two neon bars, shone on this poster, too.

4

Any name for the days, in this place where even the hours had a shape that was fictitious: fruitless was certainly Friday; fruitless, saturnine, summary, mundane, tetchy, *Weltschmerz*, and Thursday again, Bingo-Thursday, clickety-click, key-of-the-door.

Major Everard-Hopkins considered himself far too distressed and angry to go into dinner; he was also waiting for Captain Dugald to arrive, and Captain Dugald was late.

Glaring at himself in the bar looking-glass, as though Sholto Everard-Hopkins were Dugald the-cad-on-trial, the Major nevertheless drank whiskies with his reflection. To preserve this anger he entertained his *doppel-gänger* by directing another less violent rage towards the dinner he was missing.

Half-breed meals, he thought, when West meets East in the East! Compost, no more than factitiously homey compost.

Day after day, in restaurant receptacles of the Rose China which garnished every mess, club, transit hostel, and house, appeared meals which strove to achieve the toniness of lower-middle-class-three-courses but achieved more — a surrealist quality; there was something atheistic in the tastelessness, an unorthodoxy more acceptable had the frozen lamb been emerald green and the mashed potatoes crimson. The Oriental cook merely translated into another insipidity the insipidity of tinned soup, tinned peas, tinned plums, frozen steaks and corned beef, dehydrated parsnips, public raspberry jam and coffee essence: the ectoplasmic meals were served on a long table where a centre-piece of flea-bitten apples was ringed about by bottles of unsanctified Worcestershire and Mild Tomato Sauce, salt tablets, fairy bread, and numbered plastic napkin-rings.

Repulsed, repining, officers lusted for and filled up on canteen purchases: chocolate biscuits, Norwegian salmon, Bonox, gherkins, lemon butter, and tinned peanuts. It was, he thought, boarding-school all over again and no Matron, the boarding-school of delirium and welter.

Above the permanent shallows of food-fretfulness smaller other irritations put up toad snouts but, farther out, greater antipathies sliced the surface with shark-fin, bounded flying-fish-like into full view, spouted up whale-geysers. Acrimony battened on another's table noises or ceaseless whistling of several bars — and one note always wrong! — on affectations, stinginess, unwanted affabilities, on a courtesy too many, a diffidence too obtrusive, on — on anything.

At the moment, Major Everard-Hopkins hated Captain Dugald.

The insulated and dubious luxury of too many arm-chairs and coffee-tables, of central heating, *Reader's Digests*, electric fans and Oriental servants, could not temper the fact that "X" Mess was indeed a legionnaire boarding-school, a perilous enclosure in which antagonisms increased rapidly as portulaca, and moral strengths waned in the half-hour.

There was too much time to waste.

Work and the most demanding of vices, elaborate of pettinesses or tedious of hobbies, could not fully occupy this faction, for it was enclosed by an air it did not know how to breathe — leisure, and that leisure of the East in which the native folded dreams from paper, carved a saint from a nut or stared into the seductive and uncarnal eyes of nirvana.

Boarding-school, friary, barracks, old men's home, officers' mess, prison: each a unique zone having a climate of its own.

This cubicled tropic, frontiered by mirage, lay under the unflagging high noon of a male society; no cloud-shadow of wife, mother or housekeeping old-maid sister blotted the carbolic shower-rooms and coir-matted passages; men dropped cigarette-ash everywhere. Mainly self-exiled, escaped from a Western *milieu* that knew their meagre shameful failings, they pretended, in this bivouac between walls of indemnity and under the roofs of reprisal, to forget indecorums that would impair the buccaneer pose, and re-counted, as their own, depravities they had not joined in or ever even witnessed. At two a.m. what revelations!

The wallet embossed with trite Oriental designs was eviscerated on the bar counter: the snapshot of mum squinting by the backyard-fence scarlet runners, of a divorced wife in bathers concealing her corns in beach-sand, or a ten-year old Nell-Gwyn-curled daughter to whom useful gifts were periodically sent — miniature plastic water-closets, manicure sets embedded in imperial-blue velvet, scarves printed with Phar Laps or Lana Turners. Next there were the smutty postcards, the fold-worn sheets of typed pornography, ingenious as the graffiti on public-lavatory walls.

Mirage! How tremulously it hung upon the horizon, and yet its waters seemed to creep, to assume substance, lap shores and make sound: self-esteem the most garrulous of infamies, subreption, obloquy, procrastination, spite. The old personality snag by snag appeared, glamour dried off; the unrelenting glare traduced all men to the ultimate and most oblique of poses — sincerity.

Occupation-Democracy drew back its lips, as Captain Dugald had drawn back his.

Major Everard-Hopkins, in tusser shirt, dark tie, and grey suit, drank on through dinner. Anger too drank, preparing itself.

Truscott appeared first from the dining-room.

"Have you, my dear young man," said the Major, erect as a burnt tree-trunk, "seen Captain Dugald?"

What's got into the old boy? thought Truscott. Before he could answer, infamy answered for itself.

"What's the trouble?" shouted Captain Dugald, accurately spinning his cap onto the rack which stood in the hall separating bar from dining-room.

"Yours," said the Major. "A word, Dugald." Snap, snap, snap-snap. And, just too late, snap: "Please."

"Oh, really, Hopkins," brutally, "late for dinner now. After do?"

"No. Now."

Truscott, impressed by the assonance and command of these monosyllables, was startled by their — imbecile? eccentric? — vigour, knew rapiers were out, withdrew to the other end of the bar counter.

Dugald, a wolf-like solitary, unaware and unheeding of his significance in other lives, because he did not link the brute he was with the brutality he was responsible for, came to the bar counter.

Everard-Hopkins too deliberately drained his whisky and ordered another.

Dugald exempted himself from nothing: "You might ask me to have a drink." A quick and glittering sentence.

Everard-Hopkins glittered back: "I'm afraid I shouldn't care to."

"What's this?"

"You will no doubt be appeased to hear that the gardener's jaw is fractured."

"So that's it." Dugald's voice was stones dropped from a cliff-edge of insensibility; the flesh of his face petrified.

"I saw the poor man was attended to; the X-ray shows a crack that, luckily, the M.O. says will not need wiring up."

This, Truscott noticed, was intoned in the iambic pentameters of conscious Good Samaritanism. And *poor man*: really, Everard-Hopkins!

Dugald dropped more stones: "Serve the old bastard right. Serve him right. Poor man, my foot!"

"Poor man in several senses, Dugald. Old, yes. Old, and much older than you."

Aware that the officers already in from, and coming in from, dinner for pre-Bingo drinks were unable to avoid hearing, Dugald increased the volume and clarity of his voice.

"*Old* if you like. I ordered him to make a new kennel for m'dog. He mucked it up completely, wasted good material. What should I do, Major? Compliment him?"

"You're sure you made clear to him what you wanted? Did he really understand?"

"Of course he understood. They understand well enough. He understands me now, anyway."

"Does he? I confess, Captain that *I* do not always understand you. At the moment I decidedly don't. 'Old' was the word you used — the only correct one. You know perfectly well, Dugald, that the gardener is old and frail. He tries hard to do his work well."

"Why not? He's paid to do it well, and I'm the one to see that it is done well. None of this false pity for me. You seem to regard the slant-eyes as some sort of — of — salt of the earth. Sentimentalism, damned sentimentalism."

"If it's sentimentalism to point out that an officer of

your . . . your bulk, and relative youthfulness, should have
sufficient control to keep his hands off old men, then I'm
sentimental and grateful for being so."

Dugald had long ago put the final seal to his adulthood,
had passed his own examination, and honoured it.

He laughed; it was the bark of a beast of prey; he showed
savage teeth.

"Old or not old, he's one of them."

Everard-Hopkins's voice became higher, clearer, that of
Nemesis. "I warn you, Dugald, that I feel very strongly
about this and shall make a report of —"

"I am indifferent to your feelings. *Particularly* to your
feelings. One of the reasons I rarely drink here is you, people like you. I saw enough of the atrocities committed by
the —"

"Not by that old man!"

"Well, his son, grandson, nephew, the bloke next door,
the bloke in the next town. What does it matter? They're all
the same, the dirty, stinking —"

"That's enough, Dugald. The war is over."

It was not, not by any means, and so their voices duelled
on.

The other officers once or twice attempted disregarded
interference — *Put a sock in it, you two*, or *I say, you fellows,
really* — finished their drinks, and withdrew to Bingo.

Wilkinson sat by, gammoning interest in the slick assess-
ments of *Time*.

Truscott, although bored, felt an obligation to wait a
while, sipped drinks, presently could not analyze the
obligation's apparent veracity, went to the Officers' Club,
played Bingo, won a leather satchel, and enjoyed himself.

Finally, Dugald, unsustained by an evangelistic oxygen,
perceived that Everard-Hopkins was a lunatic, off his
rocker, regretted his missed dinner, remembered his dog and
the bottle of gin in his quarters, and could bear no more.

"I'm going. I don't know why I listen to you. I must be
batty. But you're battier than they are. You're soft on them,
God knows why. They know how to look after themselves."

He left.

Everard-Hopkins noticed a pain in his chest, his left arm ached.

Batty? Battier?

He had drunk too many whiskies, and drank one more. Sentimental?

That poor old codger *can't* look after himself, he thought.

In this the Major was wrong. The dynasty of Pity is lengthy; that of Revenge is longer.

As the Major was leaving, Wilkinson rose from obscurity to say, "I think you did the right thing", and said it, but the other passed him, and each stiff pace more was one pace less of those ordained to him, as he advanced to the solitude of a bed peopled with ideals, misconceptions, and doubts. Wilkinson owned one of those faces in snapshots of groups of which one would say, "Haven't the foggiest", if asked, "Who's the insipid one?"

No one ever would ask. No one even noticed that he was insipid.

A colony repulsing explorers, he had made only the humblest explorations of himself. They ended always in a sodden and windless hollow.

Ridiculous to consider the interlocking septs, the generations of coquetry, courtings, and consummations, to say nothing of long-drawn-out tragedies and comedies, of centuries vibrant with resentments, jealousies, ardours and rancours gone to seed and tossed out to produce him, the middle-sized, middle-class young man, neither hideous nor handsome.

He was recessive and passive. Even the Orientals who care to dare or accomplish little alone, least of all the felicities of self-destruction, and who might have been expected to spot his isolation and share self-mollifying sympathy, even they by-passed him.

For example, "Good night, Brig, good night, Butch," he said to the bar-boys, and there was no reply.

Butch was studying *Damned sentimentalism* and *Put a sock in it, you two* for some impressive future moment; Brigadier was occupied in foreseeing as much as he could of one aspect of his fast-approaching nearer future. And should he wear scent?

Wilkinson returned to his room, fussed about, opened and shut drawers, sighed, got out writing paper and began:

Dearest Mumsy,
    You will be delighted to know that I have been able to get you a book on Oriental Cookery which I shall post tomorrow. My housegirl got it for me.

He paused. He began to write again.

Now that I am really settled down I am enjoying the life here immensely.

He paused. He began to write again . . . more lies, more lies.

The crowd in the Mess are awfully nice chaps and . . .

Several rooms away from Wilkinson, Everard-Hopkins, in bed, seemed to himself to be anxious for footsteps that should come, voices that should be trilling ineluctable truths, blazing hands to char away not the physical pain in his heart but the extra one.

I shouldn't have lost my temper, he thought, I'm getting too old; I'm sick; I'll see the medical bloke tomorrow and get leave; I'll have a holiday in the depths of this country away from Dugalds and Messes, among old ways and old resignations.

Something was faulty in him; he had for years been an onlooker winding himself up like a watch. Now the spring unwound itself; the watch-hands scythed too violently over blankness; he talked too much and was a bore.

Yet the Orientals were not the only ones he felt sorry for: Dugald, too. Certainly Dugald seemed stronger, more bestial — was he?

The gardener, an Untouchable bred of centuries of Untouchables, and who had told Everard-Hopkins he heard the ghosts of bombed children weeping and deploring on the slope below the Mess . . . was he really weaker with his unflawed heredity?

Did he hear weeping? Were there ghosts? The rubble on the slope, was it merely voiceless shards of havoc, broken rice-bowls, roof-tiles, and rusting spirit stoves, or vociferous chunks of children's skulls, talkative smashed pelvises.

I do not even know one useful word of the language of these people who move me so, he thought. If I, for example, were to have to study Oriental trigonometry!

"That poor boy," he actually said to the ceiling, thinking of Brigadier unable not to hear what Dugald had shouted about the gardener and the nation. I must apologize to him tomorrow, try to explain . . . what? Dugald's convictions or his own?

At that moment, his bar duties over for the night, the poor boy was holding his scrubbed face and hair and his fresh other-singlet in the fumes from a stick of incense. In the empty bar he could hear Butch loudly practising on a monotone, "Damned senti-menta-rism, damned senti-menta-rism, damned . . . ."

As Brigadier came through the bar, spick, span, and scented, Butch tried to wink at him, he tried to wink back. Though this exchange had miscarried every time, for winking was not of their race, they had learnt when a wink meant something and what it meant.

Foiled, they bowed politely to each other and Brigadier, Yoshiharo Minato, naval officer's son, student of engineering, nineteen years old, heterosexual, dexterous bar-boy, intelligent, and anxious to do the right thing, crossed the Mess compound to the end room of the Quarters where, in a robe which horrified Yoshiharo Minato by its gaudiness, Padre Hamilton awaited him.

A little while later, of the six males in the Quarters between nine and ten o'clock — Major Everard-Hopkins, Captain Wilkinson, Captain Dugald, his dog, Padre Hamilton, and a bar-boy — only the dog and Padre Hamilton, in their animal fashion, seemed to consider themselves happy.

5

It was becoming hotter.

Along streets, inside the half-doors of beer-houses or the Babylonic portals of department stores, stood troughs on legs, holding blocks of ice in which were embedded aesthetically rustic compositions of shells and egg-fruit, fish and roses. On these blocks the passers-by rubbed their palms and applied them to their foreheads.

For almost a week Hoshi had been a bungling housegirl, sullen, her squint at its worst; a flower-arrangement in which she had intended negative delicacy had shifted into an unrefined symmetry that Paula Groot for once thought artistic rather than demented. She had just returned from school.

"That is very nice," she said.

Hoshi, squatted on the bedroom mat sewing, did not answer. There was no answer to give to one who condoned meaningless design. She wore her working-dress, an armless sack of cotton from whose fibres penury's design had faded. Her mind glowed like a coal.

"*Very* nice," the teacher repeated, touched a flower senselessly, and then began to draw her dress over her head.

Her eyes thus hidden did not see the housegirl's face, already boorishly passionate, turn towards her and become haggard with an assassin's grimace, but she did hear the immediately succeeding sobs — noisy and indecorous.

"Good heavens, Hoshi!"

Hoshi had utterly given her the jim-jams this week: it could be worms, hot weather, or a display to wheedle Aspros for a pretended headache and the black market — you never could tell.

Paula Groot could not know the outburst was caused by an intensification of the ah-ness of things, or that she had her own part in it. The wasp had stung yet another weeping face.

Paula Groot's face was to have no tears for a while; her wasp was yet far off.

Irked, baldly, "Come on now, what's wrong?" she said.

Dress in hand, in brassière, scanties, and high heels, she was an illustration in a Man's Magazine.

"I am wicked." The housegirl turned up her face, a drenched dish of dolour. She was an illustration in a thicker book and an older one.

"Wicked? Wicked how?"

"I have broken prate."

"Plate, Hoshi, plate. Which plate?"

"Brue p-l-ate."

"Don't be silly, girl. It doesn't matter. Stop sniffing. Wipe your face."

She reached for dressing-gown and sponge-bag: this was bogus suffering, a pennyworth of tears, and wasted ones at that.

Paula Groot considered she had long ago come to terms with fate; to be trapped into enduring, like a confidante in a tragedy, repulsive expression of grief, neither amused nor ennobled.

How could this Westerner, uncertain of the rules of the class just above hers, uncertain even of all the rules of women of her own class, unaware of the reason behind many Western chagrins, dejections, or levities, catch the outlines, let alone the overtones, of a disquiet based on individual impulse but haunted by echoes from a foreign ancestry?

Hoshi, unkempt from and inspired by the knowledge that despair and anguish are vanities, rose fawningly out of the floor to commit martyrdom and, dabbing at her face, which was ravaged with blotches, charged herself to make a confession unworked by the leaven of artifice.

She committed it with terror and the unstylishness of reality.

Six, maybe seven, days brother Kazuo was giving gift and note for kind mistress Groot. Wick-ed Hoshi was not giving note and gift as directed. So, in nerves and being not-goodness, she was not strong to support prate. So prate was smashing. Every nights she was praying to be good, but she was being wick-ed. Every nights she was dreaming badness and praying, but she was being wick-ed.

The schoolteacher, elated and venomous, was fascinated by this sketch of crooked dealing and its inter-leaves of curious suffering; she watched the housegirl's beautiful dirty hands describe incomprehensible figures — *wick-ed* — it was an identical gesture repeated; flourishes outlined obscurity with finality, rounded in the mystery of an Oriental jealousy with curves rigid as wrought-iron.

She watched the twitching figure, uncharming but terribly living and present, a stray dog to be fed or stoned away.

Then Paula Groot's riding-crop was out, that of her voice: "'What have you done with the note? Where is it?"

The mottled face became contused with more terror, also became brutally stupid.

Ridiculous.

The crop of Miss Groot's voice flashed menacingly, sliced the air as if it were a hide: "Answer me! Where is it?"

Terror outran stupidity; the housegirl stumbled giddily towards the drawer in which she kept her private and beastly scraps, and, making obeisances, desperately commanding herself *Keep mind clean, Hoshi; keep mind clean*, handed over note and gift and collapsed shuddering to the floor.

"Ach, fool," said Paula Groot, tearing at the intricate note tied with a decorative knot of red-paper string, a special one of the conventional two hundred knots.

Adroitness of knotting and folding conveyed nothing to her — the words, the words:

Dear Miss Groot,

I am speaking of you with my sister. She is telling me that you are seriously desiring visit to god-house of White Horse on Shrine Island so beauteous. I shall find it very delightful to direct you by voyaging on ferry of 14 hours during Saturday two week time,

Yours faithfully,
KAZUO TABUCHI

Fear induces attitudes resembling trance, *rigor*: Hoshi had ground her face against the mat, and was hunched in what might be some dream of vengeance that was to be succeeded by appeasement and purification, later by the hot bath and tepid rice, the contemplation of nervous maple shadow on moon-whitened paper shutters.

Nevertheless, she felt the resplendent surprise of the other woman, perpendicular, radio-active, soaring above her and smiling drunkenly.

"Hoshi!"

Hoshi listened. *Hoshi, Hoshi, Hoshi. . . .*

"Did I tell you I wished to visit Shrine Island?"

Hoshi listened still.

"Answer!"

"No, pliss."

"Look at me. Did you tell your brother I wished to? I said, look at me."

She lifted her ravaged face. Ice regarded slushy thaw.

"Yes, pliss."

"Why?" Mad, mad the lot of them. "Why, Hoshi?"

Why, Hoshi, Hoshi, Hoshi . . . ?

The housegirl did not answer because she could not: the words were there neither in her own nor the other's daily vocabulary.

Each person is her own continent, her own homeland to which she has the visa and the only visa. In that homeland, for Hoshi, played a child Kazuo whom she had loved much, and still loved so much she had easily read his desire for Paula Groot: Kazuo had not considered this important enough to reveal or disguise.

Desire is a bowl of soup, a spray of loquats, new socks, no more.

Self-sacrificingly, slave of an unnecessary greed for his esteem, she had devised an arrangement which would free him from plottings of his own.

"Groot wishes Shrine Island guide," she had said.

Love's partial eyes saw no harm in his desire; common sense said, *Mistress Groot or anyone, it doesn't matter*; but, the note written, the sudden intemperance of a jealousy from nowhere had made Hoshi agonize, and hang on to her brother's reply to a fake message.

Paula Groot need never have been told.

However, gestures of love are not decentralized, the heart has an implacable frankness of its own that ultimately cannot be out-talked by lesser and louder-mouthed motives. Blue plates are broken, and the tongue says what it can for the unbribable heart.

The Western woman narrowly examined the Oriental for signs of *arrière pensée*, motives for a future about-face move: she certainly could not understand this present duplex one.

Nor did she really need to; things were turning out as she wished: her quarry was nearer; an animal ripe for such hunting posed in open country, and with deliberation to be brought down.

Nine or ten days would bring him down.

Hoshi herself saw little farther than the maybe of a diminished and diminishing distress for herself; she curled her fingers at her forehead as though to pluck this phantom possibility from behind it.

Paula Groot lit up, every nerve shone.

"Get up from the floor," she sang. "Go to the kitchen and make tea. Weak. No sugar."

Rising, the housegirl might have been a female Peter, alone, utterly without Leader, benighted in a night with no moon and therefore no cockcrow. Twofold deprived of betrayal, it appeared she would be unable to betray even herself.

"Hurry, Hoshi," the schoolteacher chanted like a nun refreshed and propitiated by prayer. "Hurry. I want to have a shower. Weak. No sugar. Hurry, Hoshi!"

When Hoshi left the hostel at six o'clock, she bore in her carrying-cloth a lipstick, a rayon underslip, and two blocks of hazel-nut chocolate, the pitying liberality of Paula Groot.

Hoshi's face was now a sombre pool, calm; she had accepted sorrow; the conflagration of her sickness had burned down as the sunset was burning luridly down over a homing population of tattered or flowery figures. Mosquitoes smoked up from lotus ditches; twilight smoked up from the earth.

She could not foresee that the night thus foretold was to be for her the night of a malevolent primitive world. She could not foresee that she had already begun an exile in the darkening apse of her own mind, was to become lost there, an uncontrolled wraith never to rejoin the discreeter wraiths of humanity moving in endless queues on narrow roads illuminated by the phosphorescent friction of soles without number.

"Tell your brother," had cried the silver Miss Groot, the schoolteacher, the magnanimous beauty winging high above her homely servant, "that I shall perhaps meet him on the ferry."

Later, after her shower, whistling, painted, dressed and sacrificed to, she unrolled Kazuo's gift. It was an Utamaro, a remnant of diminished family treasures.

Freakish to her against the mica-speckled yellow was the frail beak, the languid shoulders down which brooks of black hair divided.

Dear, crazed, darling Kaz-u-o!

Expressionless from ignorance of what she looked at, she slid it on to the top of her wardrobe, forgetting it for ever. The Sauternes-quaffing and cake-eating woman who succeeded her in the Y.W.C.A. room found the valuable print, screwed it up, and threw it away.

Of all incidents in the brief story of Hoshi, Paula Groot, and Kazuo, this was the worst. The paper woman was irreplaceable; the three of them were not.

From his sister Kazuo received with alert negligence the answer for which, dead-pan, he had patiently waited in silence.

When night abducted the land he again visited the brothel, for night is the time when man grows in impudicity or saintliness.

The looking-glass gods were clapped at, prayed to, and fed with rice grains and chlorinated water; monkeys slept restlessly and curled their leather-lips contemptuously in hill gulches; the melancholy whistle of the blind masseur was heard in back streets; the noodle-seller made melodious hullabaloo on market-corners.

After she had locked the rain-doors to keep out ghouls and thieves, Hoshi crawled beneath the edge of the mosquito-net and fanned out her candle. It was always unwise to blow it out: superstition is a wise politeness towards possibilities. Yet, despite these precautions, minute evils inhabited the buckwheat pillow at her ear; they kept her awake; there formed before her an abominable puppet of rice-straw that was Paula Groot.

It was not Hoshi's heart that had shattered.

It is not ever the heart that shatters, but its glassy rind; the pulp within, raw and non-moral, transmits its heinous fiats to an owner still ripe for conviction.

Although Hoshi tried to prevent herself from snarling vixenishly, tried to pray with her rosary of a hundred and eight beads which assembled on one thread, as the universe itself did, the twenty-four climates, the seventy-two atmospheres, and the twelve months, the exposed heart was too potent, and forced her to see more and more distinctly, even through the black bandage of night, the straw creature which smiled superciliously and blindly, smiled like a cat.

Elsewhere, others slept and dreamed more sanely than children, stole, murdered, regretted, laughed, wondered, denied and created.

Meantime the chrysanthemums, Snow-capped Bamboo, Banked Fire, Steed under Cherry Blossoms, Voice of Metropolis, and Lethe were beginning to enlarge those buds that would unclench in a few weeks.

6

Sparks from Major Everard-Hopkins's quarrel with Captain Dugald set off surrounding minor fires: Captain This was not speaking to Captain That who had worked out, in ink, a *John o'London* crossword; Major So-and-So had conspicuously waddled from the bar, thus infuriating Captain Someone who was already feeling guilty because his women visitors had become too-noisy-in-their-cups at Major So-and-So's elbow; the Mess Sergeant, offended by a rebuke, had decided to forget ordering tinea powder, Lux soap, and aspirin, which act had the triple power of aggravating the Mess officer who had rebuked him, the hypochondriacs, and the black-marketeers. . . .

Everybody in "X" Mess was seeing each other with the wrong clarity.

Outside: another sunset, and a vividly shining Wednesday which had electrolyzed itself into a total of sadnesses that was merely a repetition of centuries of totals.

A Cleanliness Bell struck near by; then sounds — each separate one an essence scale-thin and rarefied — began to detach themselves meticulously from the coarser and richer conglomeration.

It was the Hour of the Dog.

Everard-Hopkins, enfevered by exhaustion and thought, did not even have Truscott to drench with his judgments, and stood alone under his favourite gingko-tree, that two-sexed sacred vegetable, last vestige of a primitive botanical era. He stared, beyond the agitation of electric sparklings below, at the marble calm of the sea plunged into which, like aeroliths, were Chinese-scroll islands, hundreds of them, spurred and spiked, wearing toupées of thicket, fishermen's shrines, out-of-action wireless aerials.

He could see none of them in the dark but knew them there, just as he knew that visions seen in his pre-Occupation and fancy-free daylight were hidden in the Occupation darkness.

He went on mischievously cultivating, as the sick and

irascible can cultivate, an emotion of regret, affected and tender.

Before, and for a while after, his arrival, he had possessed no faintest desire to rebuke or correct humanity, East or West, Teutonic or Slav, this or that, had no interest in defending it against itself or participating in its feckless ballet: choreography, Selfishness; *décor*, Misery; music, Barratry; costumes, Sin; *prima ballerina*, Compromise, and a *corps de ballet* composed of . . . no, no, not for him.

First views of the East were disappointing: he had imagined pagodas of vermilion lacquer, house-eaves like gilded antlers hooked in the lower boughs of forests of camellia, girl-high irises and slender women taller than irises inclining beneath and among yard-long racemes of wistaria.

Nothing like that to see. No gilt and scarcely any gingerbread: in towns that were essays in muted tones, ash and sub-ash, towns reeking of dried squid and human-manure, hundreds of faces had appeared the same face.

By and by, however, he was able to beguile himself by translating the mean of straight black hair, oak-brown eyes and blank — blank! — faces into English: word by word came right — astute, whimsical, shifty, meek, benevolent, maternal, silly, mean. No finesse of expression was absent. He saw Merry Wives of Windsor, Sentimental Tommies, Micawbers, Saint Joans, Becky Sharps, characters from Rowlandson, Daumier, Breughel, and Stanley Spencer.

Next he observed there was not merely a quaint and comic troupe of bar-boys, housegirls, peasants, fishermen, and curio-dealers, bowing and admiringly hissing to quixotic champions, but a vast success of motor-salesmen, editors of pornography, lottery promoters, brothel magnates, wireless announcers, dive-guides, film-actresses, contraception kings, drink stewards, all bowing to their influx of clients.

Reluctantly he was self-converted to the belief that the conquerors were being conquered.

As he stood, celibate and valueless, under the two-sexed tree, there came to him as strongly as to any zealot a haunting odour.

In the wake of the tide-race of flesh that had ebbed with ebbed daylight, stronger than the odours of satiety, frenzy, serenity and all states, rose the odour, tainted and exhilarating, of . . . of . . . was it living? Whatever it was, it smelled to him of a beauty he should have liked to analyze — an analysis that, expressed in his sentences, would begin to smell not of life but of Major Everard-Hopkins.

No good though, for Truscott had taken his ear and charming ploughboy attention with him to the Eastern Capital where he was to be stationed, while from "X" Mess the initial hoarse din of male revelry was increasing in volume, striking down one life's life with another's.

Irritation having mounted behind irritation, the fluid in the pressure tube of "X" Mess had risen to its danger-limit and lapped ominously there. No man could foretell when this point would be reached, every man knew when it was. Without warning or invitation therefore, as though identical clots had day by day, pique by pique, fattened in each man's machinery of nerves and needed to be dissolved now or never, a sacrament of dissolution was to take place.

They were all there, no visitors, all males, all what they called *home*, a family with dinner over, laughter pitched tones higher or deeper than usual, crowded at the bar.

Truscott had gone; Everard-Hopkins and Dugald never appeared at this sort of thing.

Everyone almost jostled, drinks were beginning to be splashed . . . who cared? . . . on clothes the housegirls daily cleaned and pressed.

That was what clothes were for, and people. To become dirty, to be cleaned.

Enemies were not yet speaking — the temporarily divorced Thisses and Thats, Someones and Thingummies — but they were already magnetized towards each other, and shouldered about in the same groups; hands were turning redder or whiter, faces thicker or more hollow, as intoxication increased, as the tide rose and they galumphed in its deepenings. Voices became louder and, soon, high or deep, had borrowed and lent quality until all had reached a common level of masculinity, recklessness, and hard jocularity.

Daredevil quantities and combinations of drinks were downed.

Higher the tide, louder the waves.

Wilkinson, emerging from the sea-cave arm-chair of his

corner, paddled half-drunk in the shallow edges of cliques, unobserved but dumbly happy, gaping troutlike at scandals and legends about absent heroes who towered on stilts of anecdote to strike resonant heads like Mardi Gras monsters against the ceiling-fans.

How these Pistols and Hectors reeled and swaggered through piratical occasions; outwitting a general in a typhoon; springing Athos-nimble through cuckolds' windows; how they hoodwinked, floored, seduced, captured, and circumvented! And how enriched with the addition of strong moustaches, thick watchbands, tattooings, heavy bellies, belts, and signet rings the hero-worshippers felt!

Wilkinson, admiring them, was incapable of observing that initiative and self-discipline had been frittered away to minimum, for he was one of them, as the egg is the alligator.

Scorched upon them to be seen, and invisibly staining the flimsiest tissues of their imaginations, were bitternesses, impotencies, deceits, the incurable sores from orgies of flesh and cunning and brutality. Most were not professional officers, but opportunists. The flamboyant dead, blown into existence as beer-stained balloons larger than life, burst to death again in epitaphs of laughter from their living kin. The dead were the living's wilder brothers.

Captain This was now friendly with Captain That who leant on the piano-top, a Marcus Stone lover who would never work out a crossword in ink again. To Captain This's music, feet were straddled and heads thrown operatically back, elbows rested on neighbour shoulders, maudlin and bawdy songs were roared. Drinking competitions were held: glasses clenched between teeth, drunk backward, emptied while kneeling and in a flash.

The tide deepened, mouth-over, eyes-over, head-over; the tide was deep above them; below its surface-waves, they swayed and boomed.

Coats were stripped off; some began worming and squeezing through the nickel legs of cocktail stools.

Wilkinson, drowning and inflamed though unregarded, took a stool into the shadow behind the writing-desk. He was inspired: would try the trick privately, get the knack, reveal his expert self. His head and his shoulders through: easy. His chest through: easy. His waist: easy. Now a twist and . . . Captain Wilkinson stuck. Ashamed and horrified, he remained stuck and unnoticed during the hour he went on modestly and guiltily attempting escape.

The party reverberated on without him.

Suddenly, the second-last stage in the purification was upon them all: the boarding-school dormitory pillow-brawl, the university college Walpurgis-night. The moment had arrived everyone had known would arrive — the first arm-chair cushion took the air.

Behind the bar counter, Brigadier and Butch edged nearer to each other — Babes in the Wood — made their bodies narrower, and set their expressions at nought.

At first, cushions only were thrown; but why only cushions? Coats then, and sodden counter-cloths then, and magazines then, and newspaper balls then.

Paper?

Now lavatory-paper rolls streamered and cometed, masonically horse-collared about necks, were trapped in strips to wing round and round in the overhead fan.

When the circular detachable tops of standard ash-trays — hoop-la! — viciously sliced through the air, the bar-boys, already thinking of stitched foreheads and split ears, expectantly bent their knees in imperceptible curtseys, but remained at facial nothing, as *one* and *one* and *one* and *one* four light-globes were smashed. In a coma of amazement, Butch said liplessly to Brigadier, "Damned senti-ment-arism."

Brigadier knew he was wrong, but could not think of the word.

Wilkinson, quietly straining in his shadow, was glad of less light, and saw little of the storm he heard. It abated, the last stage was coming; the waters were falling and ebbing.

To the Orientals, the transfixed bar-boys, the wrestling that now began lacked grace and subtlety, lacked pattern and climax, had suggestions of a hobgoblin polka performed horizontally as well as vertically and askew. Neck veins thickened; gusts of sweat-stink reached the bar-boys. Some Laocoön-like trios had found in their central member an in-termedium whose force so neutralized right and left they were for minutes stuck at heaving and panting statuedom;

teeth slashed the dimmer light in every direction from tightly carved and garish smiles.

Enemies of the past weeks and earlier hours now executed together a stumbling and almost wordless schottische, their marble eyes riveting forgiveness on each other and a red understanding, a collusion they did not themselves understand though they felt its hot power.

Here and there, a tossed-aside partner, crouching solo like a beast behind a hurled-over chair, huskily exhorted the straining and streaming others in the monosyllabic dialect of the beast, but — the waters ebbing and ebbing — *diminuendo*, until only the crunching of under-sole glass remained, the sounds of scuffling and hairy breathing.

Noise had dissolved in the same way as the tumours on their natures had; the ruck — knee-deep only, now — began to fall apart amicably, to splash enervated ashore to their coats, to cry hoarse good night like albatrosses, to tread the sands back to the Mess Quarters.

They almost marched springily.

And, as the officers almost marched springily across the compound, the twopenny-coloured page of night flickered over to the next day behind their shoulder-blades, which were opening and closing like the muscled scars of torn-out wings, opening and closing with inhalations and exhalations of relief — the relief of some unnamable orgasm, some neolothic ceremony no vocabulary of their semi-civilization could explain.

The tide was out till next time.

As the last group stamped from the dishevelled sands, the room of wreck, Wilkinson rose from his mortification and followed them slowly.

The bar-boys moved to clean up. Their public smiles unknotted like lovers' knots. Beachcombers both now, scavengers, Shire Council odd-job-men, they began to swear. Since their own language did not provide the adornments of profanity, they used the English their conquerors had permitted them to overhear. Brigadier used it more finically, more correctly, more vehemently. Butch had a wider range but used it much less appositely, and with the pleasure of someone making something from a lot of scraps of nothing.

The world turned in its sleep.

The scavengers grew quieter, dropped their last words, became mute. Circles under their eyes, they moved softly and seemed to listen. This was their world that had grown quiet and they with it. The ghosts they owned were about. There were the ghosts of crucified traitors seeking redemption and peace, of fox-women deathly beautiful seeking any lover — any late and handsome author, poet, fletcher, mayor's clerk, or bar-boy.

"Any lover, any lover," the fox-women whispered, seeking and drifting.

"One, one," whispered the ghosts of suicide lovers, drifting and seeking the one.

Captain Truscott was asleep in his train to Eastern Capital, Hoshi asleep, Kazuo asleep, Paula Groot asleep, the gardener asleep; Dugald's housegirl — an Untouchable — slept under a bitterly complacent smile; Dugald's dog asleep, its time running out, but asleep.

At the edge of the baseball ground by the rust-sown dockland, even the raped and strangled Oriental woman, with bloody shreds of skin and some blond hair in her fingernails, seemed merely asleep, for the wind that had run lightly across the waters from Sacred Island, where none may be born and none are permitted to die, hovered curiously about her, curiously touching the hair of her corpse and curiously the cotton of her dress, so that she too seemed to stir in this sleep after murder, and to breathe.

7

The Captain Truscott travelling by train to Eastern Capital was already, after three weeks of hearing it, irritated to indifference by the ululation ascending from Western crusades for and against Orientals; he sided with neither.

Everard-Hopkins's passion for them was, he decided, a sort of mental scrofula, a sophism beyond which he permitted himself to see no further than the partial truth that Occupationnaires were charlatans mis-sincerely tedding the hay of whipped-up problems on the greener fields of original and more significant ones. Certainly the victor-visitors suffered from the relative degeneracy shown in the behaviour of all bread-eating races. They were enfeebled, too, by the sloth of a prosperity which left them unprepared to admire a nation drawing, and able to draw perpetually, on lodes of ancestral vigour.

Oriental art and poetry, which Truscott had fervently dipped into, were formal and selective, mysteriously asymmetrical and, while appearing to give no more than a peephole view, nevertheless revealed blood-saturated and palaeocrystic uplands where magnificent and undoubted heroes treacherously ravaged and postured to discount Everard-Hopkinses.

Also revealed, as it were through holes in paper panes, were sleepy by-ways where unending retinues of the childlike, the modest, self-sacrificing and gentle luminously defiled past the sneers of unbelieving Dugalds.

Sweated awake at early sunrise on the oven-hot train, Truscott raised the tinny venetians of his bunk window to see unpleat a succession of exquisite scenes. These, more than great cities and ports, had for millennia inspired art and sustained economies, interlocking beauties where field, village, farmhouse, well, temple, graveyard, fence, granary, and canal were themselves richly interlocked, also woven so intimately with and upon slope, about river, around rock and through valley, that there was no hair-line division between Man's tribute and Nature's.

Truscott felt that he saw a truth beyond Everard-

Hopkins's, saw it with an almost sinister clairvoyance: the Orientals had not been strangers in their world, as others less thrifty were in theirs.

Many times throughout many decades, he thought, those appealing images the living call the dead, must have darned and re-darned this lush fabric rent by feudal forays, blazing crops, cyclones, thunderbolts, and famine. How natural, criss-crossed lovingly, and imperceptible were the darnings!

Holocaust, devastation, Armageddon itself with machine destroying machine to gain domination over a kingdom of cinders, could not utterly annihilate this interfusion of earth and seasons and person: the domestic fire small as love, that drop of ichor in the human blood, would thickly multiply on the blackest plain.

When Truscott reached the Capital, itself still half shattered from war, he reported for duty at a building whose interior was undergoing the assaults of reorganization.

Floor-boards were torn up, scaffolding showed, lift-wells rang with hammers, dozens of squat Oriental workmen laboured like gremlins at what were surely mischievous demolitions.

The Officer in Charge, whose distraction had become normal, publicly permanent, and a thing he played up, chattered in his cell, dusty and confining as a nineteenth-century vestry, "Did you say Truscott? Why *have* they sent you? I ask myself why?"

He pretended to seek frenziedly for documents he knew the exact whereabouts of.

"I don't seem to have *any* order about you, not a syllable. Truscott? I rilly don't know what is going on . . . ah!" He had sanctioned himself to find a pertinent document.

And, "Truscott!" he cried as though the word were "treasure!" and he a Jim Hawkins. "I *rilly* don't know what is. . . ."

Ultimately Truscott was made grateful to receive the information that he had been given three weeks' leave, could be quartered in a city hotel, was allowed to visit places within a day's travel of the capital. It was the stopgap gift of confusion.

"After that," said the Officer in Charge, "*if* this place *is* ready, I *rilly* don't know what's going to eventuate. Not a clue! The usefulness of this Department is over — but *over*; half of us already recalled. Why, Truscott, have they sent you? I ask myself? Why? And all this?" he indicated the gremlins in their clouds of dust. "I *rilly* don't know."

He did, of course. And he knew Truscott was a departmental might-come-in-handy-later. Departmentally, therefore, he performed warm-handshake-and-congratulation without losing his air of whimsical lunacy. When Truscott left he lost it; it faded as intoxication does; he frowned with wasted severity, and dust thickened on his shoulders.

At large! On leave! Holiday! — a quest in which mind and body have scope and leisure to justify themselves to Galahadry or betray themselves to guttersnipedom.

Truscott now began his own explorations in a world he had so far observed largely through the eyes of others, of Chiyos and Hokusais, of Everard-Hopkins the ageing partisan with adolescent-coloured glasses, of Dugald the bloodhound self-trained to track only the criminal.

Truscott was not to see far or travel far. Experience would give him some small and abiding souvenirs: happiness that could have been illusion but which memory was to regard as authentic, and the knowledge that loneliness shared is not loneliness halved but loneliness doubled: one is lonely when one looks into no other heart, lonelier when one does, for another loneliness sits there with all too human countenance.

In the city, one of Earth's largest, of Martian skyscrapers *craquelé* as Ming monstrosities, of emporiums avenued with plastic cromlechs, of street-stalls fragile as insect skeletons and shabby as primitive gunyahs, he found himself most moved by the not-yet-cleared-away wreckage of air raids.

Gothic apparatus upreared, notching the sky with vast caltrops, above objects misplaced, surrealistically juxtaposed, pluperfect, no longer cherished and surely suffering though unable to complain even mutely. These saddened him; the fingerprints and foot-wearings of the forsaking or the killed veneered them as an accidental smile does the countenance of a corpse. Past them, through the streets and alleys, swept the living: postman, van-driver, anarchist, gangster, rhetor, goldfish-seller gloved like Yvette Guilbert, rice-bran wife, exegete, negro, Queenslander, hordes of anonymous poor as awkwardly dressed as children from an orphanage.

For the illimitable dead peppering the troposphere, this passing and re-passing life must have seemed the mystery; to the dead, life must always seem so.

This city was the domain of elegancies as confirmed and permanent as those of *Vogue* are instantly anachronistic, of verities as scientifically works of art as Vermeers are; even in the dissension of a semi-Westernized noon, whose cryptic angelus might have been guilt's, there stood veteran copses about shrines built to immortalize feuds and rapine of still-stylish nicety. In these trees was entangled a twilight of yearning, a semi-dusk composed of the smoky flutterings of long-rotten robes, of black hair lived grey and cremated centuries ago, of the shadows of dead fingers that had carved tombstones for the dead, of the shadows of later fingers that had burnt incense for the dead fingers that carved the tombstones. Here remained the effluvia of ages — pure and serene, or lavish yet controlled, or of spendthrift fantasy — hovering over ruptured roofs under which stoicism had been esteemed above guile, filial sacrifice above capricious selfishness, the perfection of death above bias-distorted life.

Yet this was far from all, far from all.

One night, half drunk, city-fevered, eating fake-raspberry syruped ice-grouts in a back-street cell dominated by its ice-shaving machine — a moulded iron lathe that Albert would not have regretted in the Crystal Palace — Truscott decided his explorations must become less public, his contact with the East more personal. A woman!

Outside the iced-water shop, under creaking firkins of red paper lanterns, he picked up a pedicab and let the driver, whose scantily covered body might have been a Michelangelo model's, pedal him to the amusement section — a deliberately created pleasure area little altered in purpose from when it began five centuries before.

Convoluted about a park littered with the detritus of hedonism were the labyrinthine alleys of a market in flesh. Here, every desire was fulfilled by an organization for ever feverish; music rattled up from the pits of narrow lanes edged by freak shows, strip-tease rooms, burlesque and movie houses, circuses, pawnshops, penny arcades, brothels, noodle-stalls, temples and shrines, inferior theatres and cabarets. Acrobats, spivs, fences, thieves, masochists, masters of every conceivable aberration of sex, pickpockets, gangsters, and dancers, lived lives of gorgeous laxity in their Oriental Alsatia, to which the subway and the every-twenty-minutes-bus brought the fascinated thousands they satisfied, duped, or corrupted.

Arbitrarily Truscott paid off his Adam-muscled driver outside the neons of FLORIDA CABALET.

He descended steps to a basement-hall huger than he could have imagined; it brimmed with the raddled-and-ruby sultriness of the Demon King's Cave in pantomime.

At each end, in a sulphurous glare, squirmed a dance-band, earnestly demoniac; the hall was chock-a-block, the dancers sealed together beneath lights that, pulsing like tired hearts and revolving slowly, slapped on them the colours of burning cities. Whirling spheres of small looking-glasses dappled flak-like gleams over the dancers.

On the rim of the mass, taxi-girls performed involved tango designs with their partners; others drank at small tables. Truscott's eyes, as he sat at a table and ordered whisky, over-stepped all these to the swooning navel.

There, soldered together, boy and girl, girl and girl, boy and boy, face and mouth demented on face and mouth, body tamped to body, salted with the glue of each other's flesh, scarcely progressing except as a gelatinous mass, the young wallowed to seismic throbbing with shut eyes and calm foreheads over which the semibreves of flak-light slipped and slithered.

Here, thought Truscott, imagining Everard-Hopkins's distress, was certainly a degeneration, but it was a defiance too.

Despite the closed eyes to hide the vision they knew of grey urnings, lean and vapid, who relentlessly trailed from Pole to Pole, dithering, "Youth is nothing, splendour nothing, life nothing, death nothing", they expressed their defiance unbitterly.

"We are," they seemed to moan in tango time, "record

only of a passing era; tinged by the dyes of destruction we are the new positive and negative, the new single and double, the new obverse and reverse. Past is gone and will come again; future comes, but is not here while this music countermands. We swivel as one, a thickly wheeling stew of lawless, delinquent, neurotic youth. Oh, we are still young, still young! We are the blotted ampersand between two urbane utterances . . . young, still young."

They were, Truscott could understand, decidedly not the immobile of spirit, not lion and peony, regality and strength; they were atom bomb's children, black market's messengers, eroticism's devotees with wits and moods as entangled, facile and fictitious as Shakespeare-Bacon cryptograms.

When one orchestra ceased, the other began without a break; the more conventional outrider dancers changed partners, drank at tables, parleyed in the dialect of lust; the central dancers remained seething in their warm death until Life should halt the turbine of the Kiss Dance, divide them, point to Duty patiently waiting, recall to them the horror of the kiss, that imported indelicacy.

After several whiskies Truscott turned his attention, now carnal, to the taxi-dancers he had hitherto observed merely as ciphers in a florid illustration; through the flushed smoke-mists, one of these ciphers excited him. He imagined himself turning the pages of her gown.

She was vivacious; her smile made a seemingly accidental bee-line to Truscott. He smiled back and, remembering Everard-Hopkins again, recklessly beckoned her in the Oriental way, palm down.

She came to his table and sat with him, spoke chirping English, smoked a cigarette, did not drink in this place. They danced; in the ruddiness she seemed as enchanting as some candied and semi-aristocratic figurine; Imiko was her name.

Both she and Truscott were of the country, had been brought up in leafy rustic towns; a sort of vegetable frankness made them perhaps draw nearer to each other than is usual in these encounters. Moreover, it was his first experience, and she needed and intended to get a protector.

Later that night he went to her room where she became his first woman.

As such, the never-to-be-forgotton partner of proven virility, Truscott poetically set her also as a symbol between youth and manhood, between conjecture and revelation, between West and East and, oddly, between loneliness and fulfilment, for he had not ever thought of himself as lonely, and fulfilment he knew to be a crest he had many years' climbing to reach.

Imiko was not a symbol.

Within a few hours of meeting, they had assessed their feelings as love, for both were romantics. Once, love for him would have meant class prejudice, investment, insurance, and quibbling; love for her would have been less for an appointed husband than maternal, would have meant obedience, hard work, immolation in the back of the house.

He had been, and would remain, unsophisticated enough to misinterpret poetry and attempt to write what he thought poetry was. She was a film fan. Excited by the physical reality of their position, he delighted, she shrewd but self-fooling, they began to graft sonorous unrealities on it. Love! chameleon whose changing colours sicken to the achromatic.

Love: Truscott began to arrange for the continuance of bliss with the placidity of one plotting a tour of Paradise, not doubting that every train would run on time and keep to the lines, the weather remain divine.

8

Another part of the field.

The ferry of fourteen hours, to Shrine Island: on it, among others, Captain Wilkinson, Kazuo Tabuchi, Miss Paula Groot. She and her housegirl's brother had instantly seen each other, exchanged a look; hers had expressed "We do not *travel* together", and Kazuo, who had been uncertain only of this, nodded agreement without nodding and now waited, as she did, for fusion in privacy to follow this separation in public. Sustained by musings on their mutual hereafter they scarcely noticed the day with all its windows up and gauzes hung across distances. Since each of them nudely occupied an inner boudoir of the other's senses, they were not alone. Lust never is. It carries its object with it, discarding when that object is achieved.

Wilkinson was alone.

As much as in "X" Mess, he leaned unnoticed on the ferry charged with mortals.

What was it they did not wish to know about him, the secret he did not know himself, which made him viewless?

Even his room did not know him, it remained an hotel room, an official conception of comfort, lout's idea of splendour: he had not bothered, as the other officers had, to improve matters by displaying musical cigarette boxes, tanks of goldfish, plastic toys, indecorous pottery, collections of ties decorated with seed-catalogue roses, sacred mountains, Bernborough, *No More Atom Bombs* and hula-hula girls. In other officers' wardrobes, the housegirls' Harris tweed skirts and exotic party robes were squeezed closely as Bible pages among dress uniforms, white sharkskin coats, pinkish sports trousers, Hawaiian shirts and suits of cocoa-brown, or pinstriped flannel. Dressing-table still lifes of aspirin, tinea powder, Bonox, arm-bands and brilliantine were feminized by scent-bottles, hair-lotions, curling devices, and wire hair-brushes.

Wilkinson's housegirl, who had been the domineering mistress of the officer he replaced, forbidden to share Wilkinson's bed, wardrobe and dressing-table, was

bedevilled by a notion that nobody lived in the room, frequently discussed felo-de-se with herself, and occasionally
dusted a love-powder of charred lizard bootlessly in his underpants. Sometimes, Wilkinson home, when she had mut-
tered herself to distraction, she cleaned off just enough
make-up to leave her prettiness heart-rending, put on her
oldest dress of sad colour, crouched gracefully, making tears,
her back to him, behind the half-open wardrobe door. He
did not, from politeness, shyness, and especially indifference, question her, no matter how loudly she
restrained sobs or rustled paper handkerchiefs.

Any other officer would have shouted the thrilling
words, "Take it easy, you bloody nong!" or wrestled intimately with her and bought nylon stockings at an
American P.X.

When she pointed out she had shaved, or displayed hair
freshly goffered, he said, "Oh yes. Look here, what have
you done with my Fasteeth?"

Yet, alone, now as always, and constantly disclaiming to
himself that he cared, stroke added to stroke, gave dimen-
sion to the fact that he did care. He had to content himself
with being the only one aware of him, as though he were his
own bunion.

Even the older Orientals, squatted on the deck mats,
were unaware of him, though disapprovingly aware of three
other Australians with their skiting Oriental wives, of some
American soldiers, several negroes, two loud-mouthed
American women in suntops and gold sandals.

Aware, yet — mocked by the haze and the formlessness
beyond it, souls helpless in a mesh too subtle — they sun-
dreamed of the reigning dead, of an emperor patiently and
thriftily waiting to stir out, again godly, on a noodle-white
horse, across the sacred landscape.

It was a landscape of islands striving from veils, of forests
of vapour peopled by divinities' messengers: crane, badger,
sparrow, rat. As deities and demons do, distances transformed themselves moment by moment.

East-north, west-south, there and over there, the old
ones knew, were currents, cascades and steaming springs
startled from holy earth by the transit of holy feet. Their

work-grey wooden clogs set aside, toes still, the elders cleansed their countenances of even the stains of patience.

Babies everywhere, slung on backs; their heads drooped like dark fruit: necklets of hare-fur dyed apricot, raspberry-fool pink, heliotrope or jade-green encircled the limp stalks. Children grasshoppered about: girls showing patched knickers, and sniffling under their river-boy fringes; boys squealed, each wearing a kind of guild medal of snot; there were grey fingerprints of disease impressed in their bristly scalps.

Wilkinson felt them bound through the texture of his solitariness.

Two Oriental women, pallid from talc and tapeworm, flaunting musical comedy get-ups, seemed to flow between his vacant portals: meantime they were being disdained by the Australians' native wives who, touched up and scented by Helena Rubinstein, in Viyella and American shoes, all three contrived to look like Merle Oberons.

In their turn they were disdained by Paula Groot.

On the shabby steamer, the self-contained dispositions of bodies slackened to mere spectatorship and non-participation. Children's limbs were now hobbled with languor; the vessel appeared freighted by the supine.

Kazuo kept face, since he was still uncertain, despite Paula Groot's presence, by consoling himself with dreams of physical resurrection. The resurrection would come, although foredoomed as are all resurrections. Lazarus is dead again.

Wilkinson closed his eyes. The completeness and emptiness of his being formed overlapping shades of dark and light, the negative and the positive: neither could be closely examined.

When he opened eyes again, as even the condemned must do, the nearer land displayed itself above the roofs of shrines, pagodas, curio-stalls, and hotels as a stepping, level by level, skywards, and was painfully mortised together — table-cloth fields, scraps, wedges, stripes and polyangles — mere spoonfuls of soil moulded upon heights, driven into clefts, fitted on brinks, narrowing the already narrow roads.

The ferry strove closer.

Until almost arrival the Orientals brooded in their

lassitude, then, just before the steamer tied up, fearful of losing one second of the future they had reached, petulantly prodding those in front with parasol and closed fan, they escaped from the used-up vessel. Guides and hotel touts, with withered suspenders ornamenting their bare bandiness, shouted flocks under the advertising banners they flourished. Carrying parcels bound in purple cloth, rosaries, small towels, rice-wine bottles, and babies, flocks and shepherds merrily shuffled off.

Kazuo, concealing emotion, moved with poise towards a street leading uphill to paths remoter than those of the immelodious pilgrims.

He knew Paula Groot followed him nonchalantly but inevitably as the Hound of Heaven, first through crops of Orientals with oiled hair gleaming like dark flowers and exhaling muskiness, next through steeper alleys where fewer stirred until a last girl, wearing a navy-blue cold-germ mask and carrying a spray of blossom from which not a drop spilled, went downhill past them and left them alone to confront the problem of meeting.

No one about, in the silence of distant rejoicing, he waited until she reached him, bowed and smiled.

"How do you do?" he said.

"Where can we go?" she said.

He had purposely, his plan, come to standstill outside a little inn. Entering it both were vocally silent, though eyes and nerves kept up question and answer.

Wilkinson, far below, walked apparently unconcerned, but his spirit stumbled, flickering forward its antennae against whatever rock of affront should protrude from the Pacific of others' happinesses.

In the willows lining the streets hung fans, case-lanterns, globe-fish lanterns, gourd-shaped balloons, and celluloid masks: beneath these were cluttered stalls; long fringes of tissue-paper maple-leaves or beads, swayed before china grotesqueries, varnished wooden seagulls, plaster-of-paris Virgin Marys, plates of strawberries, verdigris-green confectionery, and photographs of Greer Garson.

Somewhere here, for Wilkinson the long Volume One of his doldrums came to miraculous finis: he was irrefutably in Volume Two walking with an Oriental girl.

How?

She had looked and smiled, he had revealed his false teeth responsively and had paused, solitary. Why?

He had moved on with the warm animal of her hand curved inside his elbow. What had melted within him to make him vulnerable and acceptable?

The trim creature sidling beside him inclined her face to say, "Hah-oo de-right-foo is sunshine!"

The sun was indeed as bright as . . . as . . . as the sun.

It was precisely then that Kazuo, closing the inn-room shutters, said the same thing to Paula Groot. Both Westerners, in answer to this statement which had been studied and rehearsed as a Western one, said, "Yes."

Kazuo and Paula Groot advanced their hands towards each other's now unnecessary clothing.

Yes.

The sun was delightful.

Wilkinson had once been off-handedly tempted, someone lifting jugs to examine the china-marks, to find what lay beneath alien notions and gestures; there seemed something, beyond policy and rivalry and the hour of the century, which might have been a different and comforting fact. He was able to decide nothing except that a meagre humanness existed — the same he already could not join in, no mystery.

Now mystery and glamour vibrated towards him from the very fan his companion artistically agitated. He did not know he walked with an intelligent beer-house waitress with a day off. In his own country he would have thought her common as dirt. He bought fairy-floss for her, and a brooch of tin stamped into a maple-leaf. They walked, and he thought he was very happy. How warm the skin, the flesh of human beings — of other human beings.

Afternoon neared its zenith.

By and by, hand in hand, they ascended to the Park of the Sacred Horse, littered with pine-shadows, food-boxes, crab-meat tins and sunburnt papers. They were encompassed by lanterns of stone, stone foxes and cat-nosed idols of stone wearing disease-speckled baby-bibs. Lukewarmly, as though bruised to torpor by the mere wandering among these antique hazards, crowds in clothes the colour of bruises strolled in the bruise-coloured thickenings of late afternoon. Seductively it had passed and was passing.

She demanded money from him in a wifely way, and bought good-luck paper-slips from a priest who smoked a cigarette called Peace. She read them slowly and femininely.

"Good-ya, good-ya," she cried.

"What do they say?" he asked.

"Good-ya me. Me many money to come. Nice felicitee." She rolled her beady eyes.

"And me?" He felt like a lover, even uxorious.

"Good-ya you. No sick-oo, no pain. You live old, old." They laughed; the breaths from her active fan blew the dust from his heart into his glowing eyes.

Everywhere, people read these commercial prayers and felicitations, then tied them to the lower granite-slab-propped branches of pines or on bronze lantern-rims. Queues plunged up the temple steps, rang the bell to arouse the Presence, clapped like cock-wings, prayed silently. Coins of inferior metal clinked through offering-chest grilles.

The waitress tugged at Wilkinson, but, fearful of sacrilege, he would not follow under the left-hand-woven rice-straw rope, beyond which evil could not pass, and beyond which again a priest rustled a dry aspergillum of paper strips over the worshippers.

Wilkinson, waiting, moved to read the notice outside the next-door temple.

> *I venture to ask you to remove your shoes according to the costom if you are going to worship the image, Kogoro Tsuboi (High Priest).*

"Pliss go up! Go up, sah," pleaded the bootblack boys; they stroked his shoes with tender filthy hands; but he looked downhill, far away, where — pieced out in all directions: Dog, Wild-boar, Younger Brother Metal — was the map crawling with trippers, worshippers, children, wood-carvers, watch-menders, thugs, photographers, drunkards — so many they spilled off the land; youths on waterwheels pedalled, and schoolgirls in sailor-collars rowed, on the reflected sunset; fishers were exaggerated to postcard figures in a confusion of radiances.

Although he knew the stinking shoreline was fringed with broken tea-kettles, decaying baskets, and tangerine skins, from above it had the curve of a wing sheltering glories. He sighed with pleasure, then again, for a heated hand attached him to the little body of his companion.

"I pray we be happee tonight," she said. "Soon ferry come — we go, eh?"

Did he say yes?

He could not decide; his whole being was answering for him, tongue no longer necessary. After all, happiness had been prayed for for him, by someone else. One's own prayers for happiness deserve no fulfilment, but someone else's!

"We bisit sacred horse?"

The horse received homage in its open-fronted house by a fire-tower. As she — the wife, the mother, the soon-to-be tart — bought a terra-cotta saucer of horse-food, Wilkinson was aware of the animal waiting in gloom; an edgeless murmuring crowd stood in shadow facing this gloom.

When he approached the dividing rail, as of a celestial ticket-box, he felt that here was a finalizing trial, a culmination requiring a flourish of hautboys.

He turned to smile at the waitress; she smiled back; the others, a simultaneous opening of mysterious blooms, a lake-like glimmering, smiled also.

Now the horse!

He understood its nocturnal glance to flow meaningly to him, then, "Good-ya horsie", he was confounded to hear himself say, extending the food.

As if a tepid rain swept down and immediately off, there arrived a silence he knew circumfused future delight, passion and profit.

Inexorably, its black gaze throbbing in advance, the head of the horse neared the offering. Brusquely, impatiently, apparently relieved to do what was destined, it bit his hand to the bone.

The Communion claret was kerosene!

There was a sweeping inhalation from the bystanders, a retraction as from explosion. The dish lay broken on the pine-needles.

Appalled at the impoliteness of blood on rail and ground, he could not pass the thing off lightly.

"Good-bye, oh, good-bye," he cried at the waitress, and stumbled away, dabbling a handkerchief in his blood. Good-bye promise and pickings!

He had left himself behind, for ever, grotesque in front of the horse's house where, a macabre woodcut, the monstrous opened-up head mocked the sprinkling blood from a hand held as a mayoress's is at a garden-party.

From this entertainment, an illimitable delta drained away of faces equivocal and sheeplike; derision and imbecile politeness were creamed together. Enjoyable contempt and inward mirth consoled the watchers. Digesting his shame, that succulent flesh, they rejected him, the flaccid rind.

Steeply downhill he escaped, escaping nothing and now too visible: trios of drunks swung back like lilies from his blazing take-off; painted lad prostitutes in capes reeled from his petals of blood in a squeaking disturbance of scent.

Fingers were splashing pump-water across twilight dust and lighting lanterns which seared comet-tails of anguish on his senses.

A public address system began Mozart's "Turkish March".

He had to wait for the ferry sparkling closer from the distance. Drying-boards leaned outside a shop; flattened on them were strips of cheap silk blotted with a pattern like squashed animals. In the shop stood ten-inch rows of xylonite statuettes of pregnant girl-children each labelled *Kilroy was here*. There was a photograph of Greer Garson, well groomed and sweet in a vile odour as from caries.

This jarred him as an incompatability beyond bearing, as though a cat should suck joyfully at the foam of salt waves.

His handkerchief was glued to his raw hand which, and his head, throbbed agonizingly.

In a pause after a fourth roaring-out of "Turkish March", laughing screams came from a beer-shop.

The ferry-whistle rent clouds: he uselessly recognized Cassiopeia.

As he went aboard: "Turkish March" again, and more vehemently.

He heard it again and again, increasing in faintness but crueller, as the Sacred Island retreated, bearing on it the irked and moneyless waitress, the snoozing horse, Kazuo and Paula Groot again physically intervolved, hundreds of human bipeds, many sacred deer, two marble magpies, and the beginning of Wilkinson's future.

9

The walls of Captain Dugald's room displayed photographs only, and photographs of nothing except himself and his dog, himself or his dog: Dugald glared in black-and-white with the hostility of an Aztec god; it was surprising he drank gin, a potion not so intoxicating as blood. In the flesh he was less attractive, for example he moved. He paced with lupine tread a terrain whose latitude and longitude he had long ago strictly drawn. To himself: *No Farther!* To others: *Keep Out!*

Of this realm the dog was the darling; it moved there with a decent and grateful ease, desiring no more than it got, and accidentally causing Dugald to love, but only itself, which is the tragedy and use of the engaging.

In photographs the dog was silly, arch and cocky, it could be imagined to utter *facetiae*. Living, it was utterly animal and made those motions which Dugald read as intelligent, affectionate, faithful and so on.

It perhaps occupied the place once occupied by Dugald's mother, a parched woman resembling an Edwardian lady's maid called Fowler. She had been feminist, educated, affectionate and faithful — perhaps was still so in Death's land.

Her successor, a Madame Bovary of a wife, half educated, affectionate, unfaithful, and divorced now, her eyes hard with jokes, ran a chain of delicatessens in New South Wales.

However, the dog, the wife's successor, was now physically as dead as the mother.

For a while Captain Dugald had cried, Plutonian tears, artesian and unique. The man caressed, while weeping, the corpse he had found in a photogenic attitude which suggested it had perished while its eyes were fixed on the door through which Dugald must enter. Or — and this was the fabrication to cause tears — the dog, knowing death imminent, had struggled doorwards, fixed its eyes pleadingly and, hopelessly-hopefully waiting, had died.

Presently, tears over, and the problem of the body to be faced, for the passion of a year or so rots and stinks as much as the hatred of two decades, Captain Dugald drank gin, and time passed.

It was again Bingo night and, had Dugald known it, a thirteenth day, also the Day of the Dog.

For a while, as he drank, he conceived ideas that the dog had been done away with by the gardener, by his housegirl, by someone Oriental. More gin revealed this could not be so; the Orientals would not have had the nerve.

He loathed them so much that he allowed them intelligence to commit unseemly crimes only: to lie, botch, pilfer, smash cups, and carry infectious disease. Magnificent doings were not for them, not while Occupation-Democracy ruled would there be arson, manslaughter, revolution or dog-destruction.

In the almost empty Quarters, he began to talk to the dead creature, drunkenly as always, but seriously, on a topic affecting both. The dog did not comment, as it usually did, on his remarks: whether it agreed or not, it was to be buried immediately, now, at night, before the other officers and their tomfool women returned from the Officers' Club. O.K., poor little doggie? O.K.?

He rose, unfolding like a hunting beast, eyes slitted, but his heart temporarily circumcised of hate.

He fumbled the door open and walked the long corridor, starkly lit and reeking of disinfectant, with idol-faced dignity. He crossed the compound to the tennis courts and garden; the House that Jack Built, highest on the hill, lent its opera-house-foyer illumination.

He decided on the burial spot and stood by it, suddenly in tears again, at the unfairness of concealing his beloved possession just here, or anywhere, in foreign dirt. Downhill, thousands of the Orientals still lived — still lived: he snapped his teeth like castanets, he was Hatred's ferocious rough again.

He heard a door grit open in the servants' quarters behind the Mess bar, and moved with his streaming face into the shadow of a camphor-laurel. The door closed.

Invisible as a demon, he watched Brigadier.

The bar-boy moved rapidly and softly across the tennis courts, through the garden past the unseen Captain, and on to the compound. He was humming "Some Enchanted

Evening". As he moved, scented eddies of air uncurled from
him, infiltrating even Dugald's gin-deadened nostrils. The
youth reached the end of the Mess Quarters, Padre
Hamilton's room, and entered.

Dugald did not wonder why the bar-boy should be going
there; housegirls left the Area before dinner, officers who
remained in their quarters often telephoned through for
drinks, Alka-Seltzer or purgatives.

A brute is he who destroys even evil unthinkingly or
wantonly, for good and evil are fashions of a few years and
fewer square miles, and brutes know nothing of these fluctuations. Hatred may do good deliberately, accidentally, or
cynically for a fee. It may do evil so, too.

Dugald's hatred was purer: the original motive being lost,
blindness was all. Had he hated light he would have struck
the sun in the face, as he had struck the gardener. Only
those who also hate dare say whether he was right or
wrong, but right or wrong, he was a brute: the scented bar-
boy was his choice; the little swine would dig the dog's
grave.

Quickly Dugald loped to his room and tore open its door;
for a moment stood astounded at its lifelessness without a
pattering and hairy quadruped to greet, then caught up the
body as madmen do a weapon. Reason volatilized, he glared
about for something to swathe the corpse in, a shroud; with
operatic gesture plucked the cloth from the table which held
his drinking apparatus. Gin-bottle, glass, water jug, ash-
tray flew about the room, crashed to wall and floor.

As he got into the corridor, the absurd parcel under one
arm, Everard-Hopkins appeared at his door two rooms
away, his voice ready to ask, "What's up?"

The other strode unseeingly by, a flesh-and-bone
Minotaur. He reached the Padre's room. What was to be
done was done: before Everard-Hopkins had closed his
door, a gross scene began.

Dugald had expected to find nothing except an Oriental
grave-digger; he was unprepared to discover a plumpness
and rawness of situation he could instantly hack at like a
hooligan butcher.

He saw; did not believe what he saw, but asked no questions.

Fool, the Padre had not locked the door through which Dugald burst with drunken uncouthness. Everard-Hopkins heard Brigadier scream and ran down the corridor. He immediately believed what he saw.

The hero! he thought and, with repugnance, inefficiently yet firmly grabbed Dugald back from his kicking of the bar-boy he had felled.

"Dugald!" he cried. "Good God, man, control yourself! You're an officer. *Control* yourself."

Amnesty, said Brigadier's posture, stillness and silence.

"Outrage! Outrage! This is an outrage!"

Thus the Padre, a clown in a kimono of carnival colours, Nero on a bed, Heliogabalus disconcerted and far too rosy.

After his scream of shock the bar-boy had remained in a coil where Dugald had hurled him. The Earth continued rotating; half-loosed from its shroud, the dog lay by the bar-boy.

Dugald struggled in the Major's nauseated grasp:

"Let-me-go, Hopkins. The dirty little swine — I'll kill him . . . kill him . . . kill him. . . ."

"Then kill him," said Everard-Hopkins, and released the other whom he could no longer have borne to grip in violent embrace. Dugald fell over.

"Kill him. I'll watch."

From the floor Dugald shouted, "Ask the little swine what he was doing! Ask him!" And, as he got up, once more, "Just ask him. Filthy goings-on, that's what!"

"You're mistaken, Captain Dugald." The roses of shock faded a little on the Padre's forehead. "You've misinterpreted."

"Misinterpreted! By God, the C.O.'ll hear about this. I'll have the dirty little swine kicked out of —"

"Misinterpreted," repeated the Padre.

"I saw what he was doing. . . ."

"Brigadier," said Everard-Hopkins, "Get up and put on your trousers."

"Pliss," said Brigadier, and took his neatly folded trousers from a chair.

"You see, Major —" the Padre bundled himself more firmly into his appalling attire. His excuse was not quite ready. "You see, the lad wanted me to examine. . . ."

"Moral examination, Padre, gains in value at discreeter hours and in more discreet habiliments."

Why, thought Everard-Hopkins, why in the name of God am I talking like this? These people, I, what we are doing, all insane.

"Brigadier," he continued, "hurry up. And when you're dressed get straight back to your quarters. Come on out, Dugald."

They were one of those badly composed quartettes, graceless, and novelistic, which had had no intention of meeting at the crossroads of melodrama but, having met, were so unprepared and unpoised that possibilities of grand-eur or dispassion went unnoticed. They were, in short, amateurs. Everard-Hopkins, nearest to professional, did say, "Your dog, I think", as Dugald was leaving, but then wrangled with him in Dugald's room, which stank of gin.

"You must realize, Dugald, that the Padre is to blame. Get that clear — the Padre."

"Filthy little scented rat . . . do anything for a tin of con-densed milk."

"Exactly. Oh, *exactly*."

"Whatever *exactly* means he's not going to get away with it."

"Get away with being seduced, you mean?"

"He knew what he was after."

"Dugald, can't you see that this is better dropped? Much, much better dropped. You see that?"

"I do not."

"I'll speak to the Padre and I'll warn the boy off him. . . ."

"I'm going to report him."

"The Padre?"

"The boy."

"For being fooled around with? I did not, you may recall, report the gardener with the fractured jaw."

Dugald did not understand.

Everard-Hopkins became voluble. "You must see the connection. The gardener and the bar-boy are under an obligation to keep their mouths shut about what the con-queror does to them. *Personally*, I mean. You and the Padre are the conquerors; you've misbehaved. Although I sometimes regrettably do, I'm not here to assess moralities. However, if you and the Padre will just stop at this stage and . . . ."

"The Padre and me! Two different kettles of fish. I'm going to report that bar-boy."

"Dugald —" Everard-Hopkins made his stand at last — "if you report him, then I shall report the gardener. Do you understand? I'll report the victim."

"You won't blackmail me."

"Since by reporting the bar-boy you will also report the Padre — or are you going to call him a Certain Officer? — I shall speak up for the boy. And vigorously."

"Get out," said Dugald. "Get out of here. You're probably after the boy yourself. My dog's worth all of you."

Indeed, thought Everard-Hopkins, closing the door behind him, that is true; we have all manured your viciousness, the dog never did that.

Brigadier was badly bruised but very interested. Why had the Captain thrown a dead dog at him?

Not until next morning was the grave dug by the gardener.

The gardener was an Untouchable. So was Dugald's housegirl. Together, both hounded by Dugald, they had planned and carried out the killing.

This gave the gardener the chance to dig a hole of such flawless shape that his pleasure in its beauty quite outran his pleasure in revenge and his remorse at the dog's death. He said apologetic prayers for it.

How delicious and plentiful the fruit on the boughs of Vengeance, oldest of vines!

10

Away they went, Truscott and his Imiko who appeared more seductive to him than to men of her own race.

Hectic and prodigal, he had swept her from her clay-and-paper cabinet in which the scent of semen was interlarded with the musk of indigence; this was her second escape and a prospering one.

The first had been from her childhood and the country town which contained it.

Wilfully she had hankered for cities, for high-heeled shoes, for the moving-picture nostrums of cosmopolitanism and modernity.

Astray at night she had shuddered at the forms of women bent stitching scraps in the lamplight of frugality; hers had been the wooden clogs fretfully stumbling late on cobbles, hers the lonely figure looking from the bridge into planet-struck shallows from whence the flaring boats of the cormorant-fishers had packed up and gone, and where old-fashioned stars committed suicide. Mountain winds slipped over tiled roofs and the shrine of the Water God; the mountains were high, hinged against heaven and boogie-woogie; the clock-shop was crammed with dark clocks that chimed darkly . . . they, and the darkly manifesting toads, doled out nothing except dire time. All day, long, long, nothing was sold in the souvenir stalls.

Truscott, too, had engineered an escape from his country town in Western Australia, from the sandy streets at the outlets of which the Indian Ocean ceaselessly dissipated, the shore-weeds thick with blanched snail-shells that a southerly rattled like sexless seeds, from the pioneer houses askew behind oleanders higher than they, and hedges of dis-traught plumbago, from the gravestones of grandparents and great-uncles in the churchyard by the green river, from his doctor father egging him to inherit provincialism and placidity. For Truscott, this Oriental country, and its country girl tricked out as a city woman, relieved a home-sickness of the spirit; his poetic intuition smelt the flowers under the rouge. He did not think of the earth under the flowers.

Through the doorway of Imiko's body he glimpsed a congregation foreign enough and human enough but a congregation not of deaf hearts. He saw that a complex faith justified their taboos.

No Everard-Hopkins, he was willing to help break them.

Now, together, Truscott and Imiko travelled on Oriental trains past marigold and tobacco farms, past olive-trees Manzanillo, Lucca and St Catherine; at rustic stations the exalted cry of "Ice-cand-ee" was merely the intensification of their platitudinous, "I love you!" "I-ruv-you!"

She was honeymoon-dressed in Western clothes, and swaggered like an usherette, scorning her shabby compatriots with their trivial damp towels tied round foreheads or necks, tucked in belts. They wetted these at railway-station taps and drinking-fountains, waved them with a circular motion. All their gestures and mincings were exhilarating to Truscott, as were the cellophane sachets of dried peas and the bottles of cider sold by the vendors who importuned along the lane between the carriage seats.

They were travelling to Western Capital; the line sometimes ran beside or crossed the ancient road between the two capitals, and it was at one of these crossings they saw the first of the four important men. He seemed to Truscott more venerable than myth itself.

The scene was composed of ordinary-seeming and circumspect elements: the dramatic cryptomeria avenue of the old road gapped to display a farmscape whose horizon was pointilliste, Seuratized, and whose middle distance and foreground contained fields set with umbrella pines, sweet chestnuts, and beech, and farm-houses wherein comfort and suffering remained at bygone level, unchanging, unchanged for centuries.

Comfort and suffering, neither diminished, elaborated, nor altered in value — what more should be hoped for, or could be?

Time himself, Truscott thought, might live in one of these thatched places; might even be the decrepit man, hoop-shaped in a gown of black scraps sewn on black scraps sewn on black scraps. Time himself: yet he at least had not had to face death, as Jason had amid the hurtling timber of

Argo, and face it in an agony, dying gradually as his house did, stick by stick.

Yes, the decrepit man, so sable and vivid, was the first of the four.

They reached Western Capital.

City!

Meanwhile the fruit ripened in those oceanic fields of which the city was an island; the fruit of their liaison also ripened. Soon it would be the tint of mockery; soon the gong would sound from twilight, but for a while the convections of portent moved by as soundlessly as the wind in a horse's ear, and Truscott bought Imiko underwear, handbags, blouses, and dresses. Next, suitcases were bought to pack the increasing wardrobe in.

They enjoyed the voltage of each other's body, the locked tongues, the unsecret pale moss of each other's skin. For the time, their behaviour was sustained by an underlying argument of spirit that said, "I with my flesh must bless this companion flesh."

He had perceived the swiftness of her understanding him, a racial quality, an extra sense. To him, however, the marvel was a quietism beyond this acuteness that made him suspect some braking mechanism — the mystery of womanhood (he had heard of this), or a reserve of deeper water for him to navigate ecstatically at her chosen moment?

She was to him the branch thick with blossom, he to her the sonata that quiets the clock of the Poverty Insect.

City! City!

Two cities: the one Truscott saw, the one Imiko saw. These two cities, and others they would never see, were inextricably combined to form the real one of doors never to be opened, walls for ever opaque, intonations too elusive to be understood, verities too high-pitched for hearing.

On Truscott's behalf, Imiko radiated fake interest in *his* city: the shops of lantern-menders, seal-makers, the places selling wigs and box-wood combs, Buddhist requirements, Rice Goddess shrine crockery, dwarfed trees, books and lavatory paper, tea and the ritual paraphernalia of tea-drinking.

Truscott did not know how much more avidly she tracked down *her* city: the shops of copy-cat Viennese sweets or French pastry, of superior fans and sashes, the traders' depots of imported clothing, the contemporary fluorescent-lit cocktail-bars called Ronsard, Soireé, Prunier, Bel-Ami or New Look. In these places, Imiko, attempting always to improve her own rustic patois, picked up a little of the fastidious accent of the Western Capital and some of the new affectations, Gallicisms, and dockings. They were to have some use and bring some happiness no more unreal and fleeting than another.

In the skilfully done tawdriness of one of Imiko's streets, they saw the second of the four men. At sundown of the same day they were to see the third. About him there was to be no doubt; about the second there was much confusion.

He was a beggar squalidly swathed, a Quasimodo upon whose hump clung a louse-like child chattering its litany. Truscott was appalled: grossness has its line to draw as much as loveliness has. Too much of one or the other trips up the eye. Thus, with Truscott: was this Time, this freak demanding dues from the ordinary man; not in pity to give but in disgust? Unfair!

Imiko was not horrified; she opened her handbag and gave gaily. The child took the money — did its hand have six fingers? was it a growth itself on the spine of this larger growth, an articulate and child-shaped wen?

As the lovers walked on, "Stud-ent," said Imiko.

Truscott did not know what she meant.

She became laboriously informative.

"Stud-ent," she giggled, for it had seemed to her a wonderful make-up, "stud-ent is beggar. Beggar is stud-ent. Understand-oo?"

"No," said Truscott.

And then, thinking he did understand, "Oh, *no!*"

That a student! Earning money to *study*! To study what?

"No," he said again.

"Beggar is stud-ent . . . is gradu-ate. Young man, *handsome* man. Boy is hire-boy, one-day hire-boy."

It took time for Imiko to make Truscott see what she did mean: the beggar was a university student; to help pay his fees he begged — this was a proper thing because charity was well esteemed: without the catalyst how can surplus virtue re-form itself into an admired act? The student had made himself up, this so well that Imiko considered he would be wiser to drop the university for the movies. The hired boy? All beggars owned or hired a boy.

That was all.

Imiko could not convince Truscott. And he could not convince her that the monstrosity was really one. Finally he began to have his own doubts.

There were none for either of them to have about the third man; he lay on the edge of the half-dried-up river beneath their hotel room. He was dead, was found, was carried away as they watched.

After the dead man they had only one more man to see.

Why think on and on of the dead who are always carried away, tucked away, grilled away or who dissolve away themselves to an iridescent muck? So they had their last meal in Western Capital, one of those meals in which the material aspect was minified and other features emphasized — pattern, colour, the semi-sophistry of sub-saltiness, tepidity, rawness, and the constrained flavours of the soil and the sea.

Here was the ethos of a race.

It was revealed too in the slid-back shutters: the world was to be looked out on.

How different, Truscott thought, from the West where for centuries a portion only of outside light had been allowed in, and then through venetians, Muranese glass, dusty curtains, stained-glass windows, grilles and gratings. How lovingly malevolent or perkily benign the faces at these openings; how soothed his face and Imiko's as they watched the divinely cut silhouettes of the thieves' kitchens and cat-houses across the river. How unvexed the surface of the river that had killed the man; it thridded its velvet sand, creamy, flaxen, fatigued by the burden of an almost unbearable loveliness.

Chastened by the view, they drank from porcelain thimbles a rice-wine the colour and temperature of pee.

The next day they reached one of the most sacrosanct of cities, classic, and abandoned to holiness and tourism.

Anciently, its gigantic images, pagodas, temples, and vast parklands had been a swarming-place: it was still so, for its extent yet catered for the human need to run together, raindrops forming a swimming-pool. It was Pyramid, Colosseum, Lord's, any boxing stadium, football ground, race-track, cathedral, or bear-baiting pit.

Imiko and Truscott were lucky to strike an off-day; they had left behind the subways clotted with crushed white shirts, the fibre satchels, plastic handbags, pointed ox-blood shoes, the loud-speaker advertising and the fetors from gratings.

Now, only the notices *It is forbidden to wound dear trees* and *Garlic and wine prohibited beyond temple gate* softly practised reprimand for the hordes that had been coming for a millennium and would keep on coming.

In the parks of arch little waterfalls and, what to Truscott seemed despotic, marshallings of menhirs; among the ornamental creeks where small workmen on bamboo pruning-ladders scissored at pines; among saplings in stays of corroding wire; on lawns dirtied by ice-cream spoons and persimmon-skins, they now and again confronted an archaic effigy whose sneer of sagacity was weather-blunted to incomprehension — fitting expression to wear above public kisses. Here and there other lovers, consciously sentimental, strolled yearningly.

Equally conscious of their freckled symmetry, the deer tripped into tourist-luring groups — father, mother, and child — close by the photographer's tripod under its de Reszke cloak, black lined with vermilion. Little boys pretended not to stare, and squeezed sound out of cicadas, as Truscott and Imiko had their first-and-last photograph taken together. How they smiled!

And the fourth man came to them.

He, too, was begging — the imitation of a Buddhist priest from a nihilistic sect; from his mouth protruded the bamboo flute out of which he fingered an ascetic and foreboding tune, brief as joy. His mouth, his whole head, was covered by a latticed basket so that the too human countenance was hidden. His outstretched hand was well-proportioned; this means nothing. What the hand does is of more importance, but Truscott still required the annotation of a facial stir: how else decide between need and skulduggery?

A little later, Truscott and Imiko, sprawling by a stream

to kiss, to fondle, and to eat oranges — for the fruit was now ripe — said something in her own language.

"What does that mean?" he asked.

"Spider . . ." she pointed.

Descending from its horizontal web, an awning weighed with dust, was a parachutist black-and-white spider.

"I say, 'Spider, Spider, go a-way; come back day before yesterday.' "

He misunderstood. "Darling, the day before yesterday *was* heaven. Today is, yesterday was, tomorrow will be. Heaven. Always will be, always."

That heaven might be perpetual dalliance he did not for one moment believe. Lust always makes a splash in fulfilment, and dazzling ripples. These die to stillness in the reeds of the mud among dragonfly corpses and decaying leaves.

Heaven and always! Truscott, too, had sat through talkies. This was the afternoon of their last night together.

Chrysanthemum petals of numerous shapes — Boat Bottom Flat, Earpick Spatulate, Lancinate, Filiform, Halberd Quilled — were opening out.

On their way back to the hotel, he bought two bunches of grapes pretentious enough to have been biblically lugged from the Brook of Eshcol or lifted from a still life of Jan Davidsz de Heem.

A telegram awaited him: promotion, immediate return to Eastern Capital, thence by plane to Australia.

Shock produces outcry, grimace, distraught semaphoring: man is too deeply of the mob not to conform. Imiko and Truscott behaved disgracefully for a while, almost as though for another beside themselves. They tasted the ambiguous richness of each other's dismay; there were two dismays as there had been two cities.

Since duty is the fetish of the East, as rights is that of the West, she understood why he must leave, but imagined him more powerful than he was either as a military employee or a man able to reject advancement for Arcadia. She, after all, had absconded from Duty. She did not realize what a tidy room he was for himself to live in.

He was surprised and miserable to know that, though certain deeds hamstring the untamed conscience, he was to commit them.

Their voices began to sound neglected on the periphery of despair. They had arrived at a frontier of their relationship beyond which they could not go. It was misty ahead. He began to feel foreign as all do when the moment arrives at which they learn they are no more to belong where they did.

In their final embrace, glorified by melancholy, he moaned, "Come back the day before yesterday!"

He had misinterpreted that saying from the afternoon, was being nostalgic for a past already sealed and stamped. Imiko had been humorously rebuking the spider with a childish saying as old as her race.

Her cry was the cry of the East, the unhappiness that shrugged shoulders: "Can't be helped!"

They became as hungry as are the lonely and deserted they presumed they were to be. The grapes had the taste of spoiled burgundy.

Like Buddha they were out of the golden cage; but they had already seen what Buddha was prophesied into seeing — the decrepit man, the diseased one, the dead, and a monk.

Truscott, departing, took with him a keepsake heart-burning he had headed towards since his arrival, arrival pointing as it does in the direction of nowhere except departure.

They were never to see each other again.

11

If it is not being cruel, humanity is deaf or blind: the infantry man, retreating, steps on the mouth of the wounded one, the wireless horse-race is louder than the atom bomb.

After Wilkinson allowed his bitten hand to become septic, it was later than it should have been when his housegirl told the Mess Sergeant he was sick; presently the Mess Sergeant strolled to look in, rang an ambulance, and that was that. He was taken to hospital.

The housegirl devoted her unexpected windfall of free time to imperfect heroics; the Mess Sergeant, involved in a catering scandal, forgot to tell the Mess President so that "X" Mess, which would not have noticed Wilkinson's absence, did not notice it.

On heat with boredom, they had abruptly decided to embellish Mess amenities; noisily and vigorously they first set about improving the standards of food and drink while, nevertheless, robustly still keeping up their standards of pride, vainglory, envy, anger, avarice, gluttony, and unchastity. No energy was withheld, except by Padre Hamilton and Captain Dugald, who kept themselves sacredly apart, the one to gnaw frustrated fingers, the other to contemplate through gin an over-abundance of dog food. Major Everard-Hopkins was planning a travel itinerary with the help of the bar-boy Brigadier, whose bruises were fading.

The Mess President, awaiting a divorce so that he could marry an air-hostess, began a useful *affaire* with a canteen attendant; the Mess Sergeant performed black-market marvels to get extra Scotch, oysters, prawns, pheasant . . . all sorts of absolute necessities. The rest of the officers continued, but now more turbulently, to call themselves Legionnaires.

When they were men and exposed themselves in the common world as commercial traveller, shearer, jackeroo, dance-band pianist, insurance agent, or taxi-driver, they might have been relatively namby-pamby, but now, night after night, they went on the rampage, the piano was violently played and dirty songs bawled in chorus to entertain a hand-felt selection of women like the more proletarian flowers, who kept on returning from *Ladies* where they had tugged at seams and shrewdly painted their masks again, more carefully than at first.

Wilkinson, of course, had always been out of this sort of thing: it had bewildered him that he had no pin in their minds; he had been downcast because he knew no one discussed him behind his back. He had never expected involvement in lust or hatred, a black-market crimination or a to-do about his Oriental affinities, oh decidedly not.

Now, however, the certainty that he had walked arm-in-arm with a woman, an Oriental one, *and* a pick-up, on Shrine Island, and the wounded hand that had put him in hospital, appeared to him together to form a permit to hobnob with, or part of a Naturalization Ceremony for, "X" Mess.

He had so often heard the other officers, their faces swollen with alcohol and homage, loudly establishing through laughter, ". . . and . . . and the silly bastard missed the bloody bar-stool and . . . and *broke his bloody arm*! And all the silly bastard said, but, was . . . all he . . . all he said. . . ." They could not go on, it was so killing; they cuffed the brownish air with helpless yelling affection, demonstrating and verifying again and again all they bothered to give attention to remembering.

Wilkinson would never have been able to fall thus strikingly in a bar, could never *ever* have arranged it; after a possible successful breakage he would have been able to utter nothing except, "Ouch!" or "I'm afraid I've broken my —"

Perhaps, however, at last, since he was amazingly sick and, he guessed, at the point of death, the now glamorous embarrassments leading to his death would cause posthumous sensation and launch a ripsnorting legend. Bitten by the Sacred Horse; it could hardly be bettered by punching the C.O. He restlessly waited for a visitor.

No one came.

Therefore, after several muddled and dreamlike days in bed, the non-appearance of visitors convinced him he was not going to die, for visitors were certainly allowed to visit the dying. Weren't they, Sister?

This unlooked-for resurrection was in a sense disappointing, he had dizzily composed what seemed to him an actual scene in the Mess: flaring faces, eyes phosphorescent with admiration, heavily beringed hands ready to slap and crash at the edge of the bar-counter, a tornado of laughter waiting to lift the ceiling, the resonant voice shouting his saga to a rapt Valhalla, ". . . that quiet bastard Wilkinson . . . a real doer when you got to know him . . . well, he was bitten by the Sacred Horse on Shrine Island . . . bloody septicaemia . . . beat it? — killed by a bloody Sacred bloody Horse. . .!"

A lost immortality!

"Sis-ter," he called, meagrely as if he *were* dying, through the willy-nilly of laughter striped by cigarette smoke and brilliant with the spinning and boomeranging of nickel-plated ash-tray hoop-la circles. "Sis-ter!"

"What is it?"

"Sister . . . the Sacred . . . oh dear, I've lost my chance of immor — immortality with the boys in the Mess."

"Now, now," she said, "be a nice chappie, Tompkinson. Matron will be here any minute."

Nevertheless, drinking gin-and-lolly water in "X" Mess that night she tried to direct her mind point-blank to . . . who was it? . . . to tell someone something about . . . what was it? . . . immorality? She could not remember.

She was tired, jealous, and half drunk, so they bought her more drinks and she lost one cultured-pearl ear-ring while they were singing "Some Enchanted Evening" for the sixth time. Removing the settee cushions to look for the ear-ring reminded them of a game; they began to throw the cushions about.

When people die, things — gimcrack things such as a coat-button or a rolled-gold safety-pin — linger on as physical reminders, not to others, not even to the bereaved or relieved, but to the impersonal and superior pattern of physical things. So it was with some bits and pieces once of importance to Wilkinson, who died the day after the cushion frolic during which a standard lamp was smashed and the nurse was sick in a wash-hand basin.

Figures he had neatly written remained; an Eversharp pencil that had dropped from his pocket during his shame outside the Sacred Horse's house continued an Oriental existence from the very moment he started leaving off (a long novel could be written on this stubborn persistence of the inanimate); the poplin of four shirts stolen by his housegirl finished up as dyed patches on a juggler's robe many years later.

There were all kinds of trivia — an eyelash fallen into his mother's copy of *The Story of San Michele*, a nail-file, a pair of slippers, fraction of his name carved inside his school dormitory wardrobe — many fragments of Wilkinson's living that long outlasted the Occupation and "X" Mess.

"X" Mess never once mentioned him.

12

Paula Groot had years ago self-indulgently decided that to be less cautious in the barter of bodies was the more enterprising and piquant move.

However, she did not delude herself that less caution in one direction did not demand more caution in the other. It was necessary to conduct her relationship with Kazuo inside a framework more scandal-proof than odd week-ends, Oriental inns and tiresome trips — the clandestine needs a time-table and thick walls as much as the condoned does.

The Y.W.C.A. Hostel was indubitably out of the question. So, hearing that a small Rainbow Village house had become vacant, she was able to organize that it became hers: Major Bruce, whose wife was rejoining him and who had say in the allotment of these houses, was glad to pull strings and place under an obligation the woman to whom he had felt he was under one.

Paula Groot moved in, taking Hoshi with her.

Houses of its sort, hotel suites as it were, retained little flavour of the lives spent in them; apart from the fact that the design was callously functional and the furnishings of unalterable ugliness, there had been no way in which these houses could from the temporary and addled domesticity of always-on-the-move families suck out a soul-forming nourishment.

Paula Groot's less customary domestic pattern was to be even more a marble fruit; the gymnastics of her nicely scheduled lust did not change the colour of the plaster walls or the placing of comfortable hideous arm-chairs. Poor house!

She hinted that her housegirl's brother was giving her lessons every evening in the Oriental language. This falsehood, carefully scattered, no one believed or disbelieved; both the cynical and the indulgent were, however, prepared for disillusion.

Hoshi, who knew what was going on, was badgered by a sense of injury, had nightmares, and improved so much in her work, was so nimble, that Paula Groot became fonder of

her daily and talked of "my housegirl" as constantly as anyone else. Hoshi was, after all, a sort of by-blow sister-in-
law.

Rainbow Village was built between mountains and a bay,
on former Oriental air-fields which had been bombed into
craters by the West, and bulldozed flat again to accom-
modate a model Western village, the like of which existed
nowhere in the West.

It was a tiled and florid Marah set on curving concrete
roadways called Avenues, and graced by unfinished public
gardens, vast spectral playgrounds and waterless fountains.
Expensively jerry-built for officers' families, its bitter
waters were hot and cold and chlorinated; one was rescued
from it by fire-escape, death, taxi-jeep or drink.

In *Saturday Evening Post* advertisement settings, job-lot
refrigerators and profiteers' central-heating systems reproduced the murmurs of defective hearts.

In each and every house were blue curtains on which
white swallows sliced after each other, quilts of rhubarb-
coloured plush, arm-chairs of brick-red corduroy.

Each shellacked sideboard paraded on the regulation
waratah-embroidered runner, or displayed through glass
doors sand-blasted with kookaburras, the Rose China
dinner service, tea-set, coffee cups and ash-trays, all ringed
by a design of mean daintiness; drawers that stuck contained
metal-handled blunt knives resembling those used in cheap
cafés run by Greeks; each kitchen had its high stool across
the wooden seat of which ran an inch-wide fissure — this
had been reproduced in thousands by an Oriental contractor
from the warped and split model provided by the West.

To embellish this repetition of basic garniture, the tenants
had tirelessly acquired collections of Oriental teapots, glass
menageries, sunsets painted on velvet, gilt-measled rice-
bowls, cigarette-lighters in the shape of miniature
telephones, water-closet pedestals, cameras, jeeps, Avro-
Ansons, refrigerators, beer-bottles, battleships, and cabin-
trunks. Artificial materials, enamelled wood, plastic, tinned
lobster, frozen eggs, surfaces and substances ending in *ex*,
added up to a total very like caricature.

Throughout this burlesque suburban reservation, the dis-
possessed toiled for the trustees; scratching ripple-marks on

gravel paths with bamboo rakes, snipping lawns with scissors, burning porridge but not eating them, cooking prawns in batter, dusting before brushing, and walking hand-in-hand the surprising and sinuous footpaths.

Here and there nostalgic Westerners had planted rose-bushes which squeezed out a bloom or two, farouche and scentless, then grew no more in the purple ground. Meanwhile, daphne, a Western luxury, expanding to bushes of a size that appalled, weighted its branches with a horrifying prodigality of flowers. About this there was something not quite right: rabbits did not produce mink.

The hills with wine-stains on them, and shadows of aster and gentian, permanently billowed up behind this encampment whose flash-in-the-pan inhabitants squinted with beer-rosy eyeballs at signposts directing them along serpentine streets and to public buildings that were letters of the alphabet.

Pinned down at its edges by the stakes of the oyster gardens, the bay lay like a cloth set for a picnic no one but the diabolic would enjoy.

Kazuo could travel by tram to the outskirts only of this travesty.

Walking in through many twilights and the symbolic incompleteness, he was of two minds: here there seemed to be luxury, comfort, privacy and organization, things for his admiration and envy — but the luxury horrified him, the trappings of comfort broke all his rules of taste, the privacy was crowded with rubbishy gadgets and ornaments made by his people to impress their conquerors, the organization was a machine that would run for a time only and on a fuel no ordinary age could afford to use.

In Paula Groot's house, he was equally rattled by the domestic restlessness, the notes of waste and dishonesty — painted wood, coarse colour, indecorous shape. Even Hoshi's flower arrangements took on a heathenish quality against the disturbed background.

The atlas of Paula Groot's body was enough for Kazuo to read, valley and well and tremor; it was merely the atlas of any woman's body; the map of her desires, too, was the reprint of any woman on heat; the map of her mind he would never understand beyond its outline.

As his liaison with her proceeded, he found she recalled wild violets he had once seen growing beneath a hornbeam: near the tree's base pale, farther out darker, beyond the hornbeam's shadow darkest, and with an indefinable scent. What this darkness and scent were he did not know except that they resembled the end-nearing syllables of a poem.

Finis would come: would one read the poem again?

She bought him shirts, ties, and a pair of brogues he loved like a pet animal. She stilled the qualms she still felt about Orientals by dressing him as a Western bank-clerk. From her he was to learn nothing except that a woman is a woman; from him she was to learn nothing except that a man is a man and can unload a burden of bad luck at the height of ecstasy; Hoshi was to learn most.

She was not on the raft; she dog-paddled in the dark ocean; she gulped the acrid foam.

The housegirl had once seen a play in which two lords had love and respect for each other.

The son of the greater lord had been sentenced to beheading. The lesser lord, as part of his duties to the greater and conforming to a custom of the period, was sent to wait while the execution of the son took place, then to recognize officially the head which would be displayed to him in a lacquer box. Compelling his own son, whom he deeply loved, to take the place of the other condemned son, the lesser lord was therefore brought the box which contained his own child's head.

His problem was to display no betraying agony as he answered formally the formal questions put to him while gazing on the countenance of the son he had sacrificed.

Although Kazuo's and Paula Groot's faces still lived, Hoshi felt that in looking on Kazuo's face she looked on a dead one from behind whose translucent husk the Western woman's body radiated a corpse-like glow. Meanwhile her face, neatly painted, satisfied, porcelain, suckled on Kazuo's bodily death, seemed to live serene and alluring when Hoshi would have had it finger-nail-grooved with thumbed-out eyes in a pail of Paula Groot's own excrement.

Hoshi's own public face, like the bereaved father's, betrayed nothing while, gradually, through the acid-bitten perforations of her increasing hatred, something seeped away, the sediment of acquired moralities, of sympathy, modern ideas, obedience, fear, of a life of rules and complex goodnesses. The primal fluid — gradually — became almost clear: only a tinge of funk remained, that and humaneness, an emotion insidious as tolerance and as tiring.

When she was alone, behind doors, the sinews of her neck winced, her eyes squinted as violently as an Oriental actor's do when he is congealed, attitudinizing to the drumbeat, eyes conventionally crossed, at the climactic moment of a play.

Each evening Kazuo travelled in the flaking and bucking tram to the rim of the boorish suburb, and then walked on its shimmering concrete footpaths, past its painted walls and multi-coloured tile roofs and ill-bred gardens, through its foreign smells of instant coffee and grilling meat, to give his alleged lesson.

Each evening Hoshi, seeing him leave, felt her hatred burnish itself freshly, shine as iridescently as a peacock's brow; the feet of her obsession were as hideous as the peacock's feet at which, catching sight of them beneath his splendour, he screams crookedly.

Each night, with infinite care and the absorption of amentia, she added a little to the Paula Groot she was constructing from straw.

13

After Truscott had returned to Eastern Capital, Imiko gave the idea of suicide proper attention.

This occupied the several days her room was paid for.

While she soaked in baths, lacquered her nails or stared through tears at the hexagonally stone-inlaid river-banks outside the hotel, soliloquies involuted as shells spiralled in her mind, and spiralled inevitably each time to the dagger-point of self-annihilation: this prescriptive death appeared to her a stylish ritual to be performed in as aristocratic, or failing that, as ladylike a manner as possible. She had to believe she felt that she craved death's faultless permanence.

Though space, which can contain shires of suffering, comes first between separated ones, time comes next.

And time is for emendations of thought no matter how much these lack distinction or modishness: Imiko was too much of the earth to be lost on it for long. Let death catch up with her when her purse was flat; at present it was packed solidly as a potato.

From inexperience and a bloated sense of equity and guilt, Truscott had been too lavish. To the actressy suitcases heavy with clothing, cosmetics, trinkets, and confectionery, he had added more money than he could really spare, a sum to Imiko at once shocking, sobering, and condoling.

As well, he had given her his wristlet watch, an impulsive gesture he immediately regretted.

So, suffering a touch of indigestion from weeping and planning while eating too many caramels in her agony, she calmed to melodious prayer, from prayer to peace. Tenderly, and radiant, she counted her money, decided to return to her father's house, counted her money, bought her mother a sale-priced kimono and sash, and spent an hour packing Truscott's watch in the traditional way to present to her father.

Reality, like Hamlet, harangues such Ophelias as Imiko to bewilderment — the bewilderment in which the mind is made up to take firmly the first steps on a track leading, they know well, to the unimaginable.

In this fashion bewildered, most skilfully made up, faultlessly robed in Oriental manner, she caught a train, enacted fragility, hoped to be mistaken for a popular film actress she somewhat resembled, silently rehearsed Western Capital affectations of speech, did not smoke, and nibbled slices of smoked eel.

When the train arrived at the home station she was feeling nervous, but, noticing a girl porter whom she had known as a child recognize her with flattering envy, was encouraged in self-esteem by being able to snub the girl.

Imiko's father, the station-master, a man who regarded himself as broad-minded but was otherwise intelligent, did not commit the depravity of revealing surprise at his daughter's return or satisfaction at her well-to-do appearance.

As her cases were lifted one by rich one from the luggage van, his expression became blank, and blanker to cover blank, but, after he had telephoned for the small town's sole wonderful taxi, he rubbed his fingers, at first with punctilious and then relaxed fervour, over their obvious leather. Ah, so?

By the time the taxi had arrived he had discussed the bronze tube of snake-gourd and daisies hung in his office, obliquely intimating by this that he assumed her opinion of the array worth not hearing.

The taxi, on whose seats a few archipelagos of blackish pile seedily and stubbornly represented a former opulence of royal-blue plush, conveyed her, apparently successful, through streets that had limited her dreams, round corners she had turned in a flurry of petulant hopelessness, to the house and the mother she had abandoned for the insecurity of freedom.

How unchanged all was, her mother too: they bowed many times, the tears that showered from her mother's eyes were from the flower-sized cloud that perpetually hangs above the country of any mother's heart when she conceives an absent child to suffer. However annealed the heart, this rain of joy can pierce instantly to the subsoil and startle the simple vegetation to freshness again.

Imiko was home. To feed her mother's revealed happiness, her father's surprised pride and her own conceit, she began a life of cautious lying. Perhaps she pitied herself and her father — of that she was unsure; she did pity her mother who needed no pity, only the sight of what she loved.

Mothers are the only goddesses the whole world has kotowed to, theirs the name most uttered; of that eternal and powerful brood Imiko's mother lived on a plane very near earth; the flesh parcelling her bones was leaf-thin, the bones themselves as important and frail as outer branches, her blood sap-like.

While the nation held soul-consoling ceremonies for the cherry-wood mutilated in engravings, for worn-out brush-pens, for temple gongs beaten morning and evening, for hares, guinea-pigs, and marmots suffering in medical experiments, for the stallions, carrier-pigeons, and dogs of the military, for all the abraded fal-lals of science and art, she made apologies to simpler things — to used needles, to her children's dead dolls, to worn-out hats, fish eaten for breakfast. She prayed to her rustic Fornax; in the days when she had been pregnant had offered wooden dippers with their bottoms knocked out to her country's Eileithyias and Egerias.

She was an old-seeming woman, a gossiper and giggler; her toothless and bawdy laugh was most called forth by jokes about the generative parts; she was smaller than Alfred Austin but humble.

She knew the exact nature of vegetables and their parings, of stripped shrimps, handfuls of rice, the texture of edible leaves, and the secrets of herbs and fruit flavours; her execution of the elaborate domestic dance was unfaltering and unchanging.

So few of her kind and generation were to be allowed to die unhaunted, unenvious, and placid, to dissolve into the uncultured air meekly as lotus pollen, but were rather to be uprooted by cyclones of change and wither under the downpours of progress. Yet she spoke with immemorial love and softness to Imiko, while fanning the stove embers as knowingly as she would a sick brow, moving the wooden lids of the anodized aluminium pots, slicing vegetable scraps precisely into custom-dictated shapes.

Imiko, burnishing her lies, began to believe herself she

was the small-part film actress she had told her parents she was: the falsehood of being a New Face in films drifted in thickening mists across the smouldering truth of the Florida Cabalet.

It was at this time she met the farmer Masao.

It was hot; winds strolled through the heat like bodies languid with fever.

Buckwheat had been already harvested and was hanging in nigger-brown bunches; lotus leaves, rearing on serpent necks from ditches and ponds, were tattered and fringed; the first cuttings of rice jolted by in carts — lolling supple sheaves that rustled like taffeta. Uncut fields were ripe, had a dusty bloom on them, were seeding, full-blown, breathing slowly or rippling with the richness of fur.

Under the fondlings of the country sun her body too stirred with a desire in which Truscott and the Florida Cabalet now reappeared from behind the fog of lies in an artificial limelight — regret purified and deepened the colours, recollection removed shadows, an eye for the dramatic lengthened perspectives towards a horizon brilliant with auguries.

Returning one afternoon from her bi-monthly shrine visit, she passed through swaying fields from which, here and there, protruded peasant gravestones composed of the five granite forms representing Ground, Water, Fire, Wind, and Sky.

The pentachords of rock seemed to stir through the heat-ripples, the dead's own grey forms watching her, calling birdlike to each other, "Is she that-person? Is she prostitute? Is she from cat-house?"

Of this she was herself unsure: the edgings of her cannier mind were frayed by vanity, doubt, day-dreaming, and diplomatic lies; moreover, she had seen too many sacred objects and ideas, tumbled by Western bomb or interference haphazardly together to junkyard stuff, for her to be clear about more than one thing at a time. She had become, as most of her race had, a puppet on slackened wires.

In the heat she felt herself to be an exquisite dancer, and essayed a dancer's evolutions as she passed under some trees and came to a stream.

Here she folded her sunshade, gracefully removed her

sandals, danced on the grass; the pain of crushed green rose with forgiving coolness. Next, she folded her summer kimono up and back from her thighs, sat on a rock at the stream-edge and lowered her legs into the waters that leniently dissolved from them the impalpable dust of tranquil summer.

It was then she saw, hung like a veronica against a tangle of castor-oil plant leaves on the opposite bank of the stream, the face of Masao.

It was a facsimile of suffering.

Now, suffering has many intonations; this was one she instantly understood — desire; this was not an Erl King but a man.

Masao was enthralled. While she partly and partly-correctly saw herself as an enchantress inviting intemperance, he saw her as something far more dazzling; the chrysanthemum Blizzard fallen crisply from a celestial bush.

A farmer, he was one of the millions living and millions dead who had made subject to man the most perilous of dragons, the earth and waters of a land whose resurrections of spitting and thundering had infected their personalities.

Matter imposes its presence, and speaks its own tongue which he understood to the final syllable: he and his kind had become the earth; no longer themselves, they fell like camellias, bowed like the wind-shocked rice, tied themselves to nature as wisely as the bindweed. He was, in fact, prudent, hard-working, virile, and had a love of inanimate things, and the predictable. In this last he resembled Imiko's mother and the saner children of earth.

Yet, dead-centre of the things he knew, of the predictable, was the unbelievable, the female, the hitherto unseen angel, whose legs were making languid upheavals like river-salamanders pale as pear-flesh.

At last, pretending to be unaware of the watcher, the legs withdrew themselves with a succinct flourish skilfully just short of immodesty — a woman's trick. Imiko, in a contrived seductive attitude, was weighing her next move when she noticed, just above her knee, the black teat of the leech she had not felt battening there.

As a country girl, this did not alarm her; as a New Face, a city butterfly, dismay was called for.

Using a Western Capital expression and accent, feigning distress with moth-stirring hands, "It hurts," she cried to the grass and water, "it hurts!" and plucked at the leech.

Before he realized it, Masao had burst through the leaves, had crossed over on the stepping-stones arranged in an order suggesting Peaceful Honour, and bowed before her, drawing in breath with a hiss of admiration and timidity.

A long-horned grasshopper began to sing as she returned his bow and said "It hurts — river-thing hurts." It did not.

"I shall help?" His accent was blurred with the heat of his blood — no machination here.

"It does not matter much. I thank you for your speed, but I can remove river-thing."

"River-thing is leech and does no harm."

"I thank you. It hurts; it hurts."

Her voice had become more mannered; she pretended to be a little faint, closed her eyes, turned her head sideways so that not only her profile could be seen and her lashes but also the virgin arc that leads to the heart-rending nape.

Should she become fainter?

She made her lashes quiver. She swayed, swayed. . . .

"I shall be grateful for removal of . . . river-thing," she whispered.

He fell on his knees with a startling thump and, controlling his unhinged fingers, removed the creature.

"Excuse me, please," he was able to whisper, and placed his mouth to the freckle of blood above her knee and began to suck.

Now, indeed, she saw herself as the New Face on the talkie-screen, she looked into the field-dust that powdered his hair, dispassionately considered the lines, curves, planes, and ridges of his smooth muscularity and masculinity, felt the beast-like fever and slime of his inner lips.

Was he, sucking at her blood, sucking also at her heart?

Heart or no heart, he did not realize, for neither did she yet, what poison he drew on. The drop or so of blood was blood only, to him it was an intoxicant because the act of sucking it was intoxicating: more and more intoxicating was the warm vessel from which he drank a disturbing future.

Masao had been prepared to tolerate women, a woman, a wife: all men did. All men needed a wife, all men needed children madder than animals, dreadful as demons: this was the family, continuance, muscles for the field, bodies containing grandsons, hands to light the cemetery lanterns, clean the graves, set food on the ancestral altar.

This was the questionable essential.

Imiko was the star-maiden, a woman of the dreams nature cruelly forces on the sleeping body, the long-haired beauty waiting like the closed morning-glory in the autumn moonlight of little poems, the enchanting mistress opening her body's secrets in the pillow-picture scrolls.

As he rose from his knees, she appeared to Masao as fabulously feminine as those most feminine of all women, the actresses who were men.

The long-horned grasshopper still singing, they parted after formal bowings, exchanges of gratitude and its honey-mouthed rebuttal.

He returned Pan-like to trees, to fields.

Her clothing re-arranged, her sunshade open again, she shuffled homewards.

A Mr-the-Deity of Thunder roared distantly — once. Many little children, hearing him, cupped hands over their navels because they knew those were what the deity was after.

These children, and Imiko, and Masao, most people, Padre Hamilton and other Occupation padres, did not know it was Lammas Day.

Despite that, in this unchristened country, the first-fruits of the fields were being presented at the altars of the Rice Goddess where her guardian-messengers, two foxes, faced each other, one holding the barn-key in his mouth, one keeping his forepaw on the jewel-ball containing the spirit of the goddess.

Oriental All Souls' Day — the Feast of the Dead — drew nearer with the inevitability of an annual Sports Meeting.

The lantern-makers were working overtime.

14

Buddhism will have its new widow or widower, its freshest orphan or bereaved parent, participate in a taboo-leave, a holiday from usual life, because death is defiling and will have left the sorrowing or elated unclean and filthy.

Truscott imagined himself likewise polluted. Nothing but departure would cleanse him from the dismay he felt at the premature death of his first *affaire* which he saw almost as another figure separate from himself and Imiko. Most irritating was the fact that this being — which resembled a transparent, cherry-blossom Primavera — need not so soon have been felled to her bier: he had been stuck for days in Eastern Capital, elastically hobbled to another Department than his own in which confusion had reached perfection.

No one knew exactly what was going on.

Planes went without him. "Next week, I think," clerks kept on saying.

He did piddling jobs and read too many books.

He was too rattled to take on another woman; besides, this thought-of other body offended some loyalty to Imiko. He wrote several inferior poems, wished to God he had never read Dylan Thomas, got drunk with men, and wandered the streets which now revealed what he had not seen before.

Silver Street, Eastern Capital's and one of the world's great thoroughfares, displayed now the inelegancies of near-starvation and the pathetic wiles of those too proud to admit they were quasi-down-and-out.

The cigarette boxes pecked and trilled, the plastic toys hopped and whirled, the high-lights on top-hats were faint, the Western shoes worn by the Orientals — a pointed last of 1924, co-respondent black-and-white, custard-and-white — were held together only by the tenacity of polish; the snail of penury was glued behind the gold-threaded ferns on robes; the servants in the Imperial Hotel smuggled out scraps of bread through the magnificent and hideous passages that sloped from floor to floor.

In the arcade below the Assyrian opulence of this hotel

Westerners haggled for asymmetrical tea-cups and ancient sword-shields made a fortnight ago in the city Level Land, for pygmy pines and Mongolian oaks, purse toggles, seal-cases, carved ivory, lacquer, *cloisonné*, damascene ware, bric-à-brac hot from the mills of Western Capital and Big Slope.

It was in the iron-floored alleys of this arcade, which gave the impression of warship corridors, that Truscott saw Everard-Hopkins just too late to see him first and escape.

He greeted the Major joyfully and was embarrassed by the fan he flicked open.

"I'm on leave," explained Everard-Hopkins, more physically charred than ever, and fanning the ashes of his face. "The M.O. says I must be. 'Softly and softly' he orders me, dear boy. Tomorrow I go . . ." and in the torrid closeness he indicated escape by a flourish of his fan: grey villages, grassy woods, weeds with dew on them, valleys of sweet potato and shrines, hinterlands and relaxation. "I shall, dear boy, travel far enough to wear out several fans." Then his eyes kindled, as though for a first or last time, at a lantern-box lacquered with Osculating Mandarin Ducks and Chasing Pine Needles. "Oh, exquisite," he whispered raptly, "exquisite produce of a wonderful people."

Hell, thought Truscott, and waited until the eyes burned down again, and transferred their filmed surfaces towards him.

"And you, dear boy?"

"I should be returning to Australia," said Truscott who felt he was in the presence of a mummy geared to speech only by some rusted inner gadget. "My department here is breaking up, apparently being absorbed into another. *I* don't know. At the moment I hang about waiting for movement orders: this week, next week, some time . . . mystery shrouds all. I don't *know*. Hanging about doing damn-all. I'll be glad to go."

"You do not care for the Orient?"

The Major paused — was it what they called significantly?

About to shatter the pause rudely by "No!" Truscott was foiled; the alloyed voice began again, "You do not care for . . . any of it?"

Truscott suspected the quizzical.

Was Imiko's face imprinted on his, had her eyelashes scored his cheek, the massage of her mouth malformed his so that inquisitorial eyes could detect the imperceptibly changed outline of his lips and the print upon them of even the nationality of the mouth responsible? Was he scented with Imiko's scent? Did the Major know of her?

"I don't care for much of it," said Truscott. Untruthful partly; he did not care to be adrift in it.

Everard-Hopkins raised eyebrows as the Sphinx might have had someone spat on *her* desert beneath her very nose.

"What about this?" The Major fan-pointed to the tables and counters set with ivory peasants, egg-sized gods, china chopstick-rests, and lacquered bean-curd bowls with lids of dead gold.

"Not much . . . indifference is my principal feeling," said Truscott, again untruthfully, surprised at his lie.

Everard-Hopkins opened his fan like a thought, "Let us then, leave this underground in which I have met you cultivating indifference," closed his fan, stuck it in his pocket. "Let us have a drink or so, and then visit some places of entertainments less static than these. That is, dear boy, if you've no other appointment."

No other appointment except with boredom. Between boredoms Truscott made his choice and went with Everard-Hopkins.

They had their drinks, Everard-Hopkins saying, "The doctor says I shouldn't, but these will be our last together."

In that he was correct.

"Tomorrow, dear boy, I take off for the places I've always been too busy to visit before and from which I may not come back. You see, Truscott, I'm so attracted to this country I may resign my commission and stay here. *Ergo*, I must find the exact place first, the — you will pardon this — the — er — well of ultimate peace. I can see it, the morning-glory twisting around the handle of the wooden pail, the village pond at noon lazily awaiting the frog. . . . You go to Australia, I may stay here. We may never be together again. Good health!" He drained his whisky.

Truscott understood the poetic reference to pond and well, to halcyon days in rural backwaters. For a moment he was moved, doubly moved, for Imiko could be, he thought, a figure in Everard-Hopkins's dreamscape, the distant woman balancing delicately on the raised path between the spiked and glassy rice flats.

Everard-Hopkins was to come, within a few days, to his well of ultimate peace. He and Truscott were also to travel together again, but neither knew this, for the future conceals itself in the blunted perceptions of men.

Their drinks downed, they caught a bus, they arrived at a destination: "This," said Everard-Hopkins, "is something you *may* care for." *Softly and softly* on the Major's behalf, they climbed broken-edged concrete steps to the fourth of the floors, on each of the six of which was a theatre.

"*May* care for!" Truscott had been piqued, defensive; glancing at Everard-Hopkins's grey face he knew from its unobnoxious passivity that the skull within was sardonic.

On a platform jutting into the auditorium and to the left of the stage, a shirt-sleeved orchestra sweated and played clockwork music to an audience of men, most of them Westerners. From the stage ran a spotlighted gangway, its surface level with the caps and heads of the seated.

"That," said Everard-Hopkins, "is the Flowery Way — and lo, they come!" for as the two of them sat, the orchestra performed a fanfare, and the flashy curtains jerked apart.

Brutally the show began.

When one nation attempts to copy another an authenticity is sometimes achieved, even a near-facsimile; often imitation outdoes original. As often, however, the result is parody.

Strip-tease women removed their motley with the brusqueness of little girls preparing to get into the bath with their brothers or the directness of tired wives disrobing. Orientals, Australians, English, Americans sat in a silence possibly of disillusionment and a sense of having wasted money; only the paler fingers of grape-black negroes moved a little, a spider-like language of frustrated tactility.

Down the Flowery Way jerked and strutted naked women with blotched bow-legs, long false eyelashes, and quaking *Folies Bergère* head-dresses; sequined nipples shuddered as they advanced; pallid bums and grubby elbows retreated; the orchestra made a platitude of noise; two small men hastened in as the last bottom disappeared.

They were Orientals imitating Crosby and Hope imitating an Edwardian vaudeville sketch; within this complex and preposterous framework they sang *"Underneath the Arches"* in their own tongue, soft-shoed, back-chatted, neck-scratched, knee-slapped, elevated and lowered George Robey — or was it Groucho Marx? — eyebrows, grabbed at each other's privates.

Orchestra and audience smoked placidly; a generation was born; a generation died of starvation or torture; guns were fired; the sun was rising somewhere on futility and setting somewhere on rancour; night was riddled with terrors; forenoon waxed; afternoon waned; elsewhere blinding high noon; the curtains stammered together to no applause.

Economically pinching their cigarettes out, the orchestra played *"You are My Sunshine"* in an Oriental-tango rhythm.

The curtains parted.

A man, obviously a doctor, for a Brobdingnagian stethoscope swung from the pocket of his draught-board suit, gabbled at an obvious nurse with transparent veil and dress and high-heeled silver shoes.

She left; the orchestra drum heavily sounded *thump, thump, thump-thump* as the nurse returned with a woman whose magnified pregnancy the abortionist doctor listened at while the orchestra played "*Soldiers of the Queen*". Then he threw her on a table; the nurse minced to him with a carpenter's saw; to *"The Blue Danube"*, one-two-three, one-two-three, he began to saw at the woman's belly. *Boom! Crash!* the orchestra.

The door shot open on a dwarfish soldier, the P of the M.P. on his armband was back-to-front. He carried a flexible truncheon. Doctor and soldier duelled with saw and truncheon. Finally, the doctor grabbed the truncheon, pursued the soldier with it phallically held.

At the moment the truncheon touched the fleeing soldier — black-out; from the black-out yells and grunts of . . . of what?

"Does all that mean," asked Truscott, "what I think it

does?" The interval orchestra was pulsating through
Schubert's "*Ave Maria*".

"Whatever it means, dear boy, they are not to blame,"
said Everard-Hopkins, and flatly. "Don't mistake me.
These people have none of the mother-of-pearl ro-
manticism of Renoir; their own vulgarity, their coarseness,
is that of the *cartes-comiques* of the *Manneken-pis*. Gross, if
you will. I am grieved that a . . . a wounded god, however
gross in his own way, should attempt to amuse his assailant
in this way. Western dress! Vaudeville Western! Oh, *non
placet, non placet*."

A wounded god!

A wounded *man*, Truscott thought, or a man with
wounded honour. Injuries to honour take longest to heal,
but the box-receipts from clownery buy soothing ointment.

Perhaps, too, "*Soldiers of the Queen*" and the M.P. had
curative power. How strong was the strongest feeling he
detected under the ribald skit? Or was insult unintended
and the act merely the clumsy effort of fifth-rate mummers
to entertain the West with a flattering suggestion they were
not being left out of anything?

"Do you think this is just a blindness in the sense of
humour?" Truscott asked. The orchestra was playing
Gossec's "*Gavotte*".

A ripple of pain that maybe ran back from the very shore
of pain crossed the Major's face.

"Dear boy," he said, fanning his face blank again, "all
nations have a blindness and —" like a rakish eighteenth-
century duke he tapped Truscott's knee with the fan — "to
another's humour as much as to anything else. We have
long ago compelled them to imitate us: navy, army, railway,
post office — why not vaudeville?"

The orchestra decisively began Rimsky-Korsakof's
"*Chante Hindu*" and the curtains again parted.

Reckitt's Blue sky, persimmon-coloured moon, palms, a
circular downstage pit were revealed; women in gauze
trousers scissored and Arabianly dancing-girled with ver-
tebrae like serpents, then ran off to leave a writhing soloist.

She whirled pitwards, twining and untwining her arms as
flies do, gesticulating into the tomato-coloured glow that
suddenly was turned on in the pit.

"*Iokanaan! Iokanaan!*" she shrilled.

"Hell," said Truscott.

"Heavens," said Everard-Hopkins, fanning away.

Gradually a papier-mâché head with bushy brown hair, eyebrows and beard grew from the pit; a disproportionately small body in monkish habit scrambled out revealing plump legs.

"*I-ok-an-aan!*"

She importuned like an octopus, grabbing at the star-spangled underwear his caperings revealed. Eluding, he pointed at the moon. It blinked out: a cymbal crash from the orchestra. Ah! a Christian miracle!

As the Tetrarch and Herodias entered to sit on sequined hunkers beneath a palm, John the Baptist descended into the pit. Now, to throbbing and thrumming, Salome did a *danse du ventre*, throwing aside her veils as the moon also turned tomato-red. The last veil: the Tetrarch acted delirium at her bath-house nudity. A soldier in armour climbed into the pit and, while Salome was tying on a *cache-sex* of one small looking-glass, reappeared with the enormous papier-mâché head.

"Wilde's additional nemesis," whispered Everard-Hopkins as the woman plunged her face into the *crêpe* beard, crying, "Iokanaan!" Black-out again.

Out, on, for immediately the pit glowed again, and from it the headless saint climbed out and played blind-man's-buff, arms outstretched for the head he had lost. Salome dodged about him with sickening grace and heliographing *pudendum*.

Once, the headless saint staggered on to the Flowery Way, pretending to overbalance into the audience; once, he staggered orchestra-wards. The shabby players pointed him back and someone even laughed.

At last she returned the head to its shoulders. Gratefully Iokanaan lifted his habit — what more could even a Christian do? — and from his now striped underpants produced a cucumber and two apples to present to her.

Everard-Hopkins snapped his fan to an exclamation mark on unspoken comment.

"Shall we go?" he said and *softly and softly* they descended the broken stairs. There was little more to say. The Major was tired; tomorrow he was off and away; good-bye, good-bye.

For a while, after the Major, looking ghastly, had gone, Truscott stood to watch the countermarching lanes of faces, the assembly belt ceaselessly weighed with forms half gross from living, half haunted by its despairs, wholly and dully human.

Stop this, Truscott rebuked himself, stop watching. Don't watch, or you'll become an Everard-Hopkins; don't watch, they're only people. Watching makes symbols, watching makes additions of the unaddable, tacks theory to perishable flesh. Don't watch!

Truscott was about to move when an old man, hunchbacked from his burden of· years, grinned too roguishly and too surely from under a crippled umbrella. Truscott, expecting a beggar's palm, made a stock move. Now the old man was sure.

"You want-oo girl?" he said.

Truscott removed the hand he had placed in the pocket of charity.

"No."

Who was *girl*? Daughter? Granddaughter? Employer?

The old man was not disconcerted, persisted in roguishly grinning: since one avenue was closed, the other must be ridden along.

"You want-oo boy," he said, unquestioningly.

"No," said Truscott and, willing to follow along a new avenue he skittishly opened up himself, ducked his head beneath the umbrella-edge and said firmly, "Look here, I want you."

The aged smile became anxious and uncomprehending.

Truscott was pitiless. He put his hand on the umbrella handle and repeated, "You, I want you. *You are*," he softly sang, "*my heart's desire. . . .*"

The grin flashed off. "No, no, no," said the old man, detached himself from his umbrella, and scampered away.

Everard-Hopkins, Dugald, that old man, thought Truscott, all the same, all symbol-makers, do-gooders, or do-badders, all showing me a price ticket first — *Civilization, Aged in the Wood; Degeneracy, Cheap and Potent; Lust, All Popular Flavours* — as though there were not human beings in the bottle but animate bipeds of flesh in whose veins ran, not blood, but an extract squeezed from *Lust* the word, from the words *Degeneracy* and *Civilization*.

"Symbols!" he said, knowing what he meant.

What to do with the symbol-maker's umbrella?

He propped it against the building and, stepping on to the production belt, went with the others, thousands and thousands, thinking of Imiko — whom he had once made into a symbol — merely as a woman, merely in fact as certain parts of a woman.

That night he wrote poetry, impure.

And the next afternoon he sat through several plays as gorgeous and ritualistic as bull-fights. More monstrous things happened, more blood fountained up, more vileness occurred in the few playhouse hours than during a decade of bull-fights; but demoniac thought was expressed by the manipulation of gold-patched sleeves and trains, purgatory by the dropping of a paper handkerchief. The closing of night-black fans revealed a ruffling on the pool of inner virtue; murder was the blossom twirled half an inch; poverty regally advanced on gilded soles — a fragile automaton obscured in a coating of snowy paint, a web of gems and the lawless embroidery of robes without price.

Truscott, was kept on the edge of his seat which squeaked like a mouse.

All was poetry, pure.

All was symbol.

While the jewelled train of poverty dragged heavily along the Flowery Way, it rained outside.

Too poor to buy an umbrella, the old man roguishly grinned in the downpour, now and again importuning some Westerner who surely had rice in his pocket: "You want-oo girl?"

15

Before Major Everard-Hopkins left for Eastern Capital he had spoken to the Commanding Officer, a Colonel. The conversation had charmingly taken place over drinks.

Everard-Hopkins said no more than was necessary about Captain Dugald, summed him up as impetuous, did not mention the gardener.

It was at the Major's suggestion that the School Captain, Maxie Glenn was being cross-examined.

Immaculate, impersonal in manner, impassive of face, the Colonel did not reveal that he enjoyed the questioning.

Handsome, a concealed egoist commanding as a doge, he was charming because sin and sinners gave him pleasure and because, to arrive at the foregone end of justice, he was able to thrill himself again and again by elongating the means in every voluptuous direction.

His face seemed bronze, his hair coarsely-carved silver and gold; he was an idol, straight-backed and horizontal-shouldered as one; the incense of backsliding, the burnt-meats of guilt, the recklessly interknotted garlands of depravity, scented his memory and littered the altar of his life long after his supplicants had been ordered to discreet deportation and the penance of their own country.

The schoolboy answered him softly; the Colonel proceeded delicately towards a fatal *I don't understand* which he regarded as the turning-point between lie and truth.

"You went to the Padre's room for these lessons?"

"Yes, Colonel."

"How many nights a week?"

"Two or three, sir."

"Always on Thursday?"

"Yes, sir."

"Why Thursday always?"

"Well, it was Bingo night and — "

"There were fewer people in the Quarters?"

"Yes, sir — it was quieter."

"Always alone?"

"Yes, sir."

"The headmaster tells me, Glenn, that your Latin was quite good. You were not the worst in your class . . .?"

"No, sir."

"I see. How long did the lessons take?"

"About an hour or so, sir."

"How much an hour did your people pay the Padre?"

"Oh, he wasn't paid."

"Not paid! Not in — any way?"

"No, sir."

"He must have . . . he must have been very fond of you."

"I don't know, sir. I suppose so. He's a friend of the family."

"Ah! Does your father know you have been in the Mess bar?"

"I don't think so, sir. But I've only been in a couple of times, when it was hot. I had lemon squash."

"Why didn't you tell your father?"

"I didn't think to."

The Colonel was pleased with the boy's colour; it had run pinkly over his face, his eyes had become brighter, an animal gleam of self-caution. The tide was turning.

The Colonel felt the introductory flash of intoxication, but continued detachedly, "You bought a camera — an expensive one."

For the first time the boy hesitated.

"Yes, sir."

"Your father gave you the money?"

"No, sir."

"Who then?"

"I . . . I got most of it on the black market."

"All that money?"

"Yes, sir."

"You're perfectly sure?"

"Yes, sir."

"The Padre didn't, shall we say, help you out?"

"I don't understand, sir."

Ah! The Colonel's exterior was no stiller, no more idol-like than before.

"You don't understand what?"

"What you mean, sir — helped me out —"

"I'm sorry. I mean this: did the Padre give you any

money to help you — to *assist* you — in buying the camera?"

"No, sir."

"There was no reason why he should give you money?"

"I don't understand, sir."

"Again? Do you understand then when I say, did the Padre give you money for doing something particularly well . . . as a reward?"

"No, sir."

"Did he give you money for any other reason?"

In too prodigal a manner, too flushed now, already lost, "I don't understand, sir," said Maxie Glenn.

The Colonel, most charming, began to enjoy himself.

The examination continued.

Later it was the turn of the bar-boy.

Brigadier had dressed himself as Yoshiharo Minato for the interview — a new discreet gown, fresh hair-oil; he had polished the brass of his watch-face and borrowed a pair of cheap, expensive-looking horn-rimmed spectacles.

Where Maxie Glenn had sat before the idol, Yoshiharo Minato stood; the Colonel austerely questioned on, seeking at the same time truth for report, special truth for his own pleasure.

"One night Captain Dugald found you in Padre Hamilton's room."

"Yes, sah. Captain ang-ree."

"I believe so."

"Ver-ee ang-ree."

"Why was the Captain angry?"

"Sadness making ang-ree."

"Sadness?"

"Sadness because Captain dog is being dead."

"Dog? Dead?"

"Oh, yes, sah. Dog dead. House-garoo kill."

"You mean Captain Dugald's housegirl killed his dog?"

"Yes, sah."

"Why?"

"House-garoo ang-ree because Captain making rudeness. Captain say not sew shirt, not wash sock, say drink gin. All not true. House-garoo *ver-ee* ang-ree. She and gardener *ver-ee* ang-ree."

"Gardener?"

"Captain making rudeness al-so to gardener. Is punching jaw-bone. Ooh — ooh — ooh, pain."

The bar-boy held his jaw, swayed in happy anguish, smiled goldenly.

"House-garoo untouchab-le, gardener untouchab-le. Dog is being dead."

"I see. I see. Angry housegirl, angry gardener, dead dog, angry captain."

"Yes, sah. You are so-o-o right." The bar-boy again displayed his burnished teeth.

"Very well. Captain Dugald was angry because his dog was dead. Why did he kick *you*?"

"Not knowing, sah."

"No idea at all?"

"No, sah. He is kicking me impolitely."

"He says you had no pants on."

"Yes, sah."

"Why?"

"Pants off for sex."

"Pants off in the Padre's room?"

"Oh yes, sah. Padre is having sex with me."

"I see. How many times before had you been in the Padre's room?"

"Maybe seban, maybe eight."

"Sex every time?"

"Oh *yes*, sah. He is wanting woman-boy."

"Are you . . . a woman-boy?"

"No, *sah*. I am poverty student for engineering. I am adoring Miss Greer Garson, Miss Moira Shearer. I am also adoring —"

"He gave you money?"

"No, sah. Aspro, Engrish cigarette, cak-ee in can, coffee, tie with immodest woman —"

The Colonel broke in — oh, politely.

"You are not woman-boy, you say. Why did you have sex with the Padre?"

"Is politeness. He is saying, 'Brigadier, show me mogusa-burning.' I am going to his room, I am showing. That is Padre's sub-ter-fuge."

"Subterfuge, eh?"

"Not *good* sub-ter-fuge. Mogusa is on sciatica place so I am guessing before I go — ha, sex!"

Yoshiharo Minato began to giggle, covering his teeth with a delicate hand.

"You knew," said the Colonel, "why the Padre was using — ah — subterfuge and yet you went?"

"Yes, yes, sah. Is democracy?"

Padre Hamilton, next day, had no chance. He was a man of perspex to the Colonel; his skull a transparent one within which the idol of metal and charm saw what the Padre condemned himself for having initiated: ludicrous postures of venery.

The Colonel, unblinking: ". . . and now we come to . . . let me see . . . the thirteenth. On that night, about twenty-one hours, Captain Dugald came to your room. . . ."

"*Burst* in, Colonel. No other word for it. Absolutely without *knocking* . . . *burst* in!"

"Burst in. Had he knocked would you have let him in?"

"Naturally, I'd have answered the door. Whether I'd have let him *in* — another matter. He was *terribly* drunk, Colonel — a lone drinker, you know. I don't think he realized what he was *doing*. He had his dog with him, dead, wrapped in a table-cloth or something. Not *himself*. Not quite — *you* know. Imagining things."

"How did he behave, Padre?"

"Well, he burst in and attacked the bar-boy . . . *hurled* him to the floor, began kicking."

"What was the bar-boy doing in your room?"

"Heavens, Colonel, it was *quite a normal* thing. He had brought across a bottle of sherry from the bar."

"At twenty-one hours or later? His time-sheet shows that he went off duty that night at 20.15 hours."

"Well . . . well, I can't explain that. I rang through to the Mess; he brought the sherry over. That's all."

"Captain Dugald then . . . burst in?"

"Yes, Colonel. Raving, *imagining* things, misinterpreting."

"Why did Captain Dugald attack the bar-boy?"

"Drunk, mad *drunk*. The lad was just leaving; they may have collided at the door and —"

"Just leaving, Padre?"

"Yes, Colonel."

"I know it was a warmish night, but surely he wasn't leaving without his trousers?"

"Without . . .!"

The Toby Belch face looked unutterably shocked, next stiffened to dignity. "I don't understand what you mean, Colonel."

Padre Hamilton had absolutely no chance.

16

Hoshi had completed the doll of rice-straw.

It was as perfect as industrious jealousy could make it; malevolence had skilfully spliced, plaited, ravelled, and wound. Neither jealousy nor malevolence had seen fit to clothe the doll's smoothness, but guile had swaddled it in cloth and concealed it to await birth.

At last the elected day arrived, waxed, shouted, became afflicted, began to peel off its toggery of brilliance and hubbub, but feverish still; fever it could not reject.

Predestined, her future already loud-mouthed within her body, Hoshi sat unoccupied.

Presently Kazuo returned from the bath-house.

She remained apart and inert; he moved ostentatiously and sang; he dressed himself, putting on the shirt she had pressed with Paula Groot's electric iron; he came to her suddenly, "Button to sew, sister."

In terror, because her body might split and let out its horrors into the house, she sewed. He was then ready to return flourishing to the woman she herself had left only two hours ago.

"Sister is pale," he said.

She helped him on with the shoes he adored; she tried to smile but did not dare exert her will too much lest it skid away and hurl her into the unexpected.

"Shirt is becoming," was all she could say as she bowed from the shoe-step.

He was gone.

She heard him running for the tram.

Now the mother.

Her mother chewed with noisy good manners at some chocolate Hoshi had brought home, and was thinking of happy shadows and some more chocolate which she had pretended to eat days ago but had kept to eat with the present supply. She was therefore glad when Hoshi said she would go to the talkies but made no reply, feigning not to hear, stared at the mended shutter behind Hoshi, thought, *It is better not to say than to say,* closed her eyes like a baby and went on chewing.

"Excuse me for departing, mother," Hoshi said.

Hoshi had changed to her oldest and darkest kimono, and looked older and darker.

At the shoe-step, she put on her wooden clogs and, holding the cloth-wrapped parcel, began to walk in the demon's world.

Twilight.

Kazuo was nearing Rainbow Village.

Warm and muted belchings of wind, as from a gorged Apollyon in unseemly gulches of the sky, made the long tails of willows by the canal lift and slide and dodge back across the wire-encaged electric lights; the buoyant paper lanterns decorated with Buddhistic fylfots breathed and hummed; the split cotton stall-hangings were unquiet as though scandalous finger-tips assessed their value.

While it is yet the time enveloping *To Come*, there is little to dominate the senses with certainty; one's god is Self, who sleep-tosses and pules in the niche, who tries to listen and hears nothing but own broken questions.

Afterwards, of course, is the time when appears that demonstrative god who hacks with cruel plectrum at the strings of every sense to slice out discord as one does cancer from the breast of silence.

Hoshi knew where *Afterwards* was.

She shuffled in its direction as quickly as was publicly decent, for *Afterwards* would not arrive until she did. She heard nothing except the woman imprisoned in her and saw nothing at all, though she was aware of infinite degrees of superimpositions receding in perspective from her in all directions.

Silhouettes of arms in gauzy kimono sleeves lifted themselves or vibrated transparent fans behind mosquito nets behind diaphanous screens behind paper shutters, so that sane domestic acts, family calm and relaxation were ashen and ghostly negatives.

The half-naked who sat on rocks along the streets wore shadows on shoulder, face, breast, and thigh: as lanterns tilted like boats, and the willow curtains shuttled, the shadows crossed and recrossed.

Wind-bells jangled when Hoshi pushed through the cob-webs of wind in which they were stuck; water drooled down shop windows and spouted laxly up from tubs of watermelon and dripped on little toys that, thus water-driven, made a blurred chirruping with tiny hammers on tiny tin plates.

Stars blew out as clouds moved upon them.

Snooker-players, indoor-fishing adolescents, and bath-house nudes swerved about in a sickly way; tender modest girls who let themselves be played on as loudly as xylo-phones — those pigeon-toed Magdalenes born to be and hoping to be Marthas — lolled beside Goths at low ebb, flaccid Roderick Randoms and Captain Bobadills.

Next, all that was behind.

She had passed through the fluttering, the dangling, the shuttling shadows and overlapping perspectives.

There were no more people.

Her mouth padlocked as Papageno's, she was climbing up the hill, a *gruyère* of air-raid tunnellings luxuriant with old claustrophobias and dog-like dark.

The wind had lain down on the pelt-warm mould. The final star closed like the eye of a weary apostle.

Silence.

Not the silence of factory, council chamber, theatre, air-port, or street — man's things — which is perfected silence when no man is in them, but the silence of stones, thorns, boles, leaves, the unpilloried earth.

This silence received her, and the noises of her gown and wooden soles and intemperate breathing, with gluttonous fervour; to make her digestion within the intestines of dark less difficult branches plunged aside or lifted themselves away from her body's path, stones crawled off, broke like bubbles, or ducked beneath the ground.

In angular spasms she toiled higher upon the incline of nightmare, preposterous pilgrim in a country generations of crazed women had sanctified with like pilgrimages.

Suddenly, a declaration was made; heaven affirmed; a bluish artery of lightning tore down from the perimeter of light; the immobile track struck out like a carving from the blindness; the gelded trees stuttered twice, like shocks, before her; the gates of her face and hatred were smashed open.

The rain hurled perpendicularly down.

Another flash, and she reached the one ancient tree she had controlled herself to reach.

Now the demon of thunder beat his arc of drums to an entanglement of explosions.

With fingers, on which the electrical lotion of rain ran like black blood she unknotted the parcel, took out the nails which she clenched between her teeth, the hammer provided by an Occupation canteen and which she had found in Paula Groot's backyard, the doll of straw with its obscenely parted legs.

Not for Hoshi, whose toque of hair now uncoiled wickedly upon her saturated shoulders, the mid-twentieth-century jealousies, quakerish and prudent, of betrayed housegirls. Not for her to crouch weeping behind wardrobe doors, doltish with milk-and-water menace, to contemplate suicide like a pretty biscuit-mould she would not buy, not for her the prayers to genial monsters or the spooks of mercy.

Medea, Jezebel, Jaël, Erinys . . . these her near-sisters, for ever fashionable, their mad hair too snaking *à la mode* on their lonely shoulders, their unsavoury hands ready to brandish aloft the gushing head, the tuber of a heart, the torn-out uterus like a raddled pear.

Her ugliness was impeccable; another kink of lightning showed her to herself as though reflected on the looking-glass of rain, showed that what the trees and rocks saw and the vermin in the leaves heard was a devil-mask, cross-eyed, cut into chevrons and carets of flesh among which a baneful mouth extruded unmentionable slogans.

She saw, too, the rust-stained bark of the tree and the black wisps of other dolls rotting here and there upon its surface.

Groping to find a smooth spot, what was it made her palm slide and slip . . . rain? blood? sweat? the oil of insanity?

Ha! — smoothness; no granulation of nail-heads.

Upon this she held the doll and, pressing the point of a

nail into the crutch of straw, hammered it into the tree.

Several strokes.

Each nail wrenched from between her teeth and driven in towards the centre took fewer strokes, even in the darkness between lightning flashes.

The thunder was not so tall as she nor the lightning so potent.

Then she fell upon the boiling slope.

Presently, she began to move, to crawl flatly, foxlike, in circles, to find at last the downhill trail.

She knew that her brush with its ballast of filth dragged encumbering behind her, thorns no longer retracted from her, but pierced and scored her muzzle, stones sliced her paws. From time to time she whimpered bestially or lay panting.

Then she continued to crawl down and down.

By coincidence, by mere coincidence, this was the night when Paula Groot first felt the scalding pain.

Kazuo had not long left her. He carried an oiled paper parasol belonging to Hoshi. The first downpour had begun.

A block away from Paula Groot's house he had removed his shoes and put one in each pocket of her mannish gaberdine coat, which she had lent him and which fitted him well.

She was not to see the coat again.

As he ran barefooted through Rainbow Village towards his tram her pain began.

Some hours later Kazuo was awakened by a scratching and whining at the closed rain-shutters of the house.

"Mother," he called, "animal is outside."

His mother pretended, even to herself, to fall into deeper sleep.

"Mother," Kazuo called again, "go to see!"

I am dreaming, thought the mother and then, *Go to see! Easy to say, hard to do.*

Kazuo crawled from beneath his eiderdowns and opened the rain-shutters. It was a while before he found his sister, part-naked, bruised by undergrowth, with bloody knees, fox-possessed.

The mother, decorated childishly with circumoral chocolate, slept with the quiet that is supposed to be that of a child, while her son-child dragged her daughter-child into the house to which Occupation-Democracy had brought chocolate, Scotch brogues, insanity and honour — for, two years ago, the father of Kazuo and Hoshi, purged by the Occupation administrators, rather than suffer under the name *purgee* had honourably committed suicide in the classic manner, eviscerating himself while his best friend beheaded him.

The father of Kazuo and Hoshi was a traditionalist.

So was Hoshi.

Kazuo?

17

Changes, changings, everybody taking a pace back into the past as the long queue of themselves added other selves in front; a continuity of transparencies through which, looking backwards, they saw the dimmer and dimmer branchings-off into ancestors with *their* infinite branchings-off into earlier ancestors.

Atoms of dust, from a stadium large as Jericho and centuries ago smashed to dust, joined other specks of dust to form a film on seats of stadia that would go to dust; Imiko's father wrestled from his station-master's uniform into his second-best kimono — one less occasion on which he would do this.

Thus, speck by speck, action by action, emotion by emotion, the using up and filling in went on.

Dressed, his tobacco-tray beside him, Imiko's father sat on the padded floor.

Imiko kneeled before him.

"You have met man — farmer," stated the father.

"I have met farmer."

She knew what was coming and what her father would say.

What would she say?

That she did not know; vanity and a sense of peace were alloyed by irritation, a feeling of being folded up genially — a too bright sash — and firmly put in a drawer.

Two and a half years earlier she had concealed hysteria so well, and whitewashed defiance so thickly, she had been able to avoid nearing this drawer, to get away without being cursed. Her own shrewdness was a little responsible but most responsible were her father's intelligence and affectation of broad-mindedness, salty wings on which he capriciously hovered just above convention. He was conceited, used Chinese-isms which are to his language what Latin-isms are to English, and could be as engaging as a monkey.

He took two puffs from the four his little pipe contained and quoted, "Feed tiger — trouble later on."

What did he mean? Monkeys were harmful.

He continued, "You have seen cities; you have been modern girl. I think that is good experience-thing. You have returned to home."

Puff, puff.

He tapped the tiny ash from his pipe, examined the spark of dottle — plenty of time.

Plenty of time for mischief.

Imiko felt that she could, at the moment, tell her confusion and have it explained, spread out the shoddy fabric of her lies and have them forgiven, exhibit the grubby postcards of her city life, have them paternally picked over and understood.

This was not so.

All through the world, Imikos have no shoulders to cry on except those of other Imikos; how deeply and unwillingly concealed from parents is the child who never dies.

Her father would decidedly have understood motive rather than deed, the notion of adventuring rather than the fly-blown adventure; he could have forgiven her personality in long-worded confabulations, but never her unkempt offences.

He was intrigued by the peacock doings of modern-boy and modern-girl, at least, the spirit of them: the letter would have enraged him as much as he would have been had he known — as her mother did — that she smoked cigarettes.

Therefore she quietly said, "I am happy."

"Is that so, is that so?"

Delay again, while vast university halls lost another granule of their anatomy, and houses, as slackly bundled together as octopus-homes, moved microscopically closer to crack-up.

"You admire farmer?" He looked merrily, wickedly at her from his brilliant pupils.

"He was polite. He relieved distress." She was gracious and careful.

Graciousness and care would not help.

"Is that so? He is eldest son." This was firm advocacy.

"So?" she said.

Eldest son was the one who could not escape — the holding was his, and he was the family; he and she were now to be planned into making another eldest son. The accidents of her own escape, by making her desirable, were now to lead back to inescapability.

"Go-between will come to discuss marriage," he said, becoming less monkeyish at this practical moment, yet taking on the long-headed look of that god of ideals who is able to live on the mists of the skies, the dew from the twigs.

"Man who wants you is good farmer. He acquires honours, many rice-honours, millet-honours, honours for his apple-pears." Then he became endearing and "modern" again, "He wins also in thumb-wrestling."

For the final time he paused, delaying speech until he had constructed the important and deadly sentence; he watched her ruthlessly over the knowledge of what this sentence was to be; peered like a merchant, and spoke.

"I thought, feed tiger *perhaps* trouble later on. But experience-thing has been taming-thing. Home country has called you back; old proverb says, *Obey customs of place where you are.*"

Then, quickly, "Farmer's wife?"

He expected no denial, was prepared to whip her; she had had her fling.

"You are indulgent and wise father: I am father's only-too-willingly obedient and insignificant daughter."

She bowed. She felt like her mother: nothing else to do except bow.

"So?" he said, and twitched his pipe at her in dismissal.

"I am grateful to my father," she said and bowed again, and bowing, backed gracefully to the door, slid it aside with citified movements and, bowing on her knees outside in the passage, slid the door to again.

She had completely forgotten to use her Western Capital accent.

She walked to the spot where she had first been seen by Masao, smoking, tossing one cigarette butt after another into the water, trying to tie a knot in the two strands of her desires, but *Here* and *Away* slipped from each other, remaining separate.

"Better the less than the more," had been said. Was *Here* less or more, was *Away* less or more?

Roof-tiles on the gable of every house were embossed with the fire-preventing character for water. Yet houses burned down.

Security and monotony, one bed and good food with Masao, the character *peace* upon her brow: would fire come to destroy?

She broke the backs of grass-stalks.

She behaved at home with filial docility, shilly-shallying within herself, privately smoking too much. The go-between came and went, her mother giggled and chattered and planned, her father was witty and sly, being very happy. Finally Masao visited her father.

When her mother knew the visit was to take place she was elated; now came the time for her to use the house-skill and kitchen-skill she admired herself for. She hurried with pride to the shops, planning and re-planning display, flavour, and colour.

Throughout the entertainment she would not be seen, but what was best of her heedful years would be — the worldly but polite daughter, the dishes and bowls in correct shades of bran and ash, delicacies of subtle formality, and symbolic of the right things: longevity, marital happiness, good fortune, loyalty, and health.

Imiko was subjected to joyous naggings; mother and daughter quarrelled judiciously about the robes to be worn. Imiko would wear one to serve the wine, another the food, a third to entertain unobtrusively as the evening finished. Decision on the propriety of the most harmonious at each stage caused a pleasure of antagonism during which robes paid for by Truscott were taken from the cases. Imiko took out also two tins of asparagus tips and a packet of Camel cigarettes for Masao to smoke.

These would confirm the contemporary effect she would herself add to the time-worn ceremony of getting rid of a daughter.

As Masao and her father drank the wine which Imiko poured, the one-and-a-half-inch crests that circumspectly decorated their black ceremonial robes stared at her with the benign expression of the beckoning cat who lured customers through restaurant windows, of the papier-mâché dog who charmed away children's night-crying, of the salt-glaze pig through whose anus drifted mosquito-repelling incense.

Could she put up with these symbolic starings, un-blinking and reasonable, instead of those wanton and cal-culating ones of the half-world of cellophane, fluorescent lights, latex and ferro-concrete?

She changed her kimono and served food — the dried persimmons, the seaweed and shrimp biscuits, the whole bream suggesting unity, the asparagus tips, all the menu her mother had so joyously designed and brought into being.

How silently forestalling Imiko was: her airs and graces had watch-like precision; she filled the wine-cups, lit the foreign cigarettes, and removed each man's meal tray, retir-ing submissively.

With her mother's excited help she changed to the third of the kimono, intensified her make-up because the men were becoming drunk, and returned unobtrusively, aware that she was more obtrusive, more beautiful and, deprived now of the advantage of wine-and-food-serving trickery, thrown back on impurer wiles.

The cheekbones of her father and Masao were flushed; her father recited poems; Masao allowed himself to look at her openly when his eyes felt that the father's eyes were acutely turned aside. Imiko drank one cup of wine with a fanciful femininity; next she deftly made paper-folded shapes — fox, tortoise, cock, and lily.

Was Masao becoming sleepy?

Her father said, "Say poems."

She said one only before Masao asked to go to the lavatory.

" 'Whether persimmon,' " she quoted, conscious of her Max Factor make-up, her father's slyness, her own coquet-tish impertinence, which her father was drunk enough to enjoy. " 'Whether persimmon is astringent I do not know, for this is my first taste.' "

Did Masao understand?

"Lavatory," said Masao. He wanted to empty his blad-der.

Rising gracefully, she slid back the shutters and went with him, politely opening the lavatory shutter, politely seeing nothing, but smelling the asparagus-reeking urine. As she handed the pine-needle-scented wet cloth for Masao to wipe his fingers, he dropped it, his first sign of the nervousness he had repressed all evening.

"Forgive clumsiness," he said. He was a large, hardworking, well-behaved child.

Imiko felt a tenderness at that moment.

"It can't be helped," she said, and dropped to her knees, and gladly held up the cloth to him. As his hand came forward, she took it in her own and, still on her knees, washed the fingers.

That night she dreamed.

Truscott was with her, dressed ceremonially as Masao had been, but the crests on his robe were not the ordinary three there for auspicious, martial, or heredity reason, they were many, they moved from place to place on the cloth and were little mouths saying, "Feed tiger, trouble later on."

She was dressed as a ballerina, yet wore the horn-concealing bandeau of a bride. Truscott hastened before her through the Eastern Capital suburb of Upper Hill; she pursued but could not catch him. Hideous creatures importuned her from the vagrants' railway tunnel, their feet turned backways like ghosts'; they stank as much as Americans and cheese, they were shaggy as Australians. Among the cherry-blossom trees of Upper Hill Park, squalid tatters hung advertising Florida Cabalet; tunny tins and cider bottles protruded from the lotus-pool morass.

Here she lost Truscott; his robe speckled with little mouths bore him away and she knew another nastiness was to take this departure's place.

Among the warrior-tall bronze and stone lanterns commemorating warriors, crab-sliding through the urinated slush, appeared the figure of an old woman. Her mother? No — Imiko knew who it was and tried desperately to escape. Useless: the veil of rotten hair parted on an overripe sucked-in face beneath whose *pourriture noble* she recognized herself.

She cried out — the face became her mother's, toothless, smiling too sweetly, for there was nothing else to do. Imiko looked up. Seated on the lantern pedestal she leaned against was Truscott with a skin of gold, a white curl between his eyebrows, a ten-foot halo. His eyes were sealed against her.

"Wake!" she cried. "Wake up! Come back!"

It was she who woke to hear the lecherous malcontent of frogs, that prophetic coronach murderers have most listened to. She heard too the ticking of the Poverty Insect.

The next morning she decided not to smoke any more.

"Mother," she said, "today I shall walk for the seven grasses."

Her mother, who was burying a bent needle in a junket-like piece of bean-curd, to give it a soft rest after its busy suffering, smiled toothlessly and too sweetly, for there was nothing else to do.

September: month of the seven autumn grasses, season of high skies and fattening horses — for the first time since returning, Imiko dressed herself in the manner of a country woman, let her breasts hang brassière-less in a worn kimono kilted up into a thin sash; in the cupboard-for-old-things she found a rush umbrella-hat and her own straw sandals among country things she had forgotten — snow-boots of rice-fibre, bamboo-root walking sticks and straw raincoats.

She did not paint her lips or bother to remove the bro-caded cloth from the looking-glass.

It was Duty herself who slid along seeking the seven grasses. Arrowroot and wild morning-glory were easy to find; pampas, Chinese agrimony, bush clover, and wild car-nation took longer. She could not find maiden-flower with its faint stink — maiden-flower, the poets called it. Petrified vinegar was its country name.

Returning home she arranged the six in a bamboo hang-ing vase bacause the display niche was still occupied by the fortune-wishing flowers arranged the day before for Masao's entertainment.

As she snipped, twisted, and wired, undramatic tears dribbled from her eyes; she did not know why, and could not imagine a part to play to them.

In the afternoon she walked to where Masao worked in one of his fields.

"Tomorrow," she said, "I shall come to help." Then she saw the maiden-flower.

"Please pick that for me," she said.

He picked it, passed it to her with the hand she had softly wiped.

She walked home, soothed by having found the seventh grass, modest and light-coloured, in Masao's field.

Convinced that her future was settled, she decided to behave as though she had always belonged only to a Present such as now encircled her in every rustic direction.

A little snake lay on the track.

"*Aburaunkensowaka!*" she cried and the snake moved away, as she knew it must when it heard the meaningless words.

I am still innocent country person, she thought, I am wisdom-and-peace person.

Imiko had no idea who Peace was.

Peace is the double-tongued brother who discreetly poisons on a saltless gruel of ennui and denial, on unsugared years, on draughts of triviality, while wrinkles tighten on his guests, arteries harden, cancer invades, the hit-run roars from a side-street, the passenger-plane falls.

Of the three brothers, War is Wisdom's child, is the most outspoken, the austere and formal eldest. He is less pennywise with gifts of death. He lavishes them. How succulent his orgies, how spiced his pastries, how matured and from-the-first-day-unchanged-in-quality the liqueur all must drink.

Most cynical is the third brother, the neuter who lolls like a street-corner tout, lisping his hyphenated name and the allurements of a little place in the next lane where one can *m-m-m* and *m-m-m* and *m-m-m*. Democratic-Occupation is his name, the evangelist handing out pamphlets of ornamented lies. Specious and venal, he bribes with delicacies of mendacity, with wafers of half-truth, with bizarre salads slimy from the oil-and-vinegar of lubricity.

Within the girdle of his embrace, victor and vanquished embrace, fondle the ex-enemy body, poke fingers in the eyes of minds.

I am still innocent country person, they might all cry, I am integrity, a wowser, enlightened, a sea-scout leader, I cook bread-and-butter pudding, keep myself to myself, write to auntie every Sunday, am pleasant to the natives but draw the line, played bridge with the Brigadier, made a coloured movie of the Hollyhock Festival, love the *quaint* lee-tle children, dismissed the cook — tipsy, my dear, went ski-ing, swimming, slumming, am going to hate Australia and no servants, am still innocent-country person, wisdom-and-peace person.

Blind, all blinded, in a camping-park of the blind.

18

At "X" Mess, Brigadier had prepared for Everard-Hopkins a flexible itinerary of travel towards the remoter, less Westernized parts of the country; and a handful of cards of insect-like calligraphy.

These bore English headings *Mayor, Station-master, Taxiperson, Inn-master*: they explained Everard-Hopkins, his hopes of comfort, his needs and fancies, his inability to speak the language, and made clear he was rich enough to pay for whatever was said to be best.

So far Everard-Hopkins had had little use for them: several times they had swiftly solved a problem gesticulation of an insensitive sort and pidgin-mouthing might never have solved at all. A week passed. An ordained day came.

Major Everard-Hopkins was perched in a third-class carriage of Orientals. He was rigid with an explicit terror. It was an incandescent mid-afternoon: the hour and the heat, hands of a supernatural timepiece, had jammed together prohibiting the future.

Earlier in the day the natives had gossiped, convulsed their fans rapidly as bee-wings, hopped up and down to the luggage-rack for cloth-bound parcels, nibbled, dabbed at lips with their towels. All this agitation had lent speed, as a flag does to its pole.

Now all of them lolled, a kiln of uncooling dead, stripes and commas on their kimono stilled, fans and eyes closed, flies prying at nostrils. In this tableau of grossness Everard-Hopkins sat at a destination from which the rest were dreaming themselves elsewhere; his heart and his arm were aching cruelly. Sometimes he forced his eyes shut but they instantly flicked open on sesame fields blanched by heat, peasants suffocated to immobility in the act of eating watermelon, an insect of falcon stuck at zenith.

During the morning's dam-burst of wind the olive-trees, rye, sweet-potato plants, river-reeds, loves-lies-bleeding, dahlias, rippling disclosures of the undersides of leaves, had strained forward at the same angle. Unrooted and more agile, the bird-scaring devices had tugged about above rice-paddocks: on cords stretched across, old sedge hats, broken-plumed sunshades, streamers, demon faces painted on tin plates had jerked in all directions.

The forenoon had been littered with people, horses, and scarecrows; the flutter-flutter of manes, tails, tatters, and robe-skirts gave meddling an appearance of industry: women tied up loofah vines, men flung ribbons of peeled melon to dry over lines of string, stallions displayed excitements of gingko leaves between their ears, children wearing vees of brocaded scraps hunted yellow butterflies and black dragonflies across shallows. Now and then a heron, hoisting its fragility from an irrigation canal, had its angel wings blown like skirts about its wiry legs. Oh, enjoyable, all of it.

Under the leaves of enjoyment, catastrophe's fruit had been mellowing.

Hour after hour he had watched the cherry-and-white of ice-cream hawkers pedalling their bicycles in the landscape. It had amused Everard-Hopkins to pretend this succession of vendors was one extraordinary being now racing parallel to the train, now diagonally across scene, round a parsley of camphor-laurels, down slopes of rice-cocks; he would disappear west behind a thatched farmhouse and immediately scorch south-east from a spruce copse.

Suddenly Everard-Hopkins saw him again, flat-out in the afternoon breakdown. "Stop," he whispered. "For God's sake. Your heart, you'll kill yourself." Uncertain he had not screamed he turned criminally to the others. They were senseless all: their fallen scurf of egg-shells, pear-cores, and caramel papers made a portentous design on the floor.

Everard-Hopkins's body seemed to borrow from the heart's malignancy the power of a fire anxious to consume what sustained it.

He knew a doctor was necessary.

He was a fool not to have had Brigadier prepare a card labelled *Doctor*. Yet words, with a doctor, should be superfluous: the doctor would touch, diagnose, prescribe — he would have existence again. Here, he did not exist even in the dreams of those knocked all ways on the seats. Besides, had he possessed the language to arouse them, any

expression of his pain and fear would be minified in value
by the mixture of pain and fear.

In a confusion of distress he struggled for independence: I
must not, he thought, consider making extravagant moan-
ings. He pictured the aftermath: stopped train, threadbare
officialdom, alien bickerings over gaunt insensibility,
quarter-hours used up while he unsatisfactorily died.

Dignity depends on health, he thought; how undignified
are the hidden or undestroyed dead.

He kept on attempting to maintain an appearance of calm
for the sleepers, but his senses wore some lopsiding fungus
and he repeatedly recalled a place he had not thought of for
years — his boyhood sleep-out where, sick in bed, he called
out, "Mummy!" An increase of pain made him unable to
play the stoic further; not caring if he were heard either by
the sleep-massacred Orientals or the great ear invisibly inclining down from the foreign sky, he implored, "Mummy,
please."

As though his years-dead mother had influence, a
sprinkle of hock-cold drops soaked the hairs of his chest,
pain closed itself to nothing, the timepiece of cessation
cracked its hands apart. The ice-cream cyclist shot past a
pock-marked desolation of salt-pans and decisively disappeared towards the violent upsteamings of the Pacific.

Eyes and fans opened; the carriage stirred as a garden
does; the train hammered through ramshackle factories, and
arrived.

Free of all except one fear, like a solitary eye accusing up
from a mine-shaft, he left the station and displayed a *Taxiperson* card.

His sense of fatality subsided. The sun was setting.

Split-bamboo blinds roofed over the streets: smoke
smouldered from pencils of incense on fish-stalls. The taxi
had to dodge blocks of ice set on stands; passer-by fingers
had gentled the edges of the blocks in which mounds of
grapes or arrangements of shells showed perverted colours;
others fostered nothing except a white core like ear-ache.
Children escaped placidly from before the car bonnet in
garments burning with tremendous blossoms; many women
wore convoluted wigs; lanterns of cut white paper moved
skirts of greenish gauze. A festival, he thought: fresh zig-zag

papers rustled on the holy ropes slung across temple arches.

All this, seated back, he eyed indulgently; as the taxi climbed uphill he thought: Perhaps here, in this town, I find my well, the convolvulus twining the bucket handle.

At the Mansion Hotel three inn-sisters slipped from behind the demon-thwarting screen at the entrance and plunged to their knees. He handed over the *Inn-master* card which one of them hurried indoors with. Presently she returned and gave it back; the maids did not begin to unlace his boots.

What was wrong?

They wagged paws as though fanning mustard-mouth, shook oiled top-knots — the gestures of negation, of *no*. He, smiling querulously: "The master! Bring the master!"

They did not understand, sniggered with embarrassment and pointed to the rows of sandals in the shelves above the shoe-removing step. He saw many with "TIG" painted on one sandal, "ERS" on the other.

Yet, even if there were many visitors, surely Brigadier's note had explained he would not object to the national custom of shared rooms. "Go," he said and pointed, "go bring-ee master." Their faces became bilious and smaller; dismally they bowed, obscuring these against the floor. Charming; but he needed refuge, so began to make definite Western movements, unlaced his boots, planked them neatly down and walked into the hotel.

The maids, disconcerted, waggled away leaving a lane of surprise in the hot air.

The Westernized foyer smelt like a native urinal, of pickled radish. Over Genoa-velvet arm-rests and on occasional tables of 1908 sea-grass lay newspaper-sallow doilies and runners of Richelieu. He sat. Cicadas drilled the air with intense gravity. A grandfather clock, showing six, struck nine.

A fat Oriental crawled in, nudging his head upon the floor.

Crawling nearer, callipers of greased hair opening and closing on his forehead, *No, no*, the fatty — master? manager? — was saying and acting, *no room, please excuse humble place, no room*.

Again Everard-Hopkins handed over the *Inn-master* card

which was read, perhaps this time more carefully, for a vision seemed to be stimulated: metal teeth glittered in the ripe face, hands were clapped, the inn-sisters appeared, now a trio of merry assent, and led him over corridors of black and white pebbles, over satin expanses of wood cleaned with tea and polished by the friction of darned socks and Oriental foot-mittens.

His room was large. While the maids uncovered the looking-glass, brought raspberry vinegar and a wet scented face-cloth in a little silver-gilt basket, he mimed fervently, palms praying together by his cocked head. They understood and spread eiderdowns. They closed shutters on rooftops crimped down-slope to a harbour palisaded by commercial chimneys, soot-tipped like used matches, which let through from leprosium islands gushes of marine air which carried Deanna Durbin's loud-speaker shrilling of "It's Raining Sunbeams".

As his senses pedalled away across twilight, Everard-Hopkins recalled need of a doctor. On the frontier of sleep he said to himself, "I must get a doctor tomorrow . . . must get . . . something will turn up . . ." then set his frown loose and all thought, all fear.

He awoke in darkness, refreshed; a webbing of thread-like veins occupied him. He felt resurrection, but each filament had its hairline shadow: alchemy of some sort had happened during sleep, waters had noiselessly risen on the Promised Land, a finger had touched, a falcon hovered — past and present were crossed esoterically with the future. Unfolding, he stalked, his own tranquil spectre, but puzzled as a lover, and drew aside a shutter and looked down.

Many separate musics, Western, twanglings and thumping of primitive quality, artless voices, steamed up from the turbination of lights. What mighty ladle stirred them? Each gust, he thought, the very wood of the shutter frame, had in it a warning. Not knowing why, he was waiting. Sleep had left a message he could not read.

Far away, spillings of the insect-luring-to-death fluorescents of the fields rimmed the sparkling brew. He pressed bone finger-tips upon the arid muscles of his arms, listening. For what listening, waiting? Were menacing certainties to crowd in on his self-compassion, his renunciation of his own world? *Absit omen*, he thought. There were no stars, not one. He waited, and time appeared to pass.

At some moment, intimately, there was a perfect tap at the external sliding door. He more avidly waited.

"May one come inside room, please?"

He was surprised at the English, its exotic flawlessness.

"Please come in," he called as a bird might.

The door slid aside; on the lighted paper barrier of the inner shutter lay a silhouette and its shadow — a slender man.

"Come in," he said again and, as the paper door slid open, "I do not know where the switch is."

The visitor switched on the light and sank to his knees with an intense burning smile.

Everard-Hopkins saw a bowing Oriental in whom there was an excess of magnetism to which only the stern and the stupid could resist abandoning themselves. He could not resist: unhampered now by exhaustion or pain he was to be plucked. From the centre of this crystal of calm balanced on the hullabaloo outside, "What . . . ?" he asked, and in politeness lowered himself to the matting.

"I am honoured you share room with me," said the Oriental. "The master could not make you com-pre-hend. Hotel is full, many visitors and five baseball teams — famous Tigers al-so. If you do not wish to share. . . ."

How powerful and aristocrat the new-comer's smile was; he cracked his finger-joints — and firmly.

"If *you* do not mind," said Major Everard-Hopkins. "It — it is — kind of you."

"I came before. At bath-time. At dinner-time. You were all times asleep."

"I was very tired. And — not well."

Something else was — not well. The visitor was captivating, obviously rich, a fan was stuck harmlessly in his sash of unpolished-silver colour, yet Everard-Hopkins seemed to himself a tight-rope walker above a gulch of doubt.

"You have been asleep a so long time; you look well now."

"I am better." No — not utterly better: he should ask this English-speaking one about a doctor.

"Better! Are you certain? Should I telephone doctor?"

His eyes grazed like black chamois on the scarp of Everard-Hopkins's face.

"No — no, thank you." The Major startled himself by this retort: a doctor, of *course*.

How many eyed this dialogue over dark flames?

Both seemed watching themselves and each other under the cynical attention of yet one more, for whose listening Everard-Hopkins's answers had consequence. Distrust of the other's allure distressed him — this delightful fellow, he thought, is one of those I am going to live among. Delightful. Silly of me.

"If you are unhealthy tomorrow, I shall telephone doctor."

"I am grateful — very grateful," he said.

Then, for no reason, "Tomorrow and tomorrow."

Tomorrow sloped a broken wing on the air. That was that, and safety.

How very wise to be safe: a rocket of tainted laughter soared from the maëlstrom without.

"Would you like re-fresh-ment?"

"No, nothing to eat."

"Green tea? Whisky-soda? Wine?"

"Nothing at all. One day's fast will benefit me."

"Ah, so!"

A pause into which the festival scrimmage foamed: the Oriental exhilarated himself, smiled proudly as a hierarch setting out moonstones, said, "You hear? Outside? It is last night of Festival of Dead. Souls of ancestors return once a year. Our women put food on household altars — potatoes, sesame, egg-plant; lanterns are lit in graveyards; everything is so jolly. We dance in all streets — children, everyone. So very old dances. An-ti-quit-y, you know."

Into the flame of that smile the Major ashenly also smiled and said, "I should like to see them."

Oh, fool! he instantly thought. Still hot; he had the rest of his life to see festivals; hot, and the streets would be jammed; it would be indiscreet to go.

"Not in-discreet to venture?"

Concern intensified the jet of the Oriental gaze.

"No, certainly not," said the Major. With a spinsterish cry of laughter, he repeated, "No!"

"I shall be delighted to be guide."

Finger-joints were again fervently cracked; how sharp and ancient was the long Chinese nail on one little finger: this man was no labourer.

Together they rose.

Everard-Hopkins felt the room drop from him like a robe; it slipped down a crack of time. Too late to return and see what flowers had slept with him, to escape from the charmer, from fascination riddled with doubts, back to eiderdowns and the quarantine of sleep. Hampered by the assistance of the inn-sisters, he got on his boots at the step and was led away.

Intricate building, maids and master, slithered behind and fell to doom.

Immediately their path was crossed by a hurrying male in zinc-coloured gown, black sash ritualistically tied, bow on rump. This remotest outrider carried a water-melon in a net of gilded string and flounced away, speeding on a current to the vortex . . . lights, music, the vertigos of teeming souls.

Soon, Everard-Hopkins knew the surf had been reached: the corsair-haired palmists whose lanterns showed a sinister black hand, the peanut-roaster corpse-bleached by her acetylene flare, beggars sprawling in a mess of straw that could have wormed from their pruned limbs — even these wretches staked to the spot emitted scraps of melody that circled away inwards on the flood-race whirlpool. A fox in a cage which it perfectly filled and from which its brush curled outside, with love enclosing prison and self, smiled and snarled.

Inwards. Leashes of drunkards essayed caricature steps of the Dance of the Dead as they moiled from the navel back to which drifted their minds unravelled by wine.

"*Sa-a-an ah yoi yoi*," they sang.

Inwards.

The Major's patron hurried, he stooped after; paper tongues of porcelain wind-bells brushed his shoulders. They edged through a swarm of impassioned children spooning bowls of shaved ice between rouged lips. Twirling as they gulped, the children lusted to be swept blind again in the dance, to raise arms in floating sleeves, to lift feet in cloven white socks.

"*Sa-a-an ah yoi yoi!*"

Inwards.

Now a pregnant woman, a baby bound unconscious on her *scapulae*, rotated like a virgin, slitting air with a circular fan shredded and eaten by use into holes as an old lotus leaf is.

Inwards.

They arrived.

"*Voilà!*" said the guide. Ah, the smile!

Everard-Hopkins's eyes might have seen, across the lurching hair, the outrageous mandrel of uproar, but hundreds of plate-like fans, sleeves and naked arms stabbed above heads, and "*Sa-a-an ah yoi yoi!*" said every stiff mouth. Decease of all emotions except the one fed on gyrating had left flesh marked only by the past, no passions to correct — dancing for the dead all wore the dead's faces.

Nearest the axis a flux of toddlers, hours ago exhausted, still uplifted sleeves, faltering and sleep-dancing. Some wore sandshoes, dirt, rags; others were floral, painted, powdered — tinselled rosy bows quivered on their meagre coiffures. Masks were worn, a female face, white, dropsical, smug, with eyebrows smudged on like moth-wing dots. Round went the teetotum of infants. Round and round, next, tirelessly raising hoof-split feet and clogs of crimson lacquer, wheeled adept boys and girls supple as lizards. Clogs sprang from dust and were drawn down; arms gashed up; hands hailed on fans. Youths in Hawaiian shirts and with cigarettes behind ears, hussies wearing crystal necklaces, a one-armed man invisibly slapping, an adolescent dressed as a gaucho . . . "*Sa-a-an ah yoi yoi!*"

The Major's mind was marred by these uprisings like the necks of an anger of swans, by layers of sound: soft heard under loud, friction and pressing of bodies caught above sourness of musical instruments. The millstone churned to Everard-Hopkins again and again the same sweat-gleety torso, foot-high clogs, closed eyelids, piratical beret, sculptured wig, spectacles, scorpion scar, hare-lip, long finger-nails through which light shone. More and more were fated into the pack: wrestlers folded gown-skirts into sashes, women clipped the ends of head-towels in their teeth, louts combed each other's scented hair and sidled in, a prostitute dressed as a woman powdered his jaw and Adam's apple, struck his fan with a red handbag. . . . "*Sa-a-an ah yoi yoi!*"

Everard-Hopkins could no longer watch the increasing spate of flesh and muscle, the hooding towels, the profiles ploughing left, renouncing right. He watched the musicians for this Dance of the Dead in which the dead danced with the living as when living they had danced with the living and the dead.

A ladder had been climbed to a platform vined with vermilion and white lanterns. Musicians jostled on high with beer and lean, stringed instruments, with narrow drums and clacking rods and blood-streaked voices. They were thick-faced, common, and mad. Intoxicated, relentless, they coughed down the potency of their music. Sometimes a creature strained from this hot-bed, udders loose, plucking greedily among fans for a bottle surging hand-to-hand towards her, not ceasing to croak emptily while the chain moaned indolently, "*Sa-a-an ah yoi yoi!*"

Poor Dugald, he thought. They are differently stronger, these . . . these barbarians.

"Barbarians," he whispered and, "Dugald."

Alas for astringency, for serenity, reserve, formality, for autumn in a dozen brush-lines and insuperable grief in seventeen syllables!

Now the lofty wigs of the women, and the men's towel-bandaged sconces, jerked back together like the heads of steeds; from the conduits of their throats each braying was louder, imperceptibly faster. It was not to be borne longer: it was as though Everard-Hopkins had himself danced, given tongue, drained tart bottles to the lees, been soused to disgust. The next moment had arrived. I must go back to "X" Mess, to Australia, he thought.

"I should like to return to the hotel," he said.

Yes, the moment had indubitably come, a double one, for at *his* moment the guide, smile blazing, detached himself like a soul, for ever and for ever, raised tentacle arms from which the evil sleeves fainted joyously back, and glided into the mass. Everard-Hopkins was alone.

Furtively, with infinite delicacy, his heart began to bounce, and pain began to glitter in him.

Holes dropped into his mind perforating it with fear;
anger against the one who had abandoned shot up like a
blind letting in a midday of hate in which stood an urgency.

As the tangle of musicians lifted adder heads, he began to
back away, turned himself from that in which he could have
no part living or dead.

Slowly and slowly, the M.O. had said, or was it *softly and
softly*?

Miserly care got him through the stingier fringes of the
whirlpool, the gesticulations trammelled by fatigue and
watered-down inspiration. With each step pain glittered
more poignantly.

Ahead, over a canal between cabarets, drink-stands, and
vaudeville booths was a bridge of crumbling concrete,
sinewed by rusty wire. Beyond it were pedicabs, towards
which he progressed with the faith of an animal. "I'm in a
bad way," he thought he said to a fissure in the parapet.

On the mirrored neons of acrid and serpent colours,
milder pink lanterns on rowboats moved by stitches. In
shoddy whitish trousers, in dresses on which summer had
bleached the flowers, rowed lovers languorously waving
silver fans in affected arcs over the filth glorified by reflections. Farther down, from a spit of ordure, a group launched
small straw boats supporting candles to light to Other-
world the guest dead who had outstayed welcome.

The pathos of little lights was, he felt, a trick.

All about were flaring signs, scribbles of neon, native
characters advertising or indicating. How could he read
them? How indeed even correctly interpret *Joe's Club, Stand
Beer, New City, Dunhill, Piccadilly*?

Tricks, tricks, trickery.

And for him the most appalling trick was his radiant
visitor solicitous as a son. He understood him now with his
inescapable smile — death's immaculate diplomat, to dance
on artfully, and knock on other doors.

On this bridge was no place for pleas no one understood.
He knew he should not move again, but over the bridge,
clustered like rocks, covered like rooks with overlapping
patches of black, were the pedicabs — under their hoods
hope and sanctuary.

Sliding his feet preciously as the senile do, he crossed and

stood over the cabmen who, the muscles of their legs gripped in snoods of thick veins, squatted watching him. "Mansion Hotel," he said gutturally. They slanted crude faces,
pleated and grimy, up to him as he mouthed in a strength of
agony. Ink eyes slid to the corner slits as they sought each
other: they did not understand. Was nothing written on his
face? He needed to say, "If you can't get me to a doctor or
my hotel at least let me rest. Help me. . . ."

It was impossible; his lips melted like flames.

Most blood and most bitter blood falls at the foot of the
Cross, that ostentatious solitude. Rage and despair, *Eloi* and
Eloi, double doors, slammed violently within him in a final
lightning of agony.

He found it necessary to force one gargantuan boot to
step forwards. He saw the boot perversely turn aside, and
his absurd Kynoch tweed with it. One sleeve jealously hug-
ged his diaphragm, too frail a bandolier to restrain what no
flesh, no bone, no body could now hold.

As though it really mattered, one of Major Everard-
Hopkins's claws snarled forth, a mean and ugly movement,
in an attempt to rend the detail-embossed curtain of loneliness that had already fallen from before the — er — well of
ultimate peace.

19

Paula Groot had syphilis.

Just as Shadrach, Meshack, and Abednego had given no thought at all to the possibility of singeing even an eyelash in Nebuchadnezzar's sevenfold bonfire, so had Paula Groot given none to the chance of being marked by any of the fires she had consigned herself to with such cold enthusiasm.

Herein lies the difference between the real flames of myth and the metaphors of fact: the god of legend fire-proofs his minions, the god of the real world is a god of luck.

Paula Groot was furious.

She was skilled in the use of the contraceptive devices she favoured and they had never let her down; she was equally skilled in the use of a caution that at its most transparent permitted no more than guess-work about her private goings-on; moreover she had stilled an incipient misgiving about Kazuo by convincing herself that, since thousands of men played the double-backed game with Oriental women, she was justified in exchanging flesh with an Oriental man.

The pharos of the Area she lived in, the hilltop beacon visible for miles, and seen as a *Harper's Bazaar* tiara from the window of her Rainbow Village bedroom, sparked out no warning to her: the House that Jack Built was for Jacks, not Jills.

Released from the hospital at which she would never have naïvely presented herself had she realized the nature of her sickness, she was called up before the Commanding Officer.

He explained with captivating and lengthy euphemism how she was to be deported.

No scarlet letter or yellow dress, no scandal: the Colonel was handsome and suave as Lucifer about it all.

There was to be no admission that an initial error had been made and a wanton imported, therefore no revealing that anyone except a valued teacher and respectable woman was returning.

"With an excellent report and reference, Miss Groot," said the Colonel.

"We shall really miss you," he added.

Everything already arranged, Miss Groot. A discreet departure in two weeks or so. In the meantime she would not be teaching. There was an office job — school records to be filed — her experience and assistance would be valuable. And since this work was to be done at Headquarters it would be more convenient for her to be nearer the centre of the cantonment — yes? A room had been allotted at the Y.W.C.A. Hostel for her; would she be ready to move from Rainbow Village within, say, three days?

"You will be missed," the Colonel said again. By whom? Did he mean anything? And how much did he know beyond the black-and-white of her syphilis?

Away from him she wondered what the unsaid might be: *Clot of a woman! You should have stuck to men you were sure of. You should have stuck to white men you were sure of. Since you would experiment with your — your language tutor — isn't Kazuo his name? isn't he your housegirl's brother Kazuo? — why couldn't you have realized what was wrong with you and have it fixed under the lap by an Oriental quack? Why must you shame our judgment of you by breaking the eleventh commandment? How boring of you, Miss Groot.*

The last remark, at least, the Colonel would never have made; disclosure was his delight.

Hoshi, of course, had not been near her.

She was still sick — "of tubercles" the housegirl who took her place had said. Although this sounded like the lie it was, the housegirl believed it, for Kazuo had seen that this was the story to be told.

Hoshi lay in her room, mostly silent and flaccid.

The priest had been several times to exorcise the fox that possessed her. So far the creature had been stubborn, awaiting perhaps the searing delight of the final abracadabra which the priest assured the mother must be withheld until an auspicious hour and day.

In the meantime, the mother visited the medicine stall and, from among the jars and bowls of dried centipedes, cock-combs, owls, moles, and soot, and the trusses of sunflower stems, seaweed, and weeds, she chose a compound of dragonflies and goldfish to lower Hoshi's temperature, dried snake and charred monkey brains for the diminishing of delusions.

The fox, however, still inhabited the body of the cross-eyed woman.

Kazuo, denied by his nationality the right to visit the hospital, did not come to Rainbow Village until Paula Groot's last night there before returning to the Y.W.C.A. — a thing he had no way of knowing.

He also did not know this was the last time in the history of the world they were to be alone together: Imiko and Truscott, Antony and Cleopatra, Man and Woman — to them all a first time alone together, and a last.

He had travelled to Rainbow Village enkindled with happiness, tender at the idea of reunion, prepared to be cheerful and benevolent as one must for those recovered from sickness, and carrying a basket of fruit enclosed in cellophane.

He tapped at the door, the *one-two-three* — *one-two* of a lover whose signal unlocked a house and a body as swiftly as a key, the rat-a-tat-tat-tat of a lover desirous of pleasing and who had his eye on a pair of French gloves.

"Although these are inferior fruit, please kindly accept them," said Kazuo, as she let him into the house which already had the blight of emptiness upon it for the few appalling curiosities she had collected were packed, and the furniture was arranged in a pattern of insensitive finality, blank shelves, chairs at unwelcoming angles.

In this setting, without touching his gift or thanking him for it, she began her pointless scene with the directness and inconsideration of an ill-bred woman.

"I have had a loathsome disease."

"Ah, so?" said Kazuo courteously, placing the basket of fruit on a bleak table. He looked sympathy.

"A disease — do you understand? — a loathsome disease."

"I am sorry you have been hospitalized." He was sincere. She flushed.

"I have had a disease which I caught from you."

He still did not understand; idiom at speed, and spitefully, was confusing; but he understood she was not happy, and put out his hand to touch her compassionately as one touches the fallen animal, the crying child, the nerve of sorrow.

Churlishly she struck at the hand and cried out, "Don't dare! Don't you dare touch me. You are the one — you gave me a . . . a sex disease."

Apt enough in the variety of audacious postures a term of physical intercourse requires, she had never used the words that give name to any of its parts or consequences; in genteelly avoiding the name of the disease, which seemed to her sewn in tart stitches over her body, she avoided facing her own guilt in the matter, her own connivance, her own rash ignorance.

Instantly, though shocked, Kazuo was wary. His impulses and reactions were more neatly classified than hers.

Once he had thought this woman of another race could edify him; every moment she behaved more like a mere woman, and more like a vulgar one. As she lost her temper he became interested in the expressions that banished the usual Blessed Virgin arrogance from her face, and listened to her.

"You're a bad lot; all rotten to the core. And you're just like the rest of your race. All the same, scroungers, treacherous, disease-ridden. . . . When I think that I. . . ."

She went on and on.

She had never had nobility to sacrifice or worthwhile pride, love she had never experienced, even the wires that carried the currents of affection were oxidized.

Resentment put into syllables must always, for people of her limitations, use the same syllables. The limited vocabulary of her sort had been sanctioned by its use for decades by women as ladylike as she.

These truisms of petulance she delivered as though she were Phaedra.

Bad-smelling beast, thought Kazuo, does not know own smell.

She pitied herself, therefore Kazuo, who could have pitied her, did not. Her insults, expressed in an accent inferior to his, were flat and unstinging, nevertheless he perceived the intention to insult and recognized its unfairness. He tired less of her accusations than of their unmannerly presentation.

Should he bother to speak to this ugly woman . . . for ugly woman she had revealed herself as . . . ?

He spoke.

"Please to wait," he said.

Astonished, she stopped and stared bluntly at him, her face regaining a little beauty in stillness.

Quietly, he began, "You are in-continent female —"

Immediately she screeched, for although it was a word she had never used, she understood what it meant.

"How dare you! Get out of this house!"

The university student was firm, he would not listen to her any more; the man was fed up, she was merely a loose woman, he would go on.

"You are incontinent woman and not any more young woman. But not old," he added urbanely. "I am young man and virile. I am incontinent, too. So together we are sex-persons in hotel on Shrine Island and many occasions in your edifice. Man. Woman. It can't be helped."

He paused as though he had stated undeniable fact, which he had.

"Why are you having anger with me? What you say before is now water on frog's face, for anger is not justice. I do what you desire. I am pleasing lover as in contemporary literature. If I am having disease, that is bad; but spilt water does not return to tray. Question, please: am I having disease from you or you from me?"

The disease had come from far in the past, very far. This section of it had come via a South Australian soldier from Manila to a girl in the brothel Kazuo visited, from Kazuo to Paula Groot.

"It can be cured — is physical disease only. Physical disease is one of many diseases." He took breath. "Your people bring diseases; eroticism is popular. I am sorry you have eroticism-disease. Is not worst disease. Worst diseases are. . . ."

Inspired by his last opportunity to reveal himself as more than a good-looking stallion, he told her, in sentences lucid and relentless, what seemed clear to him.

He did not mention his father, but it was perhaps from standing on the suicide body he was able to see a little farther than many others, a little beyond the frontiers of stupidity.

The Orientals had, he said, a proverb: Amateur tactics cause grave wounds. To islands already packed with bodies to the last tiers, little had been brought except more bodies and those bodies' demands.

This was perhaps useful; a crusade on an official working-holiday gave employment to house-builders, cooks, gardeners, jazz-pianists, typists, guides, bar-men, waitresses, jeep-drivers, prostitutes, flower-sellers, and interpreters. At the same time manufacture of many things was flourishing: silk, beer, antiques, cameras, and shopping-baskets.

The intelligences that should have come with the bodies — where were they?

Democratic slogans were to be read in books; it was adding destruction to defeat to insist on educational attitudes which had fostered juvenile delinquency in their countries of origin, to twist existing institutions out of hallowed and useful shapes into forms that fitted nothing and ruined everything, to set up as models men with hair and minds of the wrong colour, to purge, imprison, and execute leaders who had been defeated by luckier leaders.

Kazuo's father came to his mind. He stopped talking.

"Excuse me, please," he said, "I have been impolite. Life is only flame of candle in front of wind — I know little and talk too much."

His eyes glistening with tears, he picked up the basket of fruit.

"Please forgive me: Hoshi will like it," he said, and left the house.

Paula Groot who had sat, submerged, overtaken, trivial, but desirous of love, suddenly and angrily remembered the costly raincoat she had lent Kazuo. She hurried to the door, opened it.

Kazuo was walking neatly and quickly down the avenue, under the swinging lights. He carried the basket of fruit he had bought for her; he was wearing a shirt, tie and shoes she had given him.

Oh!

She ran to the gate, was going to follow him to say, "You

may remember, Mr ... Mr Whatever-your-name-is, a raincoat I lent you", when someone said, "Good night, Miss Groot."

It was Maxie Glenn, decorative, loitering, thwarting.

"A pleasant evening," she said, and was pleased to hear her voice as a soft one, though she felt like screaming.

The lights kept on swinging; Kazuo moved out of her sight, out of her physical life.

The two spoiled, corruptible and corrupting beings chatted for a while; Oriental air flowed between them as they enacted civility with whatever Western clichés came to mind.

Time is most clearly marked by ticking off what is over and done with, since what is hoped for, and what is proposed, may never arrive.

The Chrysanthemum Festival, the Ginger Festival, Moon-viewing and Fire-walking were over, done with.

The Godless Month had arrived — of eight million gods all, except one too deaf to hear the summons, had retired for consultation to the oldest of shrines. With one deaf god the Orientals might thus have been Christians all: they finished off end-of-season tomatoes, scraped and squeezed loofahs, watched cosmos and sunflower buds enlarging.

The wedding of Masao and Imiko was not far off: astrologers had found that their birthdays ensured a happy togetherness. Genethliacs, orniscopy, and palmistry — all agreed: happiness, sons, wealth.

Rusty lines of nerines grew between the fields near which Imiko worked; a priestlike building of rooks sat on a knoll watching her and the necklaces of radish-slices she had hung to dry on fences, veranda-posts and eaves. She was now picking persimmons; as she emptied the branches she hung swags of radish on them.

Her life had become inward and centralized; the silence of radishes and persimmons required no answer, no intimations of feeling, no daintinesses of speech or conventions of posture. She certainly was rustic-person of simplicity, she had decided: before she bathed in the river on hot afternoons she threw a slice of cucumber in, lest the river-boy, who lived under water and was placated by cucumber, should try to drown her.

Homely, self-controlled, and no longer petulant — that was how she saw herself.

Yet the bare feet, the throwing of the cucumber-slice, the picking of fruit in the sun, her wife-to-be responses to Masao and meritorious-daughter ones to her father and mother, had an afterthought of sufferance and self-consciousness.

Chrysanthemum of the Metropolis in Country Basket, starring Imiko — was it really this?

And would a producer say, "Enough working today, Miss New Face?"

She went on picking — persimmon, persimmon, persimmon.

Then, in her siesta of content, she remembered what she had said frivolously, "Whether persimmon is astringent I do not know, for this is my first taste", and the weather of her content changed.

For nearly a week she had objectively and with gravity noticed the change in her hands; she now saw them subjectively, stopped picking the fruit, looked at the hands with pity as though they were dirty bargain-price gloves on her real hands. With a pulse of anger and an uncountrified movement she parted her kimono front, pushed her hands beneath her breasts and examined them as though they belonged to some other woman.

She began to dream backwards: beneath the tan globes she dreamt the white peony ones that had interested Truscott — Truscott and his drawling lust, now more nettling to remember.

Her stained hands!

So white once, and why forfeit white hands and what they must do with the relentless enigmas of men's bodies?

Who had said, "Hot snow, burning snow?"

Backward and backward she dreamed, holding her breasts in the midst of the affronting and beautiful countryside: the tolerant wind recalled electric fans on nights like an oven of bliss, shimmering bead-curtains stirred by the changing colours of neons, boogie-throbbing draughts through torn paper panes, the vacillation of floor-touching sleeves of exorbitant kimono.

She looked past the tree of persimmons, the sleeve-fence hung with radish garlands, and saw the last field of Masao's uncut rice swaying west, swaying east, swaying west — the swaying movement of the long, lethargic sleeves, and the bodies of girls languidly dancing; she saw herself white of face and hand, the white of her breasts concealed in robes of insupportable taste and luxuriousness, revolving to reveal the tempting triangle of unpainted skin below her lacquered and jewel-infested hair.

She heard the melody of "Apple Song"; the persimmon leaves made the sound of paper money.

She began to cry peevishly; dream and landscape were blinded away.

She was not leading her own life which, based on fiction, was nevertheless more real than this rice-field reality in which she was to herself the fiction.

Masao, she thought, is only man, only farm-person, only field-servant; with Masao I become my mother, I wash mountain-potato to cook, I cut melon, I give breasts to children and hands to dirt.

Leaving behind the persimmon-tree, the fields and fences, the gravestones in the fields, the stream where the leech and the farmer's mouth had fixed themselves on her skin, she began to run.

She did not look back.

She would have done what she did even had her mother been home, but it was less troublesome that she was out, smoking her pipe, gossiping and gloating in the village.

Her father was at work.

Imiko moved swiftly.

Most of her clothes were still in the famous suitcases; she folded the rest hastily in with them, and packed her fans, brushes, looking-glass, and Truscott's watch, which her father wore on notable occasions only. She left out one Western dress and coat, nylon stockings, high-heeled shoes, gloves, and a dramatic hat.

How violently one escapes, and with what strength and speed: she made three hurtling trips down the track to where it touched the bus-highway.

Here squatted the chidren's god among the scented weeds, where he had stonily squatted for six centuries.

The woman of the Era of Radiant Peace, in the Godless Month of the Year of the Tiger, who had played by him as a child, hid her new suitcases behind his worn and moss-embroidered back, and it was right enough so, for the woman was still a child.

Panting, her toys hidden, she returned for the last time to the house of her childhood which had nothing to offer her except concord, sobriety, love, and monotony.

Recklessly she washed at the well under the loquat-tree.

Although the field, the railway-station, and the village would still keep Masao, her father, and her mother for two or more hours, the inorganic was not to be trusted completely.

Who knew how directly her mind might cast a line, moreover, to those other three minds, and fetch them running?

So, swiftly and more swiftly.

She dressed.

She tore the brocade from the cheval-glass.

With no time to shave her face, she painted and powdered it strongly, arranged her hat with its wicked cock-feathers and midnight veil, put on her black coat, took up handbag and gloves, and left the house.

Stuttering on the cobbles with her film-star shoes, dumpy, overpainted, flashy and ludicrous, she was now the beautiful, fascinating, and tragic woman-in-black. As such she reached the road, sidled mysteriously across it and into the cryptomeria grove that led to a shrine.

Here she waited, saw the mountains which cupped about the waning afternoon, saw the reversed cup of sky becoming less transparent, put on one of her gloves, smoked incessantly and, presently, from between the sacred boles, saw the bus twinkling like false topaz.

It was sunset.

She threw away her cigarette, put on her other glove, and sauntered, in terror of ambush or semaphoring figures converging on her from the fields, across the road to the children's god.

She set her cases by the highway, stood tall and cool and rich, Greer Garson, beside them while the bus drew nearer and nearer. It stopped.

Down swung the conductress, shabby and dusty, "Excuse please, a passenger is getting off."

This passenger was one of Masao's neighbours; they politely greeted each other — he looking at her suitcases.

Then she and the cases were in the bus.

"Or-ri', or-ri'," called the bus-girl; the accident-averting talisman oscillated jerkily on its string and kicked its lax legs against the wind-screen; the bus started.

A shade of scorn fell down her face; she crossed her legs

with Western immodesty among the dingy and withdrawn yokels, and elaborately lit a cigarette. The others deflected their eyes from her, but they had seen enough to decorate the blankness of their torpor with aquatints of vindictiveness, condemnation, and outrage.

Knowing this, as soon as one cigarette was finished, Imiko lit another.

Meantime the cigarette dropped in the cryptomeria grove smouldered among the dried needles, heartless children devoured the evening meal, part-bloods were born, innovations wheeled softly into habits, the sky over the country Imiko was leaving turned the colour of the Florida Cabalet lights and Imiko's mother in her shopping-pinafore approached the house. She had had a wonderful afternoon.

"Happy makes young," she said, and felt young.

As she scuffled blissfully nearer, and before she saw the well-cover was awry and Imiko's sandals were hysterically abandoned on the shoe-step, the sweet air suddenly and brutally overwhelmed her with the chloroform of foreknowledge.

Bad happenings, she thought, run a thousand miles.

What use to laugh, what use to love a little baby, what use to spend an afternoon telling truths of betrothal and grandchildren that were lies even as she boastfully spoke them?

She walked slowly, more slowly, but the house nevertheless came nearer and reached her.

She adjusted the wooden lid on the well, and hung the bamboo water-dipper in its right place; she put the straw sandals in order; she entered the house.

Saddest and most irrational of prevarications is the one by which people try to convince themselves that what has happened has not.

Too late for Imiko's mother to behave as though she were still enfranchised, to put the crimson-dyed ginger stems and sesame seeds neatly on the bamboo shelf in the kitchen, to pause, then to open her mouth — O wrongly — and try to wheedle back yesterday.

"Imiko."

There was no reply, except from the wind who has her

own patois in which she speaks to no one except the happy, and they not listening.

Now the mother was a wind crying to no one, each gust louder, wasted, blowing itself away with the petal from the flower, the leaf from the twig, the seed from the tortured pod.

"Imiko, Imiko! *Imiko!*"

She heard herself.

She ran to the sleeping-room.

On the floor lay the rush umbrella-hat, Imiko's wardrobe splashed with evils of well-water, the thrown-down brocade cover of the cheval-glass.

She returned the hat to the old-things-cupboard.

She got her small scissors.

Returning to the work-robe, she knelt on the floor, snipped the thread-ends of the seams, and began to unpick the garment so the strips could be washed and flattened-out on the drying-board which leaned against the back of the house. As she withdrew each thread she rolled it on a match so it could be used to sew up the dried strips.

Twilight; she looked up, for there seemed to be another woman working opposite her, a toothless old woman . . . her mother? . . . who was too old to cry and who could not be she, for she was certainly still young enough to cry, though she would not let herself.

The moon shines rounder and rounder, the moon goes thin: that is the world's manner. What use to cry?

She got up and hung the brocade over the looking-glass and the old woman.

Her husband came home.

He knew.

How?

She could not ask him, and they did not speak in words while he took off his uniform and changed to Oriental dress.

He went to the other room while, listening, waiting for what was to come, she folded his railway clothes and cap away in their drawer.

She felt sleepy. A dignity of exemption began to imbue her; night would come and she would forget.

Then he began . . . callous, still of the day, still flashing and hot.

"Food, woman!"

"Yes, I come."

She enkindled herself, moved quickly, dodged fear hastily, but made no sound.

When she brought in his tray he was sitting, not reading as usual, but staring through the pushed-back shutters.

She did not know what to do, and waited.

"Shutters," he said.

She put the tray beside him and closed the shutters on Imiko's infamous world of lies, on her ocean that was wet and deep.

"Light!"

She switched it on and, kneeling opposite, began to serve him. She did not falter, but wakefulness faltered.

For a while he ate, and her daughter drowned, and twilight pleated itself more thickly towards its darker end.

At last he said what he had decided to say, and said it quietly as though in him, too, sleep had already turned down a lamp-flame.

"Daughter is dead."

An echo, but as quiet and no quieter than his original, she said, "Daughter is dead."

He continued, "I shall tell go-between-person tonight."

Peaceful, callous, gentle, the flame turned down, but still the day.

"Yes," she said.

Silence.

She waited for what else this man could say.

He knew she waited, therefore delayed himself, lifted the lid from the lacquer bowl and drank a little fish soup.

Now, with a cool bitterness, the controlled and silver edge of a black tide just turning: "Daughter is no-daughter. Is dead."

"Dead," she said, and saw herself dressing her dead daughter, arranging the kimono right-front over left-front, slipping the mitten socks on the wrong feet. She heard the starting-crackle of the cremation fire and at the same time, in the actual world, the gong being uncharitably beaten from the fire-tower.

The cryptomeria grove was alight.

"Masao will come tonight," he said, and that was the most shocking thing he had to say.

Then he too let himself hear the fire-gong.

Fire and Masao, fire and Masao.

Masao did not come.

The neighbour who had seen Imiko's suitcases on the highway had hastened, immediately after his evening bath, to Masao's, too kind not to let the jilted farmer know his disgrace instantly.

So, while the trees burned and people ran to see, Masao took an axe in an agony of shame to his bamboo clumps.

They were tall, each bamboo nearly a foot in diameter, but Masao's muscles were huge and his humiliation volted them.

Up and back swung the axe, down with implacable sureness; the blade cut in one violence through the great stems. Sparks sprang from each cleavage; as each shaft lunged to the ground Masao exhaled a groan of abasement. He was not so much brutalized as following a line of stern conduct, his masculinity was purified and indurated as one by one the whalebone pillars crashed. Some of them were flowering, an omen of famine.

Famine had already arrived.

Imiko's father kept on saying, "Masao will come tonight," as he watched the fire through the reopened shutters.

Masao will come tonight meant *Shame is not yet over.*

Suddenly, he had an idea. "Watch! Fetch gift-watch. I shall give it to Masao."

The mother went slowly, desiring sleep again, for this task was too pointless, she was the servant of mischiefs she knew had already been done.

What use? What use?

The watch was not there.

When she returned without it, her husband leapt up, agile as a monkey, struck her and began to scream.

"Egg-plants do not grow on cucumber vines! Bad blood from your dishonourable ancestors! Bad!" And he kicked at his fallen wife with his little darned socks, calling out, "Last night I dreamt of red horses — misfortune comes and burnings of old things. Fire! The gods are away; the wind is in evil direction; I am forty-two —" That was an unlucky age to be, and he screamed more horribly, "Forty-two! Fire! Daughter is thief! Daughter is cat-woman! Daughter is that-person!"

His voice broke; his spectacles fell to the floor.

"She is dead!"

"She is dead," said the mother tonelessly, reaching for the spectacles.

"She has not been born," he shouted defiantly, snatching the spectacles from her. Then he began to cry, and she patted his foot sleepily.

The children enjoyed Imiko's fire.

On the mountain ridge, as the bus hung between ascent and descent, she saw the far-away fire and sucked in her breath at its beauty.

The bus began to go downhill and she in it proceeded to the fate of freedom.

But the children!

They ran everywhere about this demented rodeo of flame with the agility of *secondes* in a house of *haute-couture*.

The horses of flame!

The firemen, automata lassoing rose-and-golden ropes of water from their pumps, behaved peacefully; the lovely lariats uncoiled languidly. They had small chance of taming the brilliant creatures who shattered darkness with their hooves; their lunatic manes and tails lashed and lunged; small chance, for each Pegasus of fire was distorted and crazed by diseases — megrims, strangles, farcy, glanders, and founder. Yet how enthralling to see!

Grown-ups stood circularly in a fence that was an outline of statues posed with dignity.

The firemen pumped tranquilly.

The sick horses caracoled; the mad children galloped like foals, and whinnied deliriously.

Below her, on the plain, Imiko saw the netting of lights, interfretted for miles, a prostrate webbing of millions of sparks that rayed out and out from the scintillating central eczema of Eastern Capital.

21

They were all at the farewell party to Paula Groot: the rest
of the school staff; the Oriental school-servants; a group of
senior children dressed as American adolescents; the School
Captain, Maxie Glenn; some of the mothers who had not
heard, or were too cynical to believe, the gossip about her;
the Colonel's wife who had generously sown the seeds of
the gossip as far as she was able in her limited time.

Logic would have had Kazuo and Hoshi present; convention and ignorance spared them the pleasure of this embarrassment.

The Colonel had sent his wife, by suggesting to her that
it would be unwise to be present because he had conceived
the notion of smoke-screening the reasons for two ex-
pulsions by exhibiting two deportees at once: Padre
Hamilton, who had always given the schoolchildren religious
instruction, was to present the staff-and-parents' gift to the
departing teacher.

The weather was superb.

Staff-and-parents' gift had been, as it were, chosen by
Paula Groot herself.

When the dribs and drabs of money had been finally
totalled in a cocoa-tin, one of the teachers who delighted in
such crimes had been permitted the task of finding the most
befitting gift: Paula Groot was to be given the opportunity
to choose her own brand of cigarette before walking
towards the trap-door.

It had been simple: she bluntly expressed a need to the
young woman who, investigating its price, was happy to
find there was hardly sufficient money in the cocoa-tin.

"I'll fix *that*," she announced to the others, as they soaked
their morning-recess ginger-nuts in their tea, was ex-
clamatory to the headmaster, and got the afternoon off.

First, she spent the collected money at several canteens;
her shopping-basket was soon filled with cakes of bath-
soap, chocolate, powdered milk, aspirin, and English
cigarettes. These she sold to the school staff's favourite
black-market Oriental for Oriental money; this money, in

turn, was exchanged with her own special favourite black-market army captain for the currency of Democratic-Occupation.

With the much increased total she bought the chosen gift, and pocketed the change as payment for having eluded an afternoon's teaching.

The children, uncorrupted by an obligation to put legal money in a cocoa-tin, by-passed this refinement. By stealing soap and aspirins from their mothers' store cupboards, or by buying chocolate or cocoa, they had, as their teacher had, converted them into a gift — a uniquely tawdry kimono which no Oriental would have been seen alive in but was the Orient's correct summing-up of Western taste.

This garment, which Paula Groot wore for several years, feeling like a Porcelain Princess and not Sadie Thompson, was to be presented to her by Maxie Glenn.

Padre Hamilton did not know why Paula Groot was returning to Australia, he did not know she was — as he was — being returned like a faulty article, neatly parcelled and correctly stamped; nobody in the room except the Colonel's wife knew he was being returned or that this public appearance was his last.

Even Maxie Glenn, who knew almost as much about him as the Colonel did, was ignorant of the expulsion. The Padre had for him the appearance of something on which the taxidermist had skilfully worked — a ruddy animal concealing in afternoon-tea activity the bygone activity of lust. Did this stuffed bear really eat honey once?

For the youth, too mature physically, the Padre's lesson had been undisturbingly coarse because, though an un-pimpled adolescence gave him an ethereal air, Maxie Glenn was coarse also.

Coarseness had appealed to coarseness, immaturity to immaturity.

Moreover, complicity in the matter of physical pleasure had entertained him; but on this afternoon the very idea of possible public complicity in found-out guilt was frightening — he could not look at the left-over from furtive monkeyings-about.

He kept in the background and ate many sausage-rolls. The Colonel's wife was charming and watched every gesture of Paula Groot, the Padre, and the boy, so that she would be able to describe what they concealed to the Colonel, who would pretend indifference.

Tea made with chlorinated water and condensed milk was served, and sandwiches of trimmed and genteel triangularity. These, and Queen Cakes made from dehydrated eggs, and iced flesh-pink, were the foodstuffs of nightmare: their *ersatz* components, their manufacture by Orientals, their unnecessary abundance, enhanced appreciably the triteness of the ritual.

Outside the windows, beyond the never-to-be-completed avenues of Rainbow Village with their alphabetical signboards pointing this way and that to permanent-seeming examples of impermanency, sprawled the burgundy-splashed hills eternal as hills, and a rocky cape tonguing into the spangled bay.

Outside, the insects — in minute refectories, on threads of highway, in tiers of cells and towns of tunnels behaved with ruthless sanity.

Politeness, discretion, policy, and wit did not check their purpose.

Inside, the afternoon tea went on but was over, the ordained ceremony-to-come was finished, everyone had already transferred themselves to the next entertainment, and yet languished in attendance on their bodies which could not go yet. Boring, boring.

Brightly the small talk continued — no one was very fond of Paula Groot.

Brightly as blank cartridges flashing, the Colonel's wife was witty — and Paula Groot was not fond of any of them.

There was laughter, there was counter-laughter, cigarettes were butted in saucers and on sandwiches and, at last, the Padre swiped cake-crumbs from the manly bulge of his belly, and rose to speak.

Quickly Maxie Glenn, now no longer concealed enough, averted his face, revealing his heart-breaking profile.

Quickly the Colonel's wife observed this avoidance and ecstatically sucked Sobranie smoke into her incandescent, ageing face through a foot-long holder.

Quickly the Padre did not let himself see his Giton deny him, and blushed ruddier.

Paula Groot dropped her eyelids.

The rest of the Westerners flicked grotesque lighters, lit fresh cigarettes and looked at the edges of paper doilies, at a squash of icing on the Padre's uniform, at their nicotined fingers, at the enormous teapot of Nine-valleys porcelain — a salmon-coloured object with a gilt-dragon handle.

Backs to the wall, the Orientals stood and watched everybody and everything without one movement. Since they knew about Maxie Glenn, about Paula Groot and the Padre, since the knowledge of their behaviour had days or weeks ago been calmly quaffed, their faces could have displayed comprehension.

Padre and schoolmistress were being deported — why these two? What quirk of appraisement made them sinners superior to others? — their faces could have displayed incomprehension.

Comprehension, incomprehension: blind must their faces be; and blind they were.

The Padre began his speech; the eyes of the Orientals and the Colonel's Lady alone watched.

"Good friends, I know, I feel sure in my heart of hearts, that you will, one and all, most heartily agree with me when I say that, in losing Miss Groot, we are losing an active and accomplished member of the community."

The active and accomplished seemed to lower an extra pair of lids on her already lidded eyeballs.

The Colonel's wife sheathed her face in smoke as though to obscure the fleshly display of thought.

Look at me just once, Maxie, thought the Padre and cleared his throat of nothing, continuing, "Her interests have been broad; she has entered fully into all aspects of life here."

Indeed, indeed, the Colonel's wife exhaled.

"I am certain that she has, as we all have, learned something from these good people here —" his eye swept the waxwork Orientals, who all restrained themselves from blinking. "Her experience of them has doubtless been of value to her, something to be remembered in later years."

Pause.

"Here, I am reminded of. . . ."

No pause. On and on and on.

Over the crumbs and lip-sticked cup-edges, over the creased skirts, through the smoke, past dropped eyelids and dark watching eyes, his platitudes flowed easily to the profile of the boy, caught there a moment then nicked round and into oblivion.

On and on.

A kind of sick slumber possessed them all; the Padre's lullaby seemed endless but even endlessness must end.

". . . and so, on behalf of the staff and the parents, I have the greatest of pleasure, in asking Miss Groot to accept this token of their esteem and gratitude."

In a carefully executed storm of clapping, deportee handed deportee a parcel which contained the replica of the raincoat Kazuo was to wear with dash for as long as Paula Groot was to wear the kimono that Maxie Glenn, realizing his moment had come, now took up. The package rustled as the Padre said,

"And now —"

The Colonel's wife, fitting a cigarette into her holder, nevertheless missed no shade of intensification of the latest blush, and the suddenly murmuring voice.

"Now I am happy to call on the representative of the schoolchildren. The School Captain — Maxie Glenn."

Tomorrow is the new moon: and thou shalt be missed. . . .

The boy rose, was compelled to, compelled himself to, and for a moment the eyes of the burly man and the adolescent untidily hooked together, parted.

Never again, not ever again.

No man does anything consciously for the last time without a feeling of sadness; to be forced to abandon a body of which one has not tired at least quadruples this sorrow.

Joyfully through a new gossamer of smoke the Colonel's wife watched the Padre sit and shield his eyes with a large hairy hand.

Tomorrow is the new moon. . . .

Maxie Glenn was embarrassed because he had not been able to lie well enough to the Colonel. Better than those who would forgive him and not the Padre he knew the complicity had been dual; the Padre's defection was his too: he had allowed the Padre's impudicity to recognize his.

What he had had no trouble in concealing from eyes that did not seek, he had had no qualms in revealing to one who sought and was willing to pay.

The boy's embarrassment was mistranslated by the fat man shading his eyes, so that a monstrous jealous ghost uselessly detached itself, wailing, "Who will benefit from what I have taught?" and remained blind and unknowing in the Orient long after the Padre had left.

The boy: "On behalf of the pupils of Rainvow . . . of Rain*bow* Village . . . of the pupils . . . I have great pleasure in presenting Miss Groot with this . . . this. . . ."

God, thought the Colonel's wife, God, God, *God*.

The Padre said, "Token", and took away his hand, and revealed his melancholy eyes.

". . . k-k-kimono," said the boy, nonplussed and vexed.

Hate, thought the Padre, hate — and I the crucified one. *Lama sabachthani!*

The boy went on, "We are all very sorry she has to go back to Australia because she has been a wonderful example, and we thank her for what she has done."

Once again, in the administration of noisier applause — for embarrassment must have its extra helping — Paula Groot received her black-market gift, and the ceremony was over.

The Colonel's wife attached herself to the Padre; she was his self-appointed wardress to return him to "X" Mess in a staff car with her.

Falsely the women complimented Paula Groot on coat and kimono; the room emptied of all except the Oriental servants.

The Padre had forgotten to call on them to make their presentation. They had expected to be treated graciously, for the obvious importance of the expelled suggested a ceremony which would include them. They were not surprised to be disregarded, and later sold the lacquered powder-bowl gift for more than they had paid.

Meantime, they stole the sugar, the unused condensed milk, the remaining sandwiches, cakes and sausage-rolls, dividing these scrupulously among themselves as compensation for the impoliteness of those to whom they had intended making a gesture of finesse, and a present based on an aesthetic maxim.

22

It is as difficult to discern in others what nobility causes cowardice as what conceit or perversion causes bravery, what irascibility and hysteria a serenity bordering on impertinence.

Albeit, from somewhere, and not from the gods of kitchen, mountain-crest or hydro-electric station, Imiko had got a vigour that sustained. Perhaps this was from the unseen-by-others god who sits in the recesses of that fading temple the body. Poor hereditary sleepless one!

Strong in the midday of her vanity, bolstered by her wardrobe, her prettiness, her rags and tags of affectations, and the money Truscott had left her, she was able to enjoy an unusual independence and the transient consolations of the wilful.

She was able also to side-step somewhat the daily hazards of her kind of life.

She was able, finally, to say that those one had loved, even those one loved, were merely delirious shades, nothing.

Her time as this person would not be long, and would outlive the Occupation by very few years, and these each less neon-lit and music-threaded than the preceding one.

The prawn in batter must be eaten hot, the rice-wine drunk while warm, the soldier-at-play mulcted of cash before the tenor of the mid-century changed, and he was again a dockside clerk with lumbago or a truck-driver for a timber-mill. So many similar uniforms concealed these other ones of the cane-cutter, the accountant, the butcher, the barber, and the bookmaker's clerk.

All of them concealed, as Truscott's uniform had, the man who was not there, the man who wore behind his tie the invisible tag which said on one side *Here* on the other *Gone*.

Within Imiko herself were concealed the women in the dream she had utterly forgotten: her own mother whom she would have become had she married Masao and the seasons of agriculture, the husbandry and son-bearing, the hamlet and fields encircled by tilled mountains.

The other woman, the few-fanged ex-Circe, raffish and smelly as an old Dryad, was also concealed until Imiko gradually became her, as she was to do when independence, Truscott's money, her voice, her youth and impertinence, the proceeds of her pawned suitcases, Truscott's watch, the bangles, hair-ornaments, kimono, and sashes were gone.

Concealed, too, in things and people all about her, were futures as botched as her own: typhoon would smash beer-houses flat, heads fall from gods of basalt, snotty children sketching along drain edges grow to heroes with constipation, politicians, adulterous mothers, items in a continuum of respectability or evil or bewilderment, asking questions to which there were no answers, acting out answers to questions no one except poets ask.

For the moment and the next few moments, the bark of her heart having thickened, she was secure from the gangs that ran her type as they had run her type from time's discovery by man.

She was the wood of the holly that burns unseasoned; she went her own reckless way; she acquired more knowledge of guile and more skill in the ingenuities of dirty human behaviour; she preserved that inner moral calm the soldier has who knows atrocities on both sides are equal and that rehearsals for Armageddon are really skits on a first-night success aeons ago.

Orientals are given to walking hand in hand — particularly the young men, for of all human beings, Oriental or otherwise, these require most the vibration and flow from a similar being. This non-sexual proximity, this barest linking, soothes uncertainty.

Imiko, as an act of entertainment, and shrewdly though sentimentally, chose O-Kichi as her hand-in-hand.

O-Kichi, the first Foreigner's Woman, was nearly a century dead: re-echoing her satisfied Imiko's need of make-believe.

Midway through the nineteenth century, Americans forced the Orientals to admit them to their country. A consul-general arrived and set up in a village port. O-Kichi was forced to be his servant and mistress and, surrounded by a community of the resentful and taunting, play out her life in the service and arms of a barbarian.

Revilement continuing after the consul-general had left, O-Kichi drowned herself in a mountain tarn.

Imiko perfected as far as she could the dance illustrating this part of O-Kichi's life. Her own life and the lives of thousands of less fortunate Imikos were versions of O-Kichi's sufferings in the port of Lower Field.

The dance was her specialty; it brought her what little fame she was to have.

First she executed the gestures of maidenhood and modesty, of young love scuffling through the shelly sands of a summer that promised all; next she swayed and tossed from a dreadful command, bowed stricken to the obedience it required. Music was chiselled more bitterly from the strings: she farewelled her Oriental lover in heart-breaking genuflections and graceful evolutions, used her fan and long sleeves to illustrate renunciation and sorrow.

Not once did Imiko's face, mask-painted, alter its mask-like expression: this was the dancers' tradition, the Grecian ideal.

The music divided itself into uncharitable sounds; the plectrum struck at the strings like fangs, she writhed in repulsion from the beard of the foreigner, her shuddering fan showed abhorrence, her sleeves trailed in a resignation more terrible because truth had become a legend too permanent to be destroyed.

Last, she acted the climb to the mountain pool, the agony before its looking-glass, the sour peace behind it.

She performed before wrestlers with monstrous bellies, before the Bottoms and Quinces of Australian country towns set on pepper roads traversing miles of salt-bush, before suppleness-experts with their adolescent catamites, before pale-tongued drunkards, slumming colonels, the riff-raff, the body-hunters, before a succession of audiences she would never see again.

And then, while an accompanist self-pityingly sliced her tortoise-shell plectrum at the square banjo of quince-wood and catskin with its yard-long neck of oak, she sang the song of O-Kichi's port, the song of the dockside inn-girls.

She sang, she danced, as the music jerked out like water from a rock.

Hauntingly the banjo, hauntingly in the smoky air the

manual sketches of the sailors' winds, hauntingly the motion of tossing-off the imagined wine-cup that she and Truscott had drained, that countless shes and countless Truscotts had drained, hauntingly the words in the citified accent that did not belong to them and salted their pathos:

> West Wind blows you to my heart,
> Let us drink and never part:
> If you stay long in Lower Field—
> Night on night on night—
> Your pocket will be light.

> East Wind blows you to my heart.
> Let us love and never part:
> You will stay long in Lower Field—
> Night on night on night—
> Now my heart is light.

> North Wind, South Wind, West and East,
> You will finish off love's feast:
> You will depart from Lower Field.
> Stay away one thousand nights
> And I'll wait one thousand nights!
> I shall wait for you . . .
> And wait for you. . . .

She was like a poet who, fishing up a moment from the comber that would have crashed and boiled it to oblivion, congeals it to words and presents this rococo distortion to an inquisitive world.

Sorrow, like evil, has eternal youth.

Sometimes, when the eaves wept like Alice in Wonderland and she lay beside some appeased and drunken-asleep foreigner, she too wept, staining the sleeves of her sleeping-kimono with tears for Truscott.

Each tear for him was one less to be rifled from her pilfered store of them; each outburst had in it something of self-pity, a little of pain, but would finally be a merely ritualistic grief.

When the day came that she would blow like a rotten leaf past the vagrants' tunnel of Upper Hill to the flagstones slimed with urine between the tall stone lanterns, she would be weeping and have long forgotten why; she would cry, "Wake up! Come back!"

No one would come.

23

After one has lived in a certain place, sooner, later, but infallibly, one puts on one's hat, looking-glass or no looking-glass, rays the eye around to see nothing is forgotten, nothing left behind, and shuts a terminal door: nothing has been left.

Things have been left, of course, but nothing of value, nothing that will be missed or thought of again, nothing useful: a Penguin edition, half-read, of *The Way of All Flesh*, some toe-nail cuttings caught between wall-to-wall and wall, old stockings or jock-straps, toothpaste tubes, illegitimate half-caste sons or daughters.

Everything else worthwhile is packed: the pearls, the yards of silk, the sex-books, the cute sandals, the teeny-weeny glass lobsters and Scottie dogs and penguins, the bottles of Green Chartreuse one hopes to smuggle through, the pair of trousers and the cocktail dress still with the splashings of farewell drinks and tomato sauce on.

The cases of loot, too heavy for the plane, have gone ahead or are to follow by the next ship: addressed by oneself to oneself thousands of miles away — *that* is what convinces most, objectified proof of a working-holiday's end.

Sooner or *later* came every week, and every week selections of individuals converged on the airport-bus and the plane in which they were to coalesce to a locked-in group with no one else except clouds to stare at with keen indifference, for one will have seen such clouds before.

Nothing to commend in limitlessness exhausting in its impermanency: Himalayas, savannahs, Niagaras, jungles, promontories and Titicacas of cloud will slither in counter-point, guided by perverse airs, above and below each other at uncountable levels.

The plane will wilfully distend static minutes within to fluid tens of miles outside: all will spin along, trivia in the boredom of speed and space.

Lonelier than they know, all will be helpless to defy the workings of unaccountability; there is no bulwark against the inexhaustible — death, say.

Or regret.

Or guilt.

Conveyed thither by penultimate planes, by trains, by taxi-jeeps, the group containing Captain F.W.R. Truscott, Miss Paula M. Groot, B.A., Padre Stanley L. Hamilton (Capt.) was in the airport-bus.

Farewell party hang-overs — otherwise physically fit, for each had been medically sanctioned to take the air: the plane will throb as convincingly as piano wires recording the pedal and — *Adjust safety belts; no smoking, please.*

Physically fit at least they had descended on the Orient; physically fit at least they must ascend from it. On no account were returning passengers to smuggle away any disease except memory.

Two of the passengers did not even have this opportunity: Captain M.M. Wilkinson and Major Sholto Everard-Hopkins.

The china jars containing their so similar dust were separately boxed, labelled precisely by someone who dotted the capital I, lest Wilkinson's widow-mumsy and the ageing father of Everard-Hopkins should receive the wrong, now so similar, sons.

Pulverized, bottled, excelsior-embedded, cartoned, tied, addressed — no longer did the one look presbyopically over the scene and maunder, no longer did the other squinny purblindly and find no one to listen to him: baking had transmogrified them to a sort of aseptic algebra, very portable. Their tongues, the cells of their brains, their electric-wiring of nerves, the incineration of all these and everything, and of the feet that had carried them busily back to nought, were now as soft as plate-powder, garden-lime, cigar-ash, baby's talcum, bedroom-dust — *this* smuggled out no full-size memories.

Paula Groot, Truscott, Padre Hamilton, Wilkinson, Everard-Hopkins — these five and five others — were passengers on the airport-bus to the departing plane.

The other five?

Human beings merely: no more and no less human beings than the five we have learnt little enough of, but enough for the purpose: a handful of pennies makes a shilling.

Three of the five were returning as respectably as

Truscott, Wilkinson, and Everard-Hopkins; two of them were being returned prudently, as Paula Groot and Padre Hamilton were.

One was a handsome Nicholas-the-Spark with flawless teeth and no corns; the burn on his backside of detected-embezzling-while-running-a-Transit-Hotel did not show.

The other, a War Crimes Commission interpreter, who wore white hare-fur ear-muffs, had courageously trusted all the lift-boys of the Moat-Circle Hotel, when he should have trusted all except the last and most comely.

The bus therefore packeted a nice countervailing of four who had been discovered breaking no law that mattered in this place at this time, and four who had broken laws of the Year of the Tiger and been found out.

Pseudomorphs all, perhaps: at least there was no chance of telling by simply looking and listening which were which. If anything, the four deportees were healthier-looking, more active of eye, and volatile: liveliness seemed the only external brand crime had put upon them.

They wore social aplomb like a becoming fancy dress; it was the criminal Padre who joyously greeted a cautious Truscott.

As yet the important day was greyish; clouds had to gape, dissolve, step higher, do something to reveal the invisible alleys of the air.

An hour was foretold for this to happen in, two hours at most.

The bus-driver had one of those pentagonal faces cut from a template of snub-nosed masculinity, seen everywhere probing a machine, and once seen — this face of the engine's valet — always forgotten.

Now, near by there was a broken bridge.

Because he wanted to see the broken bridge, he asked the passengers if they wanted to, suggesting that he was quite willing to forgo his own . . . his own what? . . . on their behalf.

"The broken bridge? *Not* the Brocade Bridge? How awful — the Brocade Bridge!" they all said, and, "Yes, yes, yes, we've plenty of taime; have we plenty of taime?" they all said, and, "Do we have time?" said Nicholas-the-Spark, who had been subtracted from an American mistress who chewed chlorophyll tablets in Eastern Capital.

Yes, plenty of taime, plenty.

So the bus-driver swung them this way and that way on their last tourist trip in the country none of them was ever to see again.

The Brocade Bridge, unique national poem of wooden engineering, was three miles away from the aerodrome which could have been anywhere: an international doggerel of engineering.

The Brocade Bridge: after four centuries of arching, night and day, day and night, over petal-freckled calms, over the brown and furious champagne of floods, it had been fractured by the latest flood.

When the eight Westerners and their driver arrived they all descended into the freezing grey air, and walked a few steps, and looked at the freezing grey flood.

Westerners love this — the sigmoidal movement, the coiling and uncoiling, the agent of destruction withdrawing its potency but still potent.

About the flood was something Nordic, some taint in the pigmentation, something too-smoothly abnormal, yet more animal than a first glance allowed, muscles under sinuous surface, ferocity under the satin tactics of liquid.

Uncountable times, the five half-moon arches and their priapic parapet posts had been sketched with ink-brush, engraved on cherry-wood blocks, woven on sashes, neckbands and hems, pictured on fans, done in *cloisonné*, lacquer, and ivory, damascened and photographed photographed photographed, but always in dormant mood, pruinose and hooded with snow, airy against fruitless blossom, reflected in a pastel glassiness that completed by reflection the five half-circles, and made of the wooden loops a divine knuckle-duster, pretty-pretty on tinted poonah paper.

Disaster is chiding and has decorative value, but its greatest value is commercial; the record of it or the curio snatched from its bosom is what the world most relishes, enshrines, duplicates or kisses: the saint's coccyx magnetizes to it the pilgrim who could not believe one of the saint's phrases or miracles.

Families are fed on the rake-off from the sale of fused

gobbets of atom-bomb aftermath, and etchings of the torn-down abbey; fascinating are the films set in the rubble of Berlin and London; most popular the cheap tour of the past's débris; under the one-eyed glare of that empty world the full moon, how picturesque the half-harrowed-under and the spot marked X.

One of us did that; let us look; let us steal or buy a relic; one of *us* did that!

The eight travellers bought *before-and-after* photographs from the bowing and smiling with their flashy . . . was it aluminium-edged? . . . teeth: *before* with its undertones of accomplishment, of quiescence, of the floral and fragile, cherry-willow girls flexuous on crescents of wood; *after* with its central semi-lunes awry, shattered, sick from holocaust, as now.

These snapshots they slid into wallet and handbag, the useless and final pass-out tickets of all the tickets collected during the dream that was ending.

With what ease, meanwhile, they settled into each other's front rooms, for now only those front rooms were open: in the back rooms — bare boards, unpainted plaster, smells of tripe-and-onions — the spinster sister who dropped her aitches, the Mongol baby, the belching grandmother with a moustache, Kazuo, Imiko, Brigadier, Hoshi, Maxie Glenn, the American mistress, the lift-boys of the Moat-Circle Hotel, the . . . the *lot* . . . Hogarthian rogues' gallery, experience and its mutes, the serpent and the bitten apple, life.

How modishly the same each front room was; how comfortable the settee; how easy not to knock over the *objet trouvé*, the Doulton Balloon-seller or the glass-bottomed pewter tankard on the chimney-piece; how plate-glass-separated from the broken-spined bridge and the flood with eel-like manners, sizzling by discreetly.

"Such a pity, really," they said.

"An absolute beauty spot," they said.

"Picturesque," they said. "Quaintly pretty. Four hundred years? Really? Now, fancy!"

"Actual'," they said. "Actual', it's still vedy vedy attrectif. Cen it be fixed, Ai wondah?"

"I should think so. The little old slant-eyes are quite

good at patching up. Actual', it'd be moneh well invested — Ai mean petching it up — Ai mean for tourism end all thet. Yes, I should think so. . . ."

Thus they silenced those others who might be inclined to bump about in the back room and shout out, "As if *you* care!"

"Seen all you want to?"

The bus-driver had seen all he wanted to. They had seen all they wanted to.

Thank-you-ing and thank-you-ing, on preselective gears, none of them did anything except move towards the bus.

As they climbed in the sun came out.

Miss Groot now sat beside the Padre. She got out her compact, opened it.

"Going home for good?" she said.

"Think so," he said. "Yes, think so. Done all I could really. I've been here nearly three years."

Nearly three years, a thousand-odd days, twenty-four thousand-odd hours; how many sermons, communions, prayers, man-to-man talks, speeches, gin-squashes, boys?

"Me, too," she said, spreading lipstick with her left little finger-tip.

How many lessons, parties, hot showers, cups of sugarless weak tea, men and couplings?

The Padre noticed a . . . a striking Oriental youth outside in the sunshine.

"M-m-m, what a *nice*-looking kid . . . that dear little girl," he added, selecting a moving biped, any at all, to deceive himself.

"Yes. *Very* nice-looking," said Paula Groot noticing the youth and noticing the youth and noticing . . . but also, with surprise, a little girl as cross-eyed as Hoshi.

The child had a baby . . . cross-eyed as Hoshi? . . . bound on her back. On the baby's back was bound a doll-baby. On the doll's back was a baby doll.

Truscott also saw this: tried to think of it as something a poem could be written about, the little girl was the past and on her back was the . . . oh, for a drink.

"Sweet," said Paula Groot, and with cold skittishness,

"How do you like the coat you gave me, Padre?" She was wearing it.

"Gave you . . .?" he withdrew his attention from the . . . from that dear little girl. "Coat? Oh!" He laughed — he yo-ho-ed heartily. "Parents and staff?"

"Yes. It's exactly the same as one I —" Lost? Gave away? Had pinched? Deserved to lose? Wouldn't wear again if paid? Left as a momento? "— accidentally mislaid somewhere," she said.

The bus started, swung in an arc, leaving the quietening waters which had more domestic things to do than crumple up arches, leaving the bridge which would be mended to echo the clatter of everyday clogs, leaving the youth and all other youths, the burdened little girl and all other little girls, the photographers and the photograph-sellers, and all Orientals, behind in their own sunlight.

The passengers fell bluntly quiet; they had visited the wind-up beauty spot; the colophon of this old book needed not to be pored over any more.

They had not yet left the ground: it is while one has an expiring purchase on the place one is about to leave that the mind's telescope becomes focused on the place one is returning to.

Paula Groot saw the cross of snow splashed like the squirtings of milk from an elemental breast on the organ-piped mountain backing her home-city, saw the steep narrow streets of patched fanlights and clay-piped steps, the scallop-shops, the sleet-glazed slates and iced-over fountain, the cold common room of the shabby fashionable girls' school with its lesbian headmistress. Thousands of miles and two or three days separated her flesh and bones from this provincial city at the world's terminus, separated her from the past that was to be her future. Her snapshots, ugly curios, cheap trinkets, the lurid kimono, would be all that anyone else would know of the past that was ending. The high snowy voices would rise falsely from the hail-bitten Englishy faces, "Oh, Miss Groot, how super, how wondrous, how utterly wizard!"

Padre Hamilton's telescope was trained on another city, flat, four-square and grilling, hemmed in by vineyard valleys, hemmed in by parklands and olive-trees, hemmed in by deserts and treeless reaches and golgothas of thistle, hemmed in and hemming in until he escaped again: where next time? Another sort of job? Another sort of uniform? An academic gown flapping through brummy Jacobean archways? A schoolteacher's imitation Harris tweed in a wheat-belt high school? Where? The Army still? Malaya?

For Truscott? His city lay smug, Edwardian, pretty, half-civilized, in the centre of his vision. From it the road unfolded south through the tuart, karri, and peppermint boughs wrenched down by a Cockeyed Bob; and south was his home-town — querulous father nagging by the blazing jarrah in the brick fireplace; nagging uselessly to set him up in business among paddocks overrun with arum lilies, freesias, and blackboys; nattering on, and always complaining good-bye, as each departure took a prodigal way, through the cassias and the grape-arbour of the family garden, from one more possibility of a gravestone among the forefather gravestones in the churchyard by the green river.

Not for Truscott and Imiko, not for the romantic and young, the grave in the right place, but where next for Truscott?

Each of the eight passengers on the bus saw a little of the land they were returning to: vast, improvident, with its glittering forests, its unused miles and useless beauties, its dying cities and crammed cities, its arrogance and vulgarity, its tinned hopes, sporting-paper gods, and rich horses.

There, a sinister poverty of purpose inexorably weeded and seeded and weeded; a poverty more obvious showed through the vandalized fabric of a past spent in preparing for a future in which all had been foretold except retrogression.

Placidly enough, the departing advanced, second by second, towards the kindergarten loudspeaker singing "Three Blind Mice", the tomato and orange debased to vapidity, the *ersatz* vanilla, the wedding ring of milder metal, the plastic egg-cup, the tinned bean, Bluebeard the motorcyclist, and the grave edged in concrete.

Presently, they had been driven through whatever thoughts they had, and through sunny space, and through the necessary minutes; they arrived at the aerodrome.

The luggage was in the plane, and Wilkinson and Everard-Hopkins; then the mobile and thirsting eight who, with too much space, for there were seats for five times as many, arranged and rearranged themselves as though it really mattered.

Presently, thinking they were arranged, they agitated themselves again, and produced bottles and flasks and plastic cups and peanut-butter tumblers and glasses with crinolined women on the outside and naked ones inside, and poured each other hairs of the dog.

They toasted, were very vivacious, and poured themselves more hairs of the dog, and were more vivacious.

Let's have anotheree — and anotheree. . . .

Presently, the plane took off, was in the air, and away.

Ten o'clock, Hour of the Snake.

Presently, presently, it was out of sight to the few Orientals who looked, and the Orientals and their remaining Prester Johns were out of sight.

Short Stories

The Room

In the winter you come from a provincial town to the city; you have a typewriter; you are nineteen, and intend being a famous author.

By a set of romantic accidents you become possessed of a large room. You suffer at a coffee palace while furnishing this room which you call a studio. Inspired by the former lodger's legacy of white, you assume a distinction in whiteness; your vision of sunflower-yellow floor, black chairs and Van Gogh reproduction flies off like a parakeet. You have not furnished a room before, have grown up among sennett-scrolled pith hall-stands, American chairs, butchers' calendars and English tea-sets. Yet, soon, it is impossible to believe you have ever lived anywhere but alone in the room furnished as you have furnished it. White walls, white bookshelves; the linoleum is off-white and white. Bed, wardrobe, chest of drawers are white; you throw snowballs of paper into a white basket. The room, immaculate as an iceberg, you consider utterly yours as your body is. Centre, under the skylight, an invisible figure takes its stand, exaggeratedly monkish: you have done some spiritual book-keeping; you decide the room ascetic, a room woman must never enter. When you leave it, and are outside its door grey as the mail of a sea-shell, you are jolted to find the room not floating in space, but topmost of a nineteenth-century cosmos of brown offices and cedar counters exuding an odour of vanished prosperity. You descend hollowing flights of stairs past doors behind which jobless public typistes and the snide promoters of evanescent enterprises gulp Ceylon tea. In one den hides a piano which plays at all hours and as though from the depths of a mine.

Below, you wade into the city. It brawls dustily or
drones with rain; shoals of cars and buses slide through it.
Miles of people press past reflected in plate-glass acres;
routs of them torrent through topless doorways, along Col-
orados of concrete summited by electric words that fanfare
in and out. There is ceaseless in and out, high tide, low tide,
lightning of movement, echo's echo of thunder of movement. You learn the secrets of cafeterias, coffee lounges,
Chinese cafés; of dress circle, gods, bookshops; of public
libraries, public clocks and Babylonian emporiums; of rock-
eries of mesembrianthemum lost behind newspaper col-
iseums. You conceive that you play a minute instrument in
the never-ending midnight to midnight fugue. You are
thread of an infinite music by a nameless composer, one of
an orchestra whose conductor is unknown, an instrument
whose maker conceals the purpose even from poets. You
return, night or day, city-fevered, city-drunk, to the flights
of stairs. The piano plays answers to questions you cannot
put. You write. When stars are frosted upon the navy-blue
skylight, you sleep. There are no dreams; no woman of
dreams enters the room. Words have quenched. In your
heart, as in the room, stands a hermit, virgin, strict as death.
The days step backward, are blown down the corridors of
time.

You set out, Saturday afternoon, late spring, to visit
sculptured Olympians in the National Gallery or fountain
tritons of the Exhibition Gardens. You feel an inexplicable
need to explore white something and circle back by
milestones of white: Doric capitals and busts of marble,
whitewashed walls, handkerchiefs ennobling the faces of
old men on park seats. But afternoon has opened flat to
pinkness, a pink camellia, and is on the point of suspiring
away, petal by petal, and you have done nothing but
dawdle into void and muter streets, eyes darting among the
silver ladles and Mary Gregories of antique-dealers' for
exquisite junk you have no desire to own and will certainly
not buy. The first pink flake sorrows away; you are almost
in suburbs; too far off the surf of city. You return recklessly,
less avid for bleached rock. You near the Hotel Oscar which
you have never entered. From it unravels a fleshy warmth
as from convoluted electroliers blessing clandestine meet-

ings years ago. You surprise you by entering. You mount, as
one must, a gesture of nougat stairs worn by the ruches of
hansom petticoats and rag-time toe-caps and jazz heels and
the soles of virile men doused in battles and senility and
death-rooms. An automaton swings open the glass doors.
For a second there seems no one under the dome, nothing
except a violin waltz mourning the drunkards of yesterday.
Then, at tables under palms, you see the cocktail-sippers
who manure the palms with fag-ends. You search the urbane light for a table. Waiters, those animals of lamp-black
and menu-white, appear and disappear, agile yet emascul-
ated, while the waltz bleats with febrile unhappiness
through the laughter and the paint of lips and the pallor of
fingers tilting potions of amethyst and jaundice, of greens of
floe and venom.

She! You see her. You see the woman.

She sits alone, no air of waiting for anyone, under a nervous palm. She is slender, she is still. She is older than you.

Before you are aware, before your mind censors, your
body is at her table. And your voice:

Would she permit . . .? Would she mind awf'ly if . . .?

She looks into you; you know she surveys the monk and
his shuttered eyes.

She does not mind, bold young man. Do sit down. It gid-
dies her to see you swaying there like a poplar or —
or —

Her voice has a colour, and yet her voice matches her
white body. On her throat you feel with eyes the imperceptible but opulent ripple of white. This, at last, of all
whites, is *the* white.

She is alone? Your voice does not flicker as it should. She
is alone?

Quite, quite alone. Her husband will not be returning for
fifteen minutes, twenty minutes.

Oh! . . . oh, you are terribly sorry. You had no idea
that . . . it had not entered your head that she would be . . .
be . . . accompanied.

So? Why should that make you terribly sorry?

Well. . . . You don't know why you. . . . You mean you
had never done this before. Really! It wasn't that you

thought she was the sort who. . . . Please, she *must* believe you. Never ever in your life before. . . . *Really!*

She laughs. The monk exposes his eyes, deliquescent, hot. He escapes your heart which suffuses with a cobweb of veins, pink of camellia, of flamingo, of blushes, of blood.

Very well, young man, she will believe you. Really! You must drink a drink with her. What will you drink?

You've not been here before. What should one drink?

There's a cocktail she prefers to others. At the moment. It's called *Tropical*. Too *rigolo*.

Her handbag is of a material and a colour too rare to have names. An aroma emanates from its recesses and from her hand . . . camellia . . . camellia . . . even from the pure banknote.

The *Tropical* is sub-acid and, at the same time, faintly putrid. It seems that juices of jungle melons have been pressed from over-ripe flesh by coffee feet and, at the birth of ferment, transfixed by frost.

Soon you probe her eyes to disentangle the iridescence there of many emotions and experiences: disenchantment, *ennui*, cruelty, lust, knowledge. You talk of yourself.

So you write short stories, young man! You climb the ladder of art, and sell nothing. How too frightening and Latin quarter! Of course, you live in the city?

In the city, yes.

Ah! Your address? Some time, perhaps, she will introduce you to someone useful. She knows so many wretched editors, so many many people.

Would she like you to write the address?

No. Tell her. She'll remember. She does not forget. She forgets nothing.

You are compelled to enter her eyes again. And you see that she will not forget. In her eyes are all the things she has not forgotten: other addresses, expedience and jewels and tedium and sleeplessness — a thousand things — a husband, young men, a marriage of boredom, boring adulteries.

Will she have a cigarette?

She does not smoke. She abhors smoking.

Then her eyes for the first time leave you. She lifts her hand from the table . . . camellia . . . camellia . . .

This is her husband. Ralph, this is the clever young

writer-person Irma was babbling of. Drowsy with the
opium of her nonchalance, you, who have had nothing
published, feel established, brilliant, distinguished — no,
distingué. Her husband? You cannot be sure about her husband. He shakes your hand relentlessly and meaninglessly.
His pentagonal face is solidified by carnalities you are ignorant of. An oak-dark masculinity, the colour of his eyes,
runs under the shaven skin. The black tufts in his nostrils
have been trimmed. You sense the hairy toes, the massaged
ruthlessness of his body. He arranges a few platitudes for
you in a cultivated voice that has an artery of coarseness. As
he takes her and her camellia-textured hand away from you,
you notice that his feet are too small. She has gone, gone,
down the swirl of nougat.

The waltz makes a filigree under the dome, a dismal
silver-work. Then it conceals itself in the immoral loam of
the palm-pots, in the unlocked faces of the cocktail-
drinkers.

Certain as grief, you will never see her again. You will
drink yourself to death. You drink *Tropicals*, squinting into
the freezing yellow-green to see yourself drowned there,
miniature, Shelleyish, curled like a black prawn.

You feather-stitch through streets for a long time. You
begin to ascend, at last, the flights of stairs; the midnight
piano, imprisoned in the mausoleum of commerce, translates her into sin, dregs and silence. You finally reach,
chastened, high above woman and world, the door on
which grey paint is petrified wrinkles. Inside is the salt-
white of a shell's interior, the anchorite rebukes under the
skylight, and his replica returns to your heart. The days file
away. Rectangular white leaves detach from the branches of
your mind. You place white shirts in drawers, wash your
white body. A letter arrives. She has not forgotten you; and
surely you have not forgotten her? You must meet her at the
Hotel Guelph.

The suite at the Guelph is the coffer in which fervent and
somehow atrabilious afternoons are hung with curtains having heavy dusty fringes. Time has wearied the blue of the
wallpaper poppies, their pattern is as complicated as the
pattern of her body . . . white camellia . . . pink
camellia . . . flamingo camellia. . . . Hairpins drop into the

dust-grey foliage of the thinning carpet; you learn infatu-
ated way through a labyrinth of cries and silences. You seem
to be always at the Guelph, lifting furs from her shoulders
before you kiss, swooping for her fallen gloves as you leave,
expecting a rap at the door — her husband's voice,
restricted and coarse, asking admittance.

Sometimes she behaves like a girl; the velvet scum of
usage and seduction slides from her laughter, leaving it
vicious as girls'. She asks how much would be needed to
publish your stories. Days before you have mentioned an
amount. You recall this. Naked pale cat, she pads towards
the dressing-table. She takes banknotes from her handbag;
she counts out the amount; using your cigarette-lighter she
burns the notes one by one. Her face becomes intent and
smaller, an unripe fruit; black orchids drop to grey carpet
from blanched fingers. Thinking murder, you say nothing;
but she, motionless among the folds and matted fringes of
the hangings, whispers for long, grows older as she accuses
herself, while the oil of contempt glosses her eyes, and
flickers there shot with ingenuity.

One day, deliberately boyish and feeling subtle, you say
that you like violets awf'ly much; violets are the most
cracker flowers. Doesn't she agree?

No. No, no. She hates violets.

But you thought . . . were positive . . . that scent from
her breasts, hair, from the inside of her arm . . . surely
violets?

She hates them. There is no flower she hates more.

Why? You are absolutely amazed. Why, angel?

Why? Because once, years ago, when she was younger,
when she first met her husband . . . oh, *sottise* to talk of it.
And you are *not* to call her angel, *never* angel. Give her a
cigarette. She ab-*hors* violets.

When you visit her while her husband is away, there are
bowls of violets on the piano, the chimney-piece, tables.
She wears a tragic gown. It is twilight. And candlelight,
long dark candles: something is dying.

Please, please, *please*, you are not to smoke. You *do*
understand *and* remember that she cannot bear cigarettes?

She plays on the piano songs you have heard before but
cannot name. The violets emit enigmatic fragrance. The

candle flames are moveless. Watching her, you feel older than she. She stills her fingers on the keys and, without facing you, talks in a voice not her own or woman's:

You really have never loved another woman?

Never. She knows that.

She doesn't mean physically. You have never loved a woman romantically, on-a-pedestal sort of thing?

Never. And certainly never physically until you met her.

Never? Never, never, never?

Never.

Of course, she knows that you'll never forget her. You'll never be able to. Never. She knows that.

Never; she knows that.

Why never?

How could you forget her!

That is not an answer, fool. Men! *Really*! Could you, for instance, tell her why you love her?

That's difficult. Words are insects that fly in the wrong direction, to sting, to poison. You know that you are a young man and that she . . . No, you cannot find the words.

Try. Find words, Mr Writer. Tell her about yourself.

Well, you . . . you. . . . Listen: she is the quintessence of female. She is the perfect noon of femininity, of sophisticated lust . . . sophisticated *love*. She is voluptuous. No, that is wrong. Not voluptuous. But the tide of money flooding her veins, the extravagance of her trappings, the culture of herself, give her a penumbra of . . . of . . . *volupté*.

She laughs. So; *clever* young man! The tide of money! You must go now. She has a migraine; the violets — it is too revolting — have given her a cataclysmic one. She will get rid of that housekeeper. Violets! She will take some tablets, and then sleep. First, however, give her a cigarette.

Now it is a thundery day; leaves in the city gardens turn pallid undersides to the thunder. You and she stand confronting by an artificial pond with its fatigued pampas plumes and parched fountain. Her eyes are suspended, full of esoteric wisdom, in the luminous shadow of her hat-brim. She says what you feel are truths never to be forgotten; you realize she has suffered much and that, from desolation, a plant has sprung and borne distorted flowers that can live only on desolation and money. These seem,

under clouds of pewter and while a swan pedals mindlessly
in the pond, to be imperishable. But all you wish to remember is gone when she is. You decide no more than that the
complexities of her being, feminine, wilful, subtle, each has
in it a hairline of gold, of money. She is lewd, corrupt, careless and clever. It is impossible for her to be crude, unfascinating or undesirable.

The special rules of your lives decree that you must part
often: at the *altaltissimi* of hills of stairs in restaurants
devoted less to dining than to interminable and amorous
bickerings. You turn from each other, she to unimaginable
places, you to your white retreat. She expresses over-
offhand curiosity about the room; would like to love you
there. With matching off-handedness you sidetrack her.
Nevertheless, it is obvious to you that your home-spun
finesses feed curiosity, that hers grows rabid. She surely
knows that you will fight for your last celibacy, yet cannot
believe her body and money will fail. She sees herself shedding a hair on the floor, deserting a scarf. Just as clearly you
see yourself scrubbing at the exact white on which a hair has
fallen, scrubbing to remove the unseen but ineradicable, trying vainly to exorcize the odour of woman.

Suddenly, it is midsummer, hot and bronze. Outside
fumes a planet of cinders. Above the smell of the city which
is like the smell of bougainvillea, rises the smell of asphalt
and cellar chicory. She lies still, too still . . .
camellia . . .camellia. . . . Only her eyes live, pulses under
them; her eyes are black opals.

She is exhausted. She will go mad. This room . . .! Your
room, it's cool, isn't it?

Mind dry, you do not answer.

Your room is cool, isn't it? Answer her.

Yes.

Must you be such a monosyllabic oaf? Your room is
cool?

Always cool.

You must take her there.

Again you do not answer.

How can you be so Hunnish? She is dying. This place, on
a night like this — on any night — is impossible. She's tired
of it. It oppresses her: *décor* worse than the Guelph. Port-

wine-coloured carpets and mahogany beds bore her. *Pas de frisson*! She's always expecting sweaty livery to enter with full-blown tea-roses or soggy cucumber sandwiches. All on a silver salver — my God, a warm sticky salver! She is sure there are waiters in court shoes. She can smell cherry brandy and Madeira cake. The carpets are *too* stockbroker; she wants linoleum. Yes, yes, yes. She insists on going to your damned *atelier*. Instantly. See, she's going to get ready. You are to dress, *now*.

Deserted, even by yourself, you feel herring-gutted, arse-apeak. You try not to remember that in her soliloquy twists a filament, finer than one of her hairs and bitter as bought submission, of truth. Still, you sense that, for a whim, she is using herself and her unhappiness to erase restlessness, summer discontent, boredom with passion. You do not know what to do.

You telephone for a taxi.

You and she enter the taxi, the hearse. The hearse goes through the charred and suffocating canyons, and arrives too soon at the door of the stucco tomb. You open the door, the cold reek of encaustic tiles and stairs of basalt strikes your mouth. You begin to climb the stairs, your stairs. The flight of basalt changes to the second of wood. The piano, wakened by your distressed footsteps and the over-civilized fragrance from her body . . . camellia . . . camellia . . . begins to toil and mourn gently with long shudders in its throat.

She knows, wretch, you can't hide it from her, that you don't want her here.

Darling, she mustn't be silly.

But you don't.

Darling, *dar*-ling. She mustn't be absurd.

Why don't you want her?

Angel!

Why? Why? And how sweet of you to call her angel — sweet. But why don't you want her? You love her?

She knows that.

Then, why?

She wouldn't understand.

She'll understand. Of course she will.

No. First, she's a woman. And next she's not a creative woman.

Oh, not creative! Not cre-at-ive, eh? Even so, she must know.

Then — oh, *blast* it! — you'll never be able to write there again.

Nonsense!

You knew she wouldn't understand. The room is — er — consecrated. Call it a refuge, a workshop; oh, what does it matter? Maybe, after all, the idea *is* nonsense.

Utter! Arty old thing you are. A room is a room is a room. She'll disturb nothing. She will float in, holy as an abbess, sexless as a . . . as a. . . . Kiss her, right here at the stairhead. After that she'll not even speak. She'll peep at your sanctum, and gli-i-i-ide away. She'll be sexless as a . . . as a . . .

Isn't necessary. Must be herself. There's the door, that grey one. You'll not only kiss her; once inside you'll absolutely ravish her. That'll encourage her to pry into young men's apartments.

You are laughing, two strange creatures laughing strangely, when you touch the door. A pain strikes from its surface into your arm. Laughter drops. Quickly she plucks your hand away. Nothing is said. You are forced to visit her eyes.

You meet in them a number of emotions spraying up. Among them, destroying all others, is an emotion to which you must apply adjectives you would never have thought of applying to her emotions: sweet, maternal, sympathetic. The emotion is pure with the purity of newness, not with the purity of polish.

Then she is gone.

You will not see her like that again. The last untainted bubble in the cocktail of her nature has broken the surface, has volatilized outside the puckered door.

Her scent fades down corridors and stairs; an expensive wraith passes door after door. The piano, foundered in the well of stucco, sobs in its throat joyously, softly, softly.

Now, at last, you know something.

The one tear that drops from your heart is whiter than your heart, whiter than paper or camellias or flesh. And when you open the door the anchorite is unmoved as ever, eternal guest of a room which woman — now — will never enter.

Everleigh's Accent

Do you know what a rep. is?

It is what certain shop-girls and nurses, who call a man a "chappie" and a woman "another lass", dock "representative" to. I am a rep — a commercial traveller. I represent — I *work for* — a book firm and am not fond of people, but can well enough simulate the Intelligent Good Mixer. You understand?

One night, thises-and-thats delayed until ten o'clock my usual six-thirty arrival at a large country town. I was dinner-less; I was dazzled by forty miles of a road resembling a moon-congealed channel of liquid, unblotted by anything except two truck-squashed possums. From the last hill-top the over-lit town declared itself an ante-room to coruscating gaiety. I knew better; perspectives of municipal moons showed streets naked except for three Italians dressed as New Australians but gesticulating like Italians in front of a display of Volkswagens and cyclamen; the Prince Regent Theatre lassoed out hectoring talkie voices towards the gibbous moon; from the rotunda in the strip of lawns, palms, and claret ashes that divided Main Street the Shire Band was despairing its way through *Mélodie d' Amour*. On a couple of visits this Arcadia of standard roses, begonia, and Exhibition Border had been the setting for a grotesque picnic, Hogarth's not Tiepolo's. Part-blood aborigines had lain in Gin Lane contortions among the lozenge- and crescent-shaped plots, their White Port and Muscadine bottles drained, while the Hitlerish yappings of carnival spruikers exhorted vainly. The next day I had seen them paying for their lock-up night: teetering and with bunglings, they weeded and raked through the Police Station garden.

The architecture of this town's Police Station is Georgian and "Quality Street"; it would not have been surprising had the fanlighted door opened on a mincing crocodile of Kate Greenaway girls in muffs and coal-scuttle bonnets. The Police Station, the street gardens, the whole town emanated peace, had that baby-eyed, you-can-trust-me look that defied anyone to imagine its fires any other than domestic, its inner and moral weathers any more than mild. Even the Railway Hotel seemed an ark of peace as I parked my car in one of the brick-floored garages under a time-pallid sign-board LIVERY STABLES.

As usual — for the licensee and his wife were shrewd and audacious — there was an after-hours'-drinking party in the PRIVATE LOUNGE (*Guests Only*); one of those factitiously democratic gatherings into which group law-breaking injects the fever of orgy. I knew them all, their salaries, vanities, weaknesses, and reputations. I could even remember some of their names. They had been drinking for some time; their postures were relaxed towards abandonment, the room was dazed with cigarette smoke; exaltation and fatigue mingled fifty-fifty in their faces. Four timber-cutters posed as effectively as Rodin sculptures; their names such as Herb, Ern, Mac, Tim, Bob, and Tex I had to select by guile before pinning one like a Rotarian's badge on each of these dogmatic males with hairs curling over their singlet tops. There were a chattering mandrill of an S.P. bookmaker and his wife, a Cassandra of provincial disasters; two high-school mistresses, one — Art? English? — in matador pants; a bank-teller affecting leather elbow-pads; a window-dresser; two other commercial travellers; the hotel cook; the licensee's wife who sat at the piano. On this . . . this machine, jacked up at one corner by a folded sporting-paper, I had often heard her, with showy near-accuracy, play "by ear". It was a mixed bunch upon which drinks had induced the same social colouring to shine; Christian names unfolded as cheaply as eschscholtzias in the weeded acre of their acquaintance. Yes, I knew them all except one young man who, as I entered, was the crystal ball for these half-drugged gazers.

His face was mobile and, I suppose, attractive. By this I meant that my interest, being directed towards him by theirs, did not waver away. He was pale, vivacious, compelling. Using an impeccable Cockney accent he was finishing a discreetly off-colour yarn, apparently well-told and well-timed, for his final sentence caused an uproar of laughter. The ovation seemed to startle him; dark eyes opened with mock amazement as though what he had told he had himself listened to and understood for the first time. "Oh dear, oh *dear*," he said. It was the witty paraph underlining the effect of his story. Yet — remember I was a sober onlooker — did a shadow slip across the midday of his smile, a sardonic bird? He was tall; the unsavoury word *lissom* landed like a fly in my mind; a frond of soot-black hair sickled the pallor of his forehead; his face was a sea of many winds, many intelligent half-winds; expressions chased upon it like the blushings on calms of water. His name was Everleigh and he was called Everleigh; this I found immediately symbolic of . . . of what? Among these cosmical Pats, Guys, Gregs and Verns, an audience of monosyllables, why the three-pronged Everleigh? What covenant had he made with originality.

His eyes rhymed well, but I found this rhyming a little . . . what was the word? Wary? Devious? There lurked the under-sheen of another activity, a sense of craftsmanship whose motive was obscure.

"Oh, Ev-er-leigh, you poppet," the girl in matador pants was exaggeratedly moaning, "you rilly mustn't, rilly. You're killing, but *killing*!" And her *Vogue* mask let down its painted eyelids under her *gamin* hair-cut so that she looked like one or other of Fagin's boys.

"Oh, Ev-er-leigh!" This was the licensee's wife amplifying her lisp. "You mutht thing 'I'm walking bee-hind you'. Pleathe, Everleigh."

"Go worn, myte." One of the timbermen: "Giss a sorng!"

Deferentially, but expecting no denial: "Man! I must have more grog, man!" For the first time I heard Everleigh's own voice.

Now, it is generally not difficult to decide from the voice the State any Australian comes from. Sooner or later, for one thing, betraying words jump up like skip-jack: *port* or *suitcase*, *tissue* and *cordial* or *cigarette paper* and *soft drink*, *parkland. Wyandotte* or *plonk-artist, poloney* or *fritz* or *German sausage, I'm not going there, but* or *Dickin, I'm not going there*. Many pebbles can be dropped by which to track home a Hansel. Indeed, conveyed blindfolded here or mysterious there to confront, unblindfolded, notice-boards bearing *Gents for sale, Pedestrian refuge, Gas ring here* or *Cows only*, is to confront a vocabulary as localized as *Siste, viator*, or wild-flowers. As far as these pebbles can lead, an accent can also lead: at least it can lead me, and I am no Higgins. Yet Everleigh's accent discomfited me. Many, abandoning State and class crotchets, have a stylized accent; these conceal their origin behind rule and rectitude. Not so Everleigh: his voice was not Gippsland's high-pitched and laconic one, it had the harshness of northern Victoria's superimposed on an elusive lilting, a fluctuation, a something I had experienced but could not recall. This piqued. I kept thinking of *Night Must Fall* or *Birds of a Feather* but knew that, "No! No. *No!*" was the only retort to them. Therefore, drinking more whisky than I had intended, I observed him and his voice, hunted Proteus through his metamorphoses, confusing myself to standstill. An hour passed.

It was Everleigh's hour. Exalted by an oxygen of temerity or malice, he told *risqué* stories in which impropriety was graced by intonation and gesture. Before us, in the currents of smoke, his sacrifices spectrally paraded — the vaudeville Jew, the Dads and Daves and lubras, the Harry Lauder Scot, the Polish airman and his Mayfair hosts. He accepted beers as though they were illuminated addresses. He sang songs of blazing sentimentality while the licensee's wife, dressed and ear-ringed as for vice-royalty, manipulated tremolos and maudlin pianissimos from tooth-yellow keys. Oily eyes uplifted with the ludicrous poignancy of a Landseer Labrador's, he sang "Danny Boy". He sang "Galway Bay". He sang in ravishing pseudo-Irish.

Ravishing! It was perhaps the whisky, but I imagined myself to find more and clearer proofs that he was purposely *ravishing*; one extra tone, the merest flinch of his eyelid would have raised the mercury above the mark to ironic comment, satire, burlesque. During the sickliest numbers I was certain that this beer-swilling jester was agitating his bells not merely derisively but also waywardly and dis-

tractedly. "I'm walking bee-hind ye-e-w . . ." he sang. The
long-drawn, radio-talent-quest ye-e-w was sharp as insult:
after all he was a mimic. Excited by drink, the enigma of his
accent, his apparent duplicity, the mockery that edged on
fleer, I lusted to find out more, to talk to him. An opportunity came. While he was out of the room for several
minutes the licensee's wife splashed glib arpeggios from her
instrument, the others herded about her to bay "Girl of My
Dreams".

I had just time to buy another whisky-and-water and to
learn from the barman that Everleigh came from north-
central Victoria and was a timber-cutter, when he returned.
The others, enchanted by themselves in "Mexicali Rose",
did not notice him. For a fraction of eternity he and his face
were still, he was not acting someone else. Was he
Everleigh? Was he the host himself who now inhabited the
quiet and solitude of a body rented to the many and noisy,
and who looked from it at *their* admirers with a stealthy
blankness? Only this fraction: then he turned a fervid gaze
on me and swaggered across with confidence. Our meeting
had been ordained, this was *the* moment: that was the impression I got.

As though fertilized to action by his approach, "Drink,
dear boy?" I said.

"I shall be delaighted, deah boy!" He glanced at my glass:
"Whiskeh-sodah, thenks," he said. It was a Technicolor
version of my own accent.

Now the others began, elegiacally and piercingly, to sing
"Mother Macree", each one aspiring, as drunkards do, to
outwail the rest.

Everleigh appeared too pliant, elegant, and capricious to
be a timber-cutter; he was dressed with spiv-like gentility:
narrow shoes, aluminium-grey trousers with a lustrous surface, powder-blue sports coat, a long cassia-yellow tie
manacled by bar and chain. He wore two weighty rings,
and a wristlet watch on a metal band as intricate and interlaced as a decoration in the Book of Kells. His . . . his
fancy dress, as it seemed to me, had the same qualities of in-
directness that the room had — the nickel-plated supports
for the fluorescents; the walls each a different colour —
Reckitt's Blue, magenta, stewed-quince, card-table green;

the brandy-advertising ashtrays; the wire-and-paper irises stuck in troughs of sand; the white-framed reproductions of magnolias.

Feeling subtle as Father Brown, "How do you find Gippsland?" I said.

He made a *moue*, the only one I have encountered outside a 1920 romance. He exhaled the smoke of one of my cigarettes: "Not bad, man. Ye-e-s, not too bad at all, man." Again that edulcorated note, Welsh but not Welsh, intangible as fumes.

"They tell me you hail from up north?"

Infinitesimal delay.

Then, "Yes, man," he said, and, presenting me with a matinée-idol smile of such glistening chinaness that it seemed to open a door on Truth's nudity, named a small town I had passed through some months ago. It was one of those places exposed for no detectable reason miles one way from willow-lined irrigation channels, miles the other from orange orchards. It was a parenthesis on a brick-red road, a paragraph of salt-bush, dust like paprika, a senselessness of shacks whose fallen-down gates were iron bed-ends that let nothing into yards littered with oil-drums and camp-pie tins.

How could he, coming from there, have said "Not bad, man," about this shire hairy with paspalum through which matriachal queues of cows dragged their udders, a luxuriance absinthe-scented by fennel and grid-ironed Englishly by hawthorn hedges? Mountains poured creeks down through maize-flats into the river's wide highway; there were lakes, super-abundance, every shade and shape of sappy green. The town itself must have been for him a Hollywood of fish-and-chip shops, natty tailors', pubs, dance-halls, milk bars, billiard saloons, emporiums chock-a-block with cheap suède shoes. "Ye-e-es, not too bad at all, man," he had said: within my mind an extra eye artfully opened.

"Do you know that town, man?"

At this point, the extra eye, alert to some ancestral intuition, saw that I should tell a lie: "No, dear boy, I don't know it at all."

I knew that he was drunk. He seemed on the verge of

splitting like a pomegranate to exhibit a glory of seeds that could be counted one by one to an exhilarating total. I also was drunk and frustrated; his accent still eluded though the answer I had known somewhere before lurked behind the copse of memories.

"You don't know m'home tah-oon, deah boy?"

"No. Never been there." His imitation of me did not distress: after all, I had heard him imitate many, so that each mimicked personality lay over his own, making him a mystery, a symbol behind fogs.

"Ah!" His eyes widened earnestly (too earnestly?). "I love mah home town." He drained his glass. A glint of Americanism had slipped through his last sentence, the fish-gleam under a skin of water. He smiled intimately, placed his sap-stained fingers on my sleeve: "Going to purchase me a whiskeh-soda, old chappeh, old chappeh?" he said.

I had bought two rounds. I bought one more. The others were tangled in "Star Dust" but the glue between them was melting; the matador-trousered schoolmistress was involved on a moquette sofa in a Laocoön-like embrace with bank-teller and window-dresser; a voice said, "A roshe beetween two thornsh!"; eyes were glazing; the bookmaker was being denounced by his sibylline wife.

"Ah suh'nough lerv that lil ol' home-tahn . . . yeah *man*!" The American fish had broken the surface. Everleigh drank, replenishing some spiritual vat into which he lowered himself to emerge immediately glowing, to say in his own voice, "My old man owns the pub there in my home town."

Shocked, I understood why an atavistic quirk had warned me to lie, for there was no hotel in that home town, no cinema, no. . . . Well, there was nothing except the burning-down of kerosene lamps and the compline of blow-flies.

He continued reciting — yes, that is the word — reciting as though through the verse alphabet from Archer to Zany, "A pub bigger than this . . . designed by a leading Sydney bloke . . . everything, everything, man . . . fifty bedrooms. . . ." His sleep-walking voice inscribed around his lies rings that did not join to validity. His hands soaked with timber-dye no longer made succinct or even apposite comment; they sketched vague figures; his eyes no longer rhymed. "Lovely, love-ly walls . . . modern colours. . . ." He seemed to try to indicate the interior of the harlequin box in which we all thus exercised towards death. He faltered, drank, emerged from his revitalizing spa, more plangently continued: "One bad trouble though, man . . . one bad, bad trouble . . . those black men. They upset my old man; for sure they upset him . . . those blackies hanging about . . . they stink, man, those blackies . . . my dad kicks 'em out; they make him sick. . . . 'Gimme drink, man,' they say, 'gimme little cigarette, boss'. . . ." Now he foundered in dreams again; his control for an instant vanished; the glass slid from his fingers and smashed on the floor. At the same second the singers came to the end of "Sleepy Time Gal", turned shallow stares on him, focused as snakes do, and remembered him with joy. Loyally they cried, "Everleigh . . . Ev-er-leigh you old so-and-so. . . . Don't worry about that glass. . . . Buy him a grog. . . . Sing 'The Blue Bird of Happiness'. . . . Buy him another drink, Mac. . . ."

This hubbub of adulation was petrol on his sinking fire; he flared, flamed; his smile excelled itself as a more charming dogma will; he did not look at me when he moved to join them but tossed an "*Au'voir, m'sieur*! My pooblique she call me." I was farther than ever from the heart of the matter.

The cook who must have been pretty in the manner of actresses on silent films, the May McAvoy type, appeared at my elbow. Years and kitchen ranges had dried her juices so that she recalled a praying mantis. To her lower lip a perpetual cigarette was seccotined by lipstick; she squinted through the smoke that flowed up her face into her crinkled hair. "Now, did you have any dinner, Mr P.? No? You poor man. Now, I'm going out to soak the oatmeal for breakfast and have a cup of tea. Now, would you like an omelette?"

I became, immediately, Edwardian, charming, and sonorous. The cook was fond of me: I was what she had come to imagine A Gentleman to be. Hers was a finicking accent, South Australian, a little menial and worn —

digested anguish impregnated it: she was the suburban housewife tricked in a breath to widow and Cook, disorientated by a germ no bigger than a pinprick. While she cooked the omelette above which the long ash of her cigarette quivered like the sword of Damocles I sat in the kitchen and listened to Everleigh's voice distantly exhorting:

> . . . be like I,
> Hold your head up high,
> Till you find the blue bird of happiness.

Purified by space this sounded poignant; it was midnight — the song somehow fitted midnight and him, I thought; but I did not know why. Later, spooning up rubbery jelly in which slices of not-ripe-enough banana lay like Alka-Seltzer tablets, I became aware of relative silence, next of the graver silence of the moon, the river, the burdock-lined back-streets, the day's run-down dynamo, a surf of silence washing out drunken laughter and slammed car-doors. The night in the multi-coloured box was over.

I thanked Cook with the aplomb of a foreign minister and left her with her face shrouded in a gossamer of cigarette smoke through which she peered like a Chinese sage.

I groped to the stairs leading to the bedrooms. A skylight was above the stair-well; someone sat moonlit and head-bowed on the bottom step. It was Everleigh. He was deplorably drunk but, more than that, as he balanced to his feet with the flexions of some creature semi-broken but still graceful, he seemed utterly exhausted as though he had laboured desperately for a demoniacal master who was himself on a nameless field in a climate no mortal could bear. Urgency was still his, but it was a different urgency; not dedicated and self-possessed, but circuitous, feckless, and timid.

Vivacity and mobility having drained from his face, the archaic light magnified contours I should have noticed before, revealed in shadow what I could have recalled under fluorescents: the secret of his accent. I do not like people but can well enough act the Intelligent Good Mixer. . . . You remember that? But I could not act as well as Everleigh. His brilliant toil had concealed everything in light until that moment when I was forced not to ignore his outstretched hand in the hell of whose stained palm lay not only the ghastly town with its shattered verandas and the fly-besequined eye-sockets of his part-blood parents but the Main Street garden debauchees, the reeking ones, the out-skirt-walkers skinny as their mongrels, the soft-eyed beg-gars whose lilting and smoky accent Everleigh was using at the foot of the moonlit stairs, for it was his by custom, prac-tice, and heredity: "Drink, man. . . . Drink gimme. . . . Gimme little cigarette, boss."

Uncle Foss and Big Bogga

As I grow older I am increasingly fascinated by the inter-locking circles which link past with present, a remoter past to a less remote. One has constantly to revalue the quality of appearances, to give a testimony at seven thirty-two one considered grotesque at half-past seven.

Uncle Foss (Foster was his full Christian name) and Big Bogga (his correct name escapes me) — who could have foretold that in the opera of loneliness of which the music is, world over, the same but the libretti infinitely varying, these two so unlike should sing the same words to an aria?

Uncle Foss was the perfect country boy's uncle.

A photograph of the 1890's, glazed as brawn, shows a young swashbuckler, straight-nosed, with the fierce, lus-trous regard under united eyebrows of a *cinquecento* bravo. Such liquorice curls low on the forehead, such sharp-cut lips, such a Tartar moustache of almost radar vibrancy. I never knew him thus, flaunting the Aimeé-Vibert-rose-and-maiden-hair-fern buttonhole. When I first remember him he was a widower, childless, his nose bashed in some hot brawl or brawls, his moustache ravaged; his body which might well have sprawled on a Hampton Court ceiling bore the scorpion stitchings of many a bushman's gash from bowie knife, gun, barbed wire, axe, fish-hook and bicycle-spill. He shambled, tall and powerful, across my childhood and those childhoods of my brothers and boy cousins. Every school holiday, bearing oblations of khaki hand-kerchiefs, flake-cut, Madeira cakes, and sauce from dead Grandmother's recipe, we all were at Uncle Foss's, con-verged upon him from every part of the State. Only the curls, less tar-glossy lacking nineteenth-century macassar oil, remained from the photograph. The eyes were still molten but an avuncular and unimpassioned spirit occupied them as he greeted us with gorilla blarings, towering in the heat, for it seemed always hot eleven-in-the-morning then, the wind from the Kilmany Plains shuffling the loquat leaves like decks of cards, and the pomegranate-tree over the well cherishing its elegant miniature fruit as a collector his *netsuke*. We were scallawags, snorters, young Turks, sonny Jims, laddies; we were you B young B's. We worshipped him.

Of what Uncle Foss did before the lottery win released him from doing I have no knowledge — with the wisdom or shrewdness of a simple and limited man he dissipated his windfall in nothing but inexpensive leisure. He bought no chorus girls, politicians or consciences. And what could travel, bespoke tailoring, Perrier-Jouët 1921 or badger-hair shaving-brushes mean to him? Beer, and tea strong enough to walk on remained his favourite drinks, rump steak drenched in home-made tomato sauce his favourite food; he preferred a tent by a bream-river to the White Hart Hotel grandfather had preferred too much, he hunted deer and foxes rather than women or stock-market bulletins, and — I assume — compensated sonlessness by condoning periodic broadsides of nephews.

His house, scoured weekly by a char-cum-washer-woman, remained as it was when Aunt Mary died: vases in the form of white rustic fences, bamboo gipsy tables, bent-wood Vienna rockers, roods of rigid crochet — pillow-shams, table-runners, doilies, duchess sets, supper-cloths, lamp-mats, tea-cosies. The kitchen seemed an alchemist's laboratory — cannibals' iron boilers, copper preserving pans, mincers and egg-beaters ominous as instruments of torture, meat-dishes that could hold a roast yak, Mazzawattee Tea tins and earthenware bread-crocks. The house was not femininized, unsexed rather: no flower in vase, no rubber-plant in jardinière. There was a charwoman reek of phenyle. Only the chimneypiece of the front room upheld the eccentric male gesture in a house occupied by males. First, central, and our delight, was the model of the five-master *Preussen* locked in floes of greenish glass, frosted with icicles, unmoving and mesmerizing. By it slanted a photograph of Aunt Mary mournful as a pallid Clydesdale beneath a hat turbulent with poppies and wheat ears. The third object, inexplicable there, was a hexagonal stud-box of German silver. The lid-handle was a silver stud; engraved about it the statement we boys considered screamingly funny *Don't swear, here it is!* Against this background my clearest memory of Uncle Foss.

I see camp-fire *chiaroscuro* on his dishevelled face as he ladles kangaroo-tail soup into enamel plates while moon-mad swans queue across heaven; I feel again my leg-nerves run icy as he tells us of bunyips, fireballs and bushranger murders. Today, the smell of reeds, manouka or summer grassland recalls instantly that unworldly world — duck-swamp, quail-paddock, blue blink of kingfisher, aristocratic stroll of egret. I still laugh with middle-aged cousins at the grilling afternoon on the Ninety Mile Beach near The Honeysuckles where naked Uncle Foss and eight frog-naked boys, salmon-fishing, were surprised by women in floppy hats tramping over the dunes. Baying blasphemously, hands in the posture of classic modesty, Uncle Foss with lolloping buttocks cantered into the ocean, we boys, imitating modesty, with him. From the tumultuous soapsuds we glared, Triton and retinue, until the chirruping women scurried off like Touaregs through the kikuyu.

But the clearest memory is of the front room, the gasolier popping, boys lined up on the colonial sofa reading *Chums* or *Chatterbox*, Uncle Foss at his third bottle of beer, suddenly, full-stop to some secret sentence of thought, announcing in the cricket-soothed and page-turning peace, "Poor bloody old Mary! Poor bloody old Mary!"

Startled, we glanced at him, eyes skidding instantly away from his enormous, cascading tears to the Clydesdale face under its platter of flowers, next to the ice-corralled square-rigger, before retreating to stories by Frank H. Shaw, articles on *How to make a rabbit hutch* or coloured pages of flags of the world.

All this, in days when the world flew flags I knew, and Uncle Foss's country cathedral town, where now neons wince ESPRESSO, EATS, FISH AND CHIPS, MILK BAR, HAMBURGER MAX, had none, when hedges were plumbago, roses scented, tomatoes involuted, when mulberry-

trees were grown and only three or four years before had the
last calico WELCOME HOME sign been removed from the
front veranda of the ultimate, late, shell-shocked local
returning from the 1914-18 War.

By the time the next war was three years old I was Senior
English master at a fashionable school in Adelaide. E-
shaped, ivied, college-Jacobean, four-storeyed, it furrowed
the future with its freight of futures. The two-storey-high
jacaranda geysering up from the quadrangle splashed drops
of incandescent purple into form-rooms where gowned
masters wrote absurd or divine puzzles on blackboards of
slate, and every afternoon tortuous *Chopsticks* crazily rang
from all six music-rooms. Blacked-out, its basement walls
sandbagged, windows criss-crossed by paper strips, the outskirts of its playing-fields were bear-pitted with slit
trenches in which fourth-formers practised smoking.
"Where, in this day and age, do these incipient Attilas get
cigarettes of reputable make?" Big Bogga would say with
pinched and niggling accent.

Big Bogga was Junior English, and small. Little Bogga, a
Captain in Army Intelligence and Big Bogga's cousin, was,
the Common Room told me, big. The obverse of nicknames
was schoolboy wit.

Big Bogga was withdrawn, astringently tetchy, and had
the rigidity of something carved painfully from intractable
substance. His voice, shaved and bookish, mocked his pro-
fession — he denigrated himself and schoolmasters by
parodying Gunby Hadath parodies: "I fear, Westinghouse
Minor . . . that is your unseemly cognomen, is it not? . . .
that your predilection for the double negative would
scarcely merit Fowler's approval." He was a disciplinarian
tart as a guava, a collector of examination scalps. The boys
did not like him. There was a spiritual and a sniffable
mustiness about him as though he rarely showered intellec-
tually or actually. On his foolscap-white collar there was always one spot of shaving blood.

The school, like most during war, had an off-centre and
exotic atmosphere. Younger masters — Little Bogga was
one — were at the Front. So were those senior boys who
should have been rowing or cricket heroes, school- or
house-prefects, influences. The school was filleted.

Youngsters were pseudo-seniors; inferior masters with a taste for wardrobe-drinking or the maids fecklessly deputized. There were even, first time in the school's history, two women on the teaching staff. Siamese princelings, Nauru chieftain's sons and the Billy Bunter twins of a Dutch consul added a Greyfriars note. In the midst of fictitious air-raid warnings, brown-out, the white outlining of stair risers and the eternal whistling of *Run, rabbit, run*, while searchlights probed innocent chinchilla clouds with tender indecision, Big Bogga had his appendix removed. In magnanimous mood, and because I disliked a city raucous with Americans and their floozies who could always buy a table at the South Australian Hotel when I couldn't, I took over his extra duties while he was in hospital.

When he returned he insisted on the tactics of *noblesse oblige* with the truculent regality of a dauphin. He invited me to try his home-brew. Beer was as rare as pork was, then. I was inquisitive too. So I had my one, my only, night out with Big Bogga.

He lived alone in an upper-middle-class suburb. His garden, a horticultural ghetto of unpruned grape-vines, olives and poinsettias, was mysteriously littered with tea-crates — I saw MANGALATHEE, GEBROKEN ORANJE on one in the street-lamp light.

Admitted to the large house, I was immediately sure that he had altered nothing since his mother's death years ago. I sensed a behind-the-scenes bachelor messiness: egg-sulphuretted spoons, cups encrusted with dried sugar, frying-pans of stale grease in which burnt sausage-meat paraphrased the Bay of Islands. Apparently a fortnightly cowlick was all a slummocky char could manage; the drawing-room where we drank was scarcely Miss Havisham's but had the same transfixed air of having stopped when the Vulliamy clock had, years ago. Slumbering flies chicken-pocked the ceiling; their excrement and that of their ancestors was written on everything. Webs in the small chandelier were not of horror-film texture but gauzier, like thistledown, so that I blinked as though my eyes were at fault and blinking would make the chandelier and the green-stemmed hock-glasses in the Queen Anne cabinet sparkle, the vast looking-glass above the fireplace shimmer and reflect. To the end all stayed filmed, smeared, evasive. A permeating toadstool smell I recognized; it was the smell of Big Bogga. When I sat, a ghostly pepper of dust puffed from the Utrecht velvet. The evening unravelled, a ball of grubby wool, as we sampled various brews. They, at least, were fresh.

Later, he proudly guide-toured me through the cellar; its scientific cleanliness was startling, the brewing experiments arranged, dated, documented with pedantic care. Amazement and visitor-behaviour made me flatter him although I felt unnecessarily and insultingly sad. As we left the cellar he said brusquely, a decision made, "I want to show you something I've never shown a soul. Follow me." Fox-terrier perky he trotted ahead down a side passage. He fiddled out his keys and unlocked a door, embarrassing me with an out-of-character wink and "Mum's the word!"

The room was a lumber-room containing such relics as an athenienne, a plush-framed looking-glass on which bulrushes were painted, tin trunks, japanned coal-vases, lurid oleographs — *Vesuvio in eruzione, Palazzo donn' Anna*, Leaning Towers of zinc garden-labels. He mounted a Savonarola chair to grope behind a dusty reproduction of Leighton's *Bath of Psyche*. Descending, he said conspiratorially yet primly, "Discretion! Discretion! There's a war on", and displayed a key with which he began to unlock the drawers of an enormous satin-wood tallboy. "Go on, open them," he said, his shirt-button eyes aglitter like sequins. "When war started I foresaw all this slovenly rationing so. . . ." I opened the first drawer. It was weighted, full of tins of salmon. The next was brimming with tins of sardines. Eight deep top-drawers, two double-width bottom ones, were crammed with rationed goods — even boxes of matches with two striking surfaces instead of the wartime one. Astounded and impressed, I said so. Visibly gratified he locked up his hoard, climbed on the chair, replaced the key behind Psyche, extinguished the light on discarded past and accumulated future, locked the door, rattled the handle to be certain, said again, "Mum's the word!" and led me back to drinking.

It matters little what we said during the rest of the evening; drink traduces all men to the iniquity of a sham truthfulness better forgotten. I knew that, as a species of gratuity, he was offering what little of himself there was to offer outside the common room — his hobby: the clinical cellar — his fear and astuteness: the secret warehouse. He had nothing else to offer except one more thing. I was not to enter that house again. We never drank together again though we worked side by side for two more years. The next day we were as we had always been; he had tipped me — what more was necessary?

His final offering, as we got drunker pretending to distinguish brew from brew, was not merely flabbergasting as a revelation of what boarded in his heart but doubly flabbergasting as a lightning sprint through the past and the heart of one I considered an opposite sort of man.

It was late. I had no watch. The Vulliamy had stopped at twenty-five past three . . . day? night? . . . long before the war. Nevertheless I felt midnight, the page of day about to falter over.

"Music," he said. "Do you like music?"

Good God, I thought, at this hour, no, but "Yes," I said.

"Truly?" He got smaller and anxious.

"Oh, *yes*," I said, almost gushingly.

He left the room.

I listened to his goat-light footsteps, wondering what he would bring back. Musical box, glockenspiel or zither seemed the few fitting instruments for this rum but real situation.

He re-entered with a violin.

"The mater's," he said. "Glorious instrument, flawless tone. The mater played exquisitely. She taught me. I'll play her favourite piece."

Arranging himself, he lifted the bow. Perhaps he played well; I am no judge. What he played was shamefully sentimental — *Chante Hindu* or *Invitation to the Waltz* — a kindred piece, grieving and retching. Prepared to endure the fatigue of presenting an alert, absorbed, expression, I found there was no need. He was not playing just for me, perhaps not even for me. He played towards one of the many photographs in mother-of-pearl frames on the chimneypiece. A woman — the mater? — postured soulfully under much artistically bundled-up hair. As though it were the Christ Child, she nursed a violin. Same violin?

As he reached the last bars he turned to me. I was compelled to look up, to brighten, praying the dishonest praise I proposed would arrive ringing with truth.

But he spoke first, and the pattern of things broke like a necklace, its beads running wildly in all directions into dark, into the wings, away. Two rolled into the spotlight to stop side by side, dead-centre, dramatically lit. With a shock I felt the weight of *Chums* on my knees, saw the ice-bewitched Cape Horner, heard my cousins and brothers spluttering with laughter over the *Don't swear, here it is* of the stud-box. The years swung together like closing callipers; two men who would never meet stood side by side on the circle of time — lonely Goliath Uncle Foss and lonely minikin Big Bogga. For Big Bogga, whom I had never heard say so much as "Damn!", Big Bogga with one tear like a tiny snail-print on his cheek was saying, "Poor bloody old mater! Poor bloody old mater!"

Boy Meets Girl

The Koreans or the Japanese — *some* animistic nation — say, "One's love of a house extends even to the crows sitting on it." As of a house surely also so of an era. I loved the love-on-the-dole decade between 1929 and 1939. Perhaps, because I'd always been poor, I really didn't notice the crows on the ridges of that decade. If I did, well, I loved them. It was love 'em or lump 'em anyway.

I was young; I had no material ambitions, and wouldn't have minded being as barefooted as a goose and bare-bottomed as a Villon cut-throat; I was a liar of the soaring variety — Perpendicular Gothic; I was naif to the point of purblindness. Thus endowed, I was safe, even from myself. Safety encourages happiness. Happy I was.

The only recollection of a feeling against the era is of the one that zipped an electric hairline of envy through the texture of happiness when I had to scurry, running late on an incandescent day, past a beach strewn with susso Adonises already grilled walnut. There was I pounding along on the grass-plots (surely they weren't nature strips in 1937?) to save my soles, pallid under a threadbare suit that scarcely performed any function except keeping me pallid — and respectable; and there were they, straight from Delacroix, otiose, and not a jerry emptied. And smoking!

Ninety-nine point nine nine per cent of the time I was, however, incontestably happy on almost thirty shillings a week. If I eschewed luxuries such as hats, lottery tickets, cigarettes, singlets, beer, theatre tickets, copies of *Hills Like White Elephants*, and contributions to Spanish Civil War funds, it was only to afford other luxuries such as haircuts, toothbrushes, shoe-polish, soap, sale price underpants and

— for I was an artistic as well as a cleanly youth — charcoal and Michelet paper to use at the National Gallery Art Classes.

The almost thirty shillings?

My Uncle Tasker, who had the nature of Genghis Khan embedded in the shape of Alfred Hitchcock, was well-heeled enough to be mean without causing meaning looks, and mean enough to use my delusion that, come 1938, I'd be Honoré Daumier II, to employ me part-time in his business. It was heavily watered-down nepotism. "I promise you, young fellow-m'-lad, you won't be coddled," he said, richly, with relish, and exhibiting all his teeth like the Laughing Cavalier. As he was fond of saying, he never broke a promise.

Arcadia Display Specialistes was the name of his business. It was in a part of North Melbourne where streets were outnumbered by bluestone-cobbled lanes, more than usually underprivileged-looking lanes through which tomcats with tattered ears, and faces like Mr Hyde's, s-l-a-n-k instead of plumping cosily down to lick their jabots and under their armpits.

The Arcadia products were shop furnishings of elementary and depressing design: plywood display cases with one corner rounded, display boards with one corner rounded, nickel-plated *art moderne* display stands. These, though each looked the same as the other, were for ever being emotionally designed by the Head Designer (he was the only one) who was called Rexie to his pendulous off-white face, and Rosie behind his undulant back. He had melon buttocks, one or other of which now and then winced — one could almost write winked — as he stood in front of his little looking-glass combing his hair into a Cornish Pasty arrangement: up from each side with a ruffle riding the centre. He wore thick-lensed spectacles, so that his eyes seemed set in aspic. Rexie's cubicle (THE STUDIO stated his door) was as neat as a surgery but had several enlivening touches . . . a telephone he had lacquered what he said was "a soothing and *subtle* morve", a print of Van Gogh's "Sunflowers", and a Beardsleyish drawing of a young man with amaranthine tresses, but otherwise as nude and hairless as a marrow, peeking into a pond. He was on tiptoe.

I was offsider to the Head Artist, a ferocious man of fifty who must once have been very good but had drunk himself down to just good enough. Leo Ryan was his name. Brandy was his tipple. He smelt like a bar-cloth, and couldn't bear a stave of me. His foul-mouthed railings against office slip-ups, which were legion, out-Leared Lear, and enthralled me. I found it advantageous, however, to assume deafness or incomprehension when, in his down-in-the-mouth moods, he fixed me with a red eye, and *whispered* at me, "You! You haven't suffered! You don't even realize that the privilege of suffering *in the mind* is man's alone! Man's alone!" or "Look at me! Dead! Trapped! Stale! I used to be young like you! But lock up the wind — it becomes stale air, stale air! You'll find out!"

Most of my chores for this smelly and discouraging man I regarded as crass, and certainly unworthy of the Daumier just under the skin. I arranged branches of crêpe paper almond blossom in front of Leo's painted background at the South Australian Tourist Bureau; finickally dashed in the *minor* stars above his Three Wise Men . . . I wasn't up to dashing them in dashingly; daubed large white freckles on three-ply reindeer; and once painted two hundred cardboard butterflies the size of pterodactyls.

In the back regions of Arcadia Display Specialistes were three or four men who noisily constructed the display counters with rounded corners, the cut-out chefs that were stood outside cheap restaurants, and so on. They worked under perpetual electric light, and were jockey-sized, quick-tempered, weasel-quick makings-smokers with witty, dirty, whiplash tongues. They had mutton and chow-chow pickle sandwiches for lunch, and nigger-brown cups of tea almost mucilaginous with sugar. They could spit as brilliantly as llamas and, though it cannot have been so, all seemed to be called Arthur.

There were also three females on the staff. Two were, it appeared to me at the age of nineteen, mere children of six-teen or seventeen. One was Brenda, the other was Tootsie, and they were alike enough in a wizened, dank way for me never to know which was which. They shared multiple

duties, and were always on the run with their insufficient
faces stuck forward like chooks' — making the nigger-
brown tea, licking stamps, swaddling display stands in ex-
celsior, cutting silk-screen lettering, spraying stencilled
curves parallel to the rounded edges of things. Maybe they
were merely girls who'd been dabs at free-hand drawing in
Grade Six sweating it out until Mr Right fell for them on a
cable tram one dazzling Thursday; maybe they were Rosa
Bonheurs or Marie Laurencins being nipped in the bud by
Uncle Tasker's cupidity, and Miss Guildford-Maggs's
languorous nagging. Ah, Miss Guildford-Maggs! Ah, nineteen! Ah, the Nineteen-thirties! Ah, the Depression, where
one had to keep down to the Joneses! A-a-ah, Miss
Guildford-Maggs!

Right here, I must make it clear that Rexie (peevishly),
Leo Ryan (morosely), the Arthurs (busily as leprechauns),
Brenda and Tootsie (like put-upon Brontë governesses), and
even Uncle Tasker (you may miss the smiling tiger, but he
won't miss), everyone of them worked, *worked* — like
slaves, like beavers, like gins, like . . . take your pick. Even
Uncle Tasker? Even I. Have you ever played ju-jitsu in a
narrow shop window with many-elbowed real branches
covered with paper blossom, two arc-lights, a nubile
dummy in pink organdie, and a placard (with one rounded
corner) defiled with words like *picturesque, panorama,
blossom-time*, and *memorable experience* ?

I found all the workers somehow matily real, and utterly
unfascinating. Not so the third female, Miss Guildford-
Maggs. She, to me, was unimpeachably fascinating. Work?
Hardly a tap, although she was Uncle Tasker's secretary,
and oversaw Brenda and Tootsie who were ever to be seen
darting rat-like side-glances of venom at her out of their
mouse-like fiction of docility.

Miss Guildford-Maggs, cracking thirty, I thought, was
tallish, was stately and flexible with it, wandered languidly
rather than walked, and had a small flat head set on a long
neck that made me think of those herbivorous dinosaurs
that munched the uppers of prehistoric trees. A shock-proof
vanity sustained her, although her incompetence was
notable, and the *non sequitur* antics of her mind gave me the
impression that it was based in some organ small as a hazel-

nut. God knows why Uncle Tasker kept her . . . perhaps her refined telephone talks were suggestive of a superior organization to the clots who bought Uncle Tasker's products for their suburban emporiums and edge-of-the-city corner shops and country town general stores. Whyever and whatever, her contribution to herself was excessive, I could not see her for the strange offerings she piled on her own altar.

In 1937, women were plucking their eyebrows *à la* Jean Harlow, vaselining eyelids, wearing fuchsia-coloured materials, snake-skin shoes, and cyclamen lipstick. Albeit in patently cheaper stuffs, Miss Guildford-Maggs went the whole hog, with colours almost passionately wrong and distressingly vibrant. Her eyelids swam with vaseline; her eyebrows were one hair-width only from invisibility.

Externals of any sort I took in my stride. It was the inner mainspring I wanted — in the nicest sticky-nosed way — to understand. I think I thought then that, give or take a little, we all had the same one. The others at Arcadia said and did things I wasn't fazed by. Miss Guildford-Maggs was, however, the very Eiffel of fazers; and given to statements that had the flat sound of cracked truths. It was as though, in seeking her, one came on signposts that bore the correct destination but pointed elsewhere. For example, when one of the Arthurs fell down dead of a heart attack, "It was," she pronounced, "it was reelly the worst attack he ever had." On the subject of living by oneself: "If one does prefer to do so, and if one fainds . . . and Ai say *if* advaisedly, for it would be quaite unlaikely to occur in any digs of maine . . . if one fainds a hair in one's pea soup . . ." (here her protruding eyes delphically protruded a glaze-width more) ". . .one could at least be sure that it was one of one's own."

My first meeting with her was one lunchtime at the Arcadia. She sat in a swivel chair — she *reclined* in *Her* swivel *throne* — in the cubicle she called her sanctum sanctoriarium. It was opposite Rexie's THE STUDIO. With a portentous Borgia nonchalance, she was varnishing her fingernails purple. The interlaced smells of the nail varnish, of some musky scent abundantly applied to her violet dress, and of something simmering in an elderly aluminium saucepan on a gas-ring, repulsed me on the one nostril and, on the other, sent my unsteady imagination skipping in the direction of a kind of Temple of Isis occupied by love-sick priestesses up to no good with potions.

Miss Guildford-Maggs was unable to offer her hand but she offered me a fair section of a parti-coloured monologue. She indicated and named, with ennui if not distaste, Brenda and Tootsie who were playing dumb-struck Charmian and Iras to her genteel-as-buggery Cleopatra.

Brenda was stirring the greyish mess I could see heaving and pouting in the saucepan.

"Ai trust you're being careful not to let it catch, Brenda," purred the Serpent of old Nile. "Stir clockwise, and don't let it catch. It is," she said to me, looking up from under her greasy eyelids, "a delicate flesh, veal. I rather praide maiself, though Ai do say it maiself, on a rather delicate palate."

Bred in the country from which I'd just come, veal was abhorrent to me as it is to country people. I concealed a gulp of revulsion under a smile of great vivaciousness.

"It's done, I think," said Brenda through a mouthful of vanilla slice, the flakes from which ringed her feet like larger dandruff.

Miss Guildford-Maggs gave me a minuscule and qualified smile as one shrugging, "A fool, you see!" She next looked at her fingernails, oh, absorbedly . . . she was clearly putting a significant pause in parentheses. She spoke, as a sphinx might, in granite:

"It . . .is . . .*not* . . . done." She closed her eyes. "Whatever you maight think you think." She paused. "Brenda." *Brenda* implied by intonation *skivvy*, if not *idiot kitchen drab*. "Stir clockwise. It will not be done for two and three-quarter minutes." Her eyes, still closed, she nevertheless turned them elsewhere. "Ai see Tootsie, that you've set the tray with a dirty cup. There's a maite of lipstick on the rim. Ai know it's mai cup, and mai lipstick, but Ai've told you . . ." Ghost at cockcrow, Tootsie and the cup disappeared. Miss Guildford-Maggs opened her eyes which seemed luminous and more protuberant. "Ai'm sure," she said, "you'll be very happy in our happy family. Brenda, serve the veal."

Fascination! 1937! Miss Guildford-Maggs smouldering bitchily in Arcadia!

What slumbrous film star was her model . . . Barbara la Marr? . . . I'll never know: she was not a good translator. Anyway, I was green. I was emerald green.

From then on, whenever I could, I spent time in research on Miss Guildford-Maggs. Two aspects particularly led me on and on. One was that while all of us in Uncle Tasker's little web bickered *with* each other, and slammed doors behind furious exits, and found it not unpleasant, she bickered with no one. She bickered *at*, from some foxhole on a plateau of her own. It was not pleasant. Why no one told her to shut her dirty big gob, I couldn't understand. I wanted to understand. If this aspect inclined me to earnest, lines-between-the-brow moods (what is Miss G.-M.'s mainspring?), the other aspect outrightly dazzled me. She lied and lied and lied. She was as far gone a lie-addict as I was. My taste was for the elaborately detailed plot, the train of many carriages all on one branch line, and a cow-catcher ready to scoop away those rash enough to question the train. Her taste, which kept me open-mouthed, was for lies like Dodg'em Cars at Luna Park — no rails, each on its wild own, bump, bump, bump. Swapping lies with her was like swapping a finished jigsaw for the scalenes of many a puzzle.

The time came when I heard her saying, "Ai do think we've been acquainted long enough for you to call me Maevene?"

I nearly fell off my perch but, in a throbbing voice, said I'd love to; that I was very flattered; that I deemed it . . . I shut up. Then, in the unsullied, unthrobbing voice I delivered my fictions in, I said that I was par*tic*ularly intrigued by her name because one of my grandmothers had been called Maevene. Maevene Eugenie Charlotte. Paternal grandmother. The one who died in India. Tragically, but without a whimper. Bitten by a cobra. A white cobra, immeasurably ancient. A *sacred* cobra, I added with some vivacity.

"How in-ter-*est*-ing!" said Miss Guildford-Maggs — er — Maevene. "It's a very small world. Ai was named after mai grandmother." We were walking to the tram stop through the cats' maze of lanes. "She was a raving beauty in har day. The Ruse of London they called har. Ladies and gentlemen stood on the seats of Haide Park to see har sweep bai in har carriage."

Her eyelids began to droop under her cyclamen tricorne with its snippet of cyclamen ostrich feather; she was becoming slumbrous and sultry even as she steered her lizard-skin shoes through the sardine tins and dogs' turds.

I tempted myself to outrage.

"She was pregnant," I said with surprisingly unfaltering clarity for I'd never said this word before.

Maevene stopped being sultry.

"Pardon *me*!" she said sharply as though I'd plunged a hand in her bosom.

"I'm talking, Maevene, of my grandmother Maevene." I boyishly punted a camp pie tin. "The one slain by the cobra. In the winter garden of a rajah's palace. She was with child. With children, really. Before she passed away she was delivered of twins. My father was the first."

"Mai father . . ." began Maevene, recovering but still shaken.

"My uncle was the second."

"Mai father was born in . . ."

"So that is why," I cut relentlessly in, "my uncle loathes me, hates me, despises me." He was, as a matter of fact, in-differently jocular to me, and merely thought me whatever he thought a fool was.

"Ah!" said Maevene. "Ai'm glad you brought that up. Ai would never have mentioned it. But Ai do see, Ai reelly do. Ai sympathize. Ai understand. . . ."

Fascination! I hadn't the foggiest what she sympathized with, what she understood, where the signpost was point-ing. She was a drug I didn't really like, or really dislike.

Maevene and the others at Arcadia were not, of course, the only city people I was trying to learn about city people from. I didn't, for example, live at Arcadia, but in 28 Col-lins Street. I had a third-floor back room, from the window of which I could see over the high brick wall of the back-yard of the Melbourne Club wherein plane-trees, denied municipal surgery, grew like superior weeds. I paid fifteen shillings a week for my aerie, a cell which must once have been a servant's room. This payment included use of a communal kitchen I never used. As well there was a vast bathroom with water so boiling that dangerous steam jetted out when the tap was first turned on; and there was room service. This last was composed of two new experiences for me. One pillow case (the upper), and one sheet (the lower) were changed each week. Lower pillow became the upper, and upper sheet became the lower. It seemed to me dirty, and I thought of it for a long time as a mean city custom like making coffee out of what looked like gun-powder instead of out of a bottle with a turbaned Moor on the outside. The other experience was a breakfast tray which, because I lived on frugal rations, was a bracing as well as a thrilling experience. It was brought in every morning by May, a woman of about forty who could have played football but who was disguised as a sort of blown-up French maid in a bedroom farce — black dress, tiny frilled white apron, tinier frilled cap. Several mornings a week May brought a medicine glass of port wine in with the tea and toast and marmalade. I had my own ideas of what she was up to. "Now, get that into you," she would shout. "You're looking peaky. That'll bring back the roses. That'll warm the cockles." I read lustful seductiveness into this maternal din. I was terrified, and tossed the Lorelei's brew out of the window on to the wall of the Melbourne Club. She intends, I thought, to weaken my willpower, and sully my virtue. I thought in those very words. I imagined her dark magnificent eyes, although embedded in a crumpled rubber face, to be glimmering with depravity, and when, one morning, I lied that I had a headache (merely to make polite conversation), and she laid a hot hand on my cool forehead to find if it were hot, nearly bayed for help. Even had I merely squeaked, Miss Beveridge, who owned the place, would have — I was confident of this — appeared in a Fairy Godmother sunburst, and changed May into something else, a marmoset or an armadillo. Of almost the same height, weight and shape as May — solid, foursquare, high-bosomed, undumbfoundable, with legs like jeroboams — Miss Beveridge was as near to being a Grand Duchess (and a lady) as a lodging-house martinet with an eye on sheets and her lodgers' morals could be, even at the posh end of a posh street. Her fingers were kept almost as apart as frogs' fingers by thick rings, two or three to a finger, and no finger free . . . diamonds, diamonds, and diamonds. She dressed in beige, wore her stockings dull side out, and crocodile-skin shoes. Her hair was steeply terraced, a creamy pompadour ideal for aigrettes, coronets, or the basket at the base of Sanson's guillotine.

Although there must have been a dozen others in the house (we were for ever after-youing each other on the stair landings) I knew only the one who lived in the ground floor front. Her door, always rosily ajar when I came in late at night, opened off the entrance hall which was crimson-carpeted, darkly panelled, and smelt of burned toast. My knowee was also about forty (looking back it seems I was the only under-forty in the place), and her surname was Kolker, and I called her Kolker because she asked me to. No Maevene nonsense. She was a Jewess, a journalist, smoked black Sobranies so endlessly that her room fumed as if on the point of combustion, and was voluble in an elaborate cultured voice. Since, however, she looked like a gipsy queen, her intense monologues (how people *talked* throughout the Depression!) had the tone of incantations. I'd not have dared lie to *her*. Perhaps she was lying to me about liars: Hemingway, Lorca, Dos Passos, Sinclair Lewis, Upton Sinclair . . . I didn't understand, and didn't deeply listen, and was therefore a seemingly good listener. I kept my eyes intelligently wide open, directing at her the frank gaze that only the unfrank can convincingly direct. Meantime, delicately but nonetheless gluttonously, I kept on eating, for Kolker had a cupboard chock-a-block with food, terribly exotic to me, all bought at Franz the Grocer's at the Eastern Market — rollmops, anchovies, caviar, salami, olives, rye bread, incredible cheeses. I'd have preferred Irish stew, but a tight belt had driven me to caviar, and Kolker's own blend of expensive, freshly ground coffee which tasted to me as I imagine deadly nightshade would. Ah, the Depression, and caviar, and Dorothy Lamour, muted by a room or two, singing on some mysterious lodger's wireless, singing "Moonlight and Shadows" while Kolker vilified Franco!

I mention May, Miss Beveridge, and Kolker because they

resembled Uncle Tasker, Rexie, Leo Ryan, the Arthurs, Brenda and Tootsie in the possession of some quality I couldn't spring in Maevene Guildford-Maggs, and couldn't, anyway, define . . . a saltiness, an awareness of the gravitational pull in others (come down, come down, and be bored with me, my love), a proper organization of Goods and Bads.

Outside Arcadia and 28 Collins Street, I kept on adding, like a slightly dotty magpie, to my collection of people and places. Places because people wore them as snails their shells.

Kingsley Hall was a place seething with people of kinds I thought fictional because, hitherto, I'd only met them in books given to me by tangible people who, in my youth, were far too fond of this dangerous custom.

Kingsley Hall, a stucco terrace of four two-storeyed houses, was in a one-block-only street behind St Peter's Cathedral and the Eastern Hill Fire Brigade. The street's directory name eludes me. It was generally called the Street of Leaning Trees because its plane-tree avenue, aspiring heavenwards, had become so "picturesquely" skew-whiff that you could bet that, rain or shine, a middle-aged artist and a middle-aged easel would be straddling together at the end of the street.

Kingsley Hall, built *circa* 1870 for the hutching of four ma-and-pa families (children, nursemaid, cook, tweeny), went through this period. Doorways were then cut through the three inner walls to make one establishment which was, first, a private hotel for retired governesses, deaconesses, Anglo-Indian widows, and archbishops' spinster daughters. These menless women were replaced, during the reign of Edward the Seventh, by the women they could have been: Kingsley Hall became a discreetly opulent brothel which left as heritage a number of looking-glasses set high at an angle between wall and ceiling. It was next a boarding house for entertainers of the barn-storming sort: bell-ringers, contortionists, Shakespearian monologuists looking like Liszt in old age, raddled soubrettes, buck-and-wing dancers, tattooed ladies, itinerants of all sorts whose theatrical baskets could hold anything from a ventriloquist's doll, ageing as its master aged, to a brace of world-weary carpet snakes with

blasé eyes. By 1937 . . . ah, the Depression, and Three
Course Meals for Sevenpence, and Ursula Jeans singing
"Twentieth Century Blues" seated on a grand piano
(white)! . . . it housed those huddling on the fringes of the
Arts and the outskirts of spivvery: empty-bellied music students, piece-work commercial artists, door-to-door sales-
men from photo-enlarging firms, chorus boys rooming in
petulant couples, makers of china masks, amateur confidence men.

I had come to know them fairly well. Indeed, my part-
time world much resembled theirs except that my address
was less raffish, my desires were less bacchanalian, my
country ingenuousness less a hazard than their city guile. I
can't recall why my best friends among them were a disappointed writer called Erik who had turned to petty crime,
and his voluptuous fast-talking wife . . . or mistress . . .
Sybil, an usherette in a cinema.

Sybil was a cut-'em-down gossip. Kingsley Hall was a
chest-of-drawers into which a variety of defective, gaudy,
shabby, glass-eyed dolls had been shoved out of conventional sight. She dragged them forth, and held them up to
me, privately, deriding their excesses and distresses, their
tattered nobilities and scruffy *amours* and tinsel exultations.
She did this vivaciously enough, but with a tribal affection.
For one only her acridity was undiluted: I had heard her
teeth jar often on his name — Max Komesaroff. I'd met
many and most of Sybil's subjects but had somehow always
missed him. I was befuddled that she ranted most against
his openhandedness, and was inclined to agree with Erik
whom I'd heard protest in a bai-jove accent straight from a
sparkling three-act comedy: "Reahlly, dahling, Max is a
Jew-boy and a Russniak and all that, but he reahlly does
scatter the old largesse. He could be J.C., you know, the
Second Coming and all that. Lay off, old gel."

I arrived one twilight to find Sybil alone. The room, in
which I'd seen not even a waxed-paper poppy before,
reeked of a plethora of jonquils jammed into borrowed
vases, a brass jardinière that usually lived on a pedestal in
the hall, a jug, a chamber-pot without a handle, and an
enamel milk-billy. Reflected in the canted looking-glasses
left over from Kingsley Hall's more lushly improper past

this display made a considerable impact. Sybil made a more considerable one. She held a tumbler of wine. She was flaring.

"That ghetto rat!" she cried. "That Komesaroff eunuch! Tapping at my door like a charity-worker! Smirking over a great armful of these stinking bloody funeral parlour things!" I was learning not to flinch when women (that is, pretty women) swore. "Erik the fool's been picked up for conning some peasant from Woop Woop, and's been popped in the lock-up." I expressed regret.

"Don't be grotesque," she said. "The great oaf's only got himself to blame. He's conned himself in; he'll con himself out. But Big-ears Komesaroff hears the sad tidings, and comes running, pitter-patter, pitter-patter, pitter-patter, laden with a . . . *Look!* A million of these whatever-they-ares! That great fat box of sick-making chockies! Four jars of caviar!" I thought of Kolker pressing midnight snacks of caviar on me. "And a bottle of muscadine! Muck! As though the wife of the accused should celebrate. As though Komesaroff wanted to pop under the covers with me while Erik's behind the bars. But he doesn't want me to celebrate — he wants me to be wailing and keening. And as for slap-and-tickle — I think he's neuter. How dare he!"

She scolded on, meantime mopping up the muscadine muck. No one knew where Komesaroff worked. Sybil suggested a sewer. By day he was free; between seven and midnight he was invisible, and apparently earning the money with which he lavished impractical gifts — crystallized fruit, sweet wines, boxes of chocolates the size of the Koran — on penurious donees who, she said with vehement sincerity, abhorred him. Since I didn't much mind the unpopular Maevene Guildford-Maggs who *took*, I thought I mightn't much mind the Komesaroff who *gave*. I said I'd like to meet him.

"Erik doesn't mind him, and look where he is tonight. You and Erik are dingbats. He's corrupted you. Komesaroff's a creepy-crawly, but if you want to, you can meet the little runt tomorrow. He'll be at the morning session — there's a new Loretta Young film showing, and he just adores her and those great big tear-filled eyes. You be there, and I'll *give* him to you."

I pointed out that I couldn't afford Loretta Young at the Plaza.

"Don't be grotesque," said Sybil. "Your old aunt, Señorita Sybil, will get you in free, gratis, and for nothing. But wear a fur coat: the caviar king will make your blood run cold."

Señorita Sybil! Ah, the cinemas of the Depression! The Wurlitzers and chandeliers and statues and urns of authentic flowers, the ankle-deep carpets and marble staircases! Palaces for the orgies of Tiberius!

The Plaza, where Sybil and her sister usherettes were dressed like musical comedy señoritas (flounced skirt, Spanish shawl, lofty comb, black lace mantilla, red velvet roses), was all Cordoba tiles, iron grilles, seats of embossed crimson leather, and wall-fountains tinkling from the jaws of blue ceramic lion-masks. It was in this superbly executed phoniness that I met Max Komesaroff. In three minutes I knew what Sybil meant about the fur coat.

I shook his little bony chilled hand, the back of which was decorated by ginger freckles and ginger hairs of the same ginger as those, apparently knitted in moss stitch, on his spherical head. His eyes were of the same tintlessness as Maevene Guildford-Maggs's, but whereas her glance slid across the air above one's head as if eyes and mind were on a train always pulling out, his drove into one as immediately and as offensively as a harpoon.

He drew a tin of fifty cigarettes from his pocket, and offered me one. I said I didn't smoke.

"Vhy do you not?" His voice had a metallic note. It implied that non-smokers were non-humans.

No one should, suddenly, question liars. I was so startled that, instead of fictionizing ("My guardian — an eccentric paralytic who infinitely prefers gerberas to people — has forbidden me ever to smoke anything except a narghile"), I told a shameful truth: "I hate smoking."

Not for a twink removing the harpoon, he began to smile, slowly to construct a smile in which I was appalled to discern disbelief flowering into utter disbelief. A second or an aeon later I saw compassion break the surface; I spotted *pity*.

"Vhy," he said, with sorrow, "do you say this thing? It is not the truth."

Upon this, my mind instantly ceased to register anything more than that he was wearing a suit of pin-striped Vandyke brown material of eye-cutting richness.

"Vhy you do not smoke is the reason you are much too poor. Eh?"

I stood, an ossified gawk, unable to believe the evidence of my senses.

"I speak, you see, alvays the truth. It is because I have this vish to be kind and loving," continued the monster, the degenerate, the . . . the . . .

Oh, put down your electric torch, Señorita Sybil, scented and beautiful and all-seeing in your shadowy mantilla and roses of red-black velvet, put it down! Leave your caramel-chewers, and glide to my help with your dragon-slaying tongue!

"I have much experience, and see you are not vealthy. I must help you."

That did it. I took coarse measures — and, lying little gent to the last, delicatized them with High School French, *"Je ne suis pas jamais à court d'argent. Jamais! Jamais!"* and, that done, "So sorry I'm leaving you, Mis-ter Markinovich. An important engagement. The Lord Mayor. I'm already late."

"You are proud; you a vilful." His eyes filled with liquid. As one slipping a thick love-letter into a letter-box, he slipped the tin of cigarettes into my sports coat pocket. "Please, I say, not to be proud because your friend is vealthy." As though it had heard him say, "because your friend is suffering," one large tear departed from his less controlled eye, and plunged dead-straight down his cheek.

"I must run, must run," I babbled. "The Lord Mayor. Forgive me. Must run." Cigarettes and horror and all, I jog-trotted across the foyer floored with imitation Moorish tiles, and out of sight which is something one can very rarely say of oneself.

Sybil told me, later, that he left the Plaza foyer almost immediately after I did. That midnight, as she was going to bed, he came tapping at her door to ask for my address, *slyly* tapping, she said.

It was over an hour later when there was a tapping on *my* door. It was not a sly tapping. There, in a kimono of such blinding gaudiness that she looked like Katisha, stood Miss Beveridge with her marchioness's coiffure enclosed and diminished in a net. She spoke, levelly, and with precision.

"Get straight back into bed. We don't want to have you with a chill." She waited. She slightly moved the bed-lamp so the light was not in my eyes. "Now, listen carefully, young man. You are in my house because I permit you to be. So long as, in my house, you conform to the rules of decent society, I ask no more. I make no enquiries about your comings and goings although you are not yet twenty-one. I am not curious about your friends or your habits, so long as I don't find them affecting the reputation of my house. I do not even mind climbing three flights of stairs at a quarter past one in the morning. I do not mind, you understand, if there's a good reason."

I couldn't see her face; it was in shadow. I couldn't help but see her score of rings — diamonds, diamonds, and diamonds — blazing whitely in the light. Their mesmeric effect, her beautifully paced and delivered sentences, my own comfortable bed, all soothed me. Although bewildered I was not disturbed, merely felt older, very man-about-town, with a mistress wearing a cascade of silver fox, and a couple of pounds avoirdupois of charm bracelets.

"I *don't* think there's a good reason," Miss Beveridge was saying, away up there above her exploding diamonds. "There was someone at the front door for you. He wanted to come up."

Miss Beveridge stopped dead. Obviously, it was my move. My mind ran empty and, oddly, absolutely silent. What to say? Who wanted to come up?

"My uncle . . .?" I meant this.

"It was no uncle, young man. It was a foreigner."

Her voice was so horizontal I still didn't cotton on.

"I will not," she said, "not in my house, not at 28 Collins Street, have a young man of your background — or of any background — accepting boxes of chocolates from foreigners. Or from older men — accent or no accent."

I cottoned on. Max Komesaroff! I steamed with mortification and anger.

"I'm terribly sorry, Miss Beveridge. I'll go down. I'll tell him to go."

"I have," she said, "already sent him about his business."

My relief at dirty work done for me was so great that my imagination began to frolic.

"Thank you, Miss Beveridge. He's not a friend, merely an acquaintance." Out came the corny French. "*C'est un original. Mais quel dindon!* He's a Russian aristocrat. White Russian. His parents were hacked to ribbons by the Bolsheviks. He escaped disguised as a vodka-driver." I think I thought, then, that a vodka was a more elegant sort of droshky, though not *exactly* certain what a droshky was — something with bells on and wolves after. "He wanders the world distributing largesse. These cigarettes. . . ." They were on my bedside table.

"I see," said Miss Beveridge. "Why did he give them to you?" She meant something I didn't understand.

I told her I didn't know. She accepted my artlessness. Her diamonds, diamonds, and diamonds picked up the cigarette tin.

"Have you taken up smoking?"

I was surprised at her. Me, smoking? Mistress-keeping, spying in Lhasa, or jewel-stealing in the Jimmy Valentine manner was possible. Smoking? Not yet, not yet.

"I can't bear them. Would you like them?"

"I shall give them to May. From you. Not, of course, mentioning where they originally came from. I'll say it's in gratitude for the invalid port wine."

"It's done me a lot of good," I prattled. "Fortifying. It warms the . . ."

"Yes," said Miss Beveridge in such a way that I knew she knew that the stain on the Melbourne Club wall was May's port wine. "I'll say good morning." She said it. She switched out the light. She closed the door. I suffered insomnia for about four minutes during which I learned that the direct and dispassionate affection of Miss Beveridge and May was a substantial meal. How right Sybil had been to squall against the jonquils and caviar, the objectification of a creepy-crawly love.

Sybil was, however, only right for Sybil. I? The young are never right.

When one is young one sleeps deep, exhausted from
carrying thistledown. One's feelings are of minimal value no
matter how theatrically one bangs the cymbals, and agitates
the tinpot tambourine. Ah, youth! with its brummy outsize
ideals, its outsize ebony heart, its outsize dreams in cheap
fancy dress, its crooked gaze, its almost criminal desire to
steal only the best from others.

What did I, for instance, having stolen Max
Komesaroff's gesture from him, care what happened to him
and his chocolates outside the door Miss Beveridge would
have just not slammed but might just as well have slammed . . . what did I care?

I cared that I had a Miss Beveridge to not-slam awkward
doors for me, that I had Kolker's caviar for a nightcap, and
May's maternal wine on my breakfast tray. That morning I
drank the port before I set out.

It was a two-miles walk from Collins Street to where
Uncle Tasker had staked out his seedy claim amid the lanes
of North Melbourne. By the time I'd reached the last lane I
had thought myself into feeling years older and sager. I was,
nevertheless, singing, although not over-loudly, with
aplomb, and a French song at that. Thus engaged, I entered
the front door of Arcadia, Rexie's THE STUDIO to the
left, Maevene Guildford-Maggs's sanctum sanctoriarium to
the right. *Mon Dieu!* My God! The song died and dried in
my throat.

Before Maevene Guildford-Maggs trilled out,
"Surpraise! Surpraise! Someone to see you!" I had seen the
someone. Max Komesaroff was seated opposite her in the
sanctum sanctoriarium. He sat at indubitable ease as if he
faced a glowing hearth. Between them, between the
refeened bitch and the creepy-crawly, on the top of her
typewriter sat the box of chocolates as large as the Shorter
Oxford. It was open. Its lid with the bow of royal blue ribbon was as it were off for ever. Max Komesaroff was no
longer looking for me. I was the accidental penultimate.
With her fingers arranged in a chocolate-choosing
gesture . . . thumb and middle finger held open-beak-like,
the other fingers in fastidious arcs . . . Maevene Guildford-
Maggs librated hostessishly above what had been turned
away from me and the door of 28 Collins Street.

"Would you," said Maevene Guildford-Maggs, "care to
trai one of mai choc-chocs that your kaind friend has
brought?"

One scarcely needs to write another word.

Boy meets girl stuff. Lonely hearts stuff. Dupes of nature,
and victims of anatomy stuff. Attraction of opposites stuff.
It could even be last-plank-in-a-shipwreck stuff.

Love at first sight?

I wasn't there early enough to see them meet. Earlier, I
could have come upon him . . . as Maevene Guildford-
Maggs had . . . lost in the cat-haunted lanes where, just as
Miss Beveridge had done, I would have sent him about his
business.

His business? A child's business; a tippity-toeing from
diminished adult to diminished adult in vain attempts to
give away his vanity and himself, his symbolic self, in the
form of too many chocolates, and wine too sweet, and
flowers too many and too sweet and too scented, and what
he called love, a thing too sickly for anyone except
Maevene Guildford-Maggs. She had given up expecting,
years ago, that a Mr Right would appear with the marsh-
mallow truths she could substitute for her terribly untidy
lies.

This story, being no more, no more at all than a happy-
ever-after one, ends, within two months after their meeting, at the Methodist Church, Footscray, the bride —
according to Brenda or Tootsie — looking very nice, for
someone as senile as thirty-four, in lilac lace: Rexie's design.
This knowledge of her age was a mere fraction of the fund
of information the Arcadia people revealed themselves as
possessed of. Max Komesaroff was forty-five, and had
owned half a gambling saloon in Exhibition Street which
she'd persuaded him to sell for a live-in pawnshop in
Russell Street. This was considered by everyone except Leo
Ryan to be an exchange both shrewd and prudent, as well as
socially advantageous. The last distinction was too subtle
for my still rustic perception. I discovered, moreover, why
these city people had never told her to shut her big nagging
gob. Although maddening them to the point of mayhem,
she remained no more than a mean, spoilt child for whom

they were sorry. Her real name was, to my amazement, Mavis Maggs.

"You didn't know!" screeched Brenda or Tootsie. "But everyone knew! How could *she* have a toff's name? Her dad's a plumber at Footscray. A real booze-artist. You must of seen him here when he used to come to borrow from her. He was in and out all the time. You've seen him."

I hadn't, and said so.

"Anyway, you'll see him at the wedding."

I wouldn't, and didn't say so. I hadn't been asked, although everyone, including Uncle Tasker, had.

As an accidental and rather tenuous kind of *deus ex machina* I felt I should almost have been best man, and still sometimes wonder if it were the strange behaviour of my paternal grandmother, Maevene Eugenie Charlotte, or the fact that I was vilful and proud at the Plaza, or that I had Katisha in diamonds as a watch-dog at 28 Collins Street, that caused me to be excluded.

Ah, the Depression! Ah, the violinists playing "Little Grey Home in the West" in the indigo wind at twilight street corners; and the prostitutes in eye-veils and silver fox in the lamplight of Alexandra Avenue; and the El Greco young men with their backs pressed to the woman-warm bricks of bakehouse walls! Ah, the three great spheres of false gold at Komesaroff's, and the people streaming along Russell Street to Komesaroff's with their gospel-true gold-cable bracelets and wedding rings and little hearts with one ruby in.

Ah, Mr and Mrs Komesaroff!

My paternal grandfather was English, military and long-nosed. He married twice, and had seven sons and four daughters. My maternal grandfather, Swiss, agricultural and long-nosed, married once but had six sons and six daughters. As a child, therefore, I was well-provided not only with ancestral aunts and uncles but also with the uncle-husbands and wife-aunts they had married. Since each of these couples was abundantly productive, long-nosed cousins of all ages, from braggart striplings and chatterbox young women to india-rubber babies like tempestuous Queen Victorias with bonnets awry congested my boyhood. It seems to me now that what my grandparents imported to Australia along with fecundity and long noses was largely noise. Noise, in their case, can be enlarged to cover vivacity bordering on uproar, devil-may-care wildness, a febrile intensity about issues of great unimportance. From the most feckless uncle to the most social aunt, from bread-line-treading aunts to rich uncles, all were afflicted by this rowdy insouciance. My mother, essentially provincial, was nevertheless giddy as a porpoise, and lived like a windmill rotating to alternate gusts of temper and charm.

In this uproarious tribal whirlpool I was odd boy out. A throwback inheritance of some less mettlesome blood braked me. I had the same passion for decorous behaviour as they had for fits-and-starts behaviour, for conversations at full pitch, for gambling and gipsying about. This perversity of self-restraint caused me to lag behind, to be a some-time observer rather than a full-time participant. Yet, oddly enough, I also had maximum *esprit de corps*. Nor was I niminy-piminy and stand-offish. Japan-shaped scabs

blotched my fruit-stealer's country boy knees; my bare soles
were as rind-like as fire-walkers'. I could swim like a toad,
swear like a cow-cocky and smoke like a *débutante*. These
abilities and simulated ferocities were, however, strictly
conventional. In their execution I went just so far. I drew a
line. Other members of the family always went farther and
further. I would not, for example, kill snakes as Uncle
Foster and cousins and brothers did by cracking them like
whips. Sticks did me. As well as affecting protective discre-
tions such as this, and making withdrawals from hereditary
bravura, I often broke the wrong rules. My brothers and
country cousins each had a dog, usually a bossy fox-terrier
or a smart-alec mong with lots of heeler in it. I had a cat. I
found its relative muteness and disdainful independence
preferable to the ostentatious servility and noisily
neurasthenic demands of dogs. Need I say that I wore spectacles and spoke in polysyllables?

Not only did I violate the clan code by visible non-
conformity but I was mentally and invisibly rebellious. This
was harder to swear at. I believed, as all we youngsters did,
that broken-backed snakes could not die until the sun set,
that warts grew where dogs licked one, that to gash the skin
linking thumb with forefinger caused lockjaw which we
translated as instant and eternal dumbness. Along with the
mob I circumspectly believed in ghosts, the end of the
world and Spring-heel Jack. Then I ran off the rails. As
logic's advocate I believed, for longer than was deemed
orthodox or manly, in Father Christmas: his leavings were
evidence. I did not believe in God who had let me down in
the matter of prayers for a Meccano set. To the terror of the
others, I said so piercingly enough for the vast ear in the sky
to take in the blasphemy. I became the tree for believers not
to stand by when lightning flashed.

More disconcerting and shaming than even blasphemy
was my most eccentric trait. I cherished the family caprices
and florid behaviour so much that I came out of my com-
parative silence to exult — in public — over what my kith
and kin accepted as one does a birthmark better hidden. I let
out, to the dirt-rimmed and contemptuous sons of the
washerwoman, that Swiss grandfather's daughters, in order
of birth, were named Rosa Bona, Adelina, Sophia, Maria,

Meta and Ida. I explained that each name, besides ending in
A, had, sequentially, one letter less. My brothers, failing to
shut me up or divert interest from my humiliating treason,
looked bleakly down their noses. I continued to rattle on,
chattily revealing my disappointment that there had not
been two more aunts born — a final aunt, a fabulous
creature called Aunt A, would have exhilarated me more
than my favourite Sago Plum Pudding. The family,
boorishly I thought, instead of these cunningly graduated
names, used Bon, Addie, Sophie, Ria, Min Min and Doll. It
irked my senses of order as much as my sense of possession
to hear my mother called not Aunt Ida but Auntie Dolly.
As a gesture, although Aunt Rosa Bona and Aunt Adelina
were mouthfuls, I prissily insisted on using the full names. I
was inflexible in not saying Uncle Whit, Uncle Gat and
Uncle Tini to my paternal uncles who had been christened
Whitworth, Gatling and Martini-Henry after firearms. My
military grandfather's other sons were Lancaster, Enfield,
Snider and Mauser.

Though pointing an attitude, my delight in these absur-
dities of baptism was a little only of the magnetism my
flamboyant relations had for me. Even a porcupine regards
its own as soft and sleek. I overdid it: my blood-porcupines
were powder-puffs and satin to me.

Each aunt and uncle had at least one dashing foible which
still, now, years later, enchants my nostalgic middle age as
much as it then enchanted me. I know now, alas, that
behind the screen of levity and animal spirits lay concealed
human imperfections, guile, improvidence, stupidity, mendacity, anguishes of every variety and even downright tragedy. In those days, however, I gaped at everything I heard
or overheard of their vivid and forthright doings. These
legends, which they dramatically recounted of themselves
and of each other, so magnified them that they swaggered
and swept by, heroes and Amazons, along the rim of my
mind's horizon, casting miles-long shadows as blinding as
searchlight rays. When these nobilities appeared before me
in the flesh I could still gape, for I was not yet ready for disillusion. Reality matched imagination. About the family,
anyway, I was the Three Wise Monkeys.

I was stimulated by Uncle Martini-Henry's waxed

moustache, and malacca, and watch-chain with its shark-tooth *breloque* as much as by the saga of his earlier bush-whacking adventures, by Uncle Whitworth's plush-lined pipe-cases, by Aunt Rosa Bona's garden gorged with flowers so large and crisp as to appear edible. I was captivated by their houses which smelt variously of strawberry jam cooking, or furniture polish and Brasso, or cut lemons, or Eau de Cologne, or boiled-over milk, or cats and cigars. Because, indeed, the mind and its shadow senses do preserve a detailed past, I still recall the smell of Uncle Mauser's Turkish cigarettes or Aunt Sophia's glycerine soap, the exact disposition of Mazzawattee tea-canisters and gilt-handled vases long destroyed, still feel the Greek key pattern embossing the rim of Aunt Adelina's fruit-plates, still hear Melba hooting *Home, Sweet Home* through the toffee-coloured, convolvulus-shaped horn of Aunt Meta's gramophone.

I seized every opportunity to stock a granary of impressions. I picked up whole and wonderful sentences thrown carelessly down among cake-crumbs and tea-slopped saucers; tucked away luminous smiles released in happy-go-lucky flights at picnics; carried off, as it were, armloads of cuttings from virile and showy plants in a garden where summer seemed perfect and unending. How cruelly endless now seems a deadlier season.

As children in a spread-out but gregariously inclined sept, my cousins and brothers and sisters and I, during school holidays, were always everywhere but in our own rowdy nests. We were interchanged like home-made tokens of affection. Those of us who were suburban were bundled off to country aunts and uncles; those who were country bumpkins went citywards. Children are pickers-up. Each child returned home bearing objects that, almost valueless otherwise, were sacred mementoes, and doubly sacred as being something for nothing. I remember my sisters bringing back shoe-buckles, wildernesses of embroidery silks, bone crochet needles, Piver's powder boxes, raped-looking dolls, and fans still releasing from their broken wings shadows of a scent long out of fashion and the name of which nobody knew. At one time or another, my brothers brought back wilting lizards in jars of spirits, cigar-boxes of

cigar-bands, a carved emu's egg, tortoise-shell pen-knives
with broken blades, a rectangular tennis-racquet and, on a
notable occasion, Uncle Snider's elderly banjo. These things
were rubbish but, like tourist souvenirs, retained enough
glamour just long enough to garnish the short interval
before, coach into pumpkin, holiday turned back to
workaday.

As the one child in this riotous shuffling to and fro who
was family-obsessed and a born archivist, I was a magpie of
a different colour. I wanted more of Uncle Snider's past
than an unplayable banjo. I wanted facts, dates, the how
and why and where, all possible information about the pasts
of the living gods and goddesses I paid homage to. My eyes
must have glittered as much as my spectacles when I was
given dated menu cards of P. and O. dinners, Masonic dinners, mayoral dinners, or old theatre programmes, ball programmes, invitations to exhibitions and weddings. It
steadied the spinning world to fix an eye on the fact that
Aunt Adelina had gone to a wedding on June 24, 1911. It
added depth and richness to my knowledge that she was
still going to weddings. Postcards were special grist to my
enthusiastic mill. Since my aunts and uncles had been young
in the late nineteenth century and early twentieth century,
that era of postcard-sending and postcard-collecting, I had
many reefs to mine. It was a fascinating find, say, that, in
Victoria Street, North Williamstown, on February 13,
1913, Uncle Gatling received a certain message on a
postcard which showed a ragged negro Topsy, her head
spiked like a battle-mace with plaits, submerging her face in
a monster semi-lune of water-melon under the words AH'S
UP TO MAH EARS IN IT. Below her toes which were
splayed out like pianist's fingers, the sentence finished AT
ST KILDA. Written on the back in violet ink was:

> *Dear Gat,*
> *Take a gander at the coon on the other side!!!! Just a line to say
> all the Jokers will be foregathering at the White Hart next Sat.
> about 3. Expecting a hot time!! Don't wear that bokker!!!! Harry.*

I begged postcards of all sorts: *Sunset on the Nile, Miss
Billie Burke, Miss Zena Dare,* cards of padded velvet roses,
cards garishly illustrating boarding-house and mother-in-

law jokes. I was, nevertheless, really hunting photographs — footballer uncles striped like barbers' poles; Aunt Sophia under a cartwheel hat of ostrich feathers, and horse-collared by a boa; Uncle Enfield, whom I knew as a well-tailored sphere with an eye-glass, as a cock-eyed skinamalink in Little Lord Fauntleroy velvet; Aunt Meta, with unpainted lips, bare shoulders and a cumulus of hair, emerging glass-eyed as a hairdresser's wax model from a nest of chiffon.

So feverish did I become, repeating my overtures as monotonously as creation, that I exhausted family teasing into recognition of my fervour. I was understood to be some sort of notary. Spring-cleaning aunts sent me packets of photographs; uncles put aside for me dim, henna-coloured snapshots (*Me at Leongatha Woodchop*, 1920) or postcards of magenta-nosed drunks with crayfish semaphoring from their hip-pockets which they had dug out of drawers holding the treasures of a lifetime . . . sovereign-cases, insurance policies, opal tie-pins, wives' first love-letters, and the halves of pairs of cuff-links. Proff became my nickname, and my bottom was pinched affectionately. On my behalf, archaeology into their own racy and cluttered pasts became an accepted pastime of my aunts and uncles.

Alas!

At the height of my miniature fame, at the unornamental age of ten, a bee-keeper stung by his own bee, I fell in love with a photograph. I fell deeply, unfalteringly and hauntedly in love.

The photograph came in a packet of postcards from Aunt Meta. Had I not been alone in the house, with nobody peering over my shoulder, I could have been saved a long ecstasy and a savage destruction. Alone I was, however, when the postman came; alone I unwrapped my gift and, among postcards of Gaiety Girls, and snapshots of bowler-hatted uncles in jinkers, and ant-waisted aunts leaning on or being leaned on by bicycles, alone I came upon my fate. Nothing can undo what was done that instant, that day.

I saw the photograph. The door of the one addled world I had known closed softly behind me. I was in the ante-room to Paradise. Its bejewelled throne was mine. I perceived that all loves experienced in the back-room past were imaginary, were delusions, were nothing. I had been wastefully librating above shadows — however spirited; visions — however cock-a-hoop; hollow beings; deceptive shapes; creatures of gauze; dresses empty of women; names without men to them. I had had merely a bowing acquaintance with love.

The photograph was of a girl about my own age. She was dressed in Dolly Varden-ish costume. Since she held a shepherd's crook feminized by a large bow I gathered she was being Bo Peep for a fancy dress party. Or was she Bo Peep herself? There was nothing on the photograph to tell. The tilted oval of hat with its rosebuds and ribbons, the black hatching of the elbow-length mittens, the criss-cross-laced bodice, all excited me romantically. What flooded into my being, however, to reveal inner depths and expanses never revealed before, was the illumination from the smile and the eyes. It did not occur to me that what really confronted the smile and the eyes was a camera like half-a-concertina on a tripod which was concealed with a nameless human under a black cloth. No! That faintly scented smile was for me. Those eyes, bottomless, and yet of dark sharpness, were looking into me. A gale of voices whirled through the galleries of my consciousness, aromatizing them, purging them of all former presences, and calling out deliciously, "Thou!"

"Thou!"

I was eavesdropping on eternity.

Eternity is time's victim.

Eternity had scarcely begun when I heard my mother at the front door. With the unflurried movements of a master criminal I put the photograph in an inside pocket. I was aware that the pocket was on the left, and the divine face deliberately turned inwards. The eyes looked directly into my heart which I imagined crimson as a playing-card heart, plump as an artichoke, and composed of a material with the texture of magnolia petals. I extinguished the lights in my face, swept up the other photographs with a gambler's gesture and, as my mother entered, cried out . . . oh, perfect imitation of a frank and guileless boy . . . "Look what Aunt Meta sent!" Not a word about the divinity staring into my heart, not a word. I said nothing then. I kept the photograph and my love hidden for seven years. I said nothing ever.

Because my pockets and chest-of-drawers were subject to maternal investigation it was necessary to be on guard against discovery. I cannot remember, now, all my love's hiding-places when I could not carry her with me. When I had to desert her under the paper lining a boot-box of silk-worms, behind a loose skirting-board or in the never-read bible, heavy as a foundation-stone, I believed the subtle smile to dissolve away and those unflinching eyes to be in sleep.

That my idolatry persisted and became more intense was — still is — astounding for, too violently soon, I was, in years, older than she. In all else but my worship I changed. She did not change, although her beauty took on other meanings; her eyes displayed truths that, at one and the same time, vacillated like the opalescence on black oil, and remained steady and mystifying as infinity.

I changed. The family changed. Their lustihood, anima-tion, over-large gesturings and vitality, if one took a quick look, were unabated. Closer examination showed the gilt flaking off, or a hair-fine crackle of flaws. Like plates left too long in the oven some older aunts and uncles illustrated that they had been long enough in the oven of life. As wrinkles darned themselves more closely around eyes, as hair wore away or became margined with white, as figures broadened or became juiceless, curving downwards towards the earth that was their destination, perhaps what I noticed most was an increase of braggadocio and hullabaloo. High spirits were larded with slangy defiance; hilarity was so constant that cause and effect were lost sight of, and no longer had value. No one seemed to dare to ask, "Why are we laughing?" but went on defiantly laughing. All those epic suns that had warmed my earlier boyhood were declin-ing in a sky flushed with stubborn anger.

Most gaudy of these declines was Aunt Maria's. For years the family had called her the Merry Widow: singular title to hold among so many married couples. Maria's hus-band had been, I endlessly kept on overhearing and was endlessly told, handsome, rich, gifted, charming, and so on. I concluded that the dead were inevitably possessed of all the attributes the living have few or none of. Luxuriance of graces seemed a necessary qualification for death. It was a tragedy, they all said, that he should have died two months after marriage. He and dear Ria, they all said, had been a perfectly matched couple, madly in love. At first, I gathered, Maria had sought consolation in travel; later, in travel and port wine; ultimately, in less travel, more port wine, and — they lowered their voices so that I listened harder and heard more — and young men.

I saw her rarely. She was sensationally made-up. Her sardonicisms were hoarsely outrageous. Scent breezed from her furs wherein glittered the mean eyes of foxy faces chiselling snouts into their own expensive bodies; rings bulged her kid gloves; she smoked baby-blue, primrose and lilac cigarettes tipped with gold. She was the clan scandal. She belonged to the family, but she belonged in the manner of some elaborate pet with unusual vices. These were understood to age her. Virtues, nevertheless, aged the virtuous others as inexorably: simplicities aged to idiosyncrasies, habits to affectations, lovable quiddities to boring eccentricities.

As for myself, I reached the stage of rubbing vaseline on a breath of moustache. I started brilliantine which my parents regarded in much the same light as opium-smoking. I whined for adult caste-marks such as cuff-links and a wristlet watch. I was, evanescently, of that self-loving, self-pitying, unbearable race which invents loneliness and boredom, and in which all the major evils of humanity are in powerful bud. I was an adolescent of sour seventeen.

From the arrogant, dirty-minded, unaesthetic and altogether unworthy side of my nature, I found absolution only in my photograph. Since I was insufferably older and in my first long trousers, mother no longer, without fair warning, rifled my pockets with cries of "How long have you been using this revolting handkerchief?" The photograph, therefore, was able to stand constantly at my heart in a morocco wallet Uncle Lancaster had given me. The eyes I had looked into so often during seven years still offered me, from the midst of their dark moonlight, a prophetic truth; the smile seemed still that of one whispering "Thou!" and promising all affirmations, all peace, all wisdom, all love.

At this stage, my moustache still unawakened, brilliantine still anathema to my mother, my wrist still watchless, and the days a passion of ennui, Aunt Maria came to the country town we lived in.

One night, while we were at dinner, the telephone rang. Mother left the table and the room to answer it. We heard her squeal ecstatically in the distance. She returned looking younger, and had gone rosy under the eyes. That rosiness said to us children, "*Rattled!*" Father was away. Mother was at our mercy. The six of us stared at her in a certain manner. Mother stared bravely back.

"Aunt Ria's here," she said at last, over-nonchalantly and not sitting down again. "And stop that. Immediately. I'll tell your father. Take that smug expression off your smug faces."

"Sit, down, mother *dear*," we said. "Relaxez-vous. Collect your thoughts. Don't be shy. Speak out. Give us the dirt, mama. Or *we'll* tell papa."

She remained standing, and said, "Stop that. Immediately. Or I'll scream the house down." She looked at the clock with a pretence of vagueness. "She's travelling through to Sydney. She's staying overnight at the Terminus."

"Ah, *ha*!" It was my twelve-year-old sister. "Is she dee-ah-you-en-kay? Is she coming to see her poor relations?"

"No," said mother, and "How dare you, miss?" and sat down as if there was nothing else to do. "She says she's too tired."

"She *is* dee-ah-you . . ."

"Stop that," cried mother. "How dare you suggest that Ria . . . how dare you, miss? She's had a very tragic life." Her eyes hinted tears, but she finger-tipped her just-marcelled shingle with gratification. Her inward eye was riffling through her wardrobe.

"What's the time? Is that clock fast or slow or right? I have to go down and see her."

Have meant, we knew, *am so excited I can hardly wait*.

As eldest son and deputy man-of-the-house, I went with mother.

The Terminus Hotel was a hive of inactivity. The Guests' Drawing-room, to which several palms gave the atmosphere of a down-at-heel Winter Garden, contained only Aunt Maria and a young man. They sat, deep in moquette armchairs, with the air of people who have been sitting for a long time. Between them a Benares-brass-tray table held their drinks, and a whisky-advertising ash-tray fuming like a rubbish-tip with butts bloodstained by lipstick.

"My loves!" cried Aunt Maria huskily, hoisting herself upright. Scarcely less loudly, out of the corner of her mouth, she also said, "Get up, you lout, when a lady enters the room."

From under the horizontal single eyebrow which served both eyes the young man spat a glance at her which I recognized for I had ejected just such a glance at my mother when she had publicly revealed that I wrote poetry or bit my fingernails. The young man, handsome in an unlit fashion, brutally stood.

Most of what happened after does not matter.

Aunt Maria was fairly drunk. For a woman of fifty she had kept enough of her figure. Her dress and shoes were in the safely faultless taste that costs money. Her hair, of dead black, was astrakhan-crinkled, and had obviously also cost, colour and design, much money.

We were an unmatched quartette but, whatever lay under the surface of the evening, Aunt Maria and my mother gave no apparent thought to it. My aunt's one rebuke to the young man had vibrated instantly to silence. She introduced him as Ivan Something but, with a kind of marital mockery, addressed him as Ee-fahn. She disregarded him but not pointedly. One felt she might, later in the evening, as she walked much too carefully bedwards, have to stop and say, "My God! My Ee-fahn! I nearly forgot him!" as of an umbrella. She had, so to speak, already walked away leaving a number of umbrellas.

The conversation was overlapping gabble between the two sisters, and was family, family, family. They giggled, they shrieked. Diagonally across their chit-chat Ee-fahn reconnoitred me with monosyllabic information about weight-lifting. It was Urdu to me. I sat egg-faced wishing his eyebrow on my lip. He lowered his eyebrow like a perambulator-hood, and withdrew under it to drink brandies. Aunt Maria drank port after port. Saying "No, *no* Ria!

Not one more drink. I'll be featherstitching!" mother had two, three and then four Drambuies. I was permitted two beer-shandies.

My adoration of family personalities and goings-on having subsided with puberty, I was not merely uninterested in Aunt Maria, but bored, shamed and revolted. Before me, I thought, were the classic lineaments of immorality. Its surface moved as though lined with decayed elastic, it grimaced, it winked, it pleated itself to laugh, and yet was dead. Its lips, from which the lipstick had worn centrally off to reveal a naked mauve, writhed about. The eyes seemed to flash darkly but that was an illusion fostered by restlessness. They dared not tarry moveless under their glistening blue lids.

So, utterly fed-up, attempting to buy escape by startling mother into awareness of me and the late hour, I took out my wallet and opened it in a manly way. This gesture stopped mother in her tracks.

"I should like to buy . . ." I could not think of the word for a number of drinks " . . . to buy some drinks."

"The naughty love!" cried Aunt Maria. "You know, Doll, he's going to be quite a good-looker, even with the gig-lamps. Dear boy, you mustn't waste your substance on filthy-rich aunts."

She reached and took the wallet from me, took it between forefinger and thumb by one corner, and held it up, and waggled it. This was no more than old-fashioned, ex-girlish playfulness, Lily Langtry skittishness, but was earthquake and annihilation to me. From the wallet on to the brass table fell my secret, my silence, my peace, my dreams, my years of devotion, the photograph with its undefiled gaze and smile, the smile of my first love.

I was too stricken to snatch, to save, to conceal.

"A dark horse, Doll," said Aunt Maria, taking up the photograph. "A Casanova. The girl friend." Focusing, she held the photograph at arm's length.

"Who? Who is that? Who?" said mother, hand outstretched.

There is a moment when, for the first time, Life is no longer seen in exquisite profile.

Life turns full-face to one, swiftly and savagely, and

unshutters her eyes. There is nothing to be seen in their recesses but the evidence of destruction, of negation, perspectives of nullity. Peace, one sees, is perjury. The gods are down-and-out. The jewelled throne one slumbered on is no more than a rock in wasteland. The flowers one thought to have been thrown at one's feet are seen to be not flowers but the rotting wings of shapes that flew ecstatically into emptiness, and circled in emptiness, and starved there, and fell. One is, for the first time, aware of mortality, and learns in a flash that death is the one sure possession.

"Who?" said Aunt Maria, horribly smiling and smiling at the photograph. "Look, Doll. Look at the sweet, quaint little sobersides."

"Where *did* you get this?" said my mother.

"Found it. I found it," I said, my voice thick with lies and hate. "I found it in the drawer. Where the old photographs used to be. This afternoon."

"Remember, Doll?" said Aunt Maria, knocking over her wine. "Lolly Edward's party? My God, I shouldn't care to shout from the rooftop how long ago that was. You were Miss Muffet. Remember, Doll? Show Ee-fahn what a serious duck of a Bo Peep I was."

And the drunken woman with wine-scummed eyes agitated the dying muscles of her loose and painted mouth, and began to laugh hoarsely, and I heard what I heard, and saw what I saw, and my heart broke.

Brett

When Benito Mussolini was Il Duce the Milan railway station was built.

Architecture without much conscience, it is edificial, colossal, and not unfittingly dictatorial. It is also very dreary: an intention to grandeur of the sublime kind doesn't at all come off. A facade of would-be triumphal arches leads into a succession of vast, austere lobbies, seemingly limitless, and far too lofty. Here, misshapen echoes vault cumbrously and forlornly about like headaches with nowhere to settle.

Once through the first dolorous arcade the traveller is confronted and affronted by a cyclopean alp of stairs which suggests by its mathematical cruelty the incline of an Aztec ziggurat. This scarp of livid stone depresses rather than overawes: it must be toiled up to attain the platforms from one of which *l'accelerato* starts south to run through Lombardy towards Parma, Bologna, Florence, and the ever-flowing, ever-cold fountains of Rome.

On a bleak afternoon in late November, a day of drizzle from a steel-grey sky onto a seal-grey city, Jean D. and I were being farewelled at the station by the Australian Consul-General's wife with whom we had lunched. Afterwards she had come with us to a refrigerated Santa Maria della Grazie while, as our planned last sight-seeing in Milan, we looked again at Leonardo da Vinci's *The Last Supper*.

We were both wary again-lookers drifting through the Old World in the direction of the equator, and back to Australia. Middle-aged, unpassionate but firm friends, hard-bitten tourists, we were revisiting together what we had, when younger, separately visited before. To sum up our itinerary — a Harry's Bar or a Trader Vic's was as much part of it as any Gothic polyptych, Byzantine mosaic or Bernini triton.

Somewhat chastened by *The Last Supper*, we were to catch the two-fifty for Florence.

The three of us stood flinching in the maelstrom of draughts at the foot of the grim cliff of stairs while Mario the consular chauffeur unloaded our baggage from the consular Fiat.

It was I perhaps who first noticed the young woman: her face. It was the Consul-General's wife who first spoke of her.

"Now *that*," she said, "is what I should be wearing." She added, "With my impossible legs."

Jean D. and I, prudent cowards, looked neither at each other nor the legs we'd already noted as misproportionately strapping beneath the Consul-General's wife's svelte upper, and her delicately hollow face. We gave instead the keenest attention to what the young woman wore, the back-view as she ascended with much grace the Teotihuacán-like steep.

It was the year when the pitiless fashion of the mini-skirt was just giving way to a more humane one; freakish legs were returning to the seductive obscurity of longer skirts. In England, Germany, and France we had already seen numbers of women wearing the new style. The one before our eyes was the first we'd seen in Italy. A maxi-coat recalling a Ukrainian Cossack's, and worn with Russian boots, it was not only fitting wear for the untender wintriness of the day but strikingly set off its wearer's tallness and litheness. The flared skirt and its border of fur lilted romantically as she mounted the steps with all the stylish bravado of a *jeune premier* in a Graustarkian operetta. The two women with me went into analytical raptures which I did not interrupt with:

"But did you see her face?"

Useless to interrupt: had they seen it they would by then have forgotten: the Cossackian coat had become headless to them.

It was clear that what had caught my eye had not caught theirs: a face so like Eleanor da Toledo's in the Angelo Bronzino portrait that I felt myself go actually open-mouthed with amazement. It was, in effect, double amazement. There I was, about to board *l'accelerato* for Florence where one of the reasons for a proposed trek through the endless little salons of the Uffizi Gallery was to moon yet again, for the fifth or sixth time, in front of that very portrait with its sealed, cool countenance, its eyes depthless with indifference. Extraordinarily alike, portrait and passer-by: for an absurd moment it seemed reasonable to accept that Eleanor da Toledo could be a sixteenth-century ancestress of the supple stranger whose face was not only too impassive and impenetrable, a courtly mask, but whose hatless black hair was arranged much as the woman in the painting had arranged hers — was that looking-glass still alive? — more than three centuries ago.

Reason alone, I knew, is too fallible. That glimpse of her, fleeting yet charged, was no more than one from which a poem might be made, taut with regret because both the world and the Milan railway station were boundless enough for me and Eleanor da Toledo's reincarnation never to be breathing again at the same time the same freezing air with its odour of damp metal.

Jean D. and I said good-bye to the Consul-General's wife at the bottom of the steps, and climbed — how much less buoyantly than the tall girl with the still face and swashbuckling coat! — up and up into the skirmish of echoes, and the arctic cross-currents of inexplicable little indoor winds.

It would have matched my mood of Baudelairean spleen to find every seat in the train taken, and the corridor jammed with a rain-soaked herd of pilgrims on their way to Rome. The train was far from crowded. In the eight-seater *seconda classe* compartment where we settled five minutes before departure there were only three passengers.

In one window-seat was a very fat Italian woman, fiftyish, high-bosomed, with an adolescent moustache.

Opposite her sat a stocky young man brutally handsome as a brigand.

Their attire announced that they were possibly of the lower middle class, in any country the most conventional, and therefore the most easily identified. They wore the sort of clothes seen behind the plate-glass of smaller department stores, the uniform of the hide-bound and frugal, unemphatic wear, factory-made of artificial materials. The one thing about them not *ersatz* was their behaviour; but even that, taking into consideration the melodramatic country we were in, was orthodox enough.

They were patently mother and son: a family profile jutted out of her blubber and his sullenness, and they were so engrossed in a generation tiff that they neither spared us a side-glance nor lost an impassioned syllable when we came in. They were both holding forth at the one time; her soprano railing went volubly on above his fierce baritone declaiming over and over again:

"*Non è stata colpa mia!*" — whatever it was it wasn't his fault — "*Non è stata colpa mia, mamma! Non . . . è . . . stata . . . colpa . . . mia!*"

On the badgered son's side of the compartment, plumb in the middle, the half-clock-face of the air-conditioning switch directly above his hair which was like marcelled iron, sat another Italian, perhaps seventy, perhaps only sixty: it was hard to tell. Not once in the two-and-a-half hours he was with us did we hear him speak, or catch his eye.

He sat monolithically upright as a stone Rameses, contentedly withdrawn, his scoured, sun-darkened hands inactively set on his hams. The contours and rich rustic colouring of his face reminded me of an Arcimboldi one, a composition of corn-cobs, pomegranates, chestnuts, and onions. He seemed so much of the earth that we'd have to be, one felt, famished oxen or ailing vines, before his attention would turn to us, and his unreflective eyes come to life. He could, of course, have been a rugged solitary who despised the vile world, and played Ravel exquisitely.

I sat on the so-to-speak masculine side of the compartment, in the corner next to the corridor. Jean arranged herself opposite and, as we usually did on train journeys, we began the process of retracting somewhat from each other. She opened her guidebook at, I had no doubt, the chapter on Florence. A loud-speaker voice gabbling truculently against its own several echoes announced that our train was about to leave. I experienced that sensation of feline well-being mingled with here-we-go-again boredom the experienced traveller is apt to experience at such times.

Then, at the last moment, mere seconds before the

wheels turned, the young woman in the Cossack coat flashed radiantly into sight at the doorway, scanned the compartment with lustrous heartless eyes, and appeared to find it worthy of her. From where she stood, and deftly as a basketball player throwing a goal, she tossed her valise onto the rack.

This *coup de théâtre* accomplished, she moved in, and sat with decisive aplomb between Jean D. and the fat mother who, at a climax of son-baiting, her wattles aquiver, spat out a scalding babble of insult. The victim had had enough. Harshly crying, *"Non l'ho fatto apposta!"* — I didn't do it on purpose! — he folded his arms as though barricading himself behind them, set his jaws, and closed his eyes. A door had been slammed in a face.

Furtively, as if sidling from an unhallowed cathedral, the train slipped between the soaring nave piers, through a rood screen of grimy girders, over the no-altar, and out into the Milanese rain so like all other rains, the dejected industrial outskirts that could have been anywhere.

All this, and a funereal burden of smoke lowering above a palisade of chimney-stacks, I took in from the corner of my senses. For the rest I was covertly but wholly taking in the unbelievable late arrival.

She was, I saw, years younger than Bronzino's Eleanor, but twentieth-century experiences had given her an additional gloss of age in a dimension beyond years. Self-possession's self, she lit a cigarette, and opened a Penguin. The nails of the ringless, long long Renaissance fingers were bitten. That was a touch jarringly too human and modern, and stopped me in my tracks on the poetic by-path I'd taken. The Penguin was Elizabeth Bowen's *To the North*.

So, as well as being a nail-biter, she wasn't a Latin after all! This reversed sign-post was more than intriguing: I contemplated a remark about Elizabeth Bowen. Jean D. was ahead of me.

The proximity of the fur-trimmed Cossack sleeve to her Scotch tweed one generated some electricity of intuition. My friend closed the guidebook in a final way and, with the certainty that the animal in the cage she was entering was of a familiar species, spoke to the young woman. The species certainly was familiar; the animal ready to play, and without reserve. She was also Australian. She had been working for three months, *au pair* but with a small salary, as nurse-maid to the baby twins of a Signor and Signora Russo, at Parma. Oh, she was absolutely without reserve. She abhorred Parma, she said, loathed the Signor who was, like all Dago men, sly and a sex maniac; scorned the Signora; and couldn't stand babies. And the meals! *Pasta*, no matter what shape or colour, she hated. Veal too, and sausages containing God knows what. As for the continental breakfast, that was hardly food at all, or at most:

"*Slum* food, actually. Bread-and-jam and cocoa — and I *detest* crusts!"

She was twenty going on twenty-one. Her name was Brett Something-or-Other. Had her mother been reading Hemingway when she was pregnant? I didn't ask although dying to. Perhaps, as people do to lighten the hard work of travel, she would come to telling.

Travellers, imprisoned with strangers in foreign trains, ships' bars, air-terminal waiting-rooms, chartered tourist buses lunging through Turkey or Afghanistan, are inclined to foil ennui by being as unreticent about themselves as characters in a Chekhov play.

About themselves: how else keep their identity in places they do not belong to?

About themselves: even though the impression they more often than not create is of eccentricity, recklessness, animal cunning, of an incredible toughness shot through with peculiar snobberies and almost-idiot simplicities. Perhaps Brett would later clear up why she had been named Brett. As I listened to her talking to Jean D. in an educated, extrovert voice, it was manifest she had no thought of hiding anything.

I am, her manner said, what I am: lump it or leave it.

While exchanging *dragées* and peppermints and cigarettes, the women exchanged more and more of themselves, admitting me to their confidences but off-handedly, as though I were scarcely human, a dummy on the side-line. For all her poise (the panache, for example, with which she'd entered the compartment) she seemed to live in perpetual suspense. Her version of herself was hounded and harassed, a chronic Victim of Fate. It was done humorously, yet, as I laughed, I felt alarm at what catastrophe might be just ahead: some of the past catastrophes, however hilariously she presented them, seemed to me hair-raising, rape or murder an inch off.

She was always losing things, her passport, traveller's cheques, a camera, or leaving her purse with the last of her money in it at some place so disreputable that there was no hope of its being returned. She missed trains or buses to find herself stranded among near-cutthroats at unhealthy hours, drifted solo into the back-alley haunts of criminals and prostitutes; found herself fighting off inflamed lechers in places so out-of-the-way that no Good Samaritan would have heard her scream. Once she and an Australian girl-friend, speeding through Germany in a rented car had run down a deer on the outskirts of East Berlin at three o'clock in the morning, and had spent three days and nights in a lock-up.

"The food," she said, "was miraculous — *Kaffee mit Sahne*, yet!"

She was, she said, in trouble at the moment, with not a brass razoo to her name, down to her last unbroached packet of cigarettes, and nearly three days late in getting back from the week-end she had nagged Signora Russo into letting her spend in Milan.

"Everything, but everything, happens to poor Brett," she said complacently.

Meantime, outside, a landscape like a rain-botched *grisaille*, sodden Lombardy slid murkily by between the profiles of mother and son. He had been permitted a length of sanctuary behind the barrier of his folded arms and shut-tered eyes while she dipped at mechanic intervals into a black plastic carry-all for titbits she chewed with the engrossed mien of a plot-hatcher. A moment arrived when she was sated, and had ruminated her next move into shape. She attacked again, sharply: *"Carlo!"*

No response so, more sharply, louder: *"Car-lo, Car-lo!"*

Once more, no response.

The jelly of her face stiffened: she knew he heard within the fort. From among the chattels banked up around her she groped out a chubby umbrella, and tapped his knee with the blunt ferrule. He still kept to his asylum; one felt he had his back to the door, hard. A muscle flickered on his cheek.

"*Car-lo!*"

This time she tapped viciously enough to hurt. He didn't wince but his eyes, as inexpressive as all brown eyes are, shot wide open, then immediately became slits. Politely enough, yet gratingly, threateningly, he asked what she wanted, "*Che cosa desidera?*"

She beat on the seat beside her with a fat little hand, and trilled:

"*È troppo duro; è troppo duro.*"

It wasn't hard at all; on this tourist-ridden line even the second class catered for spoiled foreigners. Anyway, had it been brown sienna marble instead of brown leatherette padded with foam rubber, Carlo's mother was her own luxurious cushions. Marble, fakir's spikes, fire-walker's coals, what could her child have done? Nurse her? Advise her to stand, or swing like a larger marmoset from the luggage-rack? He didn't even bother to answer, shut his eyes, and contemptuously, as though to exclude someone crazy.

Unbearable! Unfilial! Humiliating! — the ferrule prodding maliciously at his entwined fore-arms expressed these for her. He came to angry life, and grabbed the ferrule, far from playfully.

"*Carlo, ma no!*"

She squealed as if we other four were not there, tug-of-warring frantically as with a real snatch-thief, both hands in use. A new line, femininity, was jolted into being.

"*Fa freddo,*" she wailed, piping, frail and helpless.

"*Fa freddo, Car-lo mi-o!*" and pounded her patent-leather trotters girlishly on the floor to indicate their being violet with cold. Suddenly he let go and, as she bounced back with a squeak, stretched out for the air-conditioner switch above the hair of the Rameses man who didn't even slope his head automatically to one side but remained static and sequestered as a private image. Carlo pushed the pointer to its heat limit, *Caldo,* and, as one saying, "There, boil to death, dear mother, and leave me in peace", again immured himself behind his arms and eyelids.

Brett said very clearly, "The perverse old bitch! What

that overweight madam needs is a back-hander across the chops!"

It was fascinating. Edged with indictment as her voice was, her face remained serene. She might have been praising or blessing the brawlers. They had, however, aroused a sleeping dog. She began again to denigrate Signora Russo and all living Italians. Because of the crystal pitch of her voice, she was as embarrassing as a cruel child. It disordered me. How could she know that the Italians didn't understand English, that she wasn't committing a social atrocity? I suppose, in fact, that she didn't care if every word were intelligible, and that she looked on them as being as culpable as the next Italian.

She hadn't come to Italy to dislike it; its inhabitants had taught her to. She felt blameless: she'd earned her fare over; was paying her way, working her way, conning her way when all else failed, through an Old World she'd been lured into visiting by gilded legends, propaganda ablaze with seductive adjectives. She'd been taken in by a mirage of civilizations accounted superior to her own country's, of breath-taking landscapes strewn with gorgeous cities and enchanting villages alive with diverting and decorative people.

She had been too ingenuous to believe, had not lived long enough to learn, that the Utopias of the pamphlet are what one does one's best to avoid. Now, behind her happy-go-lucky cynicism and audacious front, disillusion stirred like Polonius behind the arras. She spared nothing: Italy was a fifth-rate vaudeville show, the Italians cheap and nasty buffoons. She was revolted by the showy clothes hiding the dismal secrets of uncleanliness; sick of the untrustworthiness, the emotionalism, and jealous pride; infuriated by the sensual, over-confident faces of those who accosted her.

"Brett's *virgo intacta*, and proud of it," she said almost ringingly. "But a wise virgin, and not a timid one."

The terrors of the flesh she held at bay: she had, it seemed, learnt well the perilous lessons of modesty and love but didn't think them shield enough.

"See here!"

She took from her hand-bag a pair of wickedly pointed little scissors.

"They're silver. My great-grandmother used them for embroidery. She'd die again if she knew, poor lamb, what I use them for."

In queues, crowded trains and trams, cinemas, and public gardens, she carried them in her hand ready to stab into men who touched her. Her intolerance was flawless. Cheek by jowl with Italians in the compartment of *l'accelerato* she was separated from them by an abyss of the spirit. The Italian woman and her son shocked her: she *hated* them, she said, her face as expressionless as a camellia — yet it might have been a serpent speaking.

Curiously, despite a force and stringency in her conversation, one became also aware of odd slacknesses, bewildering *non sequiturs*. The link between thought and thought seemed especially to dissolve at a direct question. At first I thought she was letting down a safety-curtain on some of Jean D.'s feelers, but her whole-hearted candour made that unlikely. It was just that, with one foot in sophistication, the other in naïveté, dislocations occurred. She was, for example, denouncing Signora Russo for always being underfoot, always hanging over her own babies:

"I don't know why she bothers with a nanny. I might just as well be in Saudi-Arabia. Sometimes I'd like to hit her."

Jean D., who thinks kindly of most Italians and all babies, said, "Oh, you can't mean that, Brett. She treats you very well. You have plenty of time off. After all, why shouldn't she dote on her own babies?"

"Because she'll ruin them. Besotted woman — tying and untying their ribbons all the time as if they were dolls."

"But she's their *mother*." Jean D., childless, was becoming fervent and stubborn.

"Yes, I suppose the creature is." To my surprise she spoke mildly, as if she had of a sudden seen the Signora in a new light, a kind of Crivelli Madonna dandling two Holy Children in front of an oriel window-sill crowded with porcelain-like fruit, enamelled-looking flowers, and highly glazed cucumbers.

"Then, surely," asked Jean D. more in the manner of a

sentimental deaconess than I'd have believed possible, "she can be forgiven, or at least understood?"

"I . . . don't . . . think . . . so." Brett answered lingeringly, apparently in thought. It couldn't have been thought, for she added, "No, I *don't* think so. She's far too pretty, and has varicose veins." She paused. "Anyway, she's a bank-manager's wife."

Jean D. was flummoxed enough to say, "What difference does that make?"

"My father's one, too."

On the subject of returning to Parma three days late after racketing about Milan with wanderer Australian friends on their way to Venice her thoughts were equally random and unmarried to each other.

"What on earth," Jean D. had asked, "will your Signora say?"

"I don't care a damn what she says. Or does. She can rave on like that obese dolly in the window-seat if it gives her a kick. I'll make up some taradiddle or other — tell her I ran out of lire."

While I was still trying to spot what was askew about this, Jean D. said, "Heavens, girl, *that's* hardly a convincing lie. If you'd no money how could you afford three extra days?"

"It's not a lie." How calm she was. From the handbag containing scissors but no money she languidly took her last packet of cigarettes. "I told you I hadn't a brass razoo." Finically as a good little girl, she began opening the packet. "But this morning I had lashings of lucre."

"You haven't lost your purse again?" Jean D. was getting motherly.

"No. I can't imagine why — but no, the money's not lost this time. I lent it to two blokes who were skint."

"You *lent* it!" Jean D. was maternally severe. "So now you're skint. Who were they?" She doubtless pictured a brace of confidence men from Naples pretending to be Veronese counts who'd left their wallets in other suits.

"One was an Australian."

"I see." Jean D. was now absolute mother. "And the other?"

Brett languidly lit a cigarette, languidly exhaled. "Oh, he was an Australian."

A silence had to fall. There was nothing to say. Jean D. looked at me, I at her, our eyes as it were shrugging. There was nothing else to do.

At that moment the mother in her discreet production-belt hat animated herself, and intoned with tragic intensity, "*Carlo mio, fa troppo caldo.*"

The son, perhaps truly, like a disciple at Gethsemane, slept on.

"*Io sudo,*" she whined, dabbing a pink handkerchief on her moustache which was indeed beaded with sweat. "*Io sudo, Carlo. Non posso sopportare il calda.*"

"She can't bear the bloody heat!"

Brett rose up, breathing authentic cigarette smoke, and metaphorical flame. "Neither can I. Excuse me, talkative," she said down in the coiffure of the living idol whose self-absorption remained unruffled as she abruptly turned the air-conditioning pointer right back to *Freddo.* "And I sincerely hope, Mother Machree, that you freeze to death."

Whatever the words conveyed to us Australians, the tone cannot have conveyed anything to the Italians, particularly as she uttered without a side-glance at them, and had moved to perform her ostensibly gracious act like a well-bred and mobile caryatid on whose carven tresses an invisible burden of marble acanthus leaves and a ton of architrave were being perfectly balanced. Reseating herself, her visage politely neutral, "God, I *hate* them," she said.

Beyond the windows a drenched Lombardy was running out; before many minutes *l'accelerato* would be in drenched Emilia.

Sky-scraper crags, bottomless primeval lakes, cascades frothing soapily down gorges, leagues of blue-and-white snow-dunes, unemployed nature in any guise is not to my taste. It would have pleased me, however, had the plains docile from centuries of cultivation not been veiled in vertical water, to look out at them, at the tamed rivers, the food-bearing trees and drink-bearing vines, the wounded towers and castles far-off on their hill-top aeries, the farther-off mountains like penitentiary walls still keeping in something mediaeval and feudal, the fumes of vendetta and foray and, in the veins of the last of the vine-leaves, the blood of battle-axed mercenaries, of war-horses and lords, which had long ago extravagantly irrigated the soil. Since I was unable to see what lay outside, the beauty that is feud's aftermath, I had to make do with the feud in the compartment, and await its aftermath.

It wasn't a situation about which to be flinty. Brett's naïveté was too engaging for that, and her fearlessness rather moving because what was callous in it was not inborn but a culture: necessity its spore. Her fury was, I felt, only that of the displaced and disappointed, transient enough for air to have wafted it into her mind. The faintest movement of the weather-vane, and a breath would puff it out.

Perhaps, now, she could never cry, "Open, sesame!" with the old wide-eyed expectation — she had learnt too much to want to, but she could still cry, "Open, wheat!", "Open, barley!" and not be let down. The consequences of her impercipience meant nothing to her, nothing: it proved nothing except the immeasurable distance between two national minds. She had arrived at the point where civilization (as she recognized it) was seen, by its absence, to have existed where she came from, not where she had come to. Homesickness can calcify the heart and buckle the vision as quickly and easily as vice.

The train advanced into Emilia and the melancholy border-land of twilight. Perhaps because abhorred Parma, amorous Signor Russo, the doting Signora and her be-ribboned twins, tomorrow and tomorrow, all swam nearer and nearer through the darkening rain, she fell silent, closed her eyes, and did not sleep.

Her face! — behind its composure an engagement with emotion could be guessed at, but the ivory surface, the Goddess of Mercy blankness admitted nothing: her hands with their bitten nails now and then shifted restlessly on her fashionable lap.

Jean D. opened her guidebook. Would it inform her that for nearly five centuries Florence had been, like Rome and Vienna, Madrid and Paris, a centre of fake antiquities and forged masterpieces?

Night's tide was in when Brett opened her eyes.

"Forgive me, Jean. I was out on business. Really! I've

been desperately trying to think of something heart-breaking. Hopeless!"

She gave no explanation, but went on, "I must have some money. Must. *Must*."

She was talking to Jean D. rather than to both of us but her wantonly clear voice could no doubt be heard in the next compartment if not farther off.

"Oh, dear, it's maddening. In three weeks' time I want to be out of Parma. You see, there's a promise I've got to keep. Two girl-friends are coming down from Norway. We'll join up at Milan, go down to Rome and Naples, then to Brindisi where we'll get a ship across the Adriatic to Greece. I've been there before, and *loathed* it, but a promise is a promise. Even if I have to sleep in the Parthenon, and get my Vitamin C from those sour oranges that grow on the street-trees in Athens, I'll need *real* money to get there. I was certain I'd have it by now, but everything's gone wrong. Me all over, of course. Time's running out. Poor little Brett's on the horns of a whatsis. No matter how much I try and try, I can't get my suit-case stolen. What would you do?"

"To . . . to get my suit-case stolen?" Jean D. spoke out of a fog. Suddenly it cleared: "Oh, I see. For the insurance, you mean?"

"Yes. It's money for jam. Or so I thought."

She had heavily insured everything she'd brought with her from Australia, and losing her expensive camera at a time when she was on the rocks had found the insurance money a god-send. The camera's loss had been an accident; the loss she was now set on was to be deliberate. The case she hoped to collect on was, she said, a costly monster so large that it had to be wheeled on an also-costly fold-up trolley. For the sort of bread-line travelling she and her young friends now did, invaders' skimpily-accoutred Blitzkriegs, the monster, with its attendant contraption, was a hindrance. It was also potential capital.

Her account of attempts to abandon it was very funny, illegal though her intentions. She'd done everything possible to contrive situations in which her head was morally above water, even if only just. Usually she left it on railway platforms next to the most criminal-looking people in sight while she walked conspicuously away, not looking back, to dally in station bars or waiting-rooms or buffets. Time after time she returned to find it, despised loot, exactly as she'd left it. Twice she had deserted it on buses. Once a group of men who resembled the denizens of a thieves' kitchen had yelled and whistled her back; once a wizened old man with a squint had scorched after her on a new-fangled bicycle.

"I suppose," she said, "the costly bloody monster *and* its costly trolley are too conspicuous to steal. And — " she smiled faintly, — "I'm too conspicuous to be stolen from. It bugs me. Either they're all daft, or I'm fated, or both."

In a Europe she regarded as an elaborate piece of machinery set up to bilk and pillage the tourist, an honesty she regarded as perverse dogged her.

"I'd contemplated defying the fates, and trying again in Milan, but decided no-no-*no*: better to enjoy myself than have the worry of not losing it again. I've got a better plan. When I get off at Parma . . . *hell*, where are we?"

The train was decelerating, running over points. She recognized, through the streaming panes, some reassuring combination of lights and outlines.

"Ah, thank God this isn't for me."

It was for Signor Rameses-Arcimboldi who unfolded into an unexpectedly squat man, took an old-fashioned kit-bag from the rack, slid open the door, and wordlessly, on his too-short legs, went out to wait in the corridor.

"*Carlo! Che ora è? Quanto ci fermiano qui? Ho sete, Carlo. Ho appetito!*" keened the mother.

Carlo, eyes balefully open, said cruelly that he wasn't thirsty or hungry: "*Non ho sete. Non ho appetito.*" Outraged, detonated, she released a torrent of melodious abuse. Like a lip-reader, or someone at a *film muto*, he watched, one felt, rather than heard.

The train stopped. The full-dress tirade didn't. The little platform was bare except for the silent man and his kit-bag jogging through the rain. A dog committing a dire aria could be heard. The train started.

"Oh, do shut up, you neurotic old sow," said Brett looking at the palm of one hand. "You know, it's a wonder he doesn't knife the whingeing hag. I'd like to see Signora Giovanni Russo try to bully me like that."

Right then, it came to me that for all the mother's malicious caterwauling and the son's churlishness, all the domestic discord, the two Italians with their passion-afflicted faces had quieter nerves than Brett with her un-marked brow and tender mouth. Theirs might well have been a happy partnership of hate, for hate has as many allegiances as love, and far less fallible ones. If their faces were, so to speak, chewed, their finger-nails weren't.

"You were saying," said Jean D., the orchestra-conductor tapping with the baton, "that when you get off at Parma. . . ."

"I'll show them."

Brett flicked her compact open, reviewed her lips and eyes in the glass, did nothing to them.

"I used to have lovely nails until I took to feasting on them."

She put away the compact, and gazed tranquilly at her fingers.

"They really are repulsive. It makes me shudder to look at them."

"Show whom what?" Jean D. was pedantic but persis-tent. Curiosity gnawed at her like the Spartan youth's fox: she had no intention of letting Brett's riven mind remain unwelded.

"The insurance people, of course. When I get to Parma my new plan goes straight into action." She inhaled a sigh-ing breath. "I'm going to report to the Dago station-master that I've lost the monster."

We said nothing.

"Have I shocked you? Everyone does it. *Have* I?"

Neither of us answered. I saw Jean D.'s face — and felt mine — congeal at non-committal. I said, "Will they believe you?"

"Oh, don't say that. They'll *have* to believe me. I'll make them. I used to be quite an actress at school; Portia, you know — 'it droppeth as the gentle rain', and so on."

She went into a kind of trance, enacting what she'd devised, running over her pathetic script.

"I'll tell them that the case was so enormous it couldn't fit on the mingy little second-class rack, so I left it in the corridor. What else could I do? Why didn't I book it through in the luggage-van? Because, poor maiden, I didn't get to the station in time." She dropped the mediumistic manner, and absurdly pleaded, "You saw that, didn't you, Jean, my leaping on just as the train was moving out?" Then she returned to her other fiction, "I was desperate. I'd been lost for *hours* in Milan, all all alone, and was worried frantic about getting back to the dear, sweet, lovely *bambini*. In the train I was so exhausted from trailing around Milan in the downpour that I fell asleep, and didn't wake up until we arrived at Parma. When I went out into the corridor to get my case — *mamma mia! il mio bello, bello bagaglio* — gone! I'll burst into tears. '*Mamma mia, mamma mia,*' I'll sob, '*Oh, mamma mia, il mio bagaglio!* ' "

The snatches of Italian interrupted the bickering in the window-seats; mother and son turned their simmering, feral eyes on the elegant foreigner. She sensed their attention. Without deigning to look at them, she said, "Stare, stare, monkey bear! Mind your own bloody business, slobs!"

I think Jean D. and I thought that, surely this time, some Mediterranean extra-sensory gift might have been at last brought into play, and the rudeness understood, for we both quickly spoke.

"Will it work?" was hers; "It won't work," was mine.

"It has to. I promised the girls I'd meet them outside the Milan cathedral at midday on the fifteenth of next month, traveller's cheques and all. I couldn't let them down. I've got to be a get-rich-quick maiden this time. All this mess wouldn't have happened if one of the nit-wits had had the nous to pinch the case instead of trying to pinch my you-know-what. Imagine poor Brett weeping and wailing in front of a lecherous gang of porters! '*Ah, poverina, poverina ,*' they'll croon, and pat me, and I won't be able to use my scissors. And then there'll be the police, and I'll have to repeat the entire *mamma mia* performance."

She inhaled another, deeper sighing breath.

"One must martyr oneself for oneself," she said blandly.

Jean D. was near tears. It wouldn't have surprised me if she'd drawn the regal head down to her bosom.

"But aren't you worried, Brett?"

Did she really mean morally worried? Did she mean, on

a lower plane, worried about attempting blatant perjury without any of the technique of the Duse it would require to make it work? Did she, on the lowest plane, mean worried at the possibility of being not believed? Which sort of worried did she mean?

"Worried! Of course. I spent my last lire in that clinical buffet on the Milan station to mop up a few fortifying vinos. I'm worried *stiff*."

She — which sort of worried did she mean? She consulted the compact again, this time using a lipstick, wiping powder on, fussing with her scarf, touching up the leading lady or preparing the victim. Worried? The touched-up face was as pacific as a tarn nothing is reflected in.

She put a cigarette between her lips, and struck a match. The quivering of the tiny flame made it clear that her hand was unsteady.

"Oh dear," she said, "poor Brett."

She blew out the match without lighting the cigarette, and admonished herself: "Stop that instantly, you silly maiden. Stop, right now."

The aristocratic hands with their gnawed nails, held out before her, became still.

"Anyway," she said, putting the cigarette back in the packet, "there's no time."

She stood, reached for her valise, put it on the seat, and sat again, tilting her head back, closing her eyes. She kept them closed for five minutes, ten minutes, until the train, jerking over points, passing through a lighted suburb, came to Parma, and stopped.

She opened her eyes. "Yes, Jean," she said, rising, and taking up her valise. "I'm *very* worried. I've been trying to think of something sad so that I can cry for those galoots out there. Good-bye."

At the door she spoke once again, and then went. The train started. We passed her, pliant and untouchable in the Cossack coat, moving over the brilliant reflections on the wet platform. The rain had gone. Her last words had not: we kept on hearing them.

"I'm terrified. What's going to happen now? All I need is tears, and I can't think of a single unhappy incident in my whole life."

In a prison one is no more than condemned, the fuss over, and nothing now to be forgiven for. In life one is doomed, and still needs to forgive oneself, most often for over-using a capacity for being unfaithful to oneself. I, for example, have a temperate passion for the appropriate, yet keep on finding myself up to the ear-lobes in the inhuman morass of pleasure.

This time, there I am seated on the opposite side of a mezzanine table to Tad, at what could conceivably be Belshazzar's Feast, but is merely a cabaret-cum-nightclub of top-notch vulgarity, and as noisy as the Great War. With us sit two of the club's six hundred hostesses. Mine is Number 34, the bolder slut she. Tad's is Number 379. As well it might be while brooking for the umpteenth time a bow-legged singer unclothed as a fish who is beefing out with Presbyterian vigour "My Heart Belongs to Daddy" down below on the spotlit stage, the expression on the hostesses' faces, flat as photographs, is that of those who would prefer to be elsewhere — at the dentist's, in a soundproofed Iron Maiden, stretched out on a better rack. The beefer-out at last reaches a climax resembling *râles,* shuts up, and prances away backstage, perhaps to conceal nudity's shortcomings in some sort of clothes. For the second time Number 34's hand, having with secret-agent patience, but as though accidentally, advanced from my knee along the inner side of my leg, arrives at my fly, for the second time, also seemingly by accident but less gently than the first time, and more openly, I lift the hand, and plank it, *discard* it like an unsuitable *objet d'art* among the ash-trays, tumblers, and saucers of desiccated shrimps, seaweed biscuits, and antique olives cumbering the table. At the same time I cross my legs and affect an interest in the bandy nude's successors, two pocket-edition Herculeses wearing nylon lion-skins, who are being uproariously unfunny beneath us in a burlesque of weight-lifting — the kind one used to laugh at in Harry Langdon silent comic films. It is midnight, Judas of the hours, but feels much later: the evening has already lasted longer than the Middle Ages.

To avoid being impeded by Number 34's assistance, but also intending less to not-have a cigarette lit for me than to make a puritan point to her and her hand, I light a new cigarette from the tip of the last one. As if to the drop of this coin there is a jackpot reaction. Number 34, unbidden, orders, with a gay viciousness, a round of drinks. Number 379 lights a Hi-Life filter-tip for Tad with pointed and abnormal ceremoniousness. It is now Tad's turn to make a gesture. He does not omit to do so. His disorderly features, hangdog with years of self-exploration, animate themselves by wincings of earnestness. His miniature jet eyes flash toward me in the ruddy cabaret murk.

"What does it mean in Australia," he says in his plummy, bastard-Pommy accent, "when a woman lights a man's cigarette?"

Here we go again!

"Nothing," I say. What else to say? Or does it mean something I've forgotten since leaving Australia?

"Nothing! You say a joke, I think. You make a humorous teasing of me. You cannot really mean such. True or false?"

"What could it mean?" Yes, what could it?

"In Australia it is politeness and gentlemanly for a man to ignite a woman's cigarette — isn't that so? True or false?"

"True enough."

"So!" His relief is blood-curdling. "So-o-o-o this is the polite and proper custom. This is the conventional and national style. If a woman does not follow the custom and ignites a man's cigarette, she must have a special reason for thus doing. True or false?"

The intensity! He could be pleading with me to drop the Church of England and dabble in Nichiren Buddhism.

"No other reason than that she's already got a lighter in

her hand or a match lit." I'm not nice enough to hand him the lie he wants, that the foreign woman (Australian?) who, somewhere along the line, has lit his cigarette, has invitingly lit it, lit it for love.

"No other reason!" His dismay is to take some digesting. Reluctant to begin this travail, he looks Liar! at me — almost — at least as much as doubt will let him.

"Like Shizuko-san here, or your Kiyoko-san," I say. "They're both quick-on-the-draw dolls with a match box." Hearing their names, Numbers 34 and 379 exhibit — processed and artificially flavoured charm at its most instant — a quantity of their own teeth.

"But . . ." He can hardly go on. "But they are only cabaret hostesses!" *They are only trained animals*, his horror implies, *they are not women.* "It is their *métier*. They are paid. I think I have not spoken with clarity." This means I am an uncouth fool. "My English is blemished. I talk of women who are *ladies*, perhaps Australian or German or Swiss. If one of such should be kind enough to ignite my cigarette when it is not her mode of earning the crust, she must have a special feeling, a tender emotion. True or false?"

"False." The monosyllable, served neat, disconcerts him. I may as well finish off the job and disconcert him further: "It could be, of course, that she intends a rebuke."

He is more than further disconcerted, he is flummoxed: "A rebuke? A rebuff? A discourtesy? An admonishment? I find this so difficult to believe. Explain, if you please."

Although I am beginning to bore myself and to wish I'd told the silly lie he wanted, I say, "Well, the man could have carelessly not been lighting her cigarettes, and she wants to give him a lesson in manners, to shame him."

"Please?"

O God!

"If she's a touchy neurotic or a nasty bitch she's only applying a flame to that cigarette-tip in an attempt to . . . to make him lose face."

Ah! Lose face! He gets a point.

"So-o-o-o!" He gets it, though it's not what he angled for: the empty crabmeat tin instead of the succulent carp. His face becomes briefly more dishevelled with disappointment, and the two production-belt harpies, not having understood a word, but vanes in the slightest breath, bend looks of professional sympathy on him. With heavy-footed lightness he pretends next that he is too too blasé to be discomfited, shrugs his meagre shoulders, and grins like a skull.

"They're funny people," he says.

He means, it is to be taken, women — not just foreign ladies and their eccentric and intriguing ways, but the whole box and dice of them: WOMEN! Usually, his "They're funny people" is applied to the Japanese, although he himself is as Japanese as octopus for breakfast, Tad is.

"Please, you will call me Tad, I am hoping" — this after twenty minutes, our first meeting. It's a hope hard for me to fulfil trippingly, because in no way at all does he resemble my image of a Tad, somebody drawling, American, deliberately boyish, loose-jointed, ice-blue-eyed, with Tom Sawyer hair, and a badly shrivelled mind. Tad! I should prefer to call him Mr Nakamura, but rarely call him anything. His name is Tadashi Nakamura. He's over fifty, pint-size to the point of waifishness, wears always a clergy-grey suit of man-made fibres, a drip-dry white shirt, black socks and shoes, and his hair, I'm positive, is dyed. No hair feeding on such a starvation of the ego, on such a tangle of nerves; on such notable lack of nonchalance, could have survived so blackly black.

I am landed with him as interpreter and guide for a month or more. It is not clear to me precisely what position he holds on the staff of a glossy English-language Japanese magazine which has commissioned me to write a foreigner-eye-view of one of the larger prefectures of Japan, but I gather that it was once much more important than now, that he has been outrun and overtopped by younger men, and is on a shameful last lap to the lumber room. Nursemaid to a Barbarian from Without must be a chore with all kinds of humiliating undercurrents and champagne-before-execution implications: he is little more than a dragoman, even though we shall be expense-accounting it every millimetre of the way, first-class, caviar for elevenses, and tycoon's suites where they exist. In a country addicted to Spartanism and prettied-up poverty and aesthetic discomfort, this emperor-for-a-day progress is the best way to see what I have

to see. That one has to "live like a native" to know how natives live is bosh. One doesn't have to cut off one's hand to
prove that having hands cut off is odious; one doesn't have
to nibble raw bream and sleep on the floor of a paper-paned
house odorous of its hole-in-the-floor lavatory to know
that others carry on so. Anyway, I have every intention of
living as lavishly as my frame will stand, because this all-
expense-paid rake-off is largely all I shall get for the several
thousand words promised: the cheque offered for the article
would buy little more in Australia than a bottle of whisky
or a cheap pair of shoes. In Through-the-Looking-Glass
Japan it would buy only two pounds of rump steak or,
should I need them, a couple of abortions or a set of cos-
metic-surgery breasts like Venus's.

Tad is thrown in as courier, skilled bore, and unendearing
entertainer, and has a wide knowledge, valuable to me, of
his country's dialects, quixotic whims, perverted customs,
blood-soaked legends, highways, and byways. The central
spring of his nature is, however, in bad repair. He is a
master of muck-ups, and skilled in rapidly converting mere
contretemps to nerve-singeing catastrophe. There is no
doubt anywhere that, were he successfully to entreat
celestial assistance, the Travellers' Aid angel on duty would
not descend smoothly as an Otis lift, with cornless feet
pressed primly together, halo at the correct tilt, neatly parcelled in well-laundered wings, but "Thump!", plumes as
awry as an old shuttlecock's, and with a black eye.

The prefecture he is to cosset my exploration through is
as closely sprinkled with famous freaks, animal, mineral,
and vegetable, living or dead, as Père Lachaise Cemetery is
with the tombs of other prodigies — Rossini, Adelina Patti,
Chopin, Alfred de Musset, Bizet, Balzac, Molière, La Fon-
taine, Daudet, Sarah Bernhardt, Marshal Ney, and Oscar
Wilde. The dead whose tombs Tad and I are visiting once
led more passion-gorged and sinister lives than had the dead
of Père Lachaise. Warriors obsessed by atrocious loyalties,
vixenish court-ladies as patricidal as Lizzie Borden, suicided
courtesan   poetesses,   demoniac   abbots,   aristocrat
generalissimos trebly ennobled by unutterable depravities,
their gravestones are jostled — in a landscape neither naked
nor pure — by a hundred-and-one other esteemed pilgrim-

and-tourist lures: fake mediaeval castles, sacred tors, sacred monkeys, patched-up temples, idols with more arms than a crab, villages of Caliban-like craftsmen egged on by the Japan Tourist Bureau to make gimcrack folk-art miniatures of legendary killers, and godlings with the sexual habits of billy-goats. Before setting out, Tad has done much homework, and is not only a walking Baedeker but carries always, in a plastic valise of the cheerless blue 1880 theological treatises were bound in, a Magna-Carta-sized itinerary so detailed, and set out so exquisitely, that we should be gliding with unvexed and ever-punctual ease along the strands of the cobweb joining all the Points of Interest each to each. Fate, however, looks at no timetables, certainly not at Tad's, and, indeed, looks at nothing. Fatalism is one of my few virtues. I feel that, while it is not unreasonable to depend off-handedly on tomorrow being a foreseen tomorrow, it is insane dogmatically to bet an eye on it. This is fortunate, because Tad's tomorrow, too many times and too many agains, turns out not to be the one on his Magna Carta, comes up as wortromo or troomwor or romotrow. Tad's trains leave without us. Tad's buses are not to be caught where we are waiting in the rain. Tad's ferry-steamers are in buck-jumping retreat offshore when we arrive at the jetty. Tad's Grand Hotels know nothing of a booking in the Crown Prince's suite for a Mr Tadashi Nakamura and his dog-eyed, hairy barbarian. After wailings and vilifications and intricate readjustings on a plane of exaggerated despair far beyond my interest, Tad returns to earth, shrugs, performs his exhausted skull's grin, and says throatily, "They're funny people." Though these recurring accidents seem no more than accidents, and ludicrous ones at that, I come increasingly to feel that there are larger and unsuspected issues somewhere in the offing, sly and obnoxious machinations just out of earshot. Looking back, hind-sighting in a fog, perhaps there were, perhaps there were.

Instead of being unendearing and sympathy-repelling, Tad could be a more engaging creature than he is: his knotted sad face, neat frailty, perpendicular not quite threadbare tie, and dyed hair could pluck at one of the minor strings of pity; he could arouse some of the sort of affection with which one thinks of the White Knight and his upside-down sandwich-box. He is not engaging. Pity is not stirred, nor is affection. Instead, I find myself often, if not uneasy with him, not utterly at ease, almost irked by the overweight of emotional luggage he totes. Some element of his being seems asymmetrical, as though he has not only an atavistic link with the lopsided holy rocks, wilfully tortured pine-trees, neurasthenically tasteful shrines, and bloated graven images lining our advance, but an extra kind of unhealthy union, on a racial sub-level, with the hysterical warriors, doom-dogged priests, treachery-hounded uncles, and suicide barons whose lichen-splotched headstones or time-fissured monuments also line it.

I am aware that he is made more anxious by my calm — the placidity of indifference is not, like stupidity, contagious. The mess-ups, nearly as frequent and regular as the Angelus, leave me unruffled because it does not matter to me if tomorrow is moorwort, and we do not get to this toppling temple, that famous fan-painter or pottery kiln, on time or ever. He does not really accept this attitude nor understand it or, rather since it is essentially an oriental attitude, does not accept or understand it in an occidental in whom it might be a smoke-screen, a piece of acting to conceal contempt, anger, plans of revenge. In spite of his distress at each calamity he does not seem to have foresight enough to attempt preventing the next one. Each muddle affects him as though it were the first, is unique, and has taken him by surprise.

There we are, booked out of a village inn at ten a.m., waiting in the sunlight for the taxi-cab which is to come from the nearest town to take us to an interview with a famous mask-maker half an hour's drive away. The appointment is ten-forty-five. The taxi does not arrive. People pass. One has eyes. One sees them. As they pad like tamed beasts along the ruts of the road, through an air smelling of wood-smoke and cold water, one sees that their faces are of a sort withdrawn from circulation in the city, faces charged with forces not having a twentieth-century name, and fixed in expressions as menacing as spring. At ten-thirty I go to the grog-shop opposite the inn and watch, as I drink tinned pilsener, Tad still waiting and waiting like a child while the chimpanzee-like inn servant with her besom and watering-can scours the cobbles all around his little imitation leather shoes. He will not budge an inch. He has been put out. Therefore she will be put out. This is Japan.

Japan! What *am* I doing here! A flash of homesickness — and as though to erase the cramped and piddling one-street village, the cold crags behind it, the cold waterfalls performing among the crags, the Coca-Cola signs hung outside the mean weatherboard cabins, I seem to see an Australian summerscape: miles of bleached and arefied grass as shimmering as taffeta, miles of fencing wire that glitter like filaments of platinum. Here and there a witch-doctor's washing-day of dead snakes hangs on the wires. The sky is a flawless illustration of infinity. Cockatoos flicker snowily as flakes of paper overhead, making a noise like the squeakers at the navels of old-fashioned rubber dolls. A ewe coughs like Camille in the shade of a King-Kong-shaped boxthorn. Somewhere in the glaring immensity, concealed by light, sleeps the looting fox. The grasshoppers tick like thousands of minute watches. It becomes eleven a.m. Tad has left his post. The chimpanzee scours his defilement from the cobbles. Behind the inn walls there is now, I know, high drama on the telephone, shrillnesses, exchanges of delicate venom, imperious demands made in the vocabulary of impoliteness fitting to the occasion.

Ultimately — two past noon, twenty-two past one, some time too late — Tad will reappear with the fatigued yet alert air of one who has been both filleted and reboned, and a taxi-cab will turn up out of the hinterland, somewhat sullenly, growling with resentment, its eyes glinting. Maybe it will be the one that should have turned up: maybe it will be another hysterically invoked at great cost from anywhere within a radius of thirty miles; maybe, and most likely, both original and emergency will turn-of-the-screwishly materialize at the same moment, their danders equally up. Whatever happens, I know that Tad, once he is in whichever taxi-cab, relieved and triumphant at having unsorted disorder, will smile his skull smile, emit his witch's giggle, and say, "They're funny people!" A brief relief and triumph, very brief, for almost immediately it will dawn on him that the mask-maker who expected us hours ago will

have long since scoffed the apricot-tiled *gâteaux* bought for
us, and is now much tetchier than Miss Pross, and raring to
be as socially insolent as a Natural Cultured Possession,
government-subsidized and bureaucratically ear-marked for
posterity, has the right and the particular gifts superbly to
be. There is nothing to be done but speed toward this extra
fate.

By nuances of vocabulary and subtleties of behaviour
beyond my comprehension, by insults of the most delicate
sort, by intonation, minute omissions of courtesy, smiles of
a certain species, he banishes Tad to a Coventry not even
the most humiliating of apologies can release him from. It is
fascinating, but not a pretty sight to see.

Later, his cigarette and cigarette-hand quivering with an
ague of mortification, Tad attempts to explain the precise
qualities of these insults to me. Impossible. For such
analyses of comedy and slaughter his rococo-Cola lingo is
useless. The emotions he is striving to translate are, after all,
Japanese, and untranslatable to human beings. He has no
words except, "They're funny people!"

He is, anyway, always being, he says, "insulted". Indeed,
to judge by the storms-in-teacups and raised hackles littering our progress, it truly seems so. There is always something going on between him and public underlings —
ticket-sellers, begloved station-masters, Quasimodo-like
men on the gang-planks of ferry-steamers, deadpan
reception-desk lovelies with *dernier cri* coiffures, butch
priests in thick-lensed spectacles like the bases of liqueur
glasses — some suddenly exploding quarrel, bitter-sounding
and to be elaborately prolonged, about times of departure,
seats that should have been reserved, about temples visita-
ble, museums seeable, and funiculars usable yesterday and
tomorrow, but not today, not Tad's today. We arrive at
out-of-the-way villages expecting to find centuries-old
fiestas in uproarious and garish full-swing like a Breughel
kermis or a giddy Bosch hell, but are met by a disconcerting
and mundane orderliness, like that of a well-run public execution, and an all-over stillness and lassitude almost too
perfect to be of the 1960s.

What is consistently not quite credible is Tad's external
show of quick-smart recovery after each and every miscar-

riage. It is not to be known whether he has willed the stigmata not to show or has a constitution on which stigmata do
not take: he seems, *seems*, to be, between crises, no more
than witlessly insouciant or, at least, sonkily not concerned.
At first, in the early days, I think it is vanity which protects
him from blaming himself and beating his brow, vanity,
that skittish mother of all noble and tinpot illusions, that
fever-ridden comrade of poets and prophets, of reformers,
charlatans, confidence men and incendiaries. Soon this is
seen not to be. There are humilities and diffidences in his
make-up which can have nothing whatever to do with
vanity; there are flashes, simple and eccentric enough, of
near-gaiety. Looking back, it is absurdly simple to decide
that he chooses the difficult and polite duty of appearing to
express scatter-brained unaffectedness rather than the easy
relief of being authentically put out or put upon, frustrated,
embarrassed, really wretched. Does he know — *did* he
know — that a display of unhappiness would have bored
me less than a simulation of dispassion, that *Grieve and the
world grieves with you* is a safer fact than *Laugh and the world
laughs with you*? Perhaps not.

His near-gaiety, for want of a more defining term, is
peculiar, childlike, mystifying.

Wherever one goes in his country of islands one can
hardly avoid, even if one is not the sort of magpie who en-
joys doing it, picking up scraps of evidence of where one
has been, from the poshest Hiltonized hotel to the seediest
mobile soup-stall. There are, for example, the tiny boxes of
matches even the most disreputable or hill-billy of coffee-
shops gives its customers; there are the excruciatingly artistic
stubs of admission tickets to iris gardens, zoos, puppet
theatres, art galleries, and monkey reservations; there are
the envelopes chopsticks come in at restaurants and noodle-
kiosks, the postcards in hotel writing-desks, decorative
department-store wrappings, miniature paper parasols stuck
in showy sundaes or the slices of Taiwan pineapple playing
floes in even showier drinks; there are a thousand-and-one
other trivialities of the sort.

From the start, I notice that Tad collects them, slips
them, both his and mine, into the plastic blue valise.
Although he looks indefinably unmarried or, rather, un-

cherished and unwanted, an infusion of tender care in his
manner as he gathers up and neatly puts away these bits and
pieces suggests little children at home, dumpling five-year-
old daughters with horsehair fringes, boys like minified
Tads. They are — quite conceivably — waiting at a bamboo gate, the females poker-faced in lurid kimono, the
males got up like bourgeois Parisian boys. He mentions no
children, however attired, and never mentions a wife.
Japanese men rarely do, and then only as mentioning something inescapable and trite, such as a ceiling to a room, a
handle to a kettle. It is not, I find out, for children if he has
them, nor for nieces and nephews or neighbour's brats, that
he fondly tucks away alongside the troublesome Magna
Carta the menus begged from waitresses, the beer-
advertising cardboard coasters, play programmes, tourist
pamphlets, and handbills extolling beauty salons, seaweed
beverages, horror films, or cultured pearls. Not any of this
rubbish stays long in the valise. Everything is, bit by bit,
given away to passers-by, strangers.

When I witness the first giving-away it is more than
surprising, decidedly startling, and nearly unnerving. We
are in an oozy, mossy, famed, somethingth-century garden,
all up hill and down dale. It is early morning, eight-
thirtyish, because we are visiting the saturated moss and
wizened dripping trees, Tad says "before the delightful domain is overrunning by so many tourists of vulgar nature".
We are, in truth, first there. Presently, however, two
typist-like girls (tourists of vulgar nature?), both hung like
1922 hall-stands with plastic mackintoshes, scarves,
rucksacks, cameras, shoulder-strap handbags, and telescoped
nylon unbrellas, advance through the Scotch mist towards
us. On the slippery, tortuous, narrow, steep path we are
compelled to confront them. I foresee us turning side on,
our bellies drawn graciously in, while the burdened
creatures teeter past us. It is not to be.

Tad breaks off his guide-tour soliloquy and becomes on
the instant relatively radiant. A halt is made under the
waterlogged branches. Vivacious greetings are exchanged,
we a little higher up the slope, they twittering and smiling
just below. Next, groping uncarelessly in the valise, he
selects things and, as one handing out sapphire brooches,

presents them to the girls. There are further smiles, exchanges of indubitable pleasantries, and skilfully managed bowings. This drags gaily on until finally the moment for standing side on and sucking in bellies arrives, and we part, doubtless for ever.

Completely bewildered, less by the mannered ritual than the gift-giving, I look back to see if the girls are in stitches of silent derisive laughter. No. No. They are decorously slipping and sliding up the greasy incline, one helping the other, their gifts still held like rarities in their gloved fingers. The gifts, culled with some nicety, are fit only to be discarded, and not merely unutterably trashy but utterly useless, four paper napkins from the snack-bar of a hydrofoil we have used the evening before. Meanwhile, back on the guide's monologue as though nothing has happened, nothing untoward, Tad chatters about the star-crossed and blue-blooded landscape-gardener, and the novelistic series of events leading him to design what seems to me less suited to the misty-morning scramble of trippers than the mournful twilight constitutionals of a Frog Prince. While Tad rattles on, I suggest many reasons to myself for his odd charity and its unsurprised acceptance. What meets the eye cannot be the real dirt.

He is an Oriental Man from U.N.C.L.E. handing over messages at a prearranged rendezvous. He has made a peculiar carnal tryst to be kept when I am asleep or otherwise out of the way. He is a dope-pedlar, a political fanatico of an underground movement, evangelist for a cryptic religion. He is as drunk as a skunk, and shows it only in gift-giving. He is bonkers, barmy, right round the bend.

Not true, any of it.

Day after day I watch him present his pickings to all sorts and conditions of men and women, but never — why? — to children, not ever to a child howsoever cute or crippled or on the loose. It is striking that not once does any little-old-lady-passing-by, any burly back-lane peasant, near-hoodlum, or excessively ethereal young woman reject his donations of incipient litter, or not accept them unwincingly, without amazement, and with this or that degree of elegant formality and real-looking smiles. Is it that they all read something on his face or in his eyes that I certainly do not? Not once do I ask what he's up to: knocking on doors to rooms I don't know the name of is not one of my ploys, even though it would be vastly intriguing to know what the room is, and what is in it — vastly. Once only, catching a bared expression in my eye, he tips a wink with, so to speak, his bony smile, nods his dyed poll several times, and says Pommily, "They're funny people!"

They're funny people!

Does he mean that, since he's Japanese also, he's funny too? Or does he honestly mean to hint that he, of all the millions and millions of them, is odd-man-out, and not funny? And does he mean funny-ha-ha or funny-peculiar?

If I do not knock on the door of any one of his nameless rooms, attics, laboratories cells, whatever they are, nor does he, as we travel on and the weeks pass, ever open those doors except rarely, as though accidentally, the merest fraction, and not wide enough for me to put my foot in, insolently to stare beyond him, brutally to ask follow-up questions. Usually, anyway, the questions that could be asked cannot be asked.

For instance, one evening, we are soaking ourselves in a hot-spring bath as large as an Olympic swimming-pool, just the two of us because it is off-season, and the vast hotel, practically empty, echoes like a deserted mine. Despite this the steaming, faintly sulphurous pool is abob with large red apples — the hotel gimmick, amusing but dotty. He has been telling me at length, in a pseudo-medical jargon, about his ab-do-men which appears, like a fate-hounded next-door neighbour rather than an occupant of the same building, to lead a tempestuous life of its own. This sort of revelation is neither revealing nor unusual in his country: most Japanese have a belly-fixation which seems to start in childhood with a delicious fear that the Thunder God will steal their navels, and reaches its obvious and perhaps also delicious climax in ritual disembowelment. As Tad goes on and on about his ab-do-men I am nudging apples about and boredly saying, "Really!" and "How *awful*!" and "Unbelievable!" Suddenly, without change of pitch or tone, he switches from his ab-do-men to his collar-bone. He touches a starfish-shaped scar with a wet middle finger. "This injury," he tells me "is memento of my youthful era when I was a soldier. It is bayonet-wounding on behalf of my patriotism at Nanking in 1937." Then, instanter, before I can speak, the door closes; he submerges splashily as a boy, submarines hither and yon under the apples, and surfaces talking of nothing to do with nothing. Had I, quick as a flash, jammed my foot in the door, had I even bided my time and brought up the scar and Nanking when he was wine-ridden at dinner, what really could be asked? "Did it hurt?" "Did you kill the nasty Chinaman with the bayonet?" "How *was* the massacre at Nanking?"

No. No questions — and no dyed-in-the-wool answers.

All in all, by the time our run together is reaching the finishing-tape, I know very little about him that is not common-factor, that is, Japanese common-factor. Whatever else, trying to read between the lines, I sense is too obliquely set, too amorphous in outline, too differently neurotic, too un-Australian rather than too un-Western for me to catch.

I do, nevertheless, feel his lopsidedness, his asymmetry, as well as another quality of hollowness whih makes me also feel ill at ease in a special way hard to puzzle out. It is as if, somewhere between the bloody 1937 stripling and the over-the-hill journalist (ex-editor? ex-chief-of-staff? ex-feature-writer?) playing courier to a foreigner, somewhere between the lit-up little man bestowing chopstick envelopes on stray working-class matrons and the badgered little man always being "insulted", somewhere between the one I see and the one I cannot see, between the present man and the past one, there is almost visible another man, a kind of future man who has already arrived too early where he will be later, who is already his own ghost or his own long-empty empty.

At last Tad and I come to the last night together, the last hotel, the last dinner: mid-morning next day we are to fly back to Tokyo and good-bye.

This terminus hotel, with fantastic irrelevance to the year of the century and the country it is built in, serves at hair-crinkling cost an imitation, old-fashioned, Mrs Beeton-and-roast-beef-of-old-England dinner of the kind served perhaps on the *Titanic*. This is *its* gimmick — the vast *cuisine*-French menu, the soups and entremets, entrée-dishes and sorbets and finger-bowls, fruit-knives and Cheddar and heavily starched table-napkins of fake damask.

I can face three only of the nine courses. Tad accomplishes them all, and with ease, as if he is starving, has no captious ab-do-men, or is preparing for hibernation. He accomplishes them, moreover, with the facile stylishness of one who has not only studied (has he?) a late-Victorian manual on table-etiquette but has doggedly and secretly practised (has he?) its rulings. He handles all the Lord-Mayor's-banquet array of knives and forks and spoons with the aplomb of a well-mannered duke. Meantime, not dropping one crumb or spilling one tear of gravy, his accent more fruitily English than usual, his face as earnest as a he-owl's, he questions me on the U-ness or non-U-ness of English-Western eating habits.

"It is more properly, is it not, to eat asparagus by the fingers? True or false?"

"The utensil for having consommé or chicken broth is better the tablespoon, more in correct fashion than the modern soup spoon? True or false?"

"Tell me, please, is it proper and elegant to eat fish with two forks? The fish-knife is of newly rich middle class, I think — true or false?"

As I steadily drink while he refinedly gorges on and on, it more and more seems to me that the questions are not real, that they are unattached to his mind, disembodied, vagrant, wind blowing through holes. They may sound like those the industrious apprentice could ask, but have the air of the idle apprentice's vapourings. The reason for them worries me. Does this desperate-sounding, urchin-like Japanese *really* want to know how to deal with grape-pips and olive-stones, or whether it's true or false that one drinks one's Chartreuse after *café nature* rather than before?

I suppose, after answering as amiably as I can throughout the prolonged meal, that my boredom, bordering on irritation, does begin to show, because putting down his Chartreuse, he says, for the first time in all the weeks we have been together, something almost occidentally direct:

"Excuse, please, is the etiquette questionnaire boring?"

To my astonishment and shame I say, "Yes."

It is far, far too socially un-Japanese, too savage anywhere. The passions rarely miscalculate, apathy never should. Were he hulking, bony, hairy, violent, and vigorous it would still be uncouth enough. He is the opposite, and his small shell, despite its fuel of nine exaggerated and expensive courses, has no power, no certainties. I have seen its frailty shaken by minor and incomplete humours only, petty fits of cantankerousness quickly shrugged off, emotions meagre as the smoke of a dying, nearly dead fire.

My *Yes* affects him, nevertheless, like a blow on the cheek, physically. His head actually jerks away from my unwarm eyes: he goes into profile, the over-manhandled profile on a coin of little value soon to be called in. His hand, also somehow now out of the running, trembles near the liqueur glass. He removes its offence and betrayal from sight.

"I'm sorry," I say. "I'm truly sorry, but you did ask, and I'm too tired to play polite games. Frankly, I'm not so much bored by your asking questions as by your asking questions you very well know the answers to. You must know them. How otherwise would you know how to ask them?"

He takes seconds of silence to come out of profile, to stop looking at some cul-de-sac wall, to present a blind, stiff mask to me. From this younger, sterner visage comes an arid voice:

"Excuse, please, I question because I wish verifications."

He is as uncharming and pity-repelling as ever.

I cannot restrain myself: "In God's name, why? Don't tell me you're thinking of starting a school in Western table-manners?"

He does not answer, but an inner face flinching behind the transfixed one indicates that, shooting wild and silly, I have scored, if not a bull's-eye at least a magpie. I wonder what other lunatic plans, poor devil, he has insomniacally milled over. He puts his napkin — oh, carefully-carelessly — on the table. He rises.

"You will, please, I am hoping, forgive me." It is the harassed woman seeking refuge in a trumped-up migraine. "I am fatigued. I go to bed."

A few paces in retreat he turns, comes back to the table, his inscrutability very visible. Mechanically secretarial, he addresses me in a tape-recorded manner:

"Tomorrow morning at nine o'clock, before the vulgar crowd is overrunning, we will look at the historic and breathtaking view from the cliff. It is from here, in the four-teenth century that . . ." He stops, either from fear of further boring, or to make a pause to make a point. "There will be, I think, no unfortunate errors." He giggles. The gig-gle has more than a little bitterness in it. "We have only to walk five minutes or four to the viewing-kiosk."

Leaving untouched the Chartreuse he once lifted to sip, he goes. I contemplate tossing it off but do not. I suppose the Japanese waiter, got up like one out of Simpson's or Brown's Hotel, does that. Or — true or false? — does it go back into the green bottle?

No unfortunate errors tomorrow? I shall not be surprised if the cliff is now a dell.

Next morning, as I am dressing, a bell-boy brings me a letter. It is, he says, from Nakamura-san of Suite 603. It is not on the hotel writing-paper but on a sheet of hand-made paper I recognize as being the special product, very aesthetic, of a village where, a fortnight back, one of Tad's more involved muddles made the day notable.

It is written in copperplate, and is largely an apology, neurotically detailed (points *a,b,c,d,* and so on), for inconve-niences I have found far less inconvenient than he thinks, incidents forgotten, or remembered as enlivening and amus-ing. Fatalists do not fume and fret about todays or tomor-rows, and wear no face that can be lost. He writes that "many of such contretemps were not of my cause. They are misinformations supplied to me by those in the office who wish my debasement, who wish to insult me by making the embarrassments and shames. It is thus I am desolated and unhappy for failures."

He is sorry, finally, for having bored me.

So am I, Tadashi Nakamura, so am I, although you are less boring now than you were then.

When I go to his room intending, certainly, pretence that nothing has happened, that no one has bored anyone and, equally certainly, effusive acknowledgment that he has been a mine of information and the most erudite courier in Japan, he is not there. A brisk matron at the reception-desk tells me in an American accent that he has gone to the viewing-kiosk. Inside, it is a quarter to nine; outside, a plague of swallows, skimming low, slices the grey air. Rain purposes falling.

He is not in the viewing-kiosk, with its ten-yen-in-the-slot telescopes machine-gunning the blurred horizon. He is not dallying among the yuccas and agaves and concrete benches and salmon-pink litter-tins littering the cliff-top. He is not leaning over the balustrade but, without any pricking of the thumbs, I lean, and look. It is the blue valise that catches my eye. There he is. He is far down, a hundred or more feet down, at the bottom, static among the static conical rocks and the static sea-crows perched on them rather hunched. He is far down, he and his valise and ab-do-men and threadbare tie and dyed hair, far down, arrived without disorganization at his own certified tomorrow, dead as mutton. At least, if not as dead as, as still as. The view, maybe historic, is not breathtaking, but — like so much he has steered me to — over-rated, confused, its out-lines veiled and fuzzy. The sea is as out of action as the horizon is out of focus, not a heave or ripple or twinkle, as though his plummeting down has, typically, thrown a span-ner in the works, put a stop to swirling and foaming and frivolity.

There is nothing to do but tell the hotel people that Nakamura-san has had an accident, and that somebody should do something. They, sure that I am an imperceptive foreign lout, and/or in some sort of shock, give me brandy to drink. I am fascinated that it is Greek brandy, Metaxa, and quite as fascinated to sense that they are more stimul-ated by my news than discomposed: *their* cliff has, after all, been lauded for centuries as a respectable, well-patronized, and first-class suicide place. As Tad knew, it does not take much to stimulate people, to make them happy — a paper napkin, an unused drinking-straw, a little envelope with nothing in it.

The empty seat beside mine in the aeroplane is no doubt his and, for a while, it irrationally irks me that he is not there to be perhaps apologized to, perhaps praised, perhaps asked off-handedly if he does *really* believe that "the many of such contretemps" were not his blunders but the machination of others.

It is just as well I cannot ask. It is also unimportant, because I know what, however off-handedly I frame the question, his three-word answer would be, as he rifles the pouch at the back of the seat in front of him and tenderly and neatly stows away the airline pamphlets and tourist brochures in his nasty-blue plastic valise.

Mr Butterfry

When, after eighteen years, I spot him at the Lion Beer Hall, Shimbashi, Tokyo, I suspect he is someone I knew somewhere before, but it is hard and unimportant to be certain whether he really is that unplaceable someone or merely a unit cut from the template of his type. It is a type instantly familiar because ubiquitous as sinners and dandelions, and almost invariably wears the nickname Blue, despite the fact that, in some tinkling and seemly year, 1922 or 1923 say, a working-class mother has fruitlessly attached to an already wily clown of a baby the ticket Oswald or Arthur or Francis Xavier. Here, in the Lion Beer Hall, forty-odd years after conning his way into and out of the womb, he resembles his template brethren to the last blackhead. He is short, welter weight, discreetly bow-legged, topped with ginger-and-grey curls. Nickname? Guess!

Blue's nose is snub as an *ingénue's*, and as immodestly open to the delicious wickedness of the world as a rocking-horse's. His lips, too pliant, scorched-looking, agitate themselves non-stop to eject, in a falsetto of extraordinary harshness, an overflow of obscenity, boastings not to be believed and not expected to be believed, lies too Munchausen to arouse anything but irritated pity, fly-blown witticisms, and just enough tiny and tasty (and deliberately planted?) truths to make him bearable, forgivable, even lovable. His every clause — truth or taradiddle or downright delusion — is accompanied by a simpleton's gesticulation itself in need of exegesis. His water-pale eyes, nailed into all this restlessness and garrulity, are immobile as an umlaut, unwinking as a merman's. An Australian, a refractory, Depression-toughened, war-jangled, Occupation-debased, he is the oldest inhabitant of the Lion Beer Hall.

For years — eleven? fourteen? sixteen? — the Lion has
been the weekly rendezvous of expatriate Australians in
Tokyo. No need, of course, for a sign BLOKES ONLY.
Kangaroo-pelt koalas squat on the newels of the staircase
and on top of the 1908 register ornate as a tsarina's jewel-
casket. Qantas posters and elderly photographs of Sydney
Harbour Bridge and Murray River paddle-steamers hang on
the walls between dust-furred sprays of machine-made
cherry-blossom and the other-year calendars of Hong Kong
tailors.

It is behind waitresses of implausible homeliness, and
sluts with impasted faces, frowsy false eyelashes, and
Elicon-inflated breasts that one queues for a telephone-
booth-sized lavatory of which the urinous reek unselfishly
mingles with the grey and hunger-discouraging odours from
the kitchen. Here, to the behind-scenes yowling of transis-
tor Beatles, are manufactured Japanese mock-ups of
spaghetti and tomato sauce, curry and rice, or genteel
isosceles sandwiches, or dim-sims composed of elements
better not thought about. The food's one merit is its thank-
God tastelessness. Skilfully combining Wild West Saloon
dash and oriental finickiness the barman flourishes a spatula
to slice the foam from the glass jugs of draught beer the
Australians order.

Successive proprietors, and successions of Japanese
customers meekly and long-time nibbling at the surface of a
pony of beer as though it were an inordinately pricy and
singular liqueur, have year after year concealed their contempt for the heavy-drinking invaders who, every Saturday
morning from eleven o'clock on, crowd into the Lion with
an almost delinquent bravura, louder-mouthed than they
are, twice as Australian as they could ever be in Australia.
Fog or shine, a flannel sky tenderly vomiting down grouts
of soiled January snow, August giving its imitation of a
sauna bath, Plum Rain weather or suicide month, the Barbarians from Without come roaring in — public-relations
men, back-room boys from the Australian and New Zealand Embassies, ABC employees, foreign correspondents,
traders' agents, tourists who have heard of the Lion on the
grapevine, and members of that clan of confidence-men and
near-confidence-men who are the flower of Australian *haut
cynicisme*. They come, particularly the dyed-in-the-wool

expatriates enmeshed throughout the week in webs of native dissimulation and duplicity, to re-enact themselves among their kind, to refresh their evaluations, to exchange home truths in the cryptic patois, at one and the same time profane and subtle, self-mocking and sensitive, brutal and compassionate, merciless and stingless, that only Australian men can use and understand.

Although the Shimbashi immediately surrounding the Lion presents to the polluted upper air of Tokyo its architectural crosswords of plate-glass and ferro-concrete, its vulgar rooftop fairgrounds and beer gardens, its rooftop golf-driving and baseball-pitching centres encaged in green nylon netting, down below, level with the Lion, near the fissured and buckled footpaths silkily gleaming with spittle, are the pinball parlours, noodle stalls, flop-houses, homo-sexual bars, and the hole-in-the-wall haunts of herbalists, astrologers, palmists, face-readers, acupuncture quacks, cut-rate abortionists, and third-rate cosmetic surgeons, all jam-med together behind booths displaying vegetables and ex-vegetables, azure plastic buckets, and mechanical toys in the shape of prehistoric monsters called Gappa or Godzilla or Gommola. In the mean square which separates the Lion from Shimbashi railway station one steps over rows of *rumpen*, no-hopers, vagabonds, prone and sodden with their ferocious tipple of *shochu*, the grappa-like dregs of rice wine. They and their prophet's wild manes, their gnarled feet and lice-populated beards are wrapped in tatters of straw mat-ting like parcels of stale meat. The whole area is squalid, stinking, respectably vicious, and unremittingly raucous.

Across a lane from the Lion, tucked, like a never-emptied commode beneath a bed, under the Dickensian arches of the overhead railway, its foundations vibrating in the roof of the subway, is the dive New Yorker, an ear-splitting inferno of juke-boxes, red lighting, and rough-as-bags hostesses, earthy creatures from the dwindling rural hinterland, who have scented, painted and adorned them-selves as aphrodisiacally as the law allows in cheong-sams of conjunctivitis-inducing crimsons and verdigris-greens and bale-loader oranges split to their peasant buttocks. Hefty Hokusai hussies all, as well as Hogarthian whores, their laughter is so shrill as to have almost another hideous

colour of its own. After a matriculatory grog session at the
Lion there I am, in the New Yorker, sitting numbly as a
haunch of venison on a banquette of bum-worn magenta
plush at a table awash with spilt ale, and doubly repulsive
with the spiny rubble of a Japanese meal. I am not alone.
Opposite is Blue. The others have, one by one, like the ten
little nigger boys, lurched off — "Hooroo!" "Seeya, mate!"
"Hooroo!" "Seeya, mate!" Blue and I are the last two of the
Mohicans. Of the two I, at least, am incontestably shicker,
at the stage where the slightest gesture, the mildest slip of
the tongue, or the sliver of a side-glance from a repulsive
stranger seems fraught with significance. One drink more,
one only, and the garish curtain of actuality will lift to
reveal the mountain of white gold and precious silence exploding slow-motion upwards to the knees of God. I am
perfectly capable, I feel, of the look-no-hands! feat of singing in Icelandic, rattling off the Koran, understanding what
moths gently semaphore with their powdered antennae. It is
not to be. Blue, with an extra glaze on his eyes that makes
me think of farm-house axe-murderers, says in his desecrat-
ing voice, "You don' remember me, y'bastard."

Oh dear, oh dear, dear, *dear*.

Having indubitably waited to say it, he says it flatly,
flatly just this side of hurt vanity, flatly just this side of a
perceptible necessity for bitterness. I am airborne enough to
get this, but neither sozzled enough nor sober enough to do
a *passata sotto* by something like, "Are you sure, mate?" or
"Watch it, watch it!" Instead, I sit mute as mud, and this
silence reveals all. No, it states, I don't remember you.
Icelandic, Kalmuk elegies, and a fraternal understanding of
what lies behind the caprices of all alligators may, at the
moment, be well within my scope. Re Blue, alas and alack,
my receiver is off the hook.

He perceives this. It is not not not to be borne. Dead certain, Blue is, that he is not really invisible, right *now*, and
also never was in lost-to-me *then*, some yesterday, some
foundered year. With a sudden shocking violence he uses
his execrable voice and unmatching gestures to have the
morass cleared from the table by one suety trollop, fresh
beer brought by another. Then, his eyes mesmeric, he settles
down to the self-resurrecting stint of putting me s-t-r-a-i-

g-h-t. As his own apostle he is pretty vivid, and not to be side-tracked. The trains above the roof, the trains under the floor, the killer traffic outside the bead curtain, the delirious juke-boxes and the god-damning Yankee matelots inside, none of this means a thing, could be silence. He lowers his voice as if just to show. He hangs on his every word. I, too, hang, fighting down an impulse to fold my hands on the table between us like a good little kindergartener. Patiently, truculently patiently, he lifts stone after stone from my memory and, my God, suddenly, presto, lo and bloody behold, abracadabra, the crocuses spike through, spire up, unfurl, and, in the pandemonium and fetid volcano-red gloom of the New Yorker, part of a past unhibernates. A reconstituted he and I are eighteen years younger. The scene is Kure, Occupation Japan. He is a Corporal wooing the oh-so-sweet-and-cute housegirl of a Seventh Day Adventist Major in the Officers' Mess I also live in.

I seemed, in those days, to be always bumping into him. There he was, any five-thirty, waiting for the Major's housegirl by the sentry-box at the Mess gate, meantime not wasting time by third-degreeing or selling short the giggling and cross-eyed guard. There he was, as invariably as though the fates had spun some pretty plot to cross-pollinate us, in whichever of the beer-kiosks, or trinket-shops, or tea-houses I had arbitrarily chosen to give my custom to. There he was in the pathetic two-room brothel behind the White Rose Souvenir Shoppe, where the drinking of luke-warm Asahi beer and the relief of lust took place on the threadbare matting of a room furnished with a pre-Raphaelite sewing machine, a cheval glass sheathed in frayed brocade, and an elaborate Buddhist altar of mildewed gilt in a lacquer cabinet that also contained two bottles, one of Suntory whisky, the other of a murky purgative. Cut-out magazine photograhs of Betty Grable and Moira Shearer were pinned to the walls. The room was often aesthetically misted by the fumes, very Art Photograph, of smouldering mosquito repellant. Stenches of varying felicity corkscrewed their tentacles through rents in the paper shutters from God-knows-what putrescence or cess-pit out there in a tatterdemalion town slapped together from the charred boards and singed tiles of wartime bombings.

Blue had, then, an unfailing cheeky *savoir-faire* which was engaging, but so intense that it made my mind behave like a merry-go-round it was impossible to descend from. His quips and cracks were machine-gun but not fresh, not fresh. Whenever we parted after one of these apparently predestined hook-ups he was unable to stop himself squalling out not only "Au reservoir, amigo!" but also, never a miss, "Auf wienerschnitzel, chico!" He badgered me, with the fervour of Mephistopheles, to come in on his Black Market beat: my blunt refusals seem to him crass, my lack of enthusiasm scandalous, if not perverted. He drooled romantically about his housegirl in the goody-goody tones of a Sir Lancelot, his hot little hand meantime virtually well up the kimono skirt of one or other of the three spaniel-eyed White Rose harlots.

Although our natures were, by and large, absolutely opposite, recurring encounters, destiny-engineered or not, led us to exchange little snippets of unwanted truth about ourselves. None was important, and I have a hazy impression that we were drifting apart out of mutual boredom, when it came out that we both knew Gippsland well. Home-town-I-want-to-wander-down-your-back-streets stuff was on. Our relationship now had a different climate and background, both deformed. It began to seem that we had not only lived in Gippsland but had, as well, in a terrain without horizon, outline, language, or name, together participated in an initiation ceremony esoteric to the last degree, and eternally binding. In the Oriental chaos and misery and speeded-up corruption of the time it was sufficient for us to recite the names of Gippsland places — Rosedale, Bunyip, the Haunted Hills, Herne's Oak — to make us feel we were members of the one tribe. In a way, of course, we were. Our senses had been similarly baptized, and the shared memory of beige summer paddocks speckled with raisins of sheep dung, of regiments of ring-barked eucalypts St-Vitus-dancing in the heat-ripples, of ravens carping and cursing as they probed the sun-split acres for crickets, of Princes Highway telegraph wires shrilling in Antarctic winds that smelt of brine and seals and lost floes, provided us with enough tribal counters and nostalgic cards to play a childish and empty-headed game of Strip-jack-Naked neither of us won.

In short, in the tawdry gehenna of the New Yorker, he recalls us as we are tipsily deceiving ourselves into thinking we were. Like a belligerent warlock he conjures up the ghosts of our younger ghosts. The dusk of drunkenness deepens. It is nevertheless meteorite-clear that what happened in Kure is happening again. That year, it was a common Gippsland past which decorated our cut-and-come-again relationship. Now, it is to be the common past of Occupation Kure that is to handcuff us together again. Since a conclusion must be drawn from the increasingly domestic quality of our tosspot exchanges at the New Yorker, it is as sure as nightfall that the relationship is to continue. Indeed, when I wake the next morning with a mouth that has the taste and texture of tinfoil, and start to put into order the jigsaw of now-blurred, now-blinding bits cumbering my hangover, it is obvious that the relationship has already begun to continue. His business card is in my wallet. Written on its back are the time and place of a tryst. The proper side of the card indicates that he is a sales representative for a variety of commodities: Canadian margarine and tinned milk, New Zealand frozen lamb, Japanese beef and plastic vessels, an English gin, an English rum, American sporting equipment, Australian pineapple juice. His honest-to-God name? Gregory R. Patience. R? Ronald? Ralph? Roger? Reginald? Richard? It no longer matters.

Even his nickname, although I continue to use it to him, is not what my mind uses because, after we leave the New Yorker, I discover that he is Mr Butterfry, the foul-mouthed, uncouth, embittered, loathed Mr Butterfry.

I do not remember leaving the New Yorker, but do remember feeling Anzac-tall and commando-masculine as we buffet our way along beneath the barrel-sized lanterns and sickly stripling willows of the narrow Shimbashi streets, through gaggles of squat and unripe boulevardiers with louts' jaws, and eye-brows like moustaches, who are picking *their* delicate way, puma-like, in cruelly pointed non-leather shoes, among the pools of footpath water which blaze and jerk about with the violet and saffron and venom-green and raspberry of reflected and ever-stuttering neons.

I remember a solitary geisha, outside the Shimbashi Registry Office for Geisha, entering the leatherette door of a jinricksha, and being sealed in like a fabulous idol behind its little isinglass window by her two-legged horse. She is herself already sealed in layer upon layer of opalescent kimono, bound about by a sash stiff with metallic threads. Swaddled, girdled, constricted in her almost hieratic attire, her ludicrous burden of a wig flashing like a huge orchid of black glass, her face and hands thickly frosted with white paint, her vermilion lips and jet eyebrows glistening like wet enamel, she is borne off by the man-horse, upright as a clockwork effigy, anachronistic, immoral, elegant and artificial, exquisitely grotesque.

I remember swaggering after my guide into a number of smallish night-places alive with hostesses of a coquettishness so defined as to be nearly bellicose albeit nauseatingly saccharine, each ready to mulct any man of every yen he has. Since each drink makes me seem taller to myself, each new batch of harpies in sequins seems shorter, more and more like plucked monkeys in make-up and drag. Any moment, oh any moment, they will one and all scamper up the posts of the live combo platform, or up the fluted pillars of the bar-counter, take to the rafters, and swing indolently there by spangled milk-white tails among the fake maple leaves and Gifu lanterns depending from the ceiling. I remember with a faultless and absolute clarity that, in night-spot after night-spot, it is these simian women with the raw-fish halitosis of seagulls who, baring their teeth in smiles so deliberately brilliant that one senses they abhor him, call my companion Mr Butterfry.

I step aside to make comment. Most Japanese find it vexing and difficult to distinguish between l and r sounds. In their mouths Mr Butterfly becomes Mr Butterfry, a term of particularly incalculable insult when pronounced with howsoever incandescent a smile, by bar hostesses. Spoken behind the back the expression is contemptuous enough. Spoken to the face it is an appalling insult, saturated with malice. Its open use suggests that whatever incited the use has been priced as seriously appalling, also. Unforgivable loss of face has been caused. Only one step away is the offer of the arsenic-spiced *gâteau*, the jug of petrol thrown in the face, and then ignited. From women as low in the social scale as bar hostesses any insult is trebled in value. Nearly all hostesses are essentially prostitutes in that they accept money for sexually satisfying men. This is not how they see themselves. Because they reserve the right to refuse a man, however rarely, and even if never, they view themselves as non-prostitutes — prostitutes are women without a nay. That this snobbish hallucination of superiority is no more than a distinction without a difference would never enter their heads.

Hostesses are, however, not only on the lookout for a well-heeled male as husband, love-nest sugar daddy, or one-night stand. As hostesses, as cigarette-lighting animals, drink-orderers, table-companions, hand-holders, and ego-boosters, their presence is heavily charged for by the hour. As well they get a percentage on every drink drunk in their company, on every dish of salted peanuts, celery curls, dehydrated sardines, or seaweed-infested biscuits they can wheedle onto a customer's table. They prefer, therefore and naturally, regular clients, feckless clients, mug clients, who will dally for hours nibbling and sipping and tipping, and who, when the inflated bill is presented at the evening's end, will pay it without question. *Noblesse oblige!* Face must not be lost!

Mr Butterfry has only a drink or two in each clip-joint. Why not? We are ladder-drinking, pub-crawling. He is showing me the many bars he is familiar with, the same many bars in which he is loathed. He is not loathed affectionately or off-handedly. Just inside every satin-quilted or rustically bamboo or abstract-adorned bar-restaurant door he is met with simon pure loathing, naked hatred. There is no mistaking, though sloshed I am, what the deadly eyes display above the switched-on smiles. I arrive at the idea that he is execrated not only because he rebuffs, in tonally offensive Japanese, any attempt to clip him, not only because he scorns the rules of the game to pay as he goes, and pocket the change. It is rather elsewise — the vehemence of his manner, the malevolence of his unnecessary candour. It is his own hatred. It smells of murder. With no idea of what he is saying, I can hear that his voice brandishes knives, and flourishes vitriol. When we leave, the Japanese rules of duplicity require that we are farwelled with a facsimile of politeness (anyway, *I* am doing nothing outrageous), with bows that must be hell to make, with cooings that must scald the larynx.

"Auf wienerschnitzel, y' bandy bitches!" shouts bandy Mr Butterfry and, on the way to the next duel of hatreds, bedecks the theme of Bloody Jap Women are the Bloody Scum of the Earth with "Pox-ridden bloody sluts! Bloody blood-sucking jealous bloody *tarts*, every one of 'm! 'N' they've all got false bloody tits! Bloody gold-diggers!" and worse, far worse, on and on, until the last bar shuts, and another Saturday disappears down the sewer dealing with days that have no history.

Where, meantime, is the vivaciously boring Blue who waited by the sentry-box with a *presento* of chocolate biscuits and Black Market stockings? Where is the Blue who punned abominably, and unceasingly chattered (and acutely chaffered), in the back room of the White Rose Souvenir Shoppe?

My hangover still surrounding me in the fashion of a saint's nimbus, I keep the business-card tryst, and discover from a Mr Butterfry far less injured than I that there should be an overnight bag with me because it was arranged in the New Yorker that I am coming on a commercial-traveller foray into the country. Not daring to reveal that I have no memory of this, I lie that all I need is a toothbrush which I shall buy at the chemist's in the underground town at Shinjuku, where I also propose having a draught of bottled oxygen to vaporize away my nimbus, which is steadily turning dog-coloured. Presently, nimbus-free, I and a toothbrush with a mauve handle enter Mr Butterfry's Nissan Gloria, and we take off on the first of the many meaningless, fascinating, and revelatory trips we are to make together.

"Y' little mate" is how the Lion Beer Hall mob talk of Mr Butterfry to me when it becomes apparent, after several more Saturday booze-ups, that we are spending much time together like a transmogrified version of Abbott and Costello. True enough: for a couple of months he is my little mate — coarse, sore of spirit, restless as a maggot, and perpetually steeped, even at his gayest and bawdiest, in a rage against something he has not, although he never stops talking of himself, got to the point of directly revealing.

As we drive about the countryside to get orders for margarine or pineapple juice or plastic watering-cans, miles of autobiography stream from him, a mish-mash of superhuman sexual feats, quasi-criminal triumphs of diddling and putting-over, and decelerating happinesses. I come to see that he has been unable to betray his type, his gift of the infirmities and spivvish vigours accompanying Blueness, that his life is movement but not progress and that, just as he drinks with the ritualistic appetite of children and drunks, which has nothing to do with thirst, so he snatches (or used, when younger, to snatch) with ritualistic fever at the unworthiest of satisfactions. He has, I more and more suspect, built a life not to be built on and added to but burned down, a life without consolations or myths.

When I knew him in Kure, long before he had swopped himself and cheekiness for Mr Butterfry and his strange choler, he was one of the shrewdest and most successful of Black Market operators. Myself a non-starter, I was embedded in operator friends and acquaintances: ungentlemanly Officers from my Mess, Colonels' la-di-da wives, cow-eyed mothers-of-three, acne-embossed children from the school for Officers' offspring, fluke-ridden houseboys, virgin canteen assistants from the Y.W.C.A., devirginized nurses from the Army hospital. Mr Butterfry, not yet out of his chrysalis, outshone them by many watts. His rocking-horse nostrils objectified his genius for smelling out. Even more zealously than he sniffed around the White Rose, the amateurish strip-tease shows of the Naka-dori, and the Major's housegirl, whom he courted with *presentos* of skeins of wool, lengths of Habutai silk, and scanties of imitation black lace, he sniffed around and into the Black Market heart of the back alleys, his face boyishly crinkled and winningly freckled, his eyes motionless as sixpences, his gruesome voice inexorably sawing away at any branch in the way. He had come to a dishevelled country which seemed to make promises, to drop hints. He had ears to hear and, having heard, the skill to turn promises and hints into lovely filthy money.

How he was able to stay on in Japan after Occupation troops withdrew is a triumph he missed telling me of. He became rich. At a time when the starving natives were mak-

ing hashes of cats and sacred temple deer, suburban Tokyo
houses could be bought for the proceeds from the Black
Market sale of a couple of cartons of Lucky Strike cigarettes.
Mr Butterfry owned five such houses as well as a beach
house at Atami, and a mountain retreat at Chuzenji. He
married the Major's housegirl, who was able to lady it over
housegirls of her own. Two children were born, two girls.

He had, so to speak, come all the way from Gippsland
and boyhood to catch his unicorn, had caught, and corralled
it. He could have consented to be mollified by being some
kind of expatriate *rentier*. Not he. Con-men outwit themselves. Maybe there were events outside himself, outside
idiot extravagance and jettisoned common sense, outside his
own lack of foresight, which led to downfall. The lusty
Black Market, for instance, sickened, grew worse, died.
This is not entirely as he understands it or, rather, as I understand he understands it.

As he drives through the Progress-devastated hills and
dales littered with bulldozers and concrete-mixers, now and
then interrupting his high-pitched and blasphemy-larded
monologue to gulp rum from the bottle we share like unholy
infants, it gradually becomes patent that he regards himself
as having a mystical bond with catastrophe. Some It or
They beyond conventional mishap has had it in for him
since before he was baptized Gregory R. Patience, and long
before he was the scorned Mr Butterfry. I should like to say,
"For God's sake, you've got a job, a house, a car, an air-
conditioner, an Omega watch, and a gut full of rum. Relax,
mate, relax!" or "Look here, you've been crimming around
just this side of the law for years. What did you expect to
expect?" Instead I plug my mouth with that of the rum
bottle.

He finds no repose in the absurd Victim of Fate verdict
he has come to. His dismay at being down to his last house
and last car has the quality of hostility. With an impercipience so incredible that it dazzles me as if he were a
genius moron, he has designated himself a martyr — and a
furious one.

The martyrdom, I notice, habitually has Japan as its
backdrop or, rather, always seems always to have its climax
at the core of a *contretemps*, twilight and sinister, which had

been magicked in a jiffy out of radiant high noon by an ectoplasmic but evilly Japanese agency. I suspect, however, that the faceless fate, the voodoo in the woodheap who or which enrages him, is bandily biped, *homo sapiens*, common as dirt, Mr Butterfry himself.

When his bouts of railing become too strident and dotty I want to say, "For God's sake, Blue, give it a rest. Why don't you just shut up shop here, and shoot back home before you get too decrepit to be racing around flogging frozen mutton and Pommy gin?" This is out of the question, and not to be done because it is not the thing to do: I have no licence. His having, despite the autobiographical incontinence, not stripped away all the rinds from his privacy — and, surely, deliberately — seems a warning to come no closer, to keep my shut mouth shut. It is an attentive ear he has invited to accompany him on his trips to sell condensed milk, not a questioning tongue.

Perhaps I could safely, during his maudlin outbursts of it's-just-a-little-street-where-old-friends-meet, hometown sickery, have asked why he does not cut the Japan painter, and whip his wife and daughters off to Australia. Per-haps. I decide, however, not to ask, and listen to the one-after-umpteenth edition of his dream-like passion (he does not know how dream-like, and I have no right to tell him) to retire and settle down — his words — in a little Gippsland fishing port he was last in over twenty years ago. Because I knew this Sleepy Hollow place as he knew it, I understand — at least, as much as someone who has no daydream at all can understand — his fantasy of playing the well-to-do beachcomber there, the weather forever halcyon, the fish always biting, the weatherboard pub never closed. I see what Mr Butterfry sees: the palsied red gum wharves stacked with crayfish pots, the indolent reed-fringed river seething with bream, the Shylock-bearded goats under the Norfolk Island pines, the sandy side-streets of bluestone cottages behind hedges of looking-glass shrubs and lad's love. Yes, I should like to say, "Go back!" but dare not, cannot. If he is trying to change himself into something else, he must use his own wand.

Anyway, whatever nebulous but vindictive force he accuses of hounding him into a cul-de-sac, I incline nearer to a certainty that inertia of will is to blame, that he is his own victim, his own chained and captious mongrel. From my seat there is little else to see.

Then, one night, as if he has — flash! boom! — become clairvoyant about my unput questions and secret judgment or as if he has been profoundly considering them for weeks, and has reached a decision, suddenly, utterly apropos of nothing external to his own mind, he says, with electrifying and ugly vehemence, "Yeah, by Christ, *yeah! I will.* Yeah, I'll showya; I'll bloody showya, mate."

He is drunker than I have ever seen him, maybe because I am so many undrunk drinks more ʒober than is usual in his company as to be practically maiden. We are well within the outskirts of Tokyo, driving back from Atsugi and the United States Naval Air Station where, having got much larger orders for gin and Kobe steaks and plastic baseball-team jackets than he foresaw, he has over-celebrated in the Officers' bar.

Now, early night, eight o'clock, seventy miles an hour, out of the blue: "I'll bloody showya, mate."

With not the wispiest notion of what he is getting at, "Good for you; I can hardly wait," I say, and, "Show me what?" I expect no more than some superdive as yet unknown to me, some special coven of bedizened monkey-women with unflinching snow-white smiles whose hatred of Mr Butterfry is at the peak, who are already lined up with their tumblers of petrol and an Esper electronic cigarette-lighter. "Show me what, master?"

"You'll see. You'll see." For the first time I realize that the adolescent falsetto, grating and grinding, is old, older than he is, as the noise of the glacier starting to move is older than the glacier itself. "You'll see. I'll bloody showya what it's bloody like." He stops. The primeval sound stops.

Silence . . . and silence.

Silence from him is another first-time experience, and an unnerving one. Momentarily I am aghast. The ventriloquist has left the scene. No matter, the doll drives on. The doll, worn-out and voiceless, with its ginger curls and flat glass eye, drives on, robot-perfect, at perilous speed. I am host to a nightmare fancy: he and I, the mute residue of Mr Butter-fry and I are to spend eternity together, alone together, fixed side by side in the front seat of a runaway Nissan Gloria which he will steer violently around corner after corner, cutting deeper and ever deeper into a maze of unnamed streets, a labyrinth of catless alleys, all utterly deserted and silent — locked houses, shuttered shops, unlit street-lights, blind walls, smokeless chimneys, telegraph poles propping up the dead filaments of a vast cobweb that has no edge and no centre.

It seems unreal, therefore, when he pulls up in a suburban street of real-seeming passers-by, with overhead lamps, and the television gabble of "I Love Lucy" in dubbed Japanese. The street is not much chop, but not seedy, rather claustrophobic from the eight-foot walls of grey concrete on each side in which are set the fake rural gateways leading to the houses behind. As Mr Butterfry gets out at one of the gates he speaks again.

"Home," he says. "Home sweet bloody home." This has the intonation of Hell sweet bloody hell. "Get cracking, y' bastard. Y' gonna meet the wife." In such situations I am the Pavlov rat — my hand fossicks for the comb.

As he opens the gate I ask, "What's her name?" I ask because, in the Kure days, she was one of the Mess house-girls, and it seems possible that she might expect from me the politeness of remembering if she were Fumigo-san, Kiyoko-san, Setsuko-san, or Whatever-san. I am simply after rainy day material to play the game of being well-mannered with.

Mr Butterfry behaves as though I am asking for my own name. He goes immobile and pensive and, after a pause, turns his head, arranges that his eyes are on me, as on a defective, and after an unbelieving examination of something behind my face, says fretfully, "I married the bastard, di'n't I?"

What does he mean?

"Whattay' think her bloody name is? Mrs Hirohito? Mrs Duchess of Windsor? It was for real, amigo. She's Mrs Patience all right." Ah well. Next, as though the name is other and more than authentic, as though information is not the true centre of the circle, he says it again, "Mrs Patience". His burnt-out lips make the two words the filthiest I have ever heard. His face is that of a vole in a trap. Had I any

trust in imagination I would accept, right there, outside the
gate of crooked branches, the catalogue of answers which
has flashed on the screen of my mind, and would dramatically remember any appointment anywhere, and excuse
myself to hurry off in the direction of anywhere with his
"Auf wienerschnitzel, chico!" gimleting my ear-drums. I
have no trust in the imagination. I follow Mr Butterfry
toward Mrs Patience, and the living-room.

The Japanese living-room with its floor of padded mat-
ting, its paper shutters, inconspicuous shut cupboards, sole
ornament, and no furniture, has a spartan and spurious
refinement. In attempting the affectation of making an art
of the skeletal and parsimonious, it imposes the harrowing
discomfort of poverty. It is a sort of fragile hut that can
quickly become a pigsty but, kept scrupulously shipshape,
ungarnished as an empty bird-cage, it gives the illusion of
being the acme of abominably good taste. Of such a room, a
large one obviously the total of two former rooms, Mr Butterfry and Mrs Patience, and their half-caste daughters,
Lana, seventeen, and Shirley, thirteen, have made an il-
lustrative and crudely gorgeous museum of their lives. It is
the very zenith of electrically bad taste.

The area set aside, as it were, for Mr Butterfry's exhibit is
dominated by a cocktail bar as flashily outrageous and sparkling as the altar of a Mexican cathedral, and his treasures
are arranged near the monstrosity, or festooned above and
about it; scores of goliath or obscene bottle-openers; scores
of needlessly ingenious and fantastic cigarette-lighters; the
stencilled felt pennants of Australian Navy ships, life-
saving clubs, and football teams; several richly framed
oil-paintings of Gippsland landscapes by old-fashioned,
once-esteemed Impressionist artists; and a squad of
atrocious Made-in-Japan statuettes, all either off-colour or
self-consciously pornographic — Pis-Manneken, Leda and
the Swan, Europa and the Bull, Cupid and Psyche, that sort
of thing. It is the bazaar of a rich little poor boy.

In his unpunctuated soliloquies about himself Mr Butterfry has repeatedly let fall, maybe as incidental self-tribute,
that his half-breed daughters are popular as photographic or
commercial television models. I have taken popular to mean
used twice or thrice rather than once. How wrong. In the

junk-shop congestion the most discomposing objects are the overlapping posters which, from ceiling to floor, cover the walls with bar-hostess smiles, and eyes and eyes and eyes. On every hand Lana toys with, holds up, or archly indicates Mikimoto pearls, an Instamatic camera, a deerskin purse, a Hi-Cook Fryer, a stereo-monaural tape-recorder, or a goblet of Mercian wine. Elsewhere she emerges from a scarlet Compagno Spider roadster or a mink coat, or is discovered in the company of a comely young man amid the *art nouveau* conceits of Maxim's de Paris de Tokyo. Meantime, dozens of poster Shirleys enact, from under a tar-black fringe, or from between horizontal pigtails, childish rapture over tinned beef curry, effervescing cordials, bottled tangerines, homogenized milk, seaweed drinks, and lurid sorbets.

In appearance — the posters prove it over and over again — Lana and Shirley are unsulliedly Japanese, racially untainted. No physical trace shows of the blue-eyed Mr Butterfry with the paprika-tinted freckles blotching his forehead, and sprinkled among the red-gold grass on the backs of his hands. He might never have impregnated, never have set foot in Japan, never even have existed. His daughters could be copy-cat versions of an infinity of ancestresses as they are copy-cat versions of the oh-so-sweet-and-cute housegirl one used to see mincing pigeon-toed between the canna-beds of the Mess garden towards the sentry box where her Black Marketeer lover bobbed up and down like a Jack-in-the-box. Visually, the daughters are amoeboid breakaways from no one except Mrs Patience.

Her indubitable contribution to the museum is a perfect illustration of what happens when the Japanese move one millimetre off the strait of their national taste into the complex cross-currents of non-Japanese taste. Richelieu-work antimacassars hang on obese settees of glossy brocade; the carpet arabesques of unsubdued colours pulsate and twitch beneath the light of a plethora of frilled lampshades; two china cabinets and a glass-fronted sideboard are stoked with the white-hot brilliance of cut-glass vessels; urns of blue velvet roses are disposed on pedestals of fictitious marble; little lace-shrouded tables are burdened with trinkets and figurines. The lean woman standing erect at the centre of

this intemperance is, Mr Butterfry says, *her*, Mrs Patience.
He could be introducing me to a leper.

She acknowledges me by making a cryptic minor ad-
justment to her expression, no more. Her eyes are on her
husband, as on a snake.

Out of context I should never have recognized the ex-
housegirl any more than I recognized Mr Butterfry at the
Lion, and it can only be illusion that, in the taut creature in
its dusky kimono, I think I discern vestiges of what I think
she was once like. I do instantly recognize something else.
How could I not? Outside the gate of tortured branches my
mind had in a flash warned that, just as in all the bars with
their inimical hostesses, so in the last of Mr Butterfry's
seven houses, so in this preposterously bizarre room. Here,
too, the captive air is wounded by the vixen's smile,
radiantly bitter, by the eyes implacable and pitiless. Does
she, too, call him Mr Butterfry?

He is behind his bar, under the stalactites of football and
life-saving pennants, pouring this and that to make some
show-off interfusion he calls his Special. Without looking at
her, without faltering in his mixing, "Y' bloody rude Nip-
ponese bitch," he says. "Why di'n't y' say something to
m'mate, eh? Eh? Who d'ya bloody think you are? Y'know
how to behave. She knows bloody well how to behave,
mate. She knows all right." He illustrates that he does, too.
He pours a final jigger of Parfait Amour into the turbid
Special and, his mask of malice merely slightly tempered by
hostliness, lifts one of the brimming pilsener glasses: "Come
an' get it! It's a curl-a-mo, chico. Lead in the old pencil."
As I take the glass, he continues his hostly good behaviour.
"Not t' worry, mate. It's not you she's shitty at. A-a-ah, no
no no! Home sweet bloody home, this is. I told y' I'd
showya." He has fulfilled his obligations, and abandons me
to his Special and returns to his sheep. "You s-l-u-t. Y' hate
me, don't ya? Don't ya? Don't ya, eh? Answer me, y'
scungy bitch. Answer me!"

She has been standing as she was standing when we came
in, unshakable, unshakably in the middle of the implausible
emporium, she and her quarter-smile of well-bred
repugnance, her dark-robed trimness, her iron-still hair
riveted around the invisible sorcery of her mind, her half-

seen hands in control of some monstrous engine of destruction. Disdain surrounds her like an element nothing can fog, splinter, or melt. A future as yet uncorked, she will, at any moment, in a voice pure and angular as quartz, utter a lacerating profundity, produce the flash of a lightning-blue sentence which will erase Mr Butterfry in a sprig of smoke.

"Answer me!"

She speaks. Her lips writhe, as lips in novelettes used to, and she speaks: "Watta y' doing home here at this hour? Get thrown outa somew'ere?"

The battle is joined. The brawl is on. The tainted leaves explode away from the branches. The branches snap and shatter like the sticks of a terrible fan.

At my time of life to be embrangled in the who's-afraid-of-Virginia-Woolf improprieties of a husband and wife savaging each other is still dismaying and spirit-fatiguing but no longer shocks and sickens as once it did. Too many ex-glazed lovers and ex-glossy couples have played typhoon and bloody murder under my nose. Perhaps, to be certain of double murder without murdering, they shamelessly require the brake and safety of a bystander or, at least, as exhibitionists do, the presence of a dumbstruck audience. Mrs Patience and Mr Butterfry deny me nothing. The dirty leaves and rotten branches rain down — subtle mischief, flagrant deceit, betrayal, double-dealing, and malevolent chicanery.

Regarding myself as beyond shock, I am nevertheless shocked, and it takes a while to decide why. I am certainly startled and fascinated when it comes out, piecemeal, that most of Mr Butterfry's misfortunes have not been caused by his own moral or mental debility nor by a fateful mismating of Japanese stars but by a gluttonously ambitious Japanese mother, the former oh-so-sweet-and-cute house-girl bred on rice slops and pickled radish in a penurious and primitive village in a cleft of the hills behind Kure. It is by her machinations that, one by one, Mr Butterfry's clutch of houses and, I learn, a motor-launch and a racehorse have evaporated as bribes to buy continuing prominence for Lana and Shirley in the careers she has chosen for them. It is easy to see that, to herself, she appears conventionally maternal: thousands of Japanese parents, for example, feed examiners the heavy bribes which ensure a son's or daughter's place in a university. Her bribes will have been indecently heavy for, although Japanese in appearance, the daughters are authentic half-breeds and, as such, so near to untouchable that unusual largesse can have been the only means of getting them within cooee of the limelight let alone smack in the middle of it. Yes, I am startled by the knowledge of what really happened to Mr Butterfry's ill-got riches, but not shocked.

What does shock, and so totally, so physically, that the searing Special laves my gullet like milk, is the quality of Mrs Patience's self-defensive shrillness, the freakishness of her accent and verbal obscenity. If the poster daughters, whose magnified china smiles and multitudinous immense opaque eyes glimmer all around and above the mêlée, have inherited not one perceivable scintilla of himself from Mr Butterfry, not so the wife. She has, mantis, eaten his voice from him — inflection, pitch, discordancy, the lingo itself with its oaths and mutilations. Her self-justifications match his accusations in every degraded particular. Acrid and bowelless though they are they even have the wheedling spirit of the con-man, and I stand convinced that it all, to the last and most contemptible betrayal, serves him right, that it is absolutely just that his chickens have come home to roost defeathered and septic. At the same time — and not merely because I am shocked by the *lusus naturae* effect of a burlesque Australian working-man's voice spurting from a pocket-edition foreign woman in a tastefully dour kimono — I feel that she, rigid and free of warmth as a doll, is charged with power and evil, with all the glib treachery and rancorous lunacy of her race, and that Mr Butterfry is doomed, unjustly doomed.

The mind's cigarette-lighter flicks up a single-flame glimpse of him as he was, as Blue, in those White Rose and Black Market days, chipper, impertinent, disarming, as cock-a-hoop as the village idiot boy at one of his own wretched sallies in the whiffy back-room of the Souvenir Shoppe, lecherous and unfaithful as a tom-cat yet faithful as a mongrel to his idea of love for his housegirl, his oriental Daisy Mae, of whom "I love the poor little bastard, chico.

Mate, I'm tellin' ya, she's the only bloody sheila'll ever get me by the short hairs."

Let there be no doubt that it is the fiery and filament tributaries of the Special suddenly overrunning their levees, and inundating my brain, that cause the lighter-flame to expand into a wide-screen fantasy. Despite the din of the quarrel, the strident sound-track, I see the whole lurid vision. The down-at-heel castle, Arthurian, Disneyish. Battlements bearded with weeds. A raven hunched on each and every pennant pole. Pennants like old tea-towels. Dawn — cold and cheap. Far up, in the highest turret, the faceless King of Con-men at an embrasure, behind the cobwebs, behind the smoke of a gangster cigar. Far below, just beyond the portcullis, the rabble of mounted knights on the drawbridge, Knights of the Unholy Grail waiting the J. Arthur Rank gong that will unleash the ratbag mob on its quest of swindling and duping: Sir Jeroboam the Purple Knight, Sir Jocularis the Chequered Knight, Sir Jackanapes the Pin-striped Knight, a scruffy host of others, spivs all, and . . . there! . . . younger than any, freckle-peppered, ginger-haired, *retroussé*, tirra-lirra-ing in a lamentable falsetto, our man from Gippsland, Sir Juvenilis the Blue Knight. The nags fret and caracole. Each knight, waiting there in the bilious sunrise, secretively polishes a platitude or two, practises a snide and hypnotizing smile. Ah! the ravens stir, hunch their shoulders, look down their beaks — the gong sounds. They're off! Watch the Blue Knight. Follow Sir Juvenilis, and see him by-pass the perils that topple the others. The Forest Forlorn, the Hazardous Crags, the Mere of Thin Ice, the Marsh of False Steps. Hear him whistling past Dungeon Grey where Giant Wideawake has clapped Sir Jeroboam and Sir Jackanapes. Now he gallops down the last avenue (trees of tinsel and fake crystal), radiant with his rake-offs, and shining like a prince, towards the Maiden of the Eastern Hills. In a flash the bells are ringing, the champagne bottles foam at the mouth, the maiden has become his oh-so-sweet-and-cute princess, and the screen shudders and shimmers with intimations of happy-ever-after.

It is a pity, it is always a pity, that even if one is shrewd, or lucky enough to leave in time, while the champagne and *hors-d'oeuvre* are being gulped and gutsed, that circumstances — the dropped glove, the library book left under the seat — bring one back, reluctant and fuming, in the middle of another instalment, a later reel. In this case the dropped glove can be said to be the Shimbashi Lion Beer Hall or, more pinpointedly, Blue saying, in the tones of an aggrieved and deserted deity, "You don' remember me, y' bastard". The later instalment, the latest instalment, is the one in which the Maiden from the Hills, promoted to the princess with her surfeit of antimacassars, and cabinets of cut-glass salad bowls and sandwich trays, turns out to be no more than the wicked witch, the run-of-the-mill dangerous dam, with her casque of iron hair, her stranger's mind, and the stolen voice which quadruples her power since she can annihilate her victim with his own bird-of-prey accent and tricks, his own brutal oaths.

It is time to leave again, and finally, no dropped glove. If nothing else the sound-track, and who's-afraid-of-Virginia-Woolf discord, is too boring, on and on and on. More boring than anything is the truth. The truth? Mr Butterfry, my little mate, Blue, Gregory R. Patience, Sir Juvenilis, foul-mouthed, desperately yelping behind his cocktail-bar and a palisade of on-the-nose statuettes, has really found what the Unholy Grail contains. He has come as far as he can, and that is that. Now that he has, as he said he would, bloody shown me, perhaps I can, at last, partly agree with him: a fatigue like the fatigue of metal has incurably affected whatever brand of luck he may be said to have had. There is no chance of its reviving, and no way back for Mr Butterfry, no escape hatch, secret tunnel, airlift, exit of any kind, none, and nothing.

It is just as well. It leaves him with at least one dream, one Teddy Bear to tote around, or cuddle as he ranges the country to sell Pommy gin and Yankee running-shoes. The Teddy Bear dream is the retiring and settling down one. What I had no voucher or permit to tell him is better not told. The dream is no longer worth dreaming. The Sleepy Hollow fishing village in Gippsland, where he sees his dream self fishing and lazing and earbashing and shouting drinks for well-kippered old-timers with fish scales in the salty folds of their sweaters, has been wiped off the board of reality. Goats and Norfolk Island pines, sandy streets and lad's love hedges, crayfish pots, and weatherboard pub, not any of these is there. Offshore, oil-drills straddle the former fishing grounds. The village has become a geometric townlet of metal and cement. The blue-stone cottages, one of which he pictures himself buying for a song, are contemporarized, added to, and reverberate to the habits and hallucinations and accents of Americans, and cost the earth. Ferro-concrete hostels, gardenless, glassy, glaring, enclose the institutional male horse-play and immigrant odours of escapees from the neurotic and dirty Old World, the riff-raff of degenerating civilizations.

It does not matter how I escape the costly chaos of the living-room and the walls papered with depthless eyes and shadow smiles. As a ghost does from the ignobilities of the living, escape I do, slipping away so inconspicuously that the two engaged vehemently in the drama of hatred notice nothing. The sound-track of their vilifications does not falter or blur. I close the gate of artistically deformed branches as one closing a book never to be opened again. The long long street of secluding and imprisoning walls, ill-lit, and mediaevally winding in and out of a plexus of sun-less other mediaevally winding and ill-lit streets, unravels before me, and instantly and darkly ravels and reravels itself behind me. Back there, farther and farther back, lies the room, a gaudy and inferior star caught in the meshes, enclosed in the night just as the geisha, meretricious, bizarre, and blinding, was in the black leatherette cabin of her jinricksha. Back there — caught and enclosed in the room — Mr Butterfry, the Mr Butterfry who must, tonight and any night, sooner or later, flag, run down, crack up, give in again, the Mr Butterfry with whom one has shared the fascinating exhaustions of mateship, and on whom alternately squandered contempt and pity. Not until I am almost out of the tangle of suburban criss-crossings and convolutions does it seem clear that the contempt is useless and that, even if he has to suffer alien constellations and outlandish ethics, the pity is not needed at all.

Whatever anyone thinks life is for or about, whatever fatuous prophecies are attributed to scientists, whatever abnormal skills are wished upon poets, musicians, actors, etchers, sculptors and others of the non-man-in-the-street sect, Nature has not once indicated that life is for or about anything more than an arcane necessity to breed, before one dies, others to breed and live and die. The rest is side-line, mere decoration — Rembrandt oil-paintings, penicillin, Big Berthas, graven images, Lanner waltzes, top-hats, asceticism, pacifism, football-club pennants, cut-glass salad bowls, take your pick — side-line decoration, no more. Nature's suckers are, in a final generalizing count, left one only wry consolation: to love their spawn even if the spawn detest them.

I cannot tell whether, off the posters, Lana and Shirley Patience, mobile and nubile, the flames of their smiles turned down or utterly put out, love the Mr Butterfry whose relation to them, in a country of racial snobbism, makes them nearly untouchable. A guess that they do not love him is beside the point. Whether, in a melo-dramatically changed form (Act Sixteen, Scene Ninety) from the Kure one, Mr Butterfry still loves the transformed housegirl is most doubtful. A surmise of not is also beside the point. He has decided to bloody show me something of why he viciously hunts bar-creatures through the neon nights. They are creatures of the same sex and jungle as the one he long ago foretold would have him by the short hairs. Only a tithe of his excessive despair is, in private, uselessly usable against the combination of her alien inscrutability and stolen accent and vocabulary. He has, therefore, so much to spare that a prodigality of public venom has become inevitable.

He has, as well, either by accident or with elemental subtlety, bloody shown something else.

Paper smiles and eyes, bought with other houses, remain lining the walls of his last house. In the centre of its bazaar-room, she, the classic dam as much a dupe of nature as he, remains, witch-neat in a sombre kimono, black-tongued as an Australian alley virago. He has not thrown her out. He has thrown out no one, not even himself. He has not torn down the seductively grimacing posters.

If the last house must finally go so that there is no wall at all on which to tack the extra posters the house has been bartered for, his condition of imprisonment would not alter. A beat-up Sir Juvenilis, an ageing terrier of a spiv snarling and sniffing in the daily darker corners of the prison, he is not to be pitied, neither for losing his Black Market riches nor the fishing village which no longer exists.

How else than by pretending to hate such showy losses can Mr Butterfry really and truly con himself — as con-men such as he must finally do — into accepting that he hates his guilt, and deeply loves his daughters, all smiles, safe for a year more, a week more, a moment-before-the-deluge more, on and behind their gaudy paper posters?

The Sale

Aware that an act of adulation is easy or, at least, that any-one in a hole can come to the worshipping of anything — words, liquid in a bottle, a golden calf, the blown-up photograph of a crank — he's unmoved when it becomes patent that They (he thinks of them as They) in their fashion have set sights on him.

At most he hates them tenderly, and tries to avoid the offer of their unshakable hands, their overtures which have a desperation behind them.

He?

He's a novelist, famous enough, a *petit maître*, and far from prolific, content just to keep the wolf from his rented bachelor door. He appears occasionally on the literary merry-go-round, and only to scotch a whisper that he's self-satisfied and stand-offish.

They?

They are would-be Patrons of the Arts, breakers-in on ivory towers, a childless husband and wife, frankly wealthy, as well-meaning and lavish as lunatics, and convinced that all authors, like all geese, are shoeless.

They hanker to fling open doors to him.

Their town house, a plague-spot of Culture and its camp-followers, rears Victorianly up from a gardenscape like boiled spinach through which gallivant semi-nude demi-deities of marble.

Husband (elfin, with a two-pronged beard and a Ver-cingétorix moustache) and wife (wrestler's legs; a manly, pretty face) threaten rather than merely display enthusiasm. Invitations menacing with flattery stream flak-like through the letter-slot of his old-fashioned flat in a stodgy suburb.

He can't comfortably understand what *They*, a pair like them, see in him or novels like his. He's unsure that their fervour isn't insulting. It's anyway boring and They themselves such adroit bores that he only rarely, egged on by his publisher, walks under their lintels into rooms not subtle enough to sense a predicament.

He arrives discreet; remains strikingly polite, showing his square teeth in edited smiles; leaves unrifled, with the dignity and concealed roots of an iceberg.

Enough, surely?

At last, however, at long last, They have their hour.

Drained and peaky after hermitic months on a recalcitrant novel he finds himself resigned enough to accept their often-repeated invitation to use their beach-cottage as a . . . as whatever he wants: refuge, study, convalescent home, love-nest, temple of orgies.

"Do what thou wilt," They say. "Ask anyone you want to, or everyone, or no one. Have solitude or *amour* or parties. Our house is yours."

He now knows They are immoral as well as rabid.

As frayed men will, he thinks he feels some need for the house, but solely for the ocean in front of it. His mind, at last deserted by the deadly characters so long kicking up their heels in it, is still fogged by the melancholy of their not-yet-settled dust. Remoteness, an ocean's active or inactive emptiness, will, he hopes, quickly settle this.

Do the eager parasites, garrulous with victory, sinister in their liberality (a dedication on the title page of the new novel?), guess that he's yielded also because he knows They'll be out of Australia for some months, and can't therefore descend on him, radiant with proprietary affection and stinking curiosity, and laden with romantically ill-chosen gifts of books he wouldn't read on Devil's Island (expensive avant-garde poets, *novelle* by nigger homosexuals, plays peopled by anti-war marijuana-smokers in the nude), and supplies of the fashionable food and drinks he doesn't go in for: vintage clarets, burgundy and the beef fillets to marinade in it, garlic, artichokes, coffee beans, aubergines, zucchini, Camembert?

He prefers Shakespeare and Irish stew, Jean Stafford and weak tea, Thomas Hardy and apple pie.

The scalp-hunters are never for a moment in danger of doing the correct thing for him: neither ocean nor sky is really theirs. Higher education and cookery hints by Alice B. Toklas have cluttered their minds, leaving no space for perception. They are intellectuals, and know to a nicety the difference between the time-filling-in values of Bach and Bingo.

He's crafty enough to find excuses for not driving to the beach-cottage until They are well air-borne, and arrives to find it a quasi-mansion solemnly stocked with new books for him (expensive avant-garde poets, *novelle* by nigger homosexuals, *et cetera*), with vintage clarets, burgundy and the beef fillets to marinade in it, *et cetera*. A painfully witty letter larded with over-detailed instructions for a shoeless goose leans conspicuously against a painfully asymmetrical pseudo-Japanese arrangement of dehydrated foliage.

His benefactors' compulsion to repeat a pattern is every-where in evidence. Air-conditioners, a hot-water system, glittering electric machines, are either zealously active on his sole behalf (snow has already fallen in the deep-freeze niche of the refrigerator) or ready, at the touch of a switch, to be zealous. Here he is augustly to fulfil himself: *à la carte* amenities on every hand, desires *du jour* no trouble at all. His eye, truffling through the layers of possessions, per-ceives beneath the banal magnificence and considered elegance some fixed, dreary, unrelievedly flawless dimen-sion. He's in a wasteland of taste and comfort where nothing will rot, flake or unravel in front of him or behind his back. For him this Great Indoors has no tricks of charm he can refuel himself on; trapped like a *dernier cri* caveman in an enchantment that doesn't come off he can foster only the guile, docility, and spitefulness of the prisoner.

Outside — now there's what he thinks he wants.

The few other beach-cottages set among the tea-tree behind buffalo-grass lawns, and hedges of oleander and hibiscus are not near, and are anyway shut up.

It's early autumn; the season's over; the doors and French windows seem as closed for ever as doors in a painting; a Canaletto-like film of sunset light makes it incredible that, stuck immobile behind it, are radiograms, Persian rugs, vitamizers, electric stoves, exotic beach-hats, nickel-plated medicine chests filled with sunburn lotions, arrangements of furniture and bibelots enclosed as symbolically as those in Tutankhamen's tomb.

Outside, a sunset, indifferent that the calendar season and summer are ticked off, languidly fritters itself away in a summer manner above an ocean of glass — no — looking-glass. Were he to wade out waist-deep he can only be doubled like the knave on a playing-card, the upper half fastidious, canny and tart, the lower with a touch of the orphan.

Pink oddments of cloud like larger rose petals are all the luminosity holds idly in suspension. Perhaps these are delicious auguries: here on this littoral are solitude and refreshment; Earth is nobody's but yours; tomorrow will again counterfeit summer with a mercilessly blue sky.

Tomorrow does. For nine days early autumn sticks at this dazzling imitation. He walks miles along the beach, a Crusoe finding no footprint but his own, primitive and brutal among sea-gull prints delicate as trails of ivy. He watches dolphins appear, disappear, reappear along the seam where shore-green waves fuse with off-shore-blue ones.

Are the dolphins playing or working?

When the colours of the oleander and hibiscus blooms bite like acid into the dusk, he comes to think, "Time to go inside already!" rather than, "Time to go inside at last!" Each night he cannot gulp his fill of yawns; falls instantly asleep.

The mist of dust aroused by his characters — the love-sick, the betrayed, and the jealous, all frantic, all smelling the same — weakens, finally disappears. Spring-cleaned, empty, fresh, his mind awaits the unborn.

On the tenth day he wakes to find the fake summer gone, a silver sweat on the panes, rain drifting down in cold veils on the fish-grey pleats of the ocean; on sand the colour of old armour are strewn iodine-brown coils and intestines of kelp. The surges are no longer cream and jade, Mediterraneanly tepid, but chilled and sour brine dirty as kitchen slops. The season is in truth ended. Nothing to do but turn on electric fire, twist the air-conditioner switches to HOT, and read. There's nothing to read but newly minted

authors, the latest of the latest in their unseemly dust-
jackets. Willy-nilly he opens one to confront a self-pitying
poem, political, dreary as a toad's complaint, and mottled
with dirty words. He slaps the book shut. With a jerk, as if
starting out of plaster of Paris, he comes fully to.

Where *is* he?

He makes the age-old sound of distaste, of self-
condemnation, that no dictionary records. If he has momentarily signed himself away to tuft-hunters, the contract
is not binding, the sale is over. From somewhere rush the
lines: *The attendants came in to look at their dead Emperor, and
lo! as there they stood, the Emperor said, "Good morning!"*

The situation he has permitted with such a shrewd and
selfish carelessness is now seen to have become impossible.
The beach is no longer to be his but flotsam's and jetsam's, a
wailing place for gannets and, not improbably, venerable
mermen with the bleached eyeballs of the blind, and
mange-blotched scales. Fogs are on the way; and pallid
skies sick of looking down on reeking tide-lines, trawlers
with seized-up engines, unfruitful fishing-grounds; his ear
will discover that the din of the ocean is all too exactly the
din of highway traffic. He is left with nothing but a penitentiary full of possessions; a truth without thunder or
lightning, and neuter as the taste of water, a smarminess
without nether fires.

"There are," he hears himself say to the teak-panelled
walls, the turf-thick wall-to-wall, the Nigerian masks, the
Swedish glass, the omelette pans and copper-bottomed
saucepans, "too many weevils in this rich biscuit."
Metaphorical weevils, yes, but not even one flesh-and-
blood mouse — the prisoner's accredited cell-mate; and
there'll be no tapping on the other side of any wall.

Summer at last gone to earth, this is no place to endure
leisure or renaissance in; better by far a room-without-bath
in a sleazy, cosy Private Hotel, nothing except a carafe of
dying water and a brand-new Gideon Bible to feast on.

The all-over taste of the absent host and hostess cancels
their absence, and is, he perceives, less an art than a vice. Its
assumptions — theirs — would infiltrate him through the
costly furnishings and bibelots, the fool-proof comfort and
unspeakable books, and irritate him frantic.

Possessions announce what possessors are.

Looking around, he sees that They are in all things gullible; that there's a tremendous market for prefabricated feelings; that They are willing to feel anything fabricated for them to feel, and that he, a public commodity, is for them a ready-made feeling.

"The prizes for a writer," he thinks, "are all too modest; my God, the risks are mortal."

Once again, in the rich house beset by poor weather, he makes an unrecordable sound, then says, "Immediately is almost too late for me," and begins the work of absolving himself.

Like one fleeing Pompeii just in time, he packs, and locks up the prison. A fly-wire door slams finally with the wrong sound; it's not a hot and brilliant noon; the rain falls; the blowflies and their sonorous fine-weather melody are dead.

He starts to drive inland, towards his back street and the coin-in-the-slot gas-meter, towards self-possession, towards the privacy of his own secrets and sin, his own dried rose and familiar scars.

Inland is grazing country. Mile after mile of stone fences, and hedges of boxthorn and scarlet-berried hawthorn, run in a network up hill and down dale, criss-crossing in all directions the exuberant undulations.

Without rain there is more than something English in the landscape; blurred by the Scotch mist it smacks strongly of eighteenth-century Susssex: a dripping highwayman could feasibly ride out with cocked pistol from the clump of elms at the next bend in the road; a hay-wain with a smocked and gaitered gaffer atop creak into view.

Embowered in oaks and cedars, pines and orchards, the farm-houses and their outbuildings enact seemingly pre-Industrial-Revolution peace and plenty on the crests of rain-smudged eminences, nineteenth-century arks taken root on so many lesser Ararats. Their television aerials, electric light and telephone poles are less visible than the density of their past, less eye-catching than the width of their acres, and the height of their hay-stacks.

Once he sees a hawk, contemptuous of weather, suspended in a supervisory way high above a stock-still herd of strapping Herefords and, he has no doubt, a population of plump field-mice and swallows and thrushes, and corpulent hares torpid in their forms. All is abundance and order.

Early in the afternoon, decorously rounding the base of a hill, he sees the red flag with SALE on it in white letters. It hangs, stirless and sodden, from the lowest branch of a senile elm, a branch with imperfect arteries whose much yellower leaves suggest a later autumn than the merely part-sallow other leaves do. It hangs above two gate-posts that once had pretensions. Now, both are askew, and the spherical top of one is missing. How long since it fell, and rolled away into the briers and blackberry canes? Was there no one, then, in the house to restore the dignity of the house's post? The house is doubtless uphill: an avenue of lindens whose disreputable vastness and melancholy state their age seems to lead there.

On an impulse he turns in between the posts. The avenue is steep and serpentine; the thistles growing on it, spindle-shanked and ailing things, have been only recently felled by other vehicles than his. Here, in a district of abundance and order, is abundance awry, order ruptured.

As he drives out of the almost-twilight of the tunnel of leaves and entangled branches, he finds about thirty cars drawn up among horehound and docks on a level space. Beyond this, to be reached by walking up higher yet to the hill's very top, is a large weatherboard house. Trees, an orchard, hedges, a garden, all superannuated, all run amuck, press in upon the house, accost it with a sort of malign and distraught picturesqueness.

The house itself has, as it were, suffered a mild stroke yet also has — the expression comes to him as he draws up beside the earlier cars — a dissolute vitality, a secretive self-satisfaction. The dilapidation has its rakishness. The eaves wear what-the-hell cockades of grass; window-shutters are slanted aside less with a derelict air than a tipsified one; a Mermaid rose, immoderately enterprising, rages every-where; now submerged beneath out-of-hand lilacs; next, insolently brandishing its cream-yellow petals above a moss-choked pear-tree; next, bursting out from the ventilator-louvres of a gable to darn itself through the barge-board curlicues. On all the Scotch mist placidly drizzles. There is no one in sight.

He throws his raincoat over his head; runs up towards the house; hears from within it muted bursts of an auctioneer's machine-gun gabble.

The drizzle suddenly languishes, ceases. The garden, as abnormal and impenetrable as the Sleeping Beauty's, barricades the front of the house. Seeking entrance through the yard behind it, he comes on the stinking remains of a pyre that has died midway, a hummock of part-cremated mattresses and pillows, cane chairs, bamboo what-nots, and sheets of music — old songs. This rubbish-heap resembles nothing so much as a broken attempt to incinerate the furnishings of a slum visited by plague. So many mattresses, so many pillows — whose? — that the kapok vomited from the charred ticking thickly coats the ground like a peculiar and grimy snowfall.

He picks up two scraps of music on which fire and rain haven't yet quite undone the words. He reads:

Less than the dust beneath thy chariot wheels,
Less than the rust that never . . .

and is deciphering

Till the sands of the desert grow cold,
And their infinite numbers are . . .

when a man comes vigorously out of the back door, decisive as a murderer quitting a murder, a live wire on the way to elsewhere.

He's unlikely to be a country man; his up-to-the-minute clothes intimate this; his shoes are city shoes, shoes for escalators, bistros, and the tessellated pavements of mid-metropolitan shopping arcades; he has oily Israelite eyes, and the dusk of his jaws is powdered like Turkish Delight.

Surprised in his role of scavenger, the novelist lets the wet fragments of paper drop and, for something to say, says, "Sale on here?" an inane one for which, he's aware, "Good-bye, mister" would certainly better serve.

Brakes on, the man raises his profuse black eye-brows, and performs an agreeable smile, a somehow commercial one, an office one rather than otherwise. The man is no ugly customer, although an ugly customer, a striker of hard bargains, can be sensed lurking just behind the smile, and indulgently says, "Yes, here", even if thinking, "You must've seen the flag and the cars, you clot."

His eyes have meantime set a value on the novelist who's also patently not dressed for cattle-yards and paddocks, whose raincoat is a Burberry however draped on his head like an Irish biddy's shawl, and decides to go further:

"The effects of a Miss Christine Marly. Died last week. You're not a local?"

Now's the novelist's turn to think, "Clot!" but he admits, "Just a come-by-chance. I was passing and . . ."

And what?

"There's nothing worth buying, nothing. I know. I'm a dealer."

While a quite shameless ring, jewellery rather than gentlemanly, glitters on a hairy finger, the dealer pauses, leaves a gap for the prowler-around-rubbish fires to come clean.

No?

He goes on: "There might've been something once. The Marlys apparently ran a model property, and lived high, if I'm to believe the auctioneer in there. That was years ago. I suspect the old girl flogged anything worth-while. She was nearly ninety, the last of the tribe, and lived here for thirty years or more all by herself. Never saw a soul; a lady-hermit."

"Oh."

The novelist commits no more: he's elsewhere, is by the decapitated gate-post, in the avenue of slaughtered thistles, standing baulked outside the ferocious garden.

He seems suddenly older: listening, for him, is a kind of superintended debauchery that ages the face.

The rose plaits itself through the dismembered barge-board; the chimney bricks are eaten into by winds going nowhere; it's decades since the brass handle of the back door shone like a knob of gold: what a setting for a woman with a name like a prostitute's alias, for Miss Christine Marly, to act out thirty-odd years of solitary drama in! Even if it's not like it at all he's already inside a house he must enter to see the spavined side-boards, the magenta wall-paper on which birds of Paradise bicker over pomegranates, the brown oleographs of lake-side Swiss villages.

The dealer is — is less than the dust, could belong to a sept that worships lightning, and counts no further than three.

"Oh" isn't enough for the dealer; it's unsatisfactory, bloody rude, and no grist. He enlivens his eyes, becomes Jewishly engaging to screen his curiosity, rakes up a wry dimple, and rather carries on:

"And an odd tribe it was, never a marriage, all old maid sisters and bachelor brothers living together. *Very* odd, eh?"

The novelist is actually at work. *Heroines*, his mind writes, *like goddesses, are no longer as necessary as they once were. It is almost unbelievable on what iron rations the spirit can survive*, nevertheless he compels himself to say, "Odd? Perhaps."

"No perhaps about it. *Very* very odd. The auctioneer told me that every time one of them died their bedroom was locked. Imagine that old girl living alone year after year with all those locked doors."

The dealer makes a decidedly Jew-boy grimace, *sentimentalisch*, and dramatically mimes the turning of keys in a row of doors. The gangster-boss's jewel on his ring mournfully flashes, and both men look at the funeral pile of singed and sordid bed-things.

The dealer recovers, makes a last effort, really putting himself out (but, at the same time, producing his gloves, one from each raincoat pocket):

"If you're going in, there's a photograph of the whole family in the front room, taken when they were young. One of them'll be the old girl. I don't know which one. Neither do the locals in there. Some say one, some say the other. *They*'re not buying much because there's sweet Fanny Adams to buy. They're just sticky-nosing."

"I suppose so," says the novelist, back from somewhere, and adds, with a mildness foreign to his intent, "We all do. I'm sticky-nosing too. I'm very interested in people."

He halts as if he's not going on, but does go on.

"I'm an osteopath," the novelist tells the dealer.

It's now the dealer's turn to utter a toneless "Oh." If he expected anything it isn't this. Osteopaths shouldn't look like violinists or playwrights. The dealer's bilked. Fortunately the rain indicates that it's about to descend again.

The dealer pulls on one soiled pig-skin glove.

"How bestially fearless she must have been," says the novelist thinking of locked rooms and sobbing drain-pipes.

"Who?" Taken aback by this unforeseen classiness, the dealer puts on the other cleaner glove, the right one: he's left-handed. "Oh, her."

"Miss Christ-ine Mar-ly. . . ." The novelist affectedly says this.

"Well, I'm off," says the dealer to the obvious nutcase, and off he goes into the rejuvenated rain expecting no response at all. As he reaches the corner of the house some nasty niceness makes him turn, and call out:

"See if you can find out which is Miss Christ-ine Mar-ly in the photograph. She'll be one of 'em."

He raises a gloved hand with a disappointed but Dale Carnegie smile in it, and disappears, hairy and dapper, with his icing-sugared chin.

The novelist turns from the gutted, flame-and-water-tainted mattresses towards the back door through which — the front door being barred by savage flowers, barbed-wire vines, and encampments of ancient snails — her coffin must, he's sure, have been carried. Ah well, as if that sleep were any different! It can have no more remarkable aftermath than sentimental songs burnt at the edges.

He doesn't mind at all that he's been behaving whimsically to the informative Jew, but recalls it as unfitting that, instead of announcing merely, "I'm very interested in people", he's not said, "I'm very interested in what people buy, surround themselves with, cherish, hang on to, in what they leave behind: Virgin Marys and Mary Gregorys, plough-shares and ju-jus, their blood-rusted dirks, their scent-phials and thumb-screws, gramophones and water-colours. What outlasts people, that's what people are."

As his hand closes on the chilled, ungolden door-knob there's a burst of manufactured laughter from the people inside: perhaps the auctioneer has been discreetly vulgar about a Marly chamber-pot.

He enters the house which smells forlornly of decayed linoleum and mildewed ceilings, and is crammed with vacancies. Spectral outlines on the wall-papers of absent chiffoniers, tallboys, wardrobes, hall-stands, and chests-of-drawers recall a city-slicker voice: "I suspect the old girl flogged anything worth-while."

What remains is light-weight, common as dirt, most of it fit to join the mattresses and what-nots in the backyard.

If, during the time he spends drifting from room to room, the locals, peering askance, come at first to consider him another dealer on the look-out for Coalport gravy-boats and papier-mâché tea-pots, they finish up bamboozled. He neither bids nor pays attention to the bidding. He fingers nothing. He asks no question, and meets no eye. He can scarcely be said really to look at anything, and spares a mere glance for the infirm piano, the one kerosene lamp with its cracked shade and smoke-bruised glass chimney, the seven old-fashioned china dolls as maimed as escapees from a leper colony. Once only do his eyes graze for any length of time on a family photograph. Oxford-framed behind fly-speckled glass (*Bella Vista, November 1904* states the white inscription), taken on a sunny day in front of the house, taken years before Mermaid roses are created and christened, when the eaves are spirit-level horizontal and grassless, the chimneys sharp-edged and unlichened, the weatherboards glistening with paint, the four now-unopenable French windows, opaque with algae and cob-webs, ajar to the sunlight, their panes transparent as air.

As the locals, flock-like, follow the auctioneer and his clerk from room to room, harangued into desultory bidding for an incomplete tea-set, a trite wash-stand, a tarnished meat-dish-cover, they feel nearly affronted that the stranger moves always to another room as though avoiding the genial fevers of humanity.

What's he up to?

He's observed to return to the photograph, to scrutinize it with the fretful severity of the dowser in whose hands the forked twig won't vibrate, or of one who has a remarkable headache. What *is* he up to, seeming to photograph a photograph through the intense lenses of his own eyes? There's nothing special about it: a mother and father centrally seated in wicker chairs (a carpet laid down to pro-tect the close-shaved lawn), their children standing behind them, four statuesque sons, ruffianly yet handsome, five slender daughters, maidenly and impassive. The carpet is a little rucked, but the sun shines. No one is speaking, but they have all only just stopped, and will start again when the photographer ducks his head from under the camera's cloak, and says, "Thenk yaw, thenk yaw."

Up to? The novelist's doing no more than asking the unanswerable: which one are you, Miss Christine Marly?

Are you the one hugging the square-shouldered tennis bat as if it were baby or puppy? The one with the clove carnation pinned over her heart, and wearing the beaded belt with the heart-shaped buckle? The one with the elaborately puffed out coiffure and two bangles, one cable, the other plain as a slave-girl's, looping down below the triple frill of lace at her wrist? The one with lowered lids who is nearly smiling, and holds something cylindrical half-hidden in the folds of her lawn-touching skirt — a diploma? a candle? a roll of music? Or are you the one who has her arm about a brother's waist, and leans on him, he looking quizzically down, she soppily up so that the dark butterfly bow on her nape shows, and the unwrinkled curve of her yearning, young young throat?

Which of you died a week ago, the last of the tribe, nearly ninety, after living alone for over thirty years?

In the house I've just fled from, every abstract painting, every rare liqueur, every marble wash-basin, every long-playing record, every one of a hundred buttons to press, make known outright what They think They feel, what They do and do, what They worship. Their immoderate and tedious history's cut and dried, its pattern not hidden: no need to read between lines. It's easy to know all They've done throughout the last thirty years. It's difficult to guess what you did, Miss Christine Marly, day after day during your thirty, night after night.

It's not that I pity you. There's scant truth in the notion that no experience is unholier than loneliness; there are no scales on which the value of your kind of life and death can be weighed. I seek merely, and ruthlessly, clues to how you filled in more than ten thousand solitary nights and days in this hill-top house, the provincial town five miles off twinkling after dark like a forlorn drift of embers. Or did you never look towards mankind with its embers and makeshifts and moralities? Did you listen instead to the midnight gale

in the old wooden trees, and the morning scandal-monger-
ing of sparrows or, with the calm depravity of the erratic,
not listen at all? Which of these seven blind china-faced
dolls was yours, and when last fondled? Eighty years ago?
Two weeks ago? Were yours the finger-tips that wore the
elephant-tusk-ivory of the Carl Rother piano keys down to
the wood playing *Till the sands of the desert grow cold*? Or,
since the candle-sconces have been unscrewed, did you, as
the Jew-boy dealer suspected, sell them along with
chiffoniers and tallboys and God knows what else, and
never play a single chord?

The lamp chimney is smoked thickly black; you must
have lit it time and again. To read by? Hardly likely. I hear
the auctioneer say of the glass-fronted bookcase, "Sorry
there's no key, ladies and gents. Snapped off on the lock
about a million years ago . . ." and something arch about a
lucky bidder and a Shakespeare folio. Locked in for so long,
so few books, and not an avant-garde poet, not a negro
novella: *Thoughts on Daniel and Revelations, Illustrated Bible
Geography and Atlas*, half-a-dozen Scott, half-a-dozen
Dickens, three biographies of David Livingstone, nothing of
this century.

Why light the lamp?

To listen to its flaccid yellow tongue lisping indelicate
lies, licking the chimney filthy with its black tip? To watch
yourself in the metallic murk of the cheval-glass harrowing
your hair with the worn-down bristles of the ebony-backed
brush, seeing the enormous stock of hair inside you dwin-
dle, become sparser, lose colour? To stare, intent to the
point of trance, at the never-sleeping ironic eye on a moth's
wing, and dream meanwhile of the Prince Charming who
never turned up, to think thirstily of love, without having
grown to know that love isn't worth a thought or a dream,
that its gravity and savagery don't warrant even a side-
glance of curiosity?

Did the roses battering against the sullied panes come to
smell to you of anything but roses, sickly as the excrement
of reptiles?

Did you, alone on the darkening stage, a hand on your
breast so that the heart cannot hear, think to half-hear

footsteps and the clink of tea-spoons, giggles and rustling petticoats, in the wings out of which no one ever came?

Did you, the fathoms of any one of five thousand, ten thousand, fifteen thousand nights over you, look up towards the cobwebbed ceiling, interrogatively towards the sky, as though some voice there had uttered something you ought to have heard?

Or did you chatter to yourself, hours at a time, in an eager, unnatural way as if meeting a stranger for the first time, or as if you were in command of a fragmentary language in which nothing need be ever exactly said — and not heed a syllable you were saying?

The novelist moves away from the photograph.

The auctioneer and his circumspect flock are now out of the house: his yelping comes from a distance, from a stable or a barn.

The novelist moves away from what tells him nothing while telling much. He has the house to himself, the years of grime and spiders and a neglect that goes the whole hog, the dinner services filmed by rat-grey dust, the down-and-out cups and saucers, the chairs and sofas unpolished for years and, in the kitchen, arranged for sale on a vast table, iron boilers and saucepans and frying-pans, flat-irons, ladles, pastry-cutters, cake-tins, each and all rust-diseased, sloughing off flakes as he looks.

The squalor is everywhere impressive, classic, the finished product of a super-slattern or a mad-woman, and yet . . . and here something eludes him. If there has been disaster it is, he can't help feeling, not only remote but hilarious and deliberate, a matter of enjoyment. Everything has been abandoned to itself with a witch's merry shrug, sardonically perhaps, no drag-ropes of sentiment or sorrow.

The last of the Marlys — the unmarrying, the non-mixers perched above the world of matings, the local exiles with their idiosyncrasies and alien woes, their locked death-rooms — can have expected or wished no outsider to brave the winding steeps of the linden avenue, to ascend from the business of afternoon-teas and Euchre to sip afternoon-tea and play Euchre with her: rats do not thrust themselves on the child of a cat. Why walk knowingly into a zone of unceremonious weather?

Prowling alone in a house whose contents seem to have decided not to observe a usual propriety but to be haywire and capricious, the novelist begins to consider that he's been maudlin, and has romanticized into being a Miss Christine Marly more like a thin-skinned Victim of Fate than a woman who lived to be nearly ninety. When, the key turned in the lock of the penultimate brother's or sister's door, her life breaks off from what it's been soldered to, that is not perhaps the dead-end of things he imagines. It could be the start of an era for making sallies on new experiences, for savouring unknown ecstasies and fears, for reconnoitring her dense, limited element to its outskirts.

She can do much. She can plan her own terrors, and confront unhindered her own vices; she can catapult herself into repugnant pieties and austerities which have nothing to do with a past of rules and interruptions, customs and duties; she can — with the clock unwound and stopped short, the teacup unrinsed, the garden gone mad, its weeds tall enough to conceal tigers and malefactors — dance and sing all day. She can mock her own ghost mocking her from the streaked looking-glass. She can writhe in epic rages on her bed and, unrebuked, shriek elaborate blasphemies and barrack-room obscenities, or — a low card in a high game, with no more blood on her hands than in her veins, and resigned to her own lack of temperament — she can sit hour after hour as mum as a lizard, listening and listening and listening.

Everything, some time or other, somehow or other, must have spoken to her — the cast snake-skin on the threshold, the thickening rust, the stain winding down the wall, the decomposing torso of a doll, the upturned beetle dry on the sill, the scuttle of parched leaves in the corridor, the far-off scarlet-voiced cock announcing a dawn in which all the puddles are as undrinkably red as blood, cold and still. Knowledge must have perpetually stolen up behind her.

Did she suspect, and not turn to face it, enacting ignorance, exchanging no warnings with herself?

Did she virtually never speak at all?

He receives no clear answer. It's not a house for speaking directly; its mouth is sealed with rust; its crooked smile

plays its tricks behind veils of web and mildew. He receives
no answer for it is not yet time, although it's time to go.

He leaves by a side door, and is interested to find himself
in a distorted orchard, nameless windfalls rotting everywhere in a cidery stench.

He's surprised to find rain and mistiness gone, a weakling
wind abroad, and several shafts of sunlight slanting down
through a splash-shaped rupture in the suave clouds as if
pointedly to spotlight an excessive clump of arum lilies,
sheaves of them white as white kid, and to create a mystifying dazzle beyond them. Standing in the doorway he has to
use four matches to light a cigarette — the wind keeps filch-
ing the flame — and wonders what the dazzle is. Cigarette
lit, he goes to see.

He has only to follow the path, narrow, a one-person
track deeply foot-worn, but can stop before he reaches its
terminus for there's no need to seek further or ask another
question.

Miss Christine Marly has spent the years meticulously
and artistically arranging thousands of gin bottles in a sym-
metrical and convoluted design, very geometric, of zigzag
glassy ridges, luminous circular hedges, shapely crystalline
mounds. Not one weed mars this vitreous parterre, this
maze of bottles. He doesn't bother to wonder who drained
them.

He finds his way to the car. The locals, trailing out of the
stables, observe that his face is blank from stupefaction or
contentment or, perhaps, world-weariness — one cannot
tell with aliens.

Two hours later his suburban door is shut behind him
and his still-expressionless face; his wood fire burns; a jug of
cocoa steams on his desk; the traffic on Highway One four
blocks away moans pulsatingly in precisely the same manner as the ocean They freely lent him.

He sits.

He lights a cigarette.

He dips his pen into the black phlegm of the ink-well,
and begins:

*Aware that an act of adulation is easy or, at least, that anyone
in a hole can come to the worshipping of anything — words,
liquid in a bottle. . . .*

At McGarrigle's Inn

"I did warn you, my dear," says Miss Thirza McGarrigle of Hathaway, Tasmania.

Hathaway has, even in 1977, a Village Green, a sweet-Auburn one old-Englishly embowered in titanic Constable oaks. As though it were still the eighteenth century an invitation to apply for grazing rights there is annually drawing-pinned to the post office notice board, and sticky-taped up among puppies-for-sale and Linen Tea announcements on Hogan's shop window.

Only Daft Scottie, ninety-two, oldest inhabitant but hobbledehoyishly energetic, applies. He's daily seen, a face like Lent, wearing imperishable hobnail boots and a senile tam-o'-shanter, gnarled patriarchal staff in hand, bossing — with the insufferable smug dignity of an accredited eccentric — three balloon-uddered Friesian matrons along the deep path they've trodden through plantain and teazle between the Green and his own two hectares.

Here, behind centenarian hawthorn hedges, his hens prodigally lay, vegetables wax, bees do shift-work in hives, and his three-room cottage of hand-made bricks older than he, wind-nibbled and moss-mortared, skittishly admits the outrageous twentieth century through the muck-rake of a television aerial while concealing his possibly repulsive bachelor habits from the same century as personified by the denizens of Hathaway.

His yokel appearance and little, baffling piggy eyes suggest a fragment only of the truth. He's no Robinson Crusoe in this. Other locals too have an unpierceable reticence. Outsiders' questions, however innocent, elicit no angels or explanations. In their laconic, misleading utterances, and the hole-in-space silences between them, lurk intimations of handed-down rancours, of hibernating curses already in existence before the reason for them is ripe.

In a dark quadrant of their minds where nettles sting, and the hips of the wild rose are bitter, they endure obscurity with resentment even though there's an unvandalized telephone booth in High Street, and the general store sells Fanta, polyangular sunglasses, vitaminized cat-food, and paperback smut-novels, written by American Jews, and with inflammatory covers.

Hathaway started off, in chain-gang days, as a military hamlet: those elegant stone houses class-consciously overlooking the Green were built for regimental surgeons, commanding officers, and their Dundrearied kind. They are nowadays kept in doll's-house trim by antique-shoppe-haunting lawyers and estate agents, or unmerry widows with eau-de-Cologne pasts. There are clipped box and delphiniums outside; it's perfectly safe to assume Coalport and davenports within.

Once on a highway the village no longer is but, being less than two kilometres south of the present one, and midway between two provincial cities a mere twenty-five kilometres apart, it's nearer to computer and telecom tower than a newly-arrived Martian might guess from its air of knowing nothing mentionable about the two cities and their Woolworth supermarkets, air terminals, Lebanese restaurants, jeaneries, rent-a-car depots, whining Hare Krishna gangs, late-Victorian cast-iron drinking-fountains. Yorkshire shop-stewards, and Virginia-creepered museums abundantly garnished with scrim-shawed whale's-teeth and penal leg-irons.

Nevertheless, compared with other villages twenty minutes' drive away — Mudlea, Yewvale, Snatching, Uxworthy, and Tremble Brook, with their closed-up shops, smashed window panes, last-gasp gardens bloodshot with geraniums, and dawdling-past citizens unfathomably engaged — Hathaway bustles, at least throughout the summer-tourist season. It's closer to the highway, and not far from several tripper-beguiling Regency mansions vouched for by the National Trust, and a notable 1840 church, designed by a convict forger, in the graveyard of which are

some equally notable headstones exquisitely and con-
volutedly carved by a convict pickpocket. Hathaway's three
churches, old but of paltry design, have no graveyards, only
a few primly furled pencil pines sticking straight up out of
weedless lawns. There are, instead, two opulently weedy
cemeteries, the one on the western outskirts Protestant, the
other, on the eastern, Roman Catholic.

Here, among slightly askew or acutely awry Celtic
crosses, elderly cypresses, and splashes of autumn crocus,
the family tomb of the McGarrigles stands out. It's the
roomiest. Its scrupulously vertical, austere but patently expensive, cross is the loftiest. The ever-freshly-gilded
Requiescat In Pace chiselled on it serves for the several
generations filed away under inscribed slabs of marble.

Three brothers who died in 1939, 1952, and 1965 seem
to represent the latest generation. They also represent the
last — one learns this at the inn the McGarrigles built when
Queen Victoria was middle-aged, and have run ever since.
The brothers were, says their sister Miss Thirza, bachelors
all, and dolorously intones, "*They* finished the McGarrigles
off. End of the road; end of the family." That, by the way,
is all you'll ever learn of the brothers.

Three brothers, bachelors; three sisters, old maids —
Miss Thirza, Miss Ellen, Miss Carmel. Miss Carmel, having outlived an assortment of disreputable beings —
Rasputin and Fatty Arbuckle, Roger Casement and Quisl-
ing, Isadora Duncan and Aimee Semple McPherson, died in
1967, of what no one now says. Strange: she's not inhumed
in the splendid family tomb nor, though there's ample
vacant space nearby, is her grave anywhere adjacent. Indeed, it's seemingly as far away as possible, on the other
side of the cemetery, and marked by a door-sized slab of
brawn-pink granite with a high glaze. It forms the central
panel, her name incised, of a horizontal triptych.

The other sisters' day will come, their names be incised
too, one on each flanking panel — but not just yet: Miss
Ellen and Miss Thirza are still with us, and still running the
inn in their own whimsically lavish and richly idiosyncratic
fashion as though, any day, Edward the Peacemaker might
drop in and ask — yes, *ask* — for what they can supply
without wincing: four-poster beds, Minton teapots,

Georgian cutlery, chandeliers, Courvoisier, silver cigar-boxes.

What part Miss Carmel played when, during the inn's swankiest and palmiest period, there were the three sisters to look after their eminent guests — governors-general, vice-chancellors, chief justices, august visitors from abroad who'd been ruthlessly vetted before being recommended to the choosy trio — remains unspecified. It's to be suspected she saw to the bijou touches: pleating table napkins into ornate shapes; heaping roses and smilax in epergnes; mathematically setting out Waterford wine-glasses; leaving out for late-home guests, on the console-table by the foot of the stairs, a silver entrée-dish of sandwiches, a biscuit barrel of Miss Ellen's shortbread, and a thermos flask of Droste Cacāo brewed with fresh milk from Daft Scottie's Friesians.

Little doubt, from remarks let drop by Miss Thirza after she's tossed off a sufficiency of her beloved sloe gin (her own brewing from an intricate recipe), that the "dried arrangements" of honesty, barley awns, and Cape gooseberry outbursting from mammoth Rockingham tureens were created by Miss Carmel more than a decade ago. There's added proof in their dustiness, the spiderwebs filming them with a gauze it could be desecration to brush away.

Easy to commit errors of imagination, to fancy Miss Carmel drifting past the tennis court (now weedy, its wire-netting enclosure slumped and canted), under the cedars and magnolias of the hedge-girt garden (today a tousled Sorceror's Wood domain), finically snip-snipping, aesthetic, as fragile as if her bones were as hollow as a bird's and in the grip of a nameless nineteenth-century wasting disease. Miss Carmel could, of course, have been as russet-cheeked and solidly robust as Miss Ellen, as flamboyant and forthright as Miss Thirza, and have died of a surfeit of roast sirloin and port wine.

Whatever the late Miss Carmel did, no mystery about what the Misses Ellen and Thirza do. Their roles are fixed. For how many decades have they been so? No one's clear. Declining to look their age, concealing it in agelessness, they themselves divulge nothing; and even when Miss Thirza's sloe gins and Miss Ellen's brandies with black-currant cordial somewhat defrost reserve, never hint why they, and not the brothers, inherited the inn as young women.

Miss Ellen is the establishment's Martha, the one always waiting for the kettle to boil. Up at six every morning, by seven she's pegging sheets, pillow-cases, and towels on the clothes-line. This is in the remains of a former orchard: two gouty Cox's Orange Pippin trees, a mammoth cherry-plum tree, and a rachitic pear tree with mean, morocco-skinned fruit as inedible as door-knobs.

As cook she's an old-fashioned perfectionist. Nothing leaves her kitchen — sauce, chutney, marmalade, jam, ice-cream, custard, cordial, anything — not made by her of the best ingredients. *Ready mixed, instant, deep-frozen, artificially coloured and flavoured, tinned* — such terms are dirty words and heresy to her. Vegetables and fruit, except for sanctioned hot-climate exotics, are brought direct to her from garden or orchard by regulars like Daft Scottie, or seasonal vendors: voiceless little girls pale as Cheddar offering strawberries, raspberries or red currants; boys with faces like foxes or old lags bearing mushrooms, rabbits, or a dipper of the berries stripped from hedges with which Miss Thirza, adhering to her tedious recipe, concocts galvanic sloe gin; black-finger-nailed Rowlandson clodhoppers, pimpled youths with no more brow than a Teddy Bear, turn up with the baby turnips Miss Ellen insists on, with just-picked peas, or new potatoes the size of golf balls.

Trout, quail, mountain duck, a hare to be jugged, also turn up, as it were express from the Great Outdoors, often out of season, in sugar sacks toted by reprovable and shifty men toothless as babies and with a pruned finger or two, at the fly-wire back door of McGarrigle's Inn.

Miss Ellen's skill in dealing with these was perfected in the rose-coloured days when, helped by a staff of skivvies from back-road cottages known to harbour the incestuous, she prepared five-course, forty-guest dinners for solvent sodalities, civilized spendthrifts, and pastoralists' slothful wives. Of the grimmer aspects of her art — the Aga stove almost incandescent and infernally throbbing, the fore-seeable whirlpools of chaos to be adroitly skirted, the succession of culinary climaxes to be reached with cool calm in a boiler-room swelter while maddened blowflies batter themselves punch-drunk against the fly-wire — Miss Ellen says nothing.

Miss Thirza says much, but her account starts in the dining room when the curtain rises on the two inordinate chandeliers blazing above the vast table and its burden of epergnes, Parian figurines, claret jugs, rococo silver cruets, and starrily glittering crystal. There's one sideboard ornamentally set up with urns of flowers, Copeland ewers, Crown Derby frivolities; the other bears the utilitarian decanters and three intricately chased silver champagne buckets.

Behind the embossed leather screen that conceals serving-hatch from diners two cap-and-aproned waitresses dally for the starting signal, their hands white-gloved. "Oh, for effect, naturally," says Miss Thirza, "but less for effect than to cover the hussies' chewed finger-nails, and nasty red knuckles."

As she talks, now and again excitedly brandishing a forearm girded from wrist almost to elbow by silver bracelets, her Romany-queen eyes change focus to where some inner projectionist runs a romantically edited film about the hey-day of McGarrigle's Inn, she herself doubtless the star, played by a brilliant younger creature, vivacious and reckless, titian-haired, unwrinkled, not yet harried by sciatica.

Ah, the past! The grand occasions! Fairy lights looped in the cedars and horse chestnuts; scrubbed little boys to direct cars to parking spots; drink-waiters in white monkey-jackets hired from the city; a city dance-band to play wistful cocktail music before dinner, and Golden Oldies for those who cared to attempt dancing after dinner in the vast French-windowed ballroom.

In the shadows beyond the carpets of light spreading out from the French windows there would be unbidden watchers. The Misses McGarrigle, aware of them, would know without the help of spies who the loiterers were, which sullen locals, which strange-minded starers down from Misery Farms in the poor-soil foot-hills south of Hathaway, which adolescent no-hopers deliberately retangling the tangle of false legends left over from Hathaway's era of convicts and their military guardians.

Miss Thirza's still the one to greet guests today, as she

did then, in grand-lady manner, hair dyed indigo, one of her many Cashmere shawls, half-escaped from the clutch of her bejewelled fingers, trailing across the Persian rugs like the White Queen's. She's still the one to say, even if every four-poster and tester is empty, "So sorry, but we're utterly booked out," to passers-by she instantly senses are finger-lickin', tea-bag-dunking, potato-crisp-nibbling, motel people. As she says: "I'm really doing them a service. They'd go mad here with no colour television in their room, no electric jug, no air-conditioning. They're no more for us than we are for them."

She used to be the one who, *noblesse oblige*, quipping and bantering mine-hostily, spent an hour or two each day helping behind the bar or, when the day's mood or hers seemed to require it, serenely settled down to outdrink village toughs or smart-alec commercial travellers (whom she never *ever* encouraged to stay in the house: Hathaway Hotel, other end of High Street, was the shebeen for them), and, having dismantled them, to eject them with professional charm and genial implacability.

And she it was who had to deal with peter-tickling barmen, pilfering maids and light-fingered charwomen. Although her fury was Medea-like, and the pretty little police station directly opposite, she did not, as she'd have liked to, drag the squawking felon across to it. She was always her own magistrate, behind closed doors, she and the accused alone in the kitchen. Sentence passed, the malefactor could be sure nothing will be heard of the crime by anyone else except Miss Ellen, nothing, never a word.

"Even if I'd wanted to warn the world, or felt the police should know, not a syllable! This is Hathaway. One slip of the tongue, and they'd burn us out! My God, those tiny, darkened, fumbling, hill-billy minds! And if I hadn't learned how to throw those drunken hoodlums out of the bar in the right way, well, they'd burn us out too!"

What does she mean when she says things like this to guests she knows well? Late in the twentieth century is surely too late for that Old-Country, Cold-Comfort-Farm hysteria, with wild-eyed bumpkins slavering and gibbering in a ditch while barns and ricks evaporate in flames. *This is Hathaway*, are her words. What is Hathaway? There it is:

swallows kiting preciously about over a Village Green straight from Hardy, all those spidery fanlights, and cute stables of cinnamon-red bricks, and multi-paned shop windows, and Sussexy gardens ram-jam full of asters, zinnias, pompon dahlias, Queen Ann's lace and Michaelmas daisies. Look at the hedgerows crimson with haws, the ditches blue with chicory! Listen to the goldfinches and plovers and Daft Scottie's rooster announcing that the moon has set.

Whatever Hathaway was (convicts in mustard-yellow flannel, Majors' wives in Swiss muslin) or is (packaged sliced bread, king-size filter-tips, take-away food, Opportunity Shop) there's no need now, surely, for Miss Thirza still to cry wolf. There are no maids at the inn, light-fingered or otherwise, no white-gloved waitresses, barmen, odd-job gardener, no employee except an irreproachable daily char, and the occasional helper-out.

The Misses McGarrigle muddle happily through, carry on, get by. The bar's been closed for a decade because the old maids defied a Licensing Board order to install inside lavatories off the bar with its board floor, boxing and hunting prints, framed old maps, long wooden settle, and open fireplace. They can easily be egged into telling the tale.

"I said," says Miss Thirza, "I said to this *sawn-off* little runt . . ."

"Don't exaggerate, Thirza," says Miss Ellen. "He was taller than you."

"Shut up, Ellen. I said, '*Don't* use the word toilet to *me*, young man. We absolutely will *not* ruin this dear old bar with indoor *lavatories*. We have them upstairs already. For *guests*. There's a spotless and well-constructed one for *customers*, for drinkers, five yards from the bar door. *Gentlemen* have used it for years. The Governor-*General*. Leading *barristers*. Well-known . . .'" She stops dead. Her voice becomes silken; her gipsy ear-rings hang still. "Ellen, why've you handed me this teeny drink? What happened to the glass I had?"

"You're getting tipsy."

"Don't be euphemistic. I'm getting drunk. I intend to get drunker. My sciatica's giving me Larry Dooley. From now on I'll pour my own, thank you very much."

"On your own head. So-o-o," says Miss Ellen, sipping

her empurpled drink, and blandly watching Miss Thirza pour, "we dug in our heels, and refused to build . . . "

"And that *loathsome* little pipsqueak . . . "

"Taller than you, Thirza."

"Shut *up*, Ellen . . . that *dwarf* revoked our licence. Took it away after more than a *century*."

"Ninety-four years last May, Thirza."

They enjoy the sister act they play before friends.

Delicensing meant, of course, no more bar trade, but, as wealthy women, at that time, one guesses, both nearing sixty, they were — after the first melodramatic keening and blackguarding and consolatory letters had been thoroughly enjoyed — far from unhappy about the loss.

Favoured guests came and went as before, and continue to come and go, to sleep in four-posters, breakfast under chandeliers, gossip and drink with the sisters at night in the parlour among the costly bric-à-brac, Crown Derby and Meissen and Staffordshire, the miniatures and lithographs and colonial water-colours.

Sometimes a new but endorsed guest turns up.

One such, a young woman, daughter of long-time friends, makes her first visit to Tasmania and the fabled Misses McGarrigle. She has been dossiered easy-going and artistic, and turns out to be lithe, unsmiling, and, though dove-gentle in manner, given to taking off coats, gloves and scarves as though reverently unwrapping a priceless treasure.

The sisters know they don't quite like her as much as they should like their old friends' child. Each day she drives about in her Citroën sketching and snapshotting. Each evening, without being asked, and handling them as though they were Rembrandt etchings, she shows her sketches. She can't draw at all; and her sense of humour is located at a depth beyond the range of their dowsing-rod. Appalled that they're to be stuck with her for three weeks the sisters nevertheless, faithful to her uproarious parents, admit her to the parlour, are relieved when she doesn't appear, drink more than usual when she does. Conversation is made. One evening, after much heavy work, she toying with a solitary weak gin squash, the sisters desperately drinking as though to anaesthetize boredom, the conversation reaches cats.

This subject they've eschewed for months. Now, flushed out of the primitive warren where horrors skulk, it's upon them again. Their hearts are unwrinkled, plumped out with old sorrows, denials, and losses; but the budget of their emotions is not a limited one. Remembering too suddenly what they'd forced themselves to forget, drink playing havoc with their self-control, they become distressed.

"Oh why," moans Miss Thirza, "were cats brought up. I can't can't can't bear it. Those vile monsters!"

"You see," says Miss Ellen, calmer, attempting politeness, explaining perhaps her tear-filled eyes, "the greyhound-racing men of the district use cats as training quarry."

"Men!" Miss Thirza flushes darkly. "Monsters! Subhuman freaks! Vile! Vile! Vile! Y'know what they do?" She speaks thickly, as though choking. "Cut off the poor little things' claws so that . . . " She cannot go on.

"Defenceless little pussy cats," says Miss Ellen, tears flowing, "torn to pieces . . . "

"Savaged!" shouts Miss Thirza violently.

"God will punish them," says Miss Ellen.

"Why wait for God?" says the guest in her cooing creamy voice. She makes a pause occur. The sisters become aware she's steel-lined. "There's the R.S.P.C.A."

Something happens. Gears somewhere change.

The guest senses flurry, an instant disarray within the others, as though a camera has clicked at a wrong and private moment; and sees the two sisters look at each other; but goes on: "These men must be reported. I'm going to the city tomorrow so . . . "

"No!" cries Miss Thirza harshly, the first to come to, and, "Oh no," says Miss Ellen like one suddenly made absent-mindedly sane, "no, that won't do at all. We shouldn't have told you."

The guest, amazed, wears the knowing look of one who's puzzled.

"You can't, my dear," says Miss Thirza. "As Ellen said, we shouldn't've told you. We've said too much. If they know, they'll burn us out."

"But . . . "

Miss Ellen interrupts: "You're about to say they won't know. They will."

"How can they possibly find out who . . . "

"They *can!*" This is Miss Thirza, frenzied. Immediately next, in nightmare unison, both sisters wail, "They'll burn us out!"

It is as if, looking older, they've pronounced, "The moon is down, the town dark, the streets dangerous!" with an unmistakable clarity, and yet, to the visitor, their words are as incomprehensible and absurd as the words someone ignorant of cars and their gizzards thinks she hears the motor mechanic reel off, "Either the zommer trin has uncrunkled, or there's a dittle in the ashenganter."

Their distraught behaviour and din has given her disbelief pause. She listens to them. She observes them draw up from some cistern of the senses a strength resembling the ancient peculiar strength of mothers, but less nerve-ridden, the hardened-artery strength of ageing virgins, sinister and dotty, like the strength of the Fates. Exhorted by women she now understands don't trust her she promises to do nothing. Like the ubiquitous second self who exists in dreams she callously registers she's lying outright to the — oh, yes indeed — weird and addled crones. The cruel men must be brought to heel.

Next day she drives tirra-lirra to the R.S.P.C.A.; reports the Hathaway Greyhound Club's way with cats; unblenchingly leaves her name; does refrain from mentioning the Misses McGarrigle. Immediate and discreet investigation is promised. She says nothing of her well-intentioned, sly, humane, and perfidious deed to her hostesses.

Filled in by the predictable, as corners of inferior crosswords are by out-of-date interjections and foreign monosyllables, nine days pass. Then, moonless two in the morning, it's the unpredictable's turn: outside McGarrigle's Inn pandemonium, the barking of helpfully busybody men, and, confusion's navel, the fish-face of the Citroën goggling through the acrobatic flames in which its ruin nears consummation. Miss Thirza's voice flaming within — "Ellen, wake up! Fire! Fire, Ellen! Wake up!" — is soon extinguished.

Called to order by some untouchable sect spawned in a

dirtier century, the sisters unchain and unbolt the double door, and emerge. They emerge dreamily, like deaf dancers mistakenly executing a pavan to the whirlwind music of a tarantella, and stand, shawls over their secret bedroom coiffures, between the lofty pillars of the porch. Last to appear is the guest, the dead car's owner, her hair as unruffled as a brass wig. The two sisters speak to her — too much noise to hear the words which are unlikely not to express commiseration.

Not a prolonged or really spectacular show, it's over by three-thirty, and that includes McGarrigle drinks for the policeman and the smutty helpers, and the locking, bolting, and chaining again of the double door. As well — as well, the Saturn's ring of half-seen forms dodging and flitting just beyond the bonfire's rim of illumination have returned to whatever obscurity they came from.

In the kitchen, padding noiselessly to and fro, faces unreadably calm, Miss Thirza and Miss Ellen, their graves already paid for, one each side of the late Miss Carmel, do what, as inn-keepers with a standard, they feel should be done, and prepare the guest a treble whisky and hot milk.

"A sort of posset," says Miss Ellen, not handing the mug to the guest, but putting it, like the poison-laced syllabub for a wicked duchess, on a small silver salver. Her daytime bun of grey-brown hair is four-strand plaited, and coils girlishly over one shoulder of her slate-dark woollen dressing-gown.

"Should knock you out, miss," says Miss Thirza, huskily dulcet, almost whispering, far too much like Katisha in a silken vermilion kimono plumply embroidered with white-and-silver wistaria, and looking straight at the guest while being efflorescently discourteous, "Yes, Miss Meddlesome Mattie, you'll be able to sleep like the log you are."

Miss Ellen seems, unrebuking as she is, to condone this odious lucidity on Miss Thirza's part.

The guest stands mute, though her lips wince imperceptibly as if they propose some retort but cannot be supplied with the words for it, the town that manufactures them having vanished from the map, shattered by sackbuts like Jericho, scalded with brimstone like Gomorrah, harrowed under like Carthage.

With tilted, faint, inflexible smiles in which their eyes do not participate, the sisters direct a level stare of mingled disdain and appeasement at her. It would certainly appear she's acted scurvily yet served some purpose. Their detachment becomes coolly total, though Miss Thirza has cocked her head the minutest fraction as if about to pick up a remote bird-call. Perhaps she picks one up, and classifies it with certainty, for she speaks again.

"Ere you quaff that posset, and nod off, have the goodness to tell us something. You *did* go to those R.S.P.C.A. people?" Before the guest can answer, "Ha! I see it's yes. You see that, Ellen?"

Miss Ellen nods.

"I did warn you, my dear," says Miss Thirza McGarrigle of Hathaway.

"*We* warned you," says Miss Ellen of McGarrigle's Inn. She pauses, p-a-u-s-e-s, switches to another, politer but not forgiving, lobe of her mind, adds, "They were, of course, warning us too," and leaves the sentence there lying on its side like a torso.

Film Outline and Short Story

The Jetty: Outline for Segment of the Film Libido

Martin is ten years old but his eyes, so stilled, so dark, so impenetrable, are as ageless as those of the enigmatic and impassive inhabitants of a Giorgione painting. Their regard leaves one at a loss. It could be an arraignment or, more deadly, a warning of annihilation. The 1912 world it appears to focus on could be being seen as not what it is. For instance, when he stands absolutely immobile at the end of the jetty, seeming to do no more than watch the brassy plaque of the sun slide down behind the horizon, what does he really see? What does he hear?

Behind him a distraught yet sumptuous garden cascades down from his mother's bayside house, and at sunset the suburban birds behave deliriously there, calling and counter-calling from its depths. Is it possible that Martin, transfixed in silhouette against the improbable sky, hears instead of bird-calls the thin squeals of the drowning, tattered cries for help (his father's voice among them: "Martin! Martin, my son"), and the faint and fractured sounds of a ship's orchestra playing "Nearer, my God, to Thee"? Does he see a *Titanic* upended, about to plunge from view, or his father's hand clawing up above the brazen ripples of the bay? Who knows! His profile betrays nothing; his eyes are unflinching; there is an arrested silence within him. His mind, like his baffling gaze, is dark and private.

It is always so. When he comes home each day from school there are the unfathomable eyes beneath the brim of his boater. The house is drugged, noiseless, and he enters it without a sound, soft-footed as an assassin. He takes off the boater as if someone is watching and waiting for this polite

gesture, hangs it on the hall-stand, puts his strapped-
together school-books on the console table beside the salver
littered with visiting cards. As he opens the door to his
bedroom the wind-bells hanging from the hall ceiling make
a glassy comment.

From elsewhere, from the drawing-room perhaps, comes
his mother's voice, careless, drawling: "Is that you, Martin?" He does not answer. He goes into his room, slips off
his college blazer, puts it on a hanger in the wardrobe, un-
does his tie, hangs it carefully over the curlicued end of his
bed, and then stands staring at the framed picture which
hangs above the ewer and basin on the wash-stand. It is an
artist's idea of the last moments of the *Titanic*, the liner
reared up, its lights still ablaze, like a sea-monster in agony.
Life-boats draw away from her; the waves are over-
populated with writhing forms. As he stares, his mother's
voice rises again, less careless, not so drawling, "Martin, is
that you?"

Again he does not answer, but moves from his room in
the direction of the voice. His mother in the pose of one
who lives a life of blameless monotony, is lying on the ottoman in the bay-window of the drawing-room. The venetian blinds are down but not closed: stripes of light and
shadow fall on her through the slats. He does not approach
her, walks instead to the chimney-piece, and watches her
from there. The cushions behind her back and shoulders, the
fashion magazines and yellow-backs lying on the carpet, the
palm-leaf fan on the sofa-table, the smoke writhing
languidly up from her black Sobranie cigarette, all suggest
summer indolence but she's too posed, too elegantly
corseted and dressed for the indolence to be utterly authentic. Her hair faultlessly piled up, her flower-embroidered
blouse with the whale-boned collar, the revealed *broderie-
anglaise* frills of her petticoats foaming above her stylishly
crossed ankles, the number of her bangles and rings, all the
crispness and glitter and control suggest something other
than indolence — she is alert, waiting, ready to be restless
or wilful. On the shelf of the marble chimney-piece, and
reflected in the vast, gilt-framed looking-glass above the
fireplace, are a number of porcelain figurines, Petit Trianon
shepherdesses and milkmaids, pretty swains in perukes and

ruffles. She flourishes her cigarette and holds her book, with the same over-graceful gestures they flourish their tiny porcelain posies with.

"Why didn't you answer me, Martin?" She has not lifted her eyes from the book since he came in, and does not do so as she speaks.

He says nothing. He touches, and makes tinkle, the lustres at his end of the mantel-piece. She reads a little more, puts a fringed book-mark in its place, closes the book, reaches for the palm-leaf fan, and agitates it with the artful gesture of one of the figurines, her arm curved like a porcelain one, her fingers as curled as porcelain fingers. Still not looking at him she blows smoke towards the ceiling.

"Mother," she says, "has had a dreary day . . . a very dreary day." There is a pause, empty as a vessel to be filled with a dangerous liquid. Then, his face a mask, he says:

"Mother, are you a merry widow?"

She becomes moveless, but continues to keep her eyes turned toward the ceiling.

"What makes you ask that?" She speaks very softly. "Did someone say I was?"

"Who would say? No, no one said. I wondered myself."

"Did you, indeed!" She blows smoke towards the ceiling, talks towards it. "Perhaps I am. Yes, I suppose I could be called that. The question is: what makes you think I'm a merry widow?" Her voice becomes drowsy: "Is it because I'm always going out?"

"Yes, mother."

Now she looks at him, swings her feet to the carpet, sits up. "I've nothing to stay home for." She stubs her cigarette. "During the day you're at school. At night you're asleep. If I'm out, you have Mrs Purchase to minister to your wants. That's what housekeepers are for . . . at least that's what she's for." She stands, smoothing down her skirt over her hips. "Anyway I'm home now."

His face, his eyes, show no emotion, as he says, "But someone must be coming to see you. You're all dressed up."

She does not become angry with him, but distressed at something else. Restlessness overtakes her, and petulance: her nature is too shallow for love or hate, cataclysmic rages or volcanic outbursts.

"You sound like your father. You look like your father."
She is pacing about in the striped light, but stops to say,
"Your father was a bad man, Martin, a bad, selfish man. He
left me. If he hadn't been drowned when the *Titanic* went
down, he still wouldn't be here. He wasn't ever coming
back. I'd still be a widow . . . a grass widow."

Once more, imperturbably, he touches the lustres, and
makes them tinkle.

"Stop that. Go away. You've given me a headache. Go
away. Tell Mrs Purchase to bring me some tablets . . . but
go away . . . you're a bad selfish boy."

If she's not in the drawing-room when he comes home
from school, she's out and Mrs Purchase, on her knees in
the hall, polishing the legs of the console table, says in a
close-lipped way, "Your mother's out. God knows when
she'll be home . . . at all hours. Now don't hang about inside. And don't get out of earshot either. Come in the moment you're called. Tea will be early. I'm going out tonight
too. Do you hear me, Martin?"

He does not answer.

If his mother is not on the ottoman or is not already out
she is on the point of going out. As she buttons her twenty-
buttoned gloves or fiddles with the osprey in her hair she
softly sings:

> When you dance tonight, wear a rose of white,
> It will show you'll forgive me again,
> But if instead it's a rose of red
> It will show that my hopes are in vain . . .

Sometimes he watches her drawing down the spotted veil
over her face, or lifting her arms balletically in front of a
looking-glass as she stabs in ten-inch hat-pins with jewelled
tops, or snatching up a seal-skin muff when Mrs Purchase
calls out, "The cab is here, Mrs Beaufort!" A door slams. A
cab drives away. Mrs Purchase is always calling out, or
appearing, rigid and upright, to announce coldly, as if she
abhorred cabs, "The cab is here." A door is always being
slammed; a cab is always driving away; he is always being
left with reverberations and echoes: his mother's voice . . .
"Remember, Martin, in bed by nine!" or Mrs Purchase's . . . "I've left your tea on a tray in the breakfast-
room."

When the echoes die out, and the wind-bells stop vibrating and everything is dead-still and grave-silent he stands in the drawing-room as though he has been put there by hazard, he and his expressionless face, he and his dark, undeviating eyes. His gaze sweeps over, yet neither kindles at nor seems to take in, the lustres and figurines, the occasional tables with their Richelieu covers and *bric-à-brac*, the elaborate kerosene lamps, the what-nots crowded with china boots and shoes, the jardinière-crowned pedestals, the piano with its candle-sconces . . . everything is inimically not his. He is lost among a merry widow's bibelots and canterburies, tasselled cushions and over-stuffed chairs.

What does he do on such days, what does he do on solitary evenings? He begins to play chess with himself. He deals out a game of patience. He turns the pages of a book of Doré engravings or famous shipwrecks, of windjammers with shattered masts and shredded sails foundering in a lunacy of nineteenth-century typhoons and water-spouts. Nothing, however, holds him. He seeks a someone or a something not there. He shuts the book. He pushes aside the knaves and aces of the playing cards. He flicks over the Knight, the Bishop, the chess-board Queen. He does all this impassively, but wearily, as if it's his fate to be punished by living forever solitary.

At night, late, in bed, he's not even allowed the charity of sleep. Something wakes him. There are voices and laughter in the drawing-room. His mother squeals, "Oh, Monty, you *naughty* man!", and men and women laugh. A voice sings, "Champagne Charlie is me name . . ." but someone breaks in, starts to play "Alexander's Ragtime Band". A man tries to sing it but stops at "It's the best band in the land" while the others laugh. Does he hear, at the same time, the far-off wails of people drowning in icy waters, the broken and wavering sound of the ship's orchestra playing "Nearer, my God, to Thee"? What does he really hear? What is he always searching for from the end of the jetty, or in the November magnificence of the garden? What is to be found among the huge Oriental poppies, the thickly starred jasmine, the crabapples and hawthorns clotted with blossom, the bushes freighted with roses?

He's in the garden, in the sunlight, hypnotized it seems
by the translucent roses when his mother's voice comes
from within the house: "Martin! Martin, where are you?
There's someone to see you . . ."

As he reaches the drawing-room door, Mrs Purchase,
playing maid in an embroidered apron but certainly not
wearing a cap, is wheeling in the ceremonial tray, altar-like
with its crocheted cloth, its silver kettle under which the
methylated-spirit flame already burns, its silver teapot and
jug and sugar-basin, its tiered silver stand of sandwiches and
cakes, its cups with violets painted on. She hisses, "You've a
smut on the side of your face," and sweeps past him.
Beyond her back, and the moving altar, he sees his mother.
She's sitting on the spindle-legged but full-bosomed fireside
sofa in a tea-gown and smoking a Sobranie in a holder of
carved ivory.

"Here he is, Sybil," she says. "Don't hang back, Martin.
Come in, dear. This is Miss Windsor. You won't remember
her, but she knew you when you were a little baby."

He sees her before he hears her say, "And now he's a
handsome young man."

His eyes show that he sees her, and that he sees her as he
saw the mesmerizing and luminous roses. She, Miss
Windsor, has already drawn off one glove, and stands smiling by the marble chimney-piece. His eyes kindle — to him
she must be blinding, incandescent, instantly to be fallen in
love with, a miracle. The diaphanous roses of chiffon
mounting the upturned, transparent brim of her hat are
reflected in the looking-glass. There are chiffon roses at her
waist. She extends her hand to take his heart, and, fascinated, he moves forward to offer it up.

"Rosalind, he must call me Aunt Sybil." As she speaks
there is the rippling music of the wind-bells from the bay-
window and the clock plays its brief glassy melody before
revealing that it's four o'clock of a dazzling afternoon. "I'd
like that, Martin. You must call me Aunt Sybil."

His lips silently say, "Aunt Sybil."

"You've made a conquest," says his mother, tilting the
silver kettle above the silver teapot. "He's smiling. Martin,
go and wash your face."

"It's nothing . . . nothing at all," says the goddess. She

reaches for one of the afternoon-tea napkins, and wipes the mark from his cheek. "See . . . nothing at all serious!" She kisses the cheek lightly.

Now, when the candles are lit in their sconces, he turns the music as she plays the piano and sings to him:

> She watches and waits for him, day by day,
> He sleeps in a watery grave, far, far away,
> For him her heart doth yearn,
> She prays for his return,
> As she watches and waits for him . . .

His mother, smoking while she buffs her nails, reclines on the ottoman in the half-gloom.

On the sand beside the jetty, he writes her name . . . SYBIL WINDSOR. He writes his own name beneath hers . . . MARTIN BEAUFORT. Next, he encloses the names in a heart.

He comes across a perfect rose in the garden, takes out his pen-knife, carefully cuts it, and starts towards the house in which the piano is being played. Sybil Windsor begins to sing the Sun-and-Moon song from *The Mikado*. Martin doesn't notice the portmanteau in the hall, the man's boxer and overcoat and walking-stick on the hall-stand but, as he enters the drawing-room, the rose held behind his back, he cannot help but see the man leaning against the piano, his hand ready to turn the page of the score, the good-looking young man with his waxed moustache, richly waved hair, watch-chain, signet ring. He puffs at a meerschaum. Her back is to Martin but she sees the man's eyes see Martin, and stops singing and playing.

"David," she says. "This, darling, is Martin. Mr Roberts, Martin, the man I'm going to marry."

"Dav-id!" It's his mother, all ostrich plumes and feather boa, arriving home in a rush, and sailing past Martin with her arms theatrically outstretched to the newcomer. "I'm so sorry I wasn't here when you arrived but . . ."

The boy's eyes have become inscrutable. Beyond the rim of things, backing away, he looks at the rose. A spider creeps out of it.

Again, there is no one to play chess with . . . there's an adult gabble in the background as he flicks over the White Queen, the Black King. He watches the lovers playing diabolo. He watches them walk on the jetty, far-off, arm-in-arm, the woman's head on the man's shoulder. He plays tiddleywinks by himself on the carpet. He deals out the cards for patience. He abandons everything as soon as he starts it . . . the piano distortedly jangles; the adults' laughter and conversation, excluding, are also distorted, now sharp and jumbled, now hissing and hoarse.

His mother and the lovers are playing cribbage by lamplight . . . their faces seem older, seem cruel and sinister. As he passes the drawing-room door in pyjamas and dressing-gown, his mother sees him.

"Martin, you're surely not creeping off to bed without saying good-night!"

He turns at the doorway.

"Did you leave the bathroom clean? Mrs Purchase tells me that yesterday there was sand all over the . . ."

"Yes, mother."

"He's a good swimmer, you know." All their faces are turned in his direction . . . the man's satanic, mocking. The face of his false goddess is a blur. "His father taught him." Her lips, his mother's lips, make a wry movement above the fan of cards: being able to swim was no advantage when the ship struck the iceberg, and the orchestra played on the canted deck. "I . . . of course . . . can't swim a stroke."

Sybil Windsor's voice comes from the blur: "Neither can David."

"No, not a stroke. I was brought up in the back-blocks . . . there wasn't anywhere to swim. I didn't even see a big river or the ocean until I had a moustache." The man twirls his pointed devil's moustache.

"Too late for me to learn, eh Martin?"

"Well, say something, Martin. At least say good-night, and go to bed . . . go to bed . . ."

He sees the lovers in the garden, but they cannot see him and his motionless eyes. She picks a flower, and puts it in the button-hole of his lapel. Her hand rises to touch with tender finger-tips the waxed moustache. The man takes hold of this hand and presses a kiss on its palm. He takes her in his arms. They kiss deeply.

They cannot hear or see what Martin hears and sees . . . the screaming of gulls, the uplift and downfall of monstrous

waves, all the crash and roar of lunatic seas on jagged black
rocks. He is no longer in the garden. He stands in his
bedroom looking at the picture above the washstand — the
gulls still screaming, the waves still crashing destructively
down. The fury abates, gradually, gradually. The water
becomes oil-smooth, scarcely a ripple. He is in his rowing-
boat, a little off shore from the end of the jetty. He rests on
the oars, his head bowed.

"How deep is the water?"

It's the man's voice. The man has walked to the end of
the jetty, and stands there puffing at his meerschaum. The
sun is about to set. "Very deep." There's a pause. Then the
boy says, "Would you like a row, Mr Roberts?"

"I've never learned, Martin. Thank you, though."

"I can teach you." The surface of the water is glossy,
scarcely moving. "It's quite easy."

The man puffs at his pipe. "Perhaps tomorrow, eh?"

"It might be rough tomorrow." The boy is intense . . .
what are his thoughts? "If you learn you could take Aunt
Sybil rowing . . ."

Perhaps the man has an idyllic vision . . . she lies back on
cushions under a Japanese sunshade, a baby in her arms,
while he rows dashingly. She is smiling. There is a white
swan. Snowy petals fall.

"Yes . . . yes, why not?" The man puts his pipe carefully
on the top of a mooring-post. With one thrust of the oars
the boy brings the boat into the jetty, steadies it against a
pile. The man, uncertain, somewhat awkwardly, sets one
foot on the boat.

"Never too late to learn!" he says as the boat glides away
from him. With a swift strong pull on the oars the boy
sculls the boat away from the drowning man. His face
doesn't flicker at "Martin . . . Help me . . ." and his eyes are
opaque as the water cruelly offers its services.

After a while there is silence. The smoke from the
meerschaum on the mooring-post fades from the air.

The boy rows placidly towards the shore, and does not
look back. The boat moored, he walks inexorably up
towards the house. He stops. Once only . . . a flawless rose
glows like a light at him. He takes out his pen-knife and
cuts it.

Holding the rose before him, he enters the drawing-room
which is lit only by the long rays of the setting sun striking
in hazily through the venetian blinds. Sybil Windsor is idly
playing the Sun-and-Moon song, and continues to do so as
she says, "Where's everybody?"

The boy shrugs his shoulders. He puts the rose on the
piano top with a gesture patently expressing, "This is for
you!" The woman smiles. He takes a sheet of music from
the several sheets on the top of the piano, and opens it out
on the stand before her. Once again the woman smiles, and
begins to play and sing.

She watches and waits for him, day by day,
He sleeps in a watery grave, far, far away . . .

The boy's face has hitherto been closed and dispassionate,
but is now smiling and radiant.

The Author's Afterthoughts

Whatever I'll be writing about my story ("The Jetty") and Tim Burstall's heathenizing of it into a film ("The Child") had better be prefaced by an admission. Decades before I knew of Burstall's existence I already disapproved strongly of certain sorts of directors, *strongly*. The "certain sorts" I had in mind were theatre directors. In their near-criminal ranks were such chi-chi play-manglers as infest the Royal Shakespeare Company, and far too many egoists (and egotists) who knew — oh much better than the playwright himself — what the playwright was up to. I'd once innocently thought that, since they're paid, they're patently obliged to use whatever nous and experience they may have to transmute — literally — an author's typed words into three-dimensional and oral action. The important adverb: lit-er-al-ly — at least as literally as the fallings-short of actors, set designers, electricians, stage hands, and other members of the coven allow. It was not, I thought (and still think), any director's function to so manhandle a script that transmutation becomes interpretation.

Admission made, conviction revealed, I now proceed.

When an unknown John B. Murray, on behalf of the Producers' and Directors' Guild (whatever *that* was), wrote inviting a script for a short film I was only too happy to reply that script-writing wasn't my cup of tea. The Guild was not deterred. It was, after all, not a charitable sodality with lily-white ideals, far from, but a predatory collusion of would-be Hal Roaches or Ingmar Bergmans on the hunt for writers. Without writers how can guilds of this kind survive? Therefore a further solicitation, seductively worded: would I submit ideas for a film? This was easier. I submitted three, each a *précis* of about a hundred words. One was chosen. Against a small fee (I forget how much, but there must have been some inducement) I inflated the *précis* to approximately 4,500 words, a sort of short story. It wasn't the sort I'd have written to be *printed* and *read*, but was aimed at actors with dialogue to emit, cameramen with points to make visually, and — the risk of hitting no bull's-eye very great — a director with percipience. It was, in essence, a shooting-script, rather compressed, certainly not in technical jargon, but absolutely lucid.

At the time, during an interview with some hobbledehoy offsider of the Guild, I uttered into one of those recording gadgets that I considered the story "incomparably bad" (i.e. as a short story), and not one "I would permit to be published as such". Now, several years later, a re-reading shows the thing to be, as a short story, not really "incomparably bad", merely tainted, somewhat impure. As a form of shooting-script it's more skilful, thickly clue-ridden, and useful than I'd remembered. Anyway, John B. Murray wrote another of his suave and flattering letters: "The Jetty" was to be filmed. He added a sentence that made me flinch. Tim Burstall was to direct.

I should, of course, never have got involved in the first place. I should, at this stage, have backed out like one of those anonymous Shakespearian attendants. I'd already had, you see, a couple of experiences with Burstall's work — one in London (a private screening of "2,000 Weeks"), one in Australia (the script of "Eliza Fraser") — and had every reason to deem backing out a wise move: the experiences, though more or less of a bystander nature, had been curiously bloodcurdling. Both had left me rather unnerved, and quite uneasy. For one thing, as a much older mortal than Burstall, and as an ex-film-addict still lynx-eyed and leery, I instantly spotted that what he was trying to do wasn't at all what directors of the calibre of D. W. Griffith, F. W. Murnau, Federico Fellini, King Vidor, René Clair, Sergei Eisenstein, and Josef von Sternberg had long ago convinced me was worth trying to do. It wasn't for nothing I'd sat through all those now-called-classic moving pictures, silent and sound. Long before Burstall was conceived I was subliminally garnering a comprehensive knowledge of cinematic conventions, felicitous tricks of technique, *und so weiter*. I needed no theoretical drivel to back up this acquired knowledge, and disdained Freud, Freudians, and Freudian symbolism as fervently as ever Nabokov did. I was astounded and repulsed to find Burstall awash with theories, and a great one for the symbol which he cherished nearly as much as he did the *cliché*. These revelations occurred during the one and only brief encounter we had before filming began.

This was my fault. I'd come up from the country one day, and was Qantasing off to London the next. Two hours was all I could spare to "discuss" the proposed film. Had my pride been in order, and I'd had my wits about me instead of scattered over a wide area of things-yet-to-do and last-minute threads to tie off, this really *would* have been the moment to back out. Encounter and "discussion" only pointed up how vast the distance between us. Let it be said, quite without feeling, that Burstall does shamelessly and happily belong to the "certain sorts of directors" tribe. He and I are also extreme opposites practically all along the line — politically, culturally, morally, theologically, aesthetically and — it now turns out — cinematically. The profoundest chasm separating us is the one that separates all creative men from all non-creative men, the architect, say, from the builder, the fugue-composer from the fugue-player, a Chekhov from a Stanislavski, a Shakespeare from a Peter Hall. It's a chasm only rarely bridged with a worthwhile structure.

The nastiest aspect of the Burstall-Porter encounter was our mutual disesteem. In 1969 I'd been driven to be truthful about "2,000 Weeks", and had turned down an invitation in 1970 to rewrite his own lamentable script for "Eliza Fraser". His disesteem far outran mine. As a director he was, in this, not being unorthodox. Directors, by and large, seem to regard the dramatists and script-writers who keep them employed as highly imperfect workmen. I caught inklings of the disesteem during the "discussion" but was so engaged in decoding his vogue words and mumbo-jumbo

into simple English, and in refusing to agree that the end of
the story should be changed — he seemed, unbelievably, to
be proposing something sub-aqueous and, I think, symbolic
— that I neglected to consider, and make arrangements to
forestall, whatever else he might have in his addled mind
about the rest of the story. His disesteem was, I discovered,
very much greater than I'd have believed possible. It
amounted in fact to insult.

By the time I returned from abroad the film was at a pre-
penultimate stage of processing, and was run off for me. It
was fascinating, appalling and infuriating to see the mischief
Burstall, who *believes* a director has a God-like respon-
sibility for everything, had perpetrated. It was very shrewd
mischief. Since I'd not been about either to stop his
vulgarizations, or remove the story from his high-school
hands to discreet and preferable anonymity, he had had a
field day but, although behaving like Whelan the Wrecker,
did — the shrewd bit! — leave enough of the plot's strong
scaffolding to support his jerry-built alterations. These included some very shopsoiled stuff — which made no point
except that an attempt was being made to make a point —
with staircases being wistfully sidled down, saplings
tomahawked, towers climbed, with "ominous" birds about
and a stallion doing its Freudian best for those who have
theories about stallions. I went hot and cold with embarrassment as each of these *vieux-jeu* events happened, not
because they were Burstall inevitabilities (the sort of film he
makes isn't one I'd walk across a road to see), but because
my name was being bruited about as that of the script-
writer, and they'd be laid at my feet. I went hotter and col-
der at the Burstall dialogue. I'll never be able to understand
how a man with his wordy theorizings and pretensions as a
film-maker couldn't sense that, in their particular context in
the script, statements such as "Mrs Purchase, will you help
me to my room" and "You'll understand it all when you
grow up" are more hilarious than otherwise. However, it's
more than probable that such symbolic and vocal *bêtises*,
outrageous to me, aren't even dimly apparent to Mr and
Mrs Joe Blow, and I'm wasting embarrassments.

My true distress lies elsewhere. Burstall took the tension
and chill out of the plot by pincering out the final sting, and

by making the adults blameworthy and the boy a sort of come-by-chance murderer when the whole point of "The Jetty" was that the adults were essentially harmless, the murderee particularly so, and the boy sinister, selfish — and a premeditating murderer. I found it particularly offensive when Burstall coarsened the situation by making my 1912 characters behave, not like the human beings they'd been created as, but like the imitations of characters out of any 1960s best-seller by an American Jew. In "The Jetty" an innocent and pleasant young man is deliberately lured to his death by drowning because the boy villain sees him kissing his fiancée among the roses. In "The Child" a lecherous middle-aged cad, who sleeps with the boy's widowed mother, is caught by the boy *in flagrante delicto*, and, having fallen in the river, is left to drown on a sort of boyish impulse. The story mother is merely a selfish gadabout, and her visitor friend merely a charming young woman engaged to marry an agreeable young man. They appear sinister only to the evil boy. In the film he is presented as quite unevil though rather dotty, while both the mother and the visitor are promiscuous with the one dreadful bounder, the visitor cuckolding the mother. In short my three nice enough people have to be replaced by a squalid trio filched from Iris Murdoch so that — God help us! — the audience will "go along with the boy" who, filleted of intention and taking on — by contrast with the immoral adults — a late-Victorian goody-goodiness and East Lynne quality, Burstall thinks, should have the sympathy of the general public. I still can't see why it's theatrically better to angle somewhat heavy-handedly for sympathy on the boy's behalf, by making his victim accidental as well as repulsive and expendable, than to let the boy behave as he must, and the sympathy fall where it will (on the murdered fiancé? on the bereaved girl accepting the rose from the murderer?), and the audience's feeling for the boy be other than sympathetic, be a feeling of admiration or rage or shock.

Curiously, the film, the Burstall-Porter mongrel, embarrassing to me as it was (though not to Burstall), seemed to be — according to the reviews I saw — considered the least embarrassing of the four films in "Libido". I wasn't able to judge: watching the film was like looking at a photograph printed from a negative on which two different scenes had been taken. I could keep on keening about lost opportunities, mishandled moments, permissive-age crudities — and about the insult of having a commissioned story mangled and mistranslated, but shall stop.

However, a lesson has been learned. I can draw some comfort from the fact that "The Child" is highly unlikely to tarnish any silver screen ever again; and that I now know that my long-time wary disdain of directors was justified. It has hardened into a distrust brightly striped with contempt. If a director can't do what the writer does, can't literally transmute (as Visconti, say, did for Mann in "Death in Venice") it's much much safer and wiser and kinder to leave the thing in words: "Hamlet" will always defy impeachment, and unblinkingly outlast any number of Hamlets no matter whom — Richard Burbage, Johann Brockmann, Henry Irving, Sarah Bernhardt, Ernesto Rossi, John Gielgud — and the particular Svengali each used, the diabolic director.

Would I then, the interviewing young man asked, still be interested in writing for the films again? I seem to have answered that I might be interested but that, before the chopping and changing started, I'd be on the spot to put my point of view. That was four years ago. Today I'd be tougher. If a film were to be made of something of mine I'd be boringly and maddeningly underfoot protecting the home product so that it wasn't deformed, decorated, blown up, pruned, "interpreted" in any way by some mechanic and his gang of mechanics. Soothing to know there's very little danger of again being "interpreted" (this is how directors spell misrepresented) — most of my writing, thank God, performs the deed it has to well enough not to need the expensive support of those who require its existence to support them.

Martin is ten years old but his eyes, so stock-still, so impenetrable, are as ageless as those of the enigmatic and disquieting denizens of a Giorgione painting.

The current of his gaze, not a tremor in it, seems to be switched on to an elsewhere, to a terrain not-Here and an era not-Now, to some arcane place and anonymous hour. Passing clear through those it appears to be turned on, it leaves them at a loss, baffled and humiliated before a looking-glass in which no image of their sacredness is to be found. Illegible, brilliant as jet, it is the indifferent and untamed stare of a dark angel. It could be an arraignment or, more deadly, charged as it is with off-hand presentiment, a warning of treacheries to come, hemlock in the picnic lemonade, a viper beneath the eiderdown pillow, domestic doors that will one unlooked-for afternoon open on nothing, on the depthless abyss, a vertiginous universe that has no use for a skyline.

The 1912 world it seems to focus enigmatically on, the Earth in its radiant crust of holocaust and farce, betrayal and glory, could be being seen as other than it is.

For instance, when Martin stands for a long long while, as he often does, solitary and absolutely immobile at the end of the jetty, seeming to do no more than boyishly watch the sun slither down and down towards the bay's surface, dilating by degrees into an incandescent platter and finally fitting itself behind the horizon, what does he really see?

Behind his back an unbridled yet sumptuous garden hurtles pell-mell, terrace by terrace, from the gables and bow-windows of his mother's house down towards the beach and the jetty. At sunset, any sunset, the seaside-

suburban birds behave wantonly among the leaves and
blossoms, calling and counter-calling from their depths,
each tribal chorus proclaiming with nearly musical ferocity
that the syrup within the nectarine is theirs and theirs alone,
the bug in the gullet of the lily, the caterpillar on the snap-
dragon's muzzle.

It is possible that the boy, the upright idol transfixed in
silhouette against a brazen and improbable sky, does not
hear the eisteddfod of creatures stating their claims, nor
even the racket, sourer in tone, and nearer to him, of eleven
or so sea-gulls, working-class common, bickering about
offal along the tide-line.

He could, instead, be in covert touch with another hour,
one of his own choice, and elsewhere. If so, it is surely —
oh, too surely — an hour upon which a bitter night has descended without ceremony or pity. Gobblings and shrillings
riddle it: men and women engrossed in the egalitarian
labour of drowning have no finesse and not a shred of
shame. How repulsive the antics! How unsophisticated and
full of solecisms the din! Discipline is the ocean's part. It
slaps icy hands correctively across the mouth after mouth.
One by one the unprofitable pleas and squallings are put
out. The ship's orchestra, having made its vulgar point, no
longer plays "Nearer, my God, to Thee". His father no
longer calls out after boats that draw away, no longer flails,
no longer drudges uselessly on the treadmill of the waters.

If Martin see, from the end of the jetty, a signet ring he
knows he once knew flash, again and again and again, from
the knuckle of a hand clawing up into the after-sunset from
the languid ripples in the bay; or a *Titanic* spectrally
upended on the seaside sky-line, his eyes disclose neither
this nor that. There must be some nerve of feeling he does
not want touched; he protects it without knowing exactly
where it is.

When he returns from school each day he approaches the
house and the front door secretively, as if in cloak and mask.
He opens the door with prudence, very slowly and
noiselessly, as though expecting or hoping — there is no
way at all to tell which — to find the place pillaged, a chart
of blood glistening on the Persian rug. Perhaps he wants to
do no more than catch the furniture, the gasoliers and

chromolithographs, the tureens and claret jugs, in the care-
free postures man-made objects take on during man's ab-
sences. His unfathomable eyes must find everything always
as it should be. This house, at this time of any day, is a stopped machine, its cogs locked.

As he passes under the lintel he takes off his boater with
the air of one from whom this polite-little-gentlemanly
gesture is waited for and, moreover, watched for. Yet there
are no eyes to see: those are pearls that once were; full
fathom five the father lies who taught him the etiquette of
hats and doorways. He hangs the boater on the hallstand.
He puts, he *places* just so — a right place for everything, and
everything in its right place — his satchel of school-books
on the console table beside the salver laminated with the
visiting cards of enormous and sometimes immoral persons.
His bedroom door is the first one in a corridor that turns off
at the end of the hall. As he opens it the wind-bells
dangling from the corridor ceiling emit a fragment of glassy
remark.

Part of the machine has stirred.

Now . . . now, from the drawing-room comes a voice.
Drawling, simulating nonchalance, it is nevertheless pitched
to the very bull's-eye of his hearing:

"Is that you, Martin?"

It is a woman's voice. It is his mother's voice.

He does not answer.

He becomes busy. With all the signs of a perfervid con-
scientiousness, and still as if to disarm a dubious shade or
delight a beloved overseer, he swiftly changes into other
clothes, informal older ones for the formalities of pretending
to play and be happy. When the taken-off garments are on
their hangers, and the wardrobe door is closed upon them
(its little key turned), the room is as it was when he entered,
a page without a blot, a page on which the information
written in invisible ink persists invisible.

Again that woman's voice, hers, his mother's, less drawling now, not at all uncareless, glittering with sweetness:

"Is that you, Martin?"

Again he does not answer, at least not in words, and not
even in the most subtle alteration of mien. He has his own
formula, and will strike no more right notes than it lays

down. He moves at a neutral pace, a messenger with no message, in the direction of the woman who truly is his mother, and devotes some of her time to a counterfeit of maternity.

In the pose of one who lives a life of blameless monotony she is lying on a *chaise longue* in the embrasure of a drawing-room bay-window. The Venetian blinds are down but the slats not closed. Stripes of light and shadow quiver over her, a semi-camouflage, and blur the meanness of her beauty.

Entering the room softly as an assassin he does not move towards her. He takes another path, away from her, and arrives at the chimney-piece. From there he turns his eyes, it seems, to her. If so — and it is difficult to see if he sees — it can only be to disentangle her outline from the undulant and wavering strips as, in picture puzzles, he disentangles the panther's form from an urn of peonies, the octopus from a tropical jungle, Medusa's vile lineaments from the captivating paraphernalia of an antique shop.

The cushions behind her back and shoulders, the yellow-backs shed on the carpet, the palm-leaf fan biding its time between the ash-tray and the *bonbonnière* of Paris almonds on the sofa-table, the filaments of smoke meandering away from the Turkish cigarette, all suggest summer indolence, the zenana, sweet-do-nothing; but she is too strictly whale-boned and too elegantly dressed for this to be anywhere near true. The architecture of her hair gripped in combs set with gems, her flower-embroidered muslin dress with its throat-enclosing collar of stiff lace, the revelation of starched petticoat frills — white, white, intolerably white — above her stylishly crossed ankles, the profusion of rings and bangles, the artfully disposed glitterings and immaculate crispnesses, these cancel out any notion of indolence. She is not authentically in repose. She is alert, expectant, ready to be restless or wilful, perhaps not only ripe for mischief and adultery but for callous harlotry.

On the shelf of the marble chimney-piece there is a *fête-champêtre* of porcelain figurines, Petit Trianon milkmaids and shepherdesses, girlish swains in perukes and ruffles. The gilt-framed looking-glass above the fireplace is surfeited with the reflections of these minature beings at their by-play and dumb-show. She, aping lassitude among the cushions, holds her cigarette and Charles Garvice yellow-back with the same over-graceful finickiness with which they hold their minuscule porcelain crooks and posies, tricorns and nosegays.

"Why didn't you answer me, Martin?"

Does she this time expect an answer?

She has not lifted her eyes from the printed piffle since he came in, and does not do so as she speaks.

He says nothing.

Can he, can one, say: at such-and-such an hour, of this thrust in the heart or that thrust or the other, love found it-self at last dead? Can one? Dead, and answerless for ever? Can he?

Two lustres of crystal, one each end of the mantel-shelf, flank the posturing gala, the waspish faces and tiny cold breasts, the brittle wrists and sightless eyes. A moment has arrived for him to do something. He touches the lustres at his end of the mantel-piece, and makes them tinkle — not gently, not at all gently.

The transparent shade which passes — oh, swiftly! — across her face is perhaps the wraith of an unpleasing emotion. It is gone. He has not yet spoken. She reads, or affects to read, another page of the yellow-back. She has not looked at him.

She closes the book, and drops it to the carpet. She reaches for the palm-leaf fan, and agitates it with the artful gesture of one of the figurines, her arm curved like a por-celain one, her fingers as curled as porcelain fingers. Her profile a cameo, she blows smoke towards the ceiling to which, also, she says:

"It has been a dreary day . . . a very dreary day."

He does not say, as he well might, "Indeed!" or "Fancy that now!" but, permitting first of all a pause, one as deliberately empty as a goblet to be filled with fresh venom, asks as clearly and heartlessly as any Prince Charming in an end-of-term school play:

"Mother, are you a merry widow?"

Only the smoke stays alive: she, the fan, her arm, all become stilled, absolutely moveless.

He knows how to wait.

Soon, though still moveless otherwise, she lets herself say, "What makes you ask that?"

Of course he does not answer the unanswerable, so she must speak again, "Did someone say I was?"

"Who would say? No, no one said." He risks a revelation. "I wondered myself."

She comes to life again, but continues to lie on the *chaise longue*, to look upwards and not at him though uttering, with a tincture of vexation, "Wondered! Did you, indeed!"

Now she blows smoke again towards the art-metal wreaths and ribbons of the ceiling.

"Did you, indeed! Well, perhaps I am. Yes, I suppose I could be called that. The question is: what makes *you* think I'm a merry widow?" Her voice suddenly turns dulcet and tricky: "Could it be .... could it possibly be ... because I'm always going out?"

His answer is instant, weedless, quite uncharming.

"Yes."

At this the vixen leaves the den.

She discards the fan; sits up; swings her feet to the carpet; faces him.

"I've nothing to stay home for, nothing at all." She grinds the cigarette to death. "Where are you throughout the day? At school. At night you're asleep. What does it matter if I'm out? I don't play with tops or cricket bats or ... or whatever it is you play with. It doesn't matter if I'm out. You have Mrs Purchase to minister to your wants. That's what a housekeeper's for — at least that's what she's for."

She stands abruptly, and smoothes her skirt over her mermaid hips with flashing fingers and tinkling bracelets. She kicks at a yellow-back, and — fool of a woman — says, "Anyway, I'm home now."

Although a mocking laugh would well fill the bill he does not commit that kind of unsonliness. His face, his eyes, his voice, reveal not one degree of emotion as he says, "Someone is coming to see you. Or you're going out. You're all dressed up."

She does not immediately, there and then, become angry with him but fierce and distressed at something else, something hidden behind yesterday. A postponed fever overtakes her, a restlessness and petulance. She begins to pace about, and her voice becomes mellifluous with pique.

"You sound like your father. You're an inconsiderate little horror. You look like your wretched father."

She is frou-frouing here and there through the ripples of light but stops near him to say:

"Now listen to me, Martin. Your father was a bad man, a bad, selfish man. He left me and — listen to me — he left you too. If he hadn't gone down with the *Titanic* he still wouldn't be here. He wasn't ever coming back. I'd still be a widow — a grass widow."

Once more, imperturbable of countenance, he disturbs the prisms into a crystal clinking: *mer-ry wid-ow, mer-ry wid-ow, mer-ry wid-ow.*

Now she does she-foxily snarl and snap.

"Stop that. Stop, this instant. And go away. You've given me a headache. Go away. Tell Mrs Purchase to bring me some tablets . . . but get out of my sight. You're a vile vile vile . . . ."

If she is not lolling about decorated for public display when he returns from school, she has already departed for some unsolemn and gaudy destination, leaving Mrs Purchase to dispense his allotment of butterless scraps, unspiced left-overs:

"Your mother's out. God knows when she'll be home. All hours, no doubt. Now, don't hang about inside. And don't get out of earshot either. Come in the moment — listen to me, Martin — the moment I ring the bell. Tea will be early. I'm going out tonight, too. Do you hear me, Martin?"

He does not answer.

If his mother is not arranged on a *chaise longue* or ottoman, or is not effusing the scent of rose geranium in some palm court or tea-room, she is on the point of departing for an elsewhere denied fatherless boys and pretty-pretty widows' sons. As she buttons her twenty-buttoned gloves or fiddles with the osprey plums in her hair she sometimes is to be heard softly singing, as though she is simultaneously far away and still at home, some fashionably forlorn song:

When you dance tonight
Wear a rose of white;
It will show you'll forgive me again;
But if instead
'Tis a rose of red,
It will show that my hopes are in vain . . . .

Too often, without appearing to watch, he watches her performing the final pre-flight actions: drawing a velvet-spotted veil down over her rouged cheeks and powdered chin, or lifting her arms balletically in front of a looking-glass to stab in foot-long hat-pins with marcasite tops, or, at the very last moment, snatching up a square seal-skin muff when Mrs Purchase correctly announces or, caught ungirdled, dourly calls out, "The cab is here, Mrs Beaufort."

Over and over again it happens. The housekeeper calls out. A door slams. A cab drives away.

Mrs Purchase is always calling out, or appearing, rigid and upright as a Byzantine empress, to announce chillingly, as if cabs were abhorrent to her, "The cab is here." A door is always being slammed; a cab is always clip-clopping away to oyster bars, tea dances, theatre foyers, or the Winter Garden of some still-quite-reputable but nevertheless slightly gamy hotel; he is always being deserted, left with reverberations and echoes: his mother's voice — "Remember, Martin, in bed by nine!" or Mrs Purchase's — "I've left your tea on a tray in the breakfast-room."

When the echoes expire, and the wind-bells stop, and Mrs Purchase is no longer to be seen or heard, when everything is dead-still and grave-silent, he stands where he has been discarded, most often in the drawing-room. He stands as though he has been dumped there by hazard, he and his expressionless face, he and his sombre, undeviating eyes. His gaze patiently moves over, yet neither kindles at nor seems to take in, the lustres and figurines, the occasional tables with their Richelieu cloths and burden of *bric-à-brac*, the elaborate kerosene lamps, the what-not crowded with a collection of china boots and shoes all gilt-speckled and flower-embellished, the jardinière-crowned alabaster pedestals, the piano with its excessive candle-sconces — everything is inimically not his. Everything is femininized, curlicued, expensive, and in repulsive taste. He is lost

among a merry widow's vulgar hoard of bibelots and canterburies, tasselled cushions and over-stuffed chairs.

On such a glutted desert island, on such days, what does
he do? What does he do during the solitary and long-
drawn-out evenings? As a lone prisoner might, he begins a
game of chess against himself. He deals out a game of patience. He toys with a Tangram's geometrical pieces. He
turns the pages of a book of Doré engravings or of famous
shipwrecks, of windjammers with shattered masts and
shredded sails being gored to death on rocky coasts, or
foundering in a lunacy of nineteenth-century typhoons or
water-spouts.

Nothing, however, holds him. He seeks a someone or a
something not there.

He shuts this book, that book, before *Finis.* He drops the
Tangram snippets back into their box. He pushes aside the
knaves and aces of the playing cards. He flicks over the
Knight, the Bishop, the chess-board Queen. It's all done
impassively, but wearily. Who is he not to be rebuked, for
living at the wrong time, by the fate of living solitary, in the
shade?

At night, immeasurably late to him, he is often not permitted the charitable release of sleep. Something in the
lamplight wakes him in his darkness. There are dreadful
voices and curious laughter in the drawing-room. A
creature giving a distorted imitation of his mother squeals,
"Oh, Monty, you *naughty* man!" Witches and warlocks
thereupon grossly laugh. Next, one man starts up, "Champagne Charlie is me name . . ." but someone else, at the
piano, puts a stop to that by playing "Alexander's Ragtime
Band" . . . and again . . . and again.

Does Martin, hearing this, hear at the same time the
threadbare and wavering sounds of a ship's orchestra playing "Nearer, my God, to Thee"; and the lamentations,
wordless and fearful, of his father and those others wrestling
the bitter water?

Why does he seem to be forever listening to other than
what he cannot help hearing?

What is he forever searching for as he stands at the end of
the jetty, or rows about the bay?

To reach the jetty and the rowing-boat he must descend

through the garden. In November, late spring, it goes through one of its showy periods with huge Oriental poppies everywhere, swathes of thickly starred jasmine, the hawthorns and crab-apple trees clotted with blossom, the bushes freighted with roses. He is in the garden one Saturday afternoon on his way to the jetty when his mother's voice comes from the house:

"Martin! Martin, where are you?"

He can see her at the open bay-window of the drawing-room, and moves, to be certain of being unseen, behind a lilac bush.

"Martin, darling . . . ."

He does not answer.

"Martin, come inside. There's someone to see you."

She leaves the window with the air of one who will entreat no more.

He starts to ascend. As he nears the drawing-room door, Mrs Purchase, unenthusiastically enacting maid in a lavishly embroidered apron fit for a dowager duchess, and certainly not wearing a cap, is wheeling in the ceremonial tray, altar-like with its crocheted cloth, its suspended silver kettle under which the ethereal blue flame already burns, its silver teapot and attendant vessels, its tiered silver stands of sandwiches and meringues and *petits fours*, its teaset porcelain with violets painted on.

She hisses at him, "Smut . . . side of your face!" and swerves past him. Beyond her, in the sunlit room, he sees his mother sitting very gracefully, like a cigarette-card Zena Dare or a postcard Gabrielle Ray, on the spindle-shanked but buxom fireside sofa. She wears a tea-gown, and is smoking a black Sobranie. Perhaps Mrs Purchase whispers something to her because she looks towards the door, sees him, and speaks:

"Here he is, Sibyl. Don't hold back, Martin. Come in, darling. Say how do you do to Miss Windsor. You won't remember her, but she knew you when you were a little baby."

"And now he's grown into a handsome young man," says Miss Windsor.

Standing by the marble chimney-piece she has already drawn off one glove, and is gentling off the other. It is patent that her smile, for him and only him, has had the effect of an instant hypnosis. His eyes kindle, sparkle — to him she must be dazzling, incandescent, instantly to be mesmeric and adored, a miracle. It is not only her smile, which is a true and illuminating one, but her romantic toilette. Diaphanous chiffon roses, creamy and pinkish, mount the upturned transparent brim of her hat. There are chiffon roses at her waist. Out of the luminous mistiness of her mignonette-scented attire she extends a hand to take his hand and his heart, and, fascinated, he moves forward to offer them.

"You agree, Rosalind, that he must call me Aunt Sibyl . . .? Of course you do; and of course he must."

As she speaks, still holding his hand, there is a splash of music from the wind-bells, and a frivolous cherub-cluttered clock emits a brief vitreous melody before revealing that it is four o'clock of a peerless afternoon.

"Would you like that — to call me Aunt Sibyl? I'd love to be your favourite Aunt Sibyl."

His lips silently say, "Aunt Sibyl".

"You've certainly made a conquest," says his mother, now priestessing away at the altar, tilting the silver kettle above the silver teapot. "He's smiling as I've never seen him smile before. Martin, you look like a chimney-sweep. Go, and wash your face."

"It's nothing," says the goddess, "nothing at all." She reaches for one of the afternoon-tea napkins, and wipes the mark from his cheek. "Gone!" She kisses the cheek lightly, and says . . . oh, lethal triviality . . . "Now, dear Martin, you are my young man."

Since she is to spend three months with them, and is an ever-amiable guest, he has now a divinity to teach chess to, to laugh and joke with as they play diabolo and dominoes and snakes-and-ladders, to walk along the jetty with, to row about the bay when its brine is prostrate and glossy. He no longer finds it necessary to stand alone staring long-time at . . . at what? . . . from the end of the jetty.

See, a gleaming day, she strolls the jetty with him, twirling a frilled parasol above them both, an arm about his shoulders. Refracted green-and-silver light shimmers across her face as she tells him, "You are my young man."

It is as her young man, her besotted attendant, that he turns the pages of music books while, the candles alight in their trembling sconces, she plays and sings for him. He has a particular favourite, maudlin and melancholy, of which he seems not to tire:

> She watches and waits for him,
> Day by day;
> He sleeps in a watery grave,
> Far, far away.
> For him her heart doth yearn,
> She prays for his return,
> As she watches and waits for him . . . .

On the sand of the beach near the jetty he prints her name — SIBYL WINDSOR. He prints his own name beneath hers — MARTIN BEAUFORT. Then he encloses the names in a heart.

One twilight, in the garden, she says to him that of all the flowers she loves — mignonette, wistaria, mock orange, picotees, Parma violets — she loves roses best, and of them her most beloved a yellow rose.

The next afternoon he searches until he comes across the nearest to a yellow rose in bloom at the time. It is sallow merely rather than yellow but is splendidly shaped. He carefully cuts it with his pen-knife, slices some thorns from the stem, and starts towards the house with his treasure. He can hear her somewhat angelically trilling a song he has not heard before. He cannot be expected to know it is not being sung for him, the Sun-and-Moon Song from *The Mikado*. He is to learn that his springtime was over before it began, that Miss Sibyl Windsor does not play a favourite tune for him alone. Since he and the sallow rose enter the house by a side door he misses the evidence in the front hall: portmanteau, ulster, and Gladstone bag, the Homburg hat and Malacca cane of a rival.

At the open drawing-room door, the rose held behind his back, he stops in his tracks. Facing him, a man leans on the piano, his hand ready to turn the page of the score. There is a meerschaum in the other hand. He is a very handsome young man, dark, with a carbon-black waxed moustache, richly undulant hair, and the shaven parts of his face turquoise in tone.

She, her back to the door and the boy, sees the man's eyes
see the boy, ceases to strum and trill, rises, turns about, and
radiantly thows her grenade.

"David darling, this is Martin who has looked after me
for you. Can you guess who this is, Martin? It is Mr
Roberts, the man I'm going to marry."

Before the rose-bearer's face becomes void, the eyes
unlit and illegible; before the doomed lovers can observe
there the fall of a curtain, the quenching of a glory, there is a
cry of "Da-vid!"

It is the mother being *the ever-vivacious Rosalind Beaufort*,
all lockets and ostrich plumes, feather boa and opopanax
scent, flurrying in from some corner of Vanity Fair. She
sails past the husk of the extinguished boy with her arms
crucifixionally outstretched.

"Da-vid, my love! I'm so sorry I wasn't on the doorstep
when you got here but . . . ."

Who would notice that the doorway is empty?

Martin stands at the end of the jetty from which he has
tossed the sallow rose.

Now, once more, as once upon a time, there is no one to
play chess with Martin. Once more, as once upon a time,
Martin must bleakly play Martin and, weary of defeating
himself and losing to himself, come to felling the White
Queen and the Black King with heartless fingers. There
seems an incessant adult gabble in the background, blithe
and hideous. He listens. He watches. The need to listen and
watch, to watch and wait, has returned. He watches them,
him and her, beau and sweetheart, as they murmur together
at diabolo and dominoes and snakes-and-ladders. He
watches them — from far off, from the attic window —
walk the planks of his jetty, arm-in-arm, the woman's head
on the man's shoulder. What she is saying to him is not to
be thought of.

He takes up again the dreary quirk of finishing nothing,
of abandoning too soon whatever it is he has gone to the
trouble of starting. With closed-up face but vicious gesture
he scatters the patience cards, the Tangram design, the
tiddley-winks counters; but — from behind the book he
will not reach the end of, as from within the rim of the
puzzle he will not bother to work out — he listens, he
watches, he waits.

One night the mother and the lovers are playing cribbage by lamplight. He is on his way from bathroom to bedroom in pyjamas and dressing-gown. As he passes the drawing-room doorway his mother sees him and, for no more than a whim, acts as though he were scamping a nightly ritual which in fact has never taken place.

"Martin!"

Because, usually, his going to bed is an event not worthy of notice he is surprised and, in surprise, stops.

"You're surely not creeping slyly off to bed without saying good night? How could you be so ungentlemanly to your Aunt Sibyl? And what must Mr Roberts be thinking?"

Having begun she seems unable to stop, but flutes on, adding *fioriture* of the most specious kind.

"Did you wash behind your ears? Did you leave the bathroom clean? Mrs Purchase tells me that the day before yesterday there was sand all over the . . . ."

All their faces, turned from the faces on the cards to his null and void face, are stand-still, and could seem to him charged with an adult insolence and malice — his mother's with glittering Euripidean eyes, the man's satanic, that of his false goddesss glazed by deceit.

"I must say he's a good swimmer though. Aren't you, Martin? It's about the only thing his father taught him. He, of course, was a good swimmer too . . . ."

At this her lips make a wry twitching. Of what advantage was a taste for swimming, what value had it had when the iceberg killed the ship, and the orchestra played ragtime and hymns on the canted deck?

"I," she says, making a wicked point, "I — of course — can't swim a stroke."

"Neither can I," says the man, Miss Windsor's *fiancé* Mr Roberts. "I was brought up in the back-blocks — there wasn't anywhere to swim. I didn't even set eyes on a big river until I was thirteen or fourteen. As for seas and oceans, I didn't see the briny until I had a moustache."

He twirls the right-hand spike of his devil's moustache and, because the boy's eyes seem now to be directed towards him, goes on:

"Too late for me to learn now, eh Martin?"

The boy continues to stare. The mother tires of her whim.

"Well, say something, Martin. And don't hang about in your pyjamas when grown-ups are trying to enjoy themselves. Go to bed. Say good night, and go to bed."

He does not say anything, but goes.

In his bedroom he stands for some time staring at the picture he has taken from a drawer. Cut from a magazine it is a hack illustrator's conception of the death throes of the *Titanic*, the liner rearing up, as in an immense agony, out of an ocean defiled by a scum of mortals busily engaged in accomplishing death.

He continues to wait, and, waiting, watch.

Watching, he sees the lovers in the garden. They cannot see him and his motionless eyes. They stand face to face. She has plucked a sprig of something and is putting it into the *boutonnière*-hole of the man's lapel. Of what they are chattering no sound comes to the watcher except a wordless sibilation. The sprig inserted she raises her hand to touch with indubitably tender finger-tips the waxed moustache or the lips beneath it. The man takes hold of this hand, and sows across its palm a number of kisses. Next he embraces her. Their faces meet, mouth upon mouth.

They cannot be aware of what Martin, the spy among the tiger lilies, is privy to. It is the sudden madhouse shrieking of gulls, the mountainous uplift and abyssal downfall of waves, all the blasphemy and slaughter of seas run amok.

He is no longer among the tiger lilies.

He stands in his bedroom, the magazine *Titanic* fallen from his hand to the floor. He stands until the gulls no longer scream, and the waves no longer destructively riot.

Gradually the sea becomes glycerine-smooth, without a ripple except those made by his rowing-boat.

He sits in the boat, a little off shore from the end of the jetty. It is the time of day, he knows, when the man strolls on the jetty smoking his meerschaum. As though he is not waiting, the boy rests on the oars. His head is bowed as if he is subdued by lassitude or indifference.

He is subdued by neither.

He is waiting.

He makes no move until he is spoken to.

"How deep is the water?"

It is the man's voice. The sun is about to set. The man has walked to the end of the jetty, and stands there finishing his smoke. The boy who has waited looks up.

"Very deep." He permits a pause to occur before saying, "Would you like a row, Mr Roberts?"

"I never learned, Martin. Thank you though."

"I can teach you." The boy, next instant, is vivacious and wheedling. "It's quite easy, really and truly. Look! The water's like a mill-pond." It is. The surface, marble-flat, seems also marble-solid, incapable of being indented by footprints, capable of being waltzed on.

"Oh, do come, Mr Roberts."

What a charming little boy!

"Perhaps tomorrow, eh?"

"It might be rough tomorrow." The boy is intense. He has a sparkling brain-wave. "If you learn you could surprise Aunt Sibyl, and take her rowing . . . ."

"Yes — yes, why not?"

Perhaps the man has an idyllic vision: she lies back on cushions smiling under a Japanese sunshade while he rows dashingly. There is a snowy swan. Pink petals shower down *leggiero* from overhanging branches.

Perhaps, since he is a gentle and well-bred young man, he is merely being guestly and polite to the strange son of his hostess.

"Yes, why not?"

He puts his precious pipe carefully on top of a mooring-post. A deft oar-stroke or two brings the boat close to the jetty, steadied against a pile.

"Now you can step down, Mr Roberts."

Uncertain, awkward, the man gets into the boat, standing there ill-balanced, and speaking too soon:

"Never too late to learn!"

He says this as, with a brusque and unwarranted thrust of oars, the boy jerks the boat from under the man's feet.

This done he then sculls the boat away from the drowning creature until he is far enough distant to be out of the range of being accidentally helpful, but not too far off to observe how efficient the water is as it cruelly offers its services.

After a while there is silence. By this time the sun has just set; and the meerschaum on the post has grown cold for ever. The boy rows skilfully and placidly to his usual mooring-place. The boat moored, he walks up the winding garden paths and rocky steps-and-stairs towards the house.

He stops once only. There, like a reward, a yellow rose glows upon a bush. He takes out his pen-knife, and cuts it.

Holding the rose before him in the manner of a candle he enters the drawing-room. In its hazy, tawny light Sibyl Windsor is idly playing, though not singing, the Sun-and-Moon song her late *fiancé* had a tenderness for.

"Where," she says, turning her head as she ripples away to see who has entered, "is everybody?"

The boy shrugs his shoulders. How could he know?

He puts the rose on the piano top with a gesture patently expressing, "This is for you."

She smiles. She says, still playing that man's melody:

"You really are very sweet, Martin . . . a dear, sensitive boy who doesn't forget."

He selects a sheet of music from the canterbury nearby, and places it on the stand before her. Once again the woman smiles and, quitting the other tune, begins to play and sing:

> She watches and waits for him,
> Day by day;
> He sleeps in a watery grave,
> Far, far away . . . .

The boy's face, hitherto grave and dispassionate, is suddenly smiling, radiant with an abnormal joy.

Poems

The Moon is Round, The Snow is White. . .

Perhaps their voices still sing through
the branches of December.
Why once they sang I cannot say,
or what was sung remember.
When leaves crowd thick and winds go lame
all April lovers sound the same.

My April pleas they granted in
too flash and slick a fashion—
prayer's no prayer but loss unless
no answer salts its passion;
flame is not flame that will not burn,
nor is love love that asks return.

If ever love-lorn once I wore
the rig-out of the mourner—
and mainly for Main Street to see—
I smile now in the corner
and do not grieve, not even for
the grief that I can grieve no more.

Upon a time love made time pass
with ribaldry and revel.
Now time has made love pass. No tunes
the heart's harp-strings dishevel.
Though love's be out, truth's lamp gives light:
The moon is round, the snow is white.

Elijah's Ravens

For Elizabeth Bowen

You soon enough find out. Grief brings you low:
nerves snap; there's break-down of propriety;
disdain's patrician privileges go;
finesse and pride become disorderly,
and bolt before *"A bas les aristos!"*

You know your fate — too well — when, scenting kill,
the ravens swing towards your dazzling doom:
such ones as cancer, car-smash, carnage thrill,
who to the spot marked X, the death-bed room,
dive headlong with a charnel-house good will.

They sniff the fissured mould, the split defence,
the victim struck *déclassé* and distraught,
bedaubed with common tears, bereft of sense,
and closer press — ignoble, trite, unsought —
with cliché pity, crude benevolence.

These friends-in-need you elsewhere would not dare
to show your fine-drawn fancies nor expect
your high aesthetic ecstasies to share,
now that you cannot cavil or reject,
manhandle you with wise and vulgar care.

You soon enough find out. No need to guess:
grieve and the world grieves with you! — here herds stop;
the level of their human clumsiness
below the world's low level cannot drop . . .
yet *this* ground-floor's where sorrow's shame grows less.

Here only — and as focus of the rout
you loathe more than you loathe your misery,
hub of a proletarian roundabout,
your private pain a public property —
can grief find cure and peace you soon find out.

Scene:

Alexandra Tea-room

(A Provincial City, 1968)

An East-of-Suez ceiling-fan, stopped dead
some hot, F. Scott Fitzgerald afternoon
says ten-to-nevermore above your head
while you, you bitch, and I do good-bye's deed,
stir stillborn tea with an unsilver spoon.

One other patron (naice) who's overheard
our nitric-acid truths, *art nouveau* lies
(two haters parting spare no hurting word),
in genteel autumn cocoa strives to hide
her White Queen's Church-of-England-coloured eyes.

If you and I were Alice we could climb
this nervy marble table-top and pass
into that other tea-room's Proustian time,
the Jabberwocky lovescape we disclaim,
the mimsy vistas through the looking-glass.

The White Queen there, all tousled shawl and hair,
would shrill that pins had pricked before they had,
and waste some grief on us who do not care
that love has cured to loathing, There to Here:
"I wish that you could manage to be glad."

"Consider what o'clock it is," she'd plead.
Near shut-up time, the storm-chipped cups drunk dry
(too Tenniel for tears), things run to seed.
Each city's full of cities. Hell's deployed.
All abysses are shallow. So am I.

"I must first hurt if I am to forgive."
Who says it? You. You fool! I'm silent stone
not snarling, "I'm indifferent that you live",
and "I don't feel the wound you think you gave",
or "So *that's* how you look when you're alone!"

The Married Couple

They rendered what was due, not one tithe more:
The grandee manner, the unriven mind;
Bred enough proper sons — to that resigned
More to prove usual than to hint desire.

Not tied by love but land, they aged while young
From public wearing, without smiles or frowns,
Ancestral leavings, wealth, those weighty crowns —
She queen of caution, he a wary king.

The sons, the world, admired — and ceased there
As sensing warmth's withdrawal, coolness meant
To show them free of unforeseen event,
Perfected, some hard absence at the core.

Their smiles resembled others', yet not quite:
Neither to palliate nor patronize
Theirs fell just short. Locked doors behind those eyes
Hid shut-mouth captives overspent with hate.

Alone in private night, teeth bared to wound
They balked; like turnkeys, granted hate no pass,
Loving like mimics in a looking-glass,
From themselves severed, to each other blind.

Their statues waltzed at balls, or side by side
Spanked in a landau, letting all perceive
Her hand the seeming heart upon his sleeve —
Rift never left for rumour to intrude.

To lookers-on such warranties of love
Seemed, in their keeping, love's own monument
Whose gloss the years could never dull or dent.
He died. All wondered that she still could live.

She lived for years, elusive, duty done,
Sealed in equivocation. At the last,
Inspired to break truth's long fatiguing fast,
She cried, "I hate him. Bury me alone."

To this insuavity sons must sham deaf.
They buried her beside him. Someone came
To carve a stone with decades of her fame,
And in two words exposed it: *Loving Wife*.

Within a chiselled rose-wreath hand clasps hand,
Stone trapped in stone, the costly roses stone.
Below, teeth bared, they lie once more alone,
From themselves severed, to each other blind.

Autobiography

Evening School. A drawing by Hal Porter.

It is difficult enough for me, an unmistakable Australian, albeit of the Awstralian rather than the Osstralian variety, to convey in words to other Australians the exact temper of the clan gatherings at Sale, gatherings of no importance, unrecorded because unrecordable, forgotten before begun, proof of nothing that cannot be unproved, and which, allowing for family verve and off-hand solidarity, can be nothing else in the world but Australian. It is much more difficult and almost impossible to entrap this temper in a net of words for non-Australians because it is compounded of the most complex, double-sided and deceiving, and maybe even deceitful, elements. The unwritten rules of behaviour are infinite in number, finely shaded, and subtle to the last fraction of a degree. They are not to be broken. If broken, the rules of forgiveness leading to re-establishment are equally of air and iron. I learn these rules with rather less ease than my contemporaries because, in the back streets of my being, a duel is developing and increasing in fervour between my instinct which knows why something is so, and my hen-pecking intelligence which wishes to analyze why something is so.

See a crowd of us herded together for morning tea on some occasion — the Sale Show, say — which has brought eight or nine adults, and twice as many children, together at the old house. The men wear their best watch-chains, their opal tiepins, A.I.F. badges and Sunday suits of hand-tailored navy-blue twill or pepper-and-salt Donegal tweed. They wear these, and stiff collars too, although the temperature is ninety-nine in the shade. The triangles of coloured silk handkerchiefs, largely Paisley, protrude from their breast-pockets. Boots squeak. On the back veranda, the old cedar table seemingly as large as a tennis court is half-covered (the men's half) by their panamas or high-crowned, deep-valleyed felt hats.

"Hurry up with that bloody tea, you bloody women," the uncles shout. "Stop your bloody gossiping, and hurry bloody up!" This means many things: that women are merely wives, that the men want their tea, that they recognize that the women are working while the men are idle, that they politely acknowledge this fact, that each husband is saying to all the other women what he would only say to his wife if the other wives were not there.

Next to the men's hats, the women's handbags and new gloves, beige or white, are laid out with the girls' new beige or dove-grey gloves. No female of them would consider appearing ungloved in really public public. They all wear new dresses that smell new. It is still early enough in the day for these garments to be merely on them, rather than that they have settled into the dresses. The women's hats, with imperceptibly quivering, semi-transparent brims, bear bunches of gleaming artificial cherries, clinking glassy grapes with a talc-like bloom, or coffee-saucer velvet pansies. The girls' hats are ringed with linen forget-me-nots or pink silk rosebuds. Bangles, aquamarine brooches, and necklaces of amber abound. Everyone is on superlative and high-flying behaviour, which translates into the fact that there is a considered holiday truce in any current feud, and that certain dangerous truths are, this day, to be circumspectly skirted. There is an uproar of chiacking.

"Shut up, you great lazy beasts," the aunts cry back to the uncles. "Who's robbing this coach, anyway? Just be patient, you hulking beggars." Crying out thus, the aunts do not slacken their gossiping with other aunts, and do not halt their busy hands for a second.

In the midst of what appears a typhoon of angry insult and savage cruelty, the boys stand rigidly upright, too clean and too silent, with comb-marks in their hair. They would like to be wrestling or spitting or grabbing each other by the balls, not for fun but to startle the engrossed and selfish adults. The girls titter spuriously at each other, touch each other's mother-of-pearl buttons, and show each other the lace-trimmed handkerchiefs pinned with miniature gilt safety-pins to their velvet bodices, or more fashionably stuck through their rolled-gold bangles.

When tea is poured, "Christ all bloody mighty!" shouts Uncle X, pointing with a huge segment of walnut-knobbed chocolate sponge, through the gabble, at Uncle Y's shimmering tie. "Jesus bloody Christ, look at it, will you! Look at the poor bloody bastard's tie! No, no, don't look! She'll blind you."

Uncle X is thus telling Uncle Y and everyone what Uncle Y and everyone know — that he is more than happy to see his favourite bloke again, and that he likes the tie very much.

"Take no notice of the silly bugger, Y," says Aunt X. "It's sheer jealousy. He's only jealous."

She is making it clear to any aunt who, later, could take it upon herself to think — and say — otherwise, that she has no part at all, albeit harmless, in her husband's attack, and that she sides as a sympathetic woman with the attacked albeit unharmed.

"It's a *lovely* tie," squeals Aunt Z, entering the field to compliment Aunt Y tangentially, for Aunt Y, she knows, has bought Y's tie. "Lovely! It goes with your suit beautifully. Perfect combination. Perfect taste. Don't take a scrap of notice of the silly bugger. Jealousy, that's all. Pure, unadulterated jealousy!"

"*Jealousy!*" Uncle X rolls his eyes ceiling-wards. "Jealous of that poor bastard of a bloody tie!" His shouting over, he looks fleetingly, but with meaning and expectancy, out of his raillery, at Uncle Y who is the acknowledged family jester.

The ground having been prepared by Uncle X, principal stooge, with some assistance from Aunts X and Z, Uncle Y is now ready to perform. He puts down his ham-sandwich with elaborate preciseness. He brushes his finger-tips together to remove crumbs or a pretence of crumbs. He clears his throat in the manner of actors acting throat-clearing. His face puts on the pursed-mouth blandness of a superior being.

"X," he says, curling his fingers like a tea-sipping shopgirl, and assuming an accent of rum truffle richness,

"X, mai deah, *deah* brothah-in-law, whai not be honest with me? Ai know you dote on the tai. Ai'd hev given it to you. If you'd asked naicely. If you'd been frank and open. But you're a cad, suh. You're almost a bally boundah. Your language is *foul*. In short, suh, you're a bastard of the first water, and as cunning as a bloody bagful of you-know-from-where rats. Ai see through you, mai good fell-oh. No tie for you; no bloody tie at all."

"Yes, yes," says Aunt X and Z, "we all see through you, my boy. You can't pull the wool over our eyes." Then, changing sides, partly because X has now been put in the position of underdog, partly to give Uncle Y, the wit, the funny man, the sad case, the dag, the trimmer, the one-never-lost-for a-smart-come-back, a further opportunity to set them giggling and squealing, the aunts over-act cajolement, "Now, come on, Y, don't be an old meanie. Set the poor silly bugger an example. Open your heart. Don't be stingy. *You* know he can't afford ties." This is obverse but graciously astute acknowledgment of Uncle X's keen business sense, and materially successful career. "Give the poor bugger the tie before he breaks down. Come on, Y, off with that tie."

And so on.

Exchanges of this coarsely-textured, bravura kind are merely one ingredient of the clamour, and interrupt nothing else. The eating continues as does the passing of teacups, and ham-and-piccalilli sandwiches, and thick triangles of shortbread, and strawberry tart, and the correction of children's manners, and the false praising of other women's sleeves and necklines and jabots. Each one skilfully carries on, at full belt and the top of the pitch and the same time, several conversations: hay harvest, biscuit recipes, bed-wetting, other people's pitied misfortunes and enjoyably scandalous carryings-on, pig prices, milk yields, births, deaths and marriages.

Beneath the over-large gesturings, the mock black-guardisms, the trenchant side-comments and satirical laughter, lies a calm reservoir of feeling. This is a reservoir, not too deep, not too large, but strictly family and private, to be tapped only in situations of the gravest kind. It is, indeed, rarely tapped because individuals, and smaller families within the larger widespread family, prefer to be independent, even secretively proud, in solving their own problems.

Anyway, at the age of ten, I am so in love with the hub-bub and braggadocio and seeming confidence of the family that I see them as a skylarking herd to whom nothing is ever a problem, to whom a problem has never presented itself and never will. I see them, of course, only as guests in Bairnsdale or hosts in Sale, when they and we are on show, or in holiday mood, at riverside picnics, renting adjoining beach-shacks at Seaspray on the Ninety Mile Beach, at carnival times, camping or quail-shooting or salmon-fishing or hare-hunting, and taking steamer-trips down the rivers, through the lakes to the ocean and the endless miles of wide, radiant beaches that rim it. It seems perpetual high noon, dazzling, the air like molten window-panes, and vibrating with family laughter, a laughter never menacing, two-penny-ha'penny, vicious, shallow or hollow, but jetting and splashing out in a happy-go-lucky fountain. I know, now, that what I see and hear, then, conceals behind the jocular uproar, behind the camaraderie and zest, all kinds of selfish-ness and procrastination, guiles, mendacities, multi-coloured sorrows, anguishes of every variety, even down-right tragedy.

Knowing all this now, I am nevertheless able to see them all, still not found out by Life or me, on that Show Day forty years ago, loud-mouthed and showing-off, over-hearty and carelessly high-spirited, and yet keeping meticulously to the hidden rules. Those rules! Take one rule only; take the rule that governs swearing.

Blue the air may seem to be, but it is only blue of a certain tint. *Bloody, bastard* and *bugger* are the only three swear-words they, man or woman, permit themselves and each other to use in mixed company. These words are used in the tone of voice that fillets them of offence, and gives them the quality of endearments. Beyond these three words lies the country of broken rules, of outrage and disgust and Puritan anger. Egged on by my nature to listen and watch, I note too that the swear-words most loudly and often used in the early scenes of clan-gatherings are excited substitutes for expressions of affection taboo to the blushing Australian tongue, for the revelation of deep feelings not to be admitted in a more gracious form. As day wears away to its end, and night falls, and voices soften, the women do not swear at all, the men swear far less, and in a muted way. An aunt who swears like a cockatoo at eleven a.m., at eight p.m. surprises no one by saying, without venom but with firm intention, "Really, you great hulking men ought to control your language. It's eight o'clock." My uncles do not comment on this inconsequential remark, but it is understood as consequential, and has its effect. Later in life I am able to observe those of my uncles or cousins who drink, and are usually as foul-mouthed and bawdy as they come when in male company, pruning their conversation of even some of the acceptable swear-words in the front of a barmaid whose attitude they have not yet discovered.

However much I enjoy the hurly-burly and higgledy-pigglediness of these Sale holidays, however many rules I realize, or am forced to kotow to, however much my awareness of being a small fraction only in a multiplication of ancestral flesh, my keenest enjoyment comes from being able to find on every hand three-dimensional evidence of Mother's tales. This is a means of extending myself, of spreading myself backwards in time beyond my own birth; it is the beginning of thought about myself. Hitherto, I have thought far less about the being most concrete and important to me — myself — than about other people, and the world of appearances. Now, in Sale, I appear to myself not only as the me I am discovering but also as Grandfather Ruff chasing aborigines around and away from the very house I am holidaying in — "Cut 'em! Slash 'em!" I cry through my whiskers; I am Mother being born in the room I share with a brother and two cousins; I am Father carving, in his courtship days, on a post in the barn, his own and Mother's initials, H.O.P. and I.V.R., inside a lopsided heart. The past thus surrounding me contains innumerable questions to which I attempt to find answers: here, for example, is the pomegranate tree Grandmother planted above the well; I am part of Grandmother; Grandmother is dead; I live, and the pomegranate tree lives; as I break off a pomegranate, what is the slender but indubitable connection between it and Grandmother and me? Naturally, I find no real answer. I suspect then, I more certainly suspect now, that there is an important answer.

Sale is tied by innumerable threads to many bits and pieces of my later life; I am repeatedly being reminded of Sale by fragments of the world: the waters of Tunbridge Wells have the same gassy taste as the waters of the artesian fountain in Sale Park; the Aimée Vibert roses of Kew Gardens are as white and prolific and untidy as the Aimée Vibert roses by the side-gate where Father used to kiss Mother good-night during their courting; the lilies-of-the-valley I pick in a glade in the Forest of Fontainebleau remind me instantly of the lilies-of-the-valley I smell for the first time in the garden-bed by the old pump. Again and again, my boyhood in Sale comes back to me: blood oranges in the railway buffet at Alessandria, chocolate cake at Groppi's in Cairo, a particular sort of cherries in Athens, white violets under the gingko trees of a Kyoto temple, an outsize salmon in a niffy, open-fronted Soho fishmonger's.

It is just such a salmon, in size, that Uncle Fred Ruff has caught on the Ninety Mile Beach, at the Honeysuckles, when we are surprised, Uncle Fred and seven or eight of us boys, by several women in long white dresses and floppy hats appearing over the sand-dunes. Baying blasphemously, his Rodinesque, hairy hands suddenly clamped in the classic gesture of modesty, for he is as naked as a statue, Uncle Fred caracoles with lolloping buttocks into the ocean, we frognaked boys with our hands similarly but almost unnecessarily arranged, cantering behind him. There, once decently obscured in the soap-suds of surf, but nevertheless keeping our hands in position, we all glare, Triton and his minions, until the ocean- and sand- and sun- and shock-dazzled women start into life again, and, scuttling back over the noon-flowers, disappear like routed Touaregs among the dunes. On the wet sand between the startled and the shocked lies the salmon from the Soho fish-slab.

One day, autumn I suppose, while staying in Sale, Mother and I walk three miles to the cemetery. We have a two-fold purpose: to leave flowers on Grandmother's and Grandfather's grave, and to pick mushrooms. On the way we pick so many along the edges of the ditches that we reach the cemetery with a full basket. At the grave, Mother

arranges the chrysanthemums she has brought. Although I
am fully aware that she is just not crying, she does not give
me the pleasure of the conventional tears I conventionally
expect so I wander off to watch a nun who is apparently
performing what I guess to be a Roman Catholic ceremony
at a plot of many nuns' graves surrounded by yews and
dominated by an image of the Virgin Mary in white
marble. Investigation proves that the nun's moppings and
mowings and swift dartings in a half-crouch are no more
than the movements of a nun making measurements with a
tailor's tape-measure. Is another nun about to die?

As Mother and I are leaving the cemetery, the nun is
climbing into a cab at the entrance-gates.

"Gracious God!" says Mother to herself, but loudly
enough for the world to hear, as she recognizes the nun. She
brushes nothings from the knees of her skirt, takes a little
run of excitement, and calls out, "Sister Philomena!" Sister
Philomena is the nun who teaches Mother singing at the
Convent of Notre Dame de Sion when Mother is the one
Protestant pupil there. We travel back together in the cab.

I cannot recall the conversation which is rapid-fire
reminiscence laced with the names of Sisters and Mothers
and the girls who were pupils when Mother was Ida Ruff.
It is conversation not to listen to, for the sentences have no
full-stops and reach no conclusions. My attention goes inward, playing with a name they mention several times, and
which haunts me to this day — Bridget O'Loughlin. Who
was Bridget O'Loughlin? What were Mother and Sister
Philomena saying of her? Where is she now? Occupied
with this fascinating name, I do not know by which steps
the women in the cab arrive at giving a performance I cannot forget. Suddenly, to my complete amazement, from
Sister Philomena's soft and ageless face encaged in brutal
white, emerges a clear-cut scale of beautifully formed notes.
My own mouth falls open, partly in amazement, but mainly
because hers is ovally open.

"Ah! Ah! Ah! Ah! Ah! Ah! Ah! Ah!" she sings. I see her
tongue quivering like a human being's. Next, she smiles.
Her teeth are so white, so very even, that they must be the
first false teeth I ever see if they be not the only flawless
teeth I am ever to see. The smile persisting, she says, firmly,

not intending to hear refusal attempted, "Now, Ida, you too. Come, girl."

Mother immediately folds her hands in a dutifully schoolgirlish right over left on her lap.

"Ah! Ah! Ah! Ah! Ah! Ah! Ah! Ah!" they both sing, Sister Philomena gently agitating one black-gloved hand in time. The gloves bear little scabs of super-human darning.

"A-a-a-ah!" sings Sister Philomena, schoolmistress, going higher and sweeter.

"A-a-a-ah!" sings Mother, going pink and faintly cross-eyed, and, I know by her twitching fingers, really trying hard.

"Good girl! You were always a good girl, Ida. Now, "Through forest boles". One. Two."

And, as the cab, the fringes above the doorway quivering, the wheels turning through the freshly gravelled road as through sugar, idly makes its way between the red-hawed hedges and the Kelly-green paddocks and the ditches overhung with fennel and chicory, "Through forest boles the storm-wind rolls," they sing with soaring melancholy, rocking and bounding circumspectly opposite each other on the leatherette seats, "Vext with the sea-driven rain. . ."

It is the first incident in my life that I consider unconventional or, rather, it is my first recallable experience of unself-consciousness. This correctly presupposes developing self-consciousness in me. That the happening occurs at the time I am being nudged towards self-consciousness by self-investigation, is to prove of great value. 1921 is the last year, for many years, of my early poise, and is, therefore, part of the design of me, the last year of unflawed non-innocence. I am soon to begin that long, tempting and often shocking journey through the experiences of others which is, year by year, to wear the soles of non-innocence thinner and thinner.

I should, ultimately, die innocent, if I live long enough to wear down, to have wrenched from me, to lose in a half-dream, to give wantonly away, the supply of non-innocence I brought on to earth with me. To assure myself of this desirable end, since half-way house is nowhere, I am constantly uprooting myself, climbing out of the cosy pockets, avoiding the insured cave, the bed-sitter in

Babylon, the air-conditioned foxhole with T.V. In short, I do not and must not rehearse for death under the popular anaesthetics.

However, I am still ten and, though I have caught fleeting first glimpses of myself as something rather more than an animal, I am still largely a creature of the five senses.

It is my sense of smell that presents to me, so early, one of the insoluble problems of communication, of communication by word of mouth or writing. I find myself trying to put into words, not only for others but for myself, the nature of various scents, of the difference between the scent of Mother's cabbage roses and her Frau Karl Druschkis, of the odour of a jam roly-poly baked in the oven and a jam roly-poly thumping about in its pudding-cloth in the iron boiler.

It is impossible.

On Writers and Writing

Answers to the Funny, Kind Man

Had I been invited, by no matter whom, and for no matter how many times thirty pieces of silver, to write about the work of another writer I'd flatly have refused. There are pretty reasons. I've skill in neither literary malice nor flattery, and lack the needed equipment of jargon. Moreover, not having been scalped mentally by education, I am truly unaware of what is "good" or "bad" writing. I can perfervidly like or dislike someone's work ("loathe" Dostoiëvski, for instance, "adore" Elizabeth Bowen) but yawn at the idea of finding out why. As for the Pontius Pilate game of neutrality, objectivity, *that* unhuman line . . . ! I have, anyway, no right at all, not any, none, to comment on the caperings of another mind. Who has? If so, how earned, by whom else bestowed, out of which gutter picked? To me, on the side-lines, one possible answer seems to have something in common with Jesus' "He that is without sin among you, let him first cast a stone. . . ." The stone-casters — very often the stone is in a rose — are almost invariably non-sinners: he who has not sinned by writing a play stones the playwright, the non-novelist the novelist, the non-poet the poet, and, like Augustus de Morgan's fleas, so *ad infinitum*.

Since, however, out of the clear blue, an invitation has arrived from someone I've never heard of, to write for a magazine I never read something about the works of someone I do not read — myself — it is tempting, for a piddling fee, to take part in a sport that cannot be other than eccentric. Why? To lay myself open to being once more misread by yet other non-writing theorists on the Art of Writing? De-cid-ed-ly. What a relief, too, to know that I can take even less heed of my own carping or adulation than I do of anyone else's.

In the previous paragraph I noted that I do not *read* me. That's true. When a latest poem or short story or book is printed I *examine* it, for the first and last time in this form, to see how many mechanical *gaffes* have been made by the faceless, nameless bipeds who infest the cellars and back rooms of publishing houses, and the back alleys of writers' lives. *Read* it? One does not drink one's own blood.

He who has invited me to write about my own writing has suggested a plan of attack. Having none of my own, I shall gratefully follow his.

What led me into authorship?

God knows. It is hidden from me. God? The Devil? One or other of those Muses reputedly garbed like the muscular, marble demi-deities on the top of 1884 insurance buildings? If I *were* led . . . led? . . . into authorship, it was by no mortal: I was respectably brought up. The products of certain seemly authors — Nat Gould, Gene Stratton Porter, Zane Grey, Charles Garvice, Helen Mathers — did drift into the house. They had the innocence of oatmeal porridge, the sweetness of lamingtons. Had any of the *disreputable* authors improbably appeared in the flesh — Marie Corelli, say, Elinor Glyn, Baudelaire, D. H. Lawrence or Sardou — they would not have got over the brass-covered front-doorstep. Had they, I'd have been smartly and justly sent to bed. Writers, then, had nothing to do with my defection, and that includes those sacrosanct reporters, Matthew, Mark, Luke, and John. One must seek elsewhere.

Perhaps some baleful conjunction of stars hung over Albert Park at the moment of my conception there in mid-May 1910, and, although it was not evident when I was born in the same place, and after the correct interval, in mid-February 1911, left me with the Bad Fairy gift of a kink. My kinkless, estimable, f-a-q-normal father and mother had five other kinkless, estimable, f-a-q-normal children: decent, unwriting citizens from birth. They now make money, own refrigerators, and have never even heard of Harold Pinter, Miles Franklin, or F. Scott Fitzgerald. I doubt if their fortunate children have either. They have heard of me. They do not read what I write.

My siblings and I were, give or take a little, happy-go-lucky victims of the same happy-go-lucky family life and simple schooling, ate the same sirloin, said the same prayers, caught the same modish measles, began making use of our heritage of original sin, and were subject to the same outside influences. Historically, it was all very so-so, with no Messiahs or Mephistopheleses plummeting down the drawing-room chimney in a clap of thunder, no upside-down rainbows, outpourings of ectoplasm, cubic blue apples, or stray lionesses in the pantry. No fairies at the bottom of the garden, and nothing nasty in the woodshed disturbed the even tenor of fashionable wars, famine, conventional massacres, Sunday School picnics, grandparents' deaths, insect bites, birthday parties, *et cetera*. All was ordained, and our due. We frolicked on sunny beaches, quarrelled under the lee of cow-sheds, played Ludo, robbed orchards, were poisonously polite to old ladies, learned to be wary of Jews and Greeks, to steer clear of plonk-sodden Abos, and be cheeky to Chinese market-gardeners and Afghan pedlars. We picked up, in short, a working knowledge of the thousand-and-one complex bye-laws of *la vie simple*, and stored up the necessary intolerance and inhumanity to make us fit inconspicuously into the scheme of things.

My brothers and sisters were content with all this tra-la-la. So was I. Up to this point my normality was of the correct brew for my era, class, and district. Beyond it my kink showed. No sooner had I hastened through pot-hooks and *The cat sat on the mat* than I was *driven* (led?) by whatever-it-is to engage in the vice of writing, not saccharine letters to connable aunts, and not just home-work essays on "Pride Goes Before a Fall", but poems about elves and sunsets and deserted *château* gardens, and short stories called *Phyllis and the Mermaid*, and *The Golden Tortoise*. It is shame-making though fascinating to discover that energetic people trained in this sort of busybodiness have been able to track down these childish efforts, and record their existence in a hefty bibliography.

It was somehow thus, with help from no one visible, and

somewhat in the manner of a Mathematical Idiot Boy or a
Talking Mongoose, that I began authorship. I was indubitably what I was: legitimate, christened, Church of
England, a Rechabite, a member of the Gould Guild of
Bird-lovers and the Band of Hope. I was also, and un-
ashamedly, odd-child-out, a changeling tainted by an obsession I could not (and still cannot, despite stones and
roses) shuffle off. One, of course, gets used to a chronic disease, brazens it out, and becomes, while still in knicker-
bockers, a fatalist. Nothing else can be done. There is, after
all, no salvationary Authors Anonymous.

Finally, frankly, deeply, I believe that I am not to blame,
that everything that ever happens, has happened or will
happen, has, time out of mind ago, been planned so. In the
present context the over-all plan includes one's tattier
poems, the best and worst lines in one's plays, the gremlin
in the linotype machine who, with the aid of a tipsy
machinist, and the indiligence of a flagging proof-reader,
fouls up one's most poignant clause — the one you yourself
love, and no one ever ever notices. The plan also fits in the
wake of illiterate Saturday journalists, and semi-literate
academics, and highly unintelligent intellectuals which
splashes about behind authors.

A seventeenth-century proverb likens critics to brushers
of noblemen's clothes. Too kind to both. Voltaire on the
shooting of Admiral Byng is better, if *auteur* replaces *amiral*,
thus: *Il est bon de tuer de temps en temps un auteur pour en-
courager les autres.*

What led me into authorship? *Led*, for God's sake! Why
are my eyes blue?

My aims in writing?

The aims are the simple enough ones of an innocent, aims
that are obversely simpler for my having been an innocent
at large, and gregariously underfoot, for over half-a-
century. Positively, they are (a) to placate the demon within, (b) to present what little I have experienced with what
seems to *me* direct clarity, and (c) to please myself, and such
fans as are willing to be pleased. Frisking my sleeve, I find

nothing else up it. On the negative side, there are some wildly unimportant aims. Chief of these is never to appeal to what is called the General Public, never to commit the fancy sin of writing a best-seller: acceptance by the *canaille* would shock me into self-examination, and much soul-searching, and trouble me that, in gaining a general public, I had not only lost a particular disease but had caught a sort of common cold, *very* common, very *common*. I don't want to please other people's fans: there are as many kinds of reading audiences as varieties of authors fitted to perform for them. No matter on which side of a book (novel, *belles lettres*, biography, pornography, what-you-will) one stands, writer or reader, we all have limitations. I am very limited.

I couldn't write — or read — a Western or Thriller or Romance, a Political Treatise or a Kitchen Sink Drama for all the beads in Bombay. Couldn't, not wouldn't. The machinery isn't there. I am, nevertheless, intrigued by those who can write or read what I can't, in the same way as I'm intrigued, and sometimes galvanized, by those who can do all the other things I can't do — drive a motor-car, swim the English Channel, make a model of Notre Dame in used matches, drink coffee or claret with any pleasure: the list is longer than the law's arm. As for even *watching* a funambulist or cliff-scaler, let alone . . . ! I am overcome with vertigo standing on the kitchen table to put in an electric-light bulb. A mental vertigo assails me, alas, when I try to scale what are to me the dizzy heights of many authors, Australian and foreign, it would be imprudent of me to name. These authors are for those with steadier heads, or sensibilities which differ from mine. Yes, I am very limited. So are my aims.

I never consciously think of these aims, negative or positive, and am now only fossicking for them because the funny, kind man asked me to. They must have been in the boxroom, otherwise they'd not have turned up, as they have, right here and now, and one person only can have put them there. How long ago is gone with the snows of yesteryear, but the fact that they were findable is disconcerting. What a shrewd, earnest, single-minded, self-contained, over-confident young whipper-snapper that one was! How easy to be a pace-setter, an aim-maker! As if he cared what happened to his later self!

Simple at first glance, and with the lid closed, the aim to write directly clearly makes an elegant ornament. Open that chaste lid, and Pandora's casket seems by comparison a mere Jack-in-the-Box. It's soon patent that the writer's fervent, high-falutin wish for an experience to get from him to the reader in simon-pure condition, and as though the experience has angelically magnetized to itself the most unimpeachable *mots justes*, the aptest, and therefore most pellucid and author-untainted, arrangements of words, hasn't a hope in hell of being easily granted. Authors, especially those working in English, *must* intrude, smearing the very glass they are trying to make transparent. Who said, "*Le style est l'homme même*"? Not a writer. A scientist, a Frenchman, a Count. Style is fingerprints. One doesn't start out after "style", at least a writer who isn't besotted with Pater or Hemingway or T. S. Eliot or Ian Fleming doesn't. Nevertheless, if one is trying to swim straight it's eternally a naughty night to swim in. This chatty revelation, for example, is being written, before being typed, in Sheaffer *Skrip* by an Esterbrook pen held between the thumb and first two fingers of a right-handed, fifty-seven-year-old Australian (a Victorian, a *southern* Victorian), Church of England, conservative, sober, wary, half-educated (hence the Gallicisms), puritanical, anti-intellectual, *et cetera, et cetera*. All *that's* going to leave fingerprints even on a paragraph about the equivocal amours of an oyster. It could be being written by someone else with the same absurdly decorous aim, someone molly-duked, atheist, over-educated, young, leftist, Queensland-nurtured (*northern* Queensland), *et cetera*, using a plastic BiC that writes green. Neither of these characters needs intrude, I think, but it is — so far — impossible for me to conceive what would remain, a something gutted, filleted, lopped, without odour, tintless, and — surely? — if not dead and desiccated, dishonest. Whatever whosoever's aims are, and however secretly written the novella or sonnet, in ivory tower, or bed-sitter the size of a suburban lavatory, it ultimately takes to the highway.

It is then that Burns's "cut-throat bandits in the paths of fame", and Wainewright's "reputation's blowflies" come out of the undergrowth. Sonnet, novella, whatever, the writing *per se* is not the enticement. It is the footstep of the author himself, the smell of the creature. He should, of course, keep off the highway. What good his aims now, poor reeking, loud-footed, solitary wayfarer?

Getting right down to tintacks, and where at least one aim almost impossible to accomplish lies a little trodden under, I should prefer not to have to take money for what I write. How lyrical to take dollars for a lyric! I do it, of course, and for as much as I can wheedle or brutally demand from those in collusion with authors on this or that plane of the many-planed publishing racket. Be pleased to believe that, as I do it, there is a strong feeling of being someone else somewhere else, someone displaying incurable sores or leprosy-pruned fingers, and whining, "Baksheesh! Baksheesh!"

Writing is, in the final count, like virtue, its own reward. Writing like virtue, is an expensive plight, and nowadays there seem few patrons of either virtue or writing. So one hitch-hikes.

Since one must hitch-hike, manuscript in valise, towards the little town of people imagined to be waiting, it seems to me that the hitch-hiking, the thumbing a publisher, the begging and bartering should be done, *must* be done, solo. I've nothing but disdain for writers who band together to hire a charabanc (Society of This, Fellowship of the Other), and set out with banners flapping on a trade union picnic-cum-scavenger-hunt, and a beaut donnybrook laced with the thin squeals of "Authors' Rights! Authors' Rights!" I mean, naturally, disdain for such authors' *motives*. Personally, I find Australian authors as *human beings* almost without exception trustworthy and lovable. I'll dine, pub-crawl, bicker, and sleep with them, exchange social lies and excruciating truths, dandle their babies, and help dry their wives' or husbands' tears or Noritake dinner-plates.

I'll not let them convince me that writing *for* money rather than writing, and then being paid, is morally proper, nor that writing, like self-exposure, is not its own reward.

My preoccupations in writing?

Leery though I am of Greeks, Sophocles sums up my preoccupations effectively enough for this paragraph to go no
longer than:

Πολλὰ τὰ δεινὰ κοὐδὲν ἀνθρώπου δεινότερον πέλει.

It means, roughly: Many wonders, and none of them more
wonderful than man.

Man means men, women, and children, and their cats
and cattle and catastrophes, superb slums and bashed-up
abbeys, gardens and bomb-droppings, off-moments and
on-moments, glamorous vices and threadbare virtues,
blood-chilling nobilities and heart-warming blunders, their
charm and wickedness, their unending variety and fatiguing
sameness, their alarming depth and their more alarming
shallowness.

This basic preoccupation branches off into smaller and
smaller ones, and I suppose that, if I were to be handsomely
paid to do a stint of lens-eyed research on the well-over-a-
million words I've had published, a list of the ever-chang-
ing minor preoccupations of 1937, 1941, 1946, 1953,
1959, 1962, 1968 could be drawn up for the entertainment of beetle-browed students and the Maigret-minded.
Off-hand, I should think there would not be any particularly persisting or predominating ones. What would doubtless show would be my limitations, the bars of the cage.

There are, for example, works set in Rome, London,
Athens, Venice, Tokyo, even in early-nineteenth-century
Hobart (a play and a novel set in this charmingly sinister
little city) but, by and large, it would be evident that I am,
as many Australian writers are, regional — more than that,
parish-bound, and almost pastoral. I know almost nothing
about suburbia, much more about London and San Fran-
cisco than about Double Bay or Camberwell, North
Adelaide or Subiaco. Brought up in the southern Victorian
countryside, I love it more than any place on earth: love en-
sures preoccupation. Much of the rest of Australia so
fashionable with dealers' tame artists, and Pioneer Bus
tourists, brings on severe *ennui*. I don't loathe the bush, the
outback, the never-never, call it what you will, as a city-
slicker like Henry Lawson did, and have skipped happily

enough over most of these pretty deadly areas, as well as into and out of all of the capital cities and a lot of the provincial ones: "skipped" and "into and out" indicate a flourishing distaste for enormous tracts of a country which, perversely, I love the abstract whole of to the point of "core of my heart" nationalism. In poems and short stories especially there is probably, if I checked, a wide ribbon threaded of lush green grass, hawthorn hedges, buttercups, oak avenues, weeping willows, and the whip-like flick of Antarctic winds — that's the regional thing, the visual fillip, and as limiting as any love is.

Another restricting factor is lack of imagination: pure fiction, and flights of fancy are utterly beyond me. As a result another preoccupation is necessary. This is with the mechanics of transmuting actual personal experience, or the witnessed experiences of others, into what reads (I pray!) like true-to-life fiction. No character or landscape or sailors' dive or rococo event has not been put down as such, or not been winkled from its original place in the jigsaw of time and space to be refitted, *slightly* trimmed, into its new pozzie in a book-sized book, a short-story-sized short story, or a poem-shaped poem. Because one has to (I, imaginationless, *have* to) pick up a Whole Idea which needs only to be written down, most of the time extraordinarily little change is made. Many characters, settings, and situations, already tied up in a "plot", are filched, holus-bolus, with the insolence of a shoplifter, straight out of "life". Here, a strange and maddening thing occurs. Apparently not accepting, as I with my imperfections must accept, that undiluted fact is far more *outré* than unalloyed fiction, reviewers and thesis-writers, infallibly imperceptient, castigate as fictional and contrived what is tantamount to reportage, and could be libellous if any of the characters should rise from the dead and read or, if living, could read. Among the stories, which "really happened", presumed to be Figments of the Imagination are: "Great-aunt Fanny's Picnic", "Vulgar's the Word", "Say to me Ronald", "Little Old Lady Passing By", "Boy Meets Girl", "The Letter Writer", "The Two Bachelors", "Waterfront", "Miss Brockel", "At the Galahad", "In Shadow Valley", "Uncle Foss and Big Bogga", "Miss Rodda", "Mr Butterfry", "The Two

Baronesses", and "The Cuckoo". Really happened — I was
there, snooping, or involved, to get the bricks of fact. Any
mortar of guesswork was minimal. Here and there, some
unwriterlike delicacy stirred me to alter a name. The
delicacy was demi-delicate — Miss Brockelbank to Miss
Brockel, Miss Rodger to Miss Rodda, Mr Bets to Mr Steb!
More often (Lack of Imagination leads to Lack of Fear) I
have used actual names — Ronald Wee Soon Wat, La,
Bruno Redmond-Jones, Big Bogga, Uncle Foss, Aunt Rosa
Bona, Uncle Martini-Henry, Mrs Irene Brewer, Francis
Silver. One can't make up names like that. People grow into
their names: it's a reckless writer who doesn't, in search of a
moniker for his created monster, riffle through old diction-
aries, haunt cemeteries, read bound copies of bygone newspapers, until the only name possible turns up. Characters in
books have no time to grow into their names. Statements
such as these reveal another preoccupation: getting the
details right. For me an anachronism mars all. An author
should not have *these* sorts of holes in his socks. Let him be
dirty-minded, sentimental, cynical, turgid, maudlin,
baroque, sinister, or as brutal as J. M. Barrie, but let him not
have Lalique in eighteenth-century drawing-room cabinets,
1957 Australian children saying, "Bonzer!", or upper-crust
Australians using soup-spoons, and no vegetable tureens.

In more intense forms of writing — the short story, for
instance — effects must be made quickly, and often on
many planes in immediately sequent sentences. Even if one
splurge or over-express, one dares not falter on minutiae:
dress, vehicles, customs, moral quirks, peculiar snobberies,
atmospheric tone, and — above all — conversation. Unsur-
passed at it among the moderns are J. D. Salinger, Elizabeth
Bowen, Elizabeth Taylor, Edna O'Brien, and Graham
Greene — whether they are "good" or "bad" writers otherwise is beside the point. Australian authors are the worst in
Christendom at written conversation. To write down what
is literally heard, to tape-record as it were in writing is to
miss the point: the eye does not hear. The reader has to be
tricked with a selection of words which *look* like what is
supposed to be *heard*. Acquiring the necessary illusionist's
skill, a difficult one to acquire but once acquired (like the art

of riding a bicycle no hands) easy, has been another of my preoccupations.

Certainly, at the present time, my main preoccupation is with Australians themselves. The problem of getting them down on paper with unequivocal distinctness, warts and haloes, faults and powers, is a very stiff one I haven't yet the ability to begin to solve. Australians have, over and above the common-factor equipment of all other human beings, a new and surprisingly complex quality. In less than two hundred years — it is not 1988 yet — a unique being has come on the globe. After six circlings of the globe I am just starting to see how a writer can deal with the task of portrayal. That, as a violently Australian Australian myself, I am too fully aware of this generalized being's nature, makes the task not easier but much more difficult. One day I hope to be able to put down, no holds barred, neither love nor kicks spared, this exhilarating, irritating, infinitely subtle, shrewd, wise, civilized, and dangerous creature.

Meantime, to this accelerating preoccupation with Australians my preoccupation with Man must take a back seat.

Which work of mine do I especially value?

Ultimately, I think, none more than another, and if more very little more. Anyway, one values different works differently at different times, and never always because it has been lauded by big-wig critics (some Beaujolais-bibbing, Oxford and Fleet Street homo, or dandruffy, spherical Geordie playing Dr Johnson at the Wig and Pen Club); has won a prize (what *were* the judges' qualifications?); or has come out of the creative oven cooked to a turn. Often, one values too much a piece in which one alone knows what apparently insurmountable difficulties have been overcome without leaving a drop of sweat to show. Or fools oneself into valuing something because of its nostalgic scent. Or because an emotion of agony or ecstasy has been burnt out of one while the piece was being dashed on to paper. As a rule, however, once an author's literary child is out of the womb, and briskly trundled off to the orphanage of a publishing house, one does not profoundly care if one never sees the brat again, although one retains a feeling for it, as for all one's children — quarter-relief, quarter-loss, quarter-affection, quarter-self-satisfaction — an impure feeling without a name. Howsoever easy the labour, there does remain a scar of sorts and, years later maybe, it itches in a region of the mind beyond reasonable explanation. One might, at such time, be startled by or dismayed at the memory of what one has produced. One might even, in a mood of tenderness with oneself, echo Jonathan Swift talking of *The Tale of a Tub* in his later years: "Good God, what a genius I had . . . !" If wise, one is not rash enough to re-read — the risk of disillusion is too great. Better to let the value of the offspring remain in memory as it was when one callously sold it down the river.

There is one work of mine I've not opened since it came out years ago which I value a shade more than all others, though quite without objectivity. This is *The Tilted Cross*. I esteem it for a number of reasons having nix-nought-nothing to do with its "literary merit", if any: (a) Thomas Griffiths Wainewright, the central character, fascinates me; (b) the research in London, Hobart, the British Museum, and nineteenth-century prisons (actual) led me metaphorically and literally up many strange alleys; (c) the necessity to discover, in the flesh, characters who could be transposed without loss of quality and reality to convict Hobart in the 1840s led me up stranger than strange real alleys into the still-Dickensian London underworld of pickpockets, ponces, professional perverts, and old lags, and taught me so much more of human nature than was needed for one novel that, from the material left over, I was able to treadle up a play, *The Tower*.

Even had I possessed "imagination", the novel — based on the Van Diemen's Land doings of a notorious and once-living man, whose every portrayed thought and spoken sentence were in his own words — was no place for it. A facsimile of reality was my intention. Not having been alive in the 1840s, in Hobart Town or elsewhere, I had to fit together a jigsaw of facts left behind by those who were alive then. There was much midnight-oil-burning for me to do. I loved the chore, and pored happily through books, prison records, Mayhew, disintegrating newspapers and pamphlets, memoirs and diaries in search of the period's most spot-on appropriate costumes, furnishings, slang, legal procedure, surgical technique, smells, background noises, vices, affectations, and so on. I chose an actual Sandy Bay house, *Ashfield* for the Sandy Bay *Cindermead* of the book, and alive-and-kicking people of 1960 (the year the book was written) as models for my 1847 characters. To find precision-fitting names for them I sieved hundreds of the time, and came up with ones I could never have magicked out of nothing: Queely Sheill, John Death Sheill, Mr Creamly, Asnetha Sleep, Pretty Dick (no, that was a 1960, London underworld one that was not amiss), Tidswell Green, Orfée Maka, Polidorio Smith, and Rose Hartnell.

The original of Polidorio Smith turned up in a seedy but amusing, spiv-haunted club called *Chez Alicia* in Westbourne Grove, W2, London, not far from Portobello Road, and with Wormwood Scrubs appropriately looming in the west. His dance, the incident of Pretty Dick, and many elements of his personality are gospel-true. I had little to do but change his present-day language and dress, not his temperament or tone of thinking or way of life. The model for Queely Sheill, a cockney of impressive nobility of outlook, still lives in London. The crippled Asnetha, Teapot the black boy, John Death Sheill, and even the minor characters, are all based on living people provided, as Polidorio and Queely were, with the trappings and accents of the era.

Doubtless my affection for *The Tilted Cross* stems from the pleasure got from working on it. Perhaps it is not, as I feel, "better" than works for which I am praised far more. An author is as inept a judge of his child as the publisher who adopts it, and the public and the reviewers who flatter or denigrate it, but I do value it a little more, even, somewhat immodestly, for reasons not given here. This valuation is a fresh one. I haven't opened the book since 1961 and though, in this case, I shouldn't really mind reading it to see what I was really up to, am either too wary and wise or too conceited and cowardly to do so.

Commentary on Thomas Keneally as Novelist

Since his first novel, *The Place at Whitton*, Thomas Keneally has been responsible for five other published novels, three or more plays, and at least one abandoned novel about an Australian writer caught up with Sydney peace-marchers and political larrikins. Of this work, Keneally said in 1968, "I don't know which way to turn." In a sense this remark sums up a certain quality pervading much of his published work. The abundance of this, in less than a decade, would appear to make him successful, publisher-esteemed, prize-winning, and what is known on dust-jacket blurbs as "a prolific writer", that is, by and large, the sort of writer of whom the sharp-minded and fastidious reader needs must be wary even though the writer be a Dickens or a Balzac. In Keneally's case wariness is particularly justified. He is a quick-change artist of undoubted skill, presents a wide range of unusual and impressionistically drawn settings occupied by unusual and guilt-ridden people, is generally an alert entertainer, and dabbles earnestly or mischievously with problems of "conscience", the sentimental, limited, and up-to-the-minute conscienceless "conscience" of present-day trouble-makers. The observer finds himself backing towards wariness because he is compelled, in book after book, to be conscious of some lack, some so-to-speak vitamin deficiency, in Keneally's writing. No matter how engaging the felicities they are gap-toothed. Precisely what the lack is is difficult to define. It's not talent, it may be heart; it's not ingenuity, though it could be taste; it's not education, but perhaps percipience or clarity of vision; it's not fact or organized fantasy, both of which he juggles with, yet could be truth.

What adds to the observer's uneasiness, and is disconcerting, is to discover, in each successive novel, that the author has not advanced, is merely making an almost wilfully self-conscious break in yet another direction, is starting to wander off into a different sort of formlessness, to reveal a new brand of sloppiness in technique, to invest in other arrangements of clichés, to blur what seems a highly romanticized realism with a coating of symbolism. Perhaps these are the results of Keneally's never working out a detailed plot before starting to write. Perhaps they are the indirect outcome of a deeply embedded uncertainty, a quasi-fecklessness. Keneally is a Roman Catholic priest *manqué*. This fact would not be worth the recording if the hang-over did not patently, and constantly, infect his work — incertitudes both of vision and technique keep on cropping up.

Since Keneally brazenly confesses to being worried whether "the conventional novel has had it", and to wondering publicly if he should "cast off into a sea of pure fantasy" and "move forward into surrealism", it is scarcely surprising that, despite certain titillating qualities, and an engagement with fashionable (and, therefore not-to-be-trusted) "moral" issues, most of his novels are neither flesh, fowl, nor good red herring. Most, not all: *Three Cheers for the Paraclete*, a brisk and comic chess game of a book, seems more planned. Each move in the game is clear-cut; the prose so well fulfils its purpose that the actors in the comedy take on the semblance of flesh-and-blood creatures howsoever actorish and word-perfect, howsoever adroit with the brilliant riposte and superb exit line.

Usually, however, Keneally is not so deft. Many of his characters are inclined to blur not only at the edges but at the core, are literary hippogriffs neither convincingly human nor assuredly symbolic. Indeed, in his latest novel, *A Dutiful Daughter*, he has cast off into a sea of fantasy (impure rather than pure), and manufactured two symbolic freaks. The dutiful daughter's parents turn, minotaur-like, into half-bull and half-cow, and become victims of their sinister, perverted, part-insane, Joan-of-Arc-haunted monster of a child. Keneally's machinery for dealing with such a grotesque situation is ill-chosen, and handled amateurishly

— the product is his most aggressive failure as an artist. Embellishments to the situation (incest, perversion, bestiality, a triple suicide) are dealt with in the coarsely gen-teel manner which is the one ear-mark of Keneally's style which is otherwise so unjelled that he could be said to have little style at all.

Patrick White's influence is responsible for earlier affectations, for images patently injected, like borrowed penicillin, into the Keneally main-stream. Later admitted influences, Angus Wilson and Evelyn Waugh, are less vis-ible. Waugh is, indeed, quite invisible as an influence, is — surely? — too civilized and exquisitely controlled an artist for the hearty, unsophisticated, texturally coarse, and "conscience"-shackled Keneally to catch. Even Wilson's garrulity has more edge than the present Keneally can use.

Having produced in less than ten years a substantial number of printed pages, Keneally stands today on the danger line most young and fecund writers reach. If it be disturbing that, so far, he has shown few signs of maturity, it may be that it is really too early to expect more. His own stated indecision about what a novel is (or, rather, what a Keneally novel should be) tempts one to hope that a con-scious doubting will give way, as such a doubt should, to the assurance an active and gifted writer must have if he seek the immortality Keneally acknowledges he is in pursuit of.

Interview with Hal Porter[1]

ML: The first question I'm going to ask you is how satisfied you are with your work — how you assess it.

HP: Very satisfied, particularly with certain pieces, because, always realizing my limitations, I have accomplished within those limitations exactly what I could at that stage of the game. This goes for many of the short stories, some of the poems, a couple of the plays. Whatever powers I had at the time, I did the best with them. I couldn't do any more, so therefore I'm satisfied.

ML: What, in your opinion, is your least satisfactory work, and why?

HP: My least satisfactory work I would say is (counting out my first novel, *A Handful of Pennies*, which has only the obvious, run-of-the-mill imperfections) a book that should have been better because I had enough technique, I had enough information. *The Right Thing* was partly written under interruption so I wasn't able to see clearly what I was doing. I was old enough in the game for it to have been better. Other people's problems caused a certain amount of darting about, and the pattern of steady writing was broken, though I kept on coming back to it. There were, in the end, flashes of very good writing and some quite ghastly bits because I wasn't able to hang on. So I think *that* — and a couple of rather cheap short stories I've done for the *Bulletin*, and a not very good one I once did for Kylie Tennant,[2] are my least successful. I can't pick out which are the best short stories — the ultimate best — but I can pick out the ones which were obligatory things, so I would say about four short stories are conspicuously bad and the thing that satisfies me least is *The Right Thing*.

ML: What do you regard as your most serious work?

HP: I would say my most serious work really has been the best of the short stories. The connection between them makes them a serious work as a whole. *The Tilted Cross* is probably the best enclosed work, but if you were to string together a dozen of the short stories I would say they are my best contribution so far to Aust. Lit.

ML: What do you think of your reception by the critics?

HP: All things considered, pretty good, pretty good. I don't expect all of them to completely understand what I'm after. Indeed, a lot of them haven't the faintest idea, but, in general, I have been far less savaged than I could have been over the years. There are critics who have been following me around (although some of them have gone to their Maker now) since the late thirties and even before that. There are here and there fools, who are jealous or absurd; but there are a few of them, like Geering, I trust, like Leonie Kramer. I think I've had, considering what I was doing, pretty good treatment.

ML: What do you enjoy writing most?

HP: Short stories. Possibly I might enjoy trying myself out on writing *novelle* but I would love to have the time — I would most enjoy being able to write superb poetry. I haven't time for that.

ML: What do you think of other Australian short story writers?

HP: Well I don't read many of them. Now and again I have read some superb ones but most of the good work seems to me to have been done in the past. I haven't kept in touch. The last batch of Australian short stories I read was in 1970 for that book, *It Could Be You*,[3] and that's the last solid reading. Now and again I've read one in a *Quadrant* or something, and I frankly don't think there are any young ones about. You mean modern ones don't you — I mean you don't mean Australian short story writers in general, right from the start?

ML: No, I mean the ones who are writing at the present time.

HP: Well I'm not enough in touch, dear — not since 1970.

ML: What makes you think that some experiences will make a short story?

HP: I don't really know. If I'm writing a short story I've obviously accidentally somewhere along the line got some sort of pattern stuck in my mind. When I was a kid at school and William Fearn-Wannan was the English teacher, he introduced me to the first *real* short stories I ever read . . . Mansfield particularly. She did affect me deeply. So it means a pattern has been set by reading when I was a boy — the stories of Maupassant and, since they were easy to read, the "O Henry" stories, and then Mansfield, and then on to Chekhov. From them I've picked up hints about what makes a good short story. The first "real" short story I wrote was the first one I had published in the *Bulletin*[4]. I think I Chekhoved about someone wanting to escape from the city to the country and finally finishing up knowing that neither was good . . . . I've forgotten the name of it, "Holiday" or something, I can't quite recall, but I had got over my first period when the stories were about non-existent people — duchesses, countesses — unreal people.

Now most of the short stories *happen*. To me the perfect example of that — I don't mean it's a perfect short story — was "Brett"[5]. Did you read "Brett"? That was dead true. I had been with Jean Dyce at Milan, and we were on the train, and the girl did pop in, and it was all happening. As I was sitting there, and she opposite, I was thinking "Oh, how beautiful, beautiful, beautiful, but I don't know the punchline" and the girl did that herself. This, in most cases, happens with what I write about. You have to prove what has occurred to you. Why did I pick *That* out rather than *Something Else*? Probably one picks out something finished, that is there, that forms itself before you get into the business of being the intermediary between other people's (or your own) experiences, and the reader waiting to read them. Other writers taught me to select. Chekhov dealt with people. Mansfield dealt with people. For them people were the central point, and something would happen. You've got to surround the person with all the snippets from other people; and you have to prove a point. You have to get somewhere. I usually work towards a punch-line and although I know what it's going to be I never know what I'm going to write *about* the punch-line. I know where it is, I know where Z is, *exactly* where Z is. The end of that story about the little boy in love with the photograph — "First Love"[6] — when I got to the end I didn't know what I should say but found out when I got there. To make the punch-line — there's no skill or art — this is being a writer — I wrote "and I something and something and something — and my heart broke". Those are the things I knew I had to reveal. It was all true, but it wasn't true the way "Brett" was. Perhaps stories like "First Love" are better. I don't know.

ML: Presumably, what is revealed to you when you see the short story in life, or in your head, is revealed to the reader of the story.

HP: Oh, this is the kinky bit about writers: they are talking to themselves, but to have a thing published, they have to talk to the other people too. I think I really should have been a poet, but while I've written five or six heavenly poems, that's about all. Much of the poetry goes into the short stories, if you watch carefully, in the mood, in the arrangement of words. At least that's the way I see it.

ML: Why do you think you have been less successful as a novelist than in any of the other literary forms you have tried?

HP: Because I need a framework and a novel isn't a close enough cage. I work better in a cage. I'm a performing monkey — when I'm *not* running up to the top of the tree and disappearing out of sight. I'm better when I'm confined, so that is probably the reason. The novel gives a chance to waffle on — I waffle, I indulge. To keep within the frame of a short story — if you've *got* to indulge yourself — you've got to be pretty bloody good at indulging, say, in two sentences instead of three enormous paragraphs or several pages, as in a novel.

ML: This raises the question about autobiography, specially *The Watcher*. You have an unlimited space to play with. There's no set form for autobiography.

HP: In an autobiography I'm restricted in another way. I'm restricted by keeping to the facts as much as I can. I don't mind the restriction of facts.

ML: But also you can be as self-indulgent as you like.

HP: Yes, but there is the odd occasion when you have to

be pretty factual. Facts, or as far as I see them as facts, are a restriction too, inside the form.

ML: In the writing that you are proposing to do in future, are you thinking of experimenting with style or with form or with content?

HP: Well, they all tie up together. I'll be carrying on the experimental things I started doing in *Fredo Fuss Love Life*. One of the stories which is probably better than I thought it was, was called "The Other Woman". Now *there* were nice little experimental bits although it was a bad short story. The one about the goat in the town:[7] there were some good bits of experiment.

ML: What are your ambitions as a writer?

HP: Very limited. The ultimate thing I want to write (from the terrifying limitations I have) is something about Australians, more than Australia. Australia fascinates me completely and I want to make a contribution to posterity. It makes it more difficult as one gets older (because more things are crowded in and the field of selectivity is wider) to pick out the things that make the point. There were fewer people and fewer incidents and so on when I was younger, therefore it was easier to pick out. At this stage of the game I do want to pick out what makes Australians as they are *now*, particularly the way in which Australians can get right through to each other in all sorts of certain ways — and this is very, very, *very* hard to write, shockingly hard to write.

ML: But is this why you persist in writing when you might have stopped, say?

HP: I can't stop. I wouldn't be happy if I weren't writing. I wouldn't know what to do.

ML: Why do you think that you write mainly about Australian women and hardly at all about Australian men?

HP: Because Australian men are rather harder to write about. Because I haven't had the revelation.

ML: Well, I don't think it would be a distortion to suggest that you take an attitude of objectivity and detachment probably to the point of satire in a great many of the stories that you write. Do you think that you are unable to take that kind of attitude in relation to men?

HP: No. I can get through to *men* almost instantly. About the Australian male *character* — look at what has been done by writers before me — the Lawson tradition or the *Bulletin* tradition or the Dad and Dave tradition or the ocker tradition. What has been put down about Australian men, by and large, is fairly one-dimensional. There are things I could say but, supposing I wanted to explain the deep bond between Les Tanner and me, I would be hard put to it. I can't put down my affection of another sort with Mal Walden or Kev Cullen. Now here are three Aussies — I'm speaking of three that you know — and with each of them my relationship is different.

ML: And this doesn't happen with women?

HP: No, with women, the relationship is — I am — always the same. Women see through me so it's quite pointless having to do anything else about it. I don't mean women are easy — God! — but they are more transparent. The relationship I have with them is more transparent. — I know *too* bloody much about men. I know *sufficient* about women. I'll never know everything about women; any man knows that; you simply don't. You learn a great deal from your mother without her particularly teaching you. You can pick up the lies, you can pick up the enchantment, you can pick up the agony. Christ knows what you hear when you're a babe all curled up like some prawn, the lodger in the basement. Oh I'll do it sometime. I'll make a male character sometime. I'd love to, but there isn't a sort of summation in Australian man yet for me.

ML: Do you think you have a theme running through your work?

HP: No, I would think not. The possibility is that in the final terms I do believe in people. Even if I say dreadful things about them they usually survive it. How can I sum it up? Looking at the old girl in "First Love": she's had it, but she's still got the young man; she's still optimistic although drowned in grog. I don't do that awful yearning Chekhov did. You *know* the three sisters will never get to Moscow; and in *The Cherry Orchard* you can hear the axes chopping down, chopping down. No, I *am* optimistic. I think that might be a bit of a theme. Any political theme, anything I say (I'm anti-communist and anti-academic) never appears in a short story or novel. Autobiography, yes. I'm surely entitled *there* to state these silly little things, as I do at parties. In general I don't make *any* comment unless it is in the mind or the mouth of the character.

ML: Does this mean that your characters don't express your point of view ever or that you don't identify with them?

HP: No, no, no. Even the times where there's a sort of Hal Pal air you usually find if I put an "I" in, it obviously isn't me — I make him pretty invisible, even if he's got to be cynical and *dégagé*. I think I even once called him a "brown dog" in a story, a long, long time ago. In some there will be tiny bits of me, you can't avoid that, but they'd be *very* tiny bits. The "I" is usually the sort of person I want for a special reason.

ML: Technically you mean?

HP: Precisely, yes, yes. In almost every case as a technical device. If he is actually me, I make me practically invisible except as the recorder.

ML: Do you think your writing is distinctive, easily distinguishable — say from the writing of other Australian short story writers or Australian writers generally?

HP: Hard for me to judge, but I think it might be. I suppose it is possible. Through the years, I think there are Porter touches here and there which would make it distinct from — here I don't know enough — certainly distinct from Frank Moorhouse, from Frank Dalby Davison. I'm trying to think of short stories — certainly distinct from Lawson, certainly distinct from Ethel Anderson, from Norman Lindsay. I would not say all the time, but there were obviously Porter mannerisms or *something*. I might be able to define it if I had to write a thesis on myself: I'd be as detached as anything.

ML: Is there anything in the way you picture experience which leads you to decide that this should be a short story and not a play or not a novel or not a poem?

HP: Oh, the old-fashioned thing. I can't get away from the fact that the best short stories I've ever read are in a certain form — even the best novels I've read are in a certain form. Some of my ideas for novels have gone into plays. *The Professor* was first an idea for a novel. *The Tower* one wasn't quite one — that was a play. *Eden House* — that was an idea for a novel. What I mean is *Eden House* could be a novel. So there have been novels I have given away because I preferred — oh because, anyway, plays take a shorter time to write. Plays take two or three weeks, a month at the most, whereas a novel — all those words — five months, six months. I haven't time, I haven't that sort of time. I would only have time to write a novel if I were so obsessed by the topic, had thought myself into a novel of a certain sort, had researched, got all the information, and could stay within the form. Usually there's somewhere along the line where you think, "That's a good short story". This is because this material, this experience, has all the feeling, all the taste and flavour, no restriction needed, of a short story. This other stuff, this novel thing, you've got all these people crowding about and carrying on. It's not a form for me, unless something, some situation makes me think, "Oh well, these people *are* for a novel, and this house, or this situation *is* for a novel", then I could do it.

ML: I wanted to ask you a question about editors. In the note you wrote as a preface to *The Bachelor's Children* I think it was, you made it very clear that you think they have a considerable influence on public taste, or what is exposed to public taste, but what I wanted to ask you was, how influential, or how important are they, to writers?

HP: Well, the only thing I can say in my own experience, it was Ron McCuaig who gave me the great lift over. It just happened that the editors of the "Red Page", some names I've completely forgotten, turned me down. I think Douglas Stewart did publish my first short story, called "Holiday" in 1937, but then he turned down the one that won the Sydney competition; this was called "Waterfront".[8] I thought "This is editors". I wasn't fazed even then about that sort of thing, and thought "Well, O.K., to hell with him". The years passed and the next short story I had published was in 1954 or '55. All those years I had still gone on writing short stories. There had been little things published in Adelaide, but that was sheer nonsense. There had been a brilliant one or two published in magazines called *Phoenix* and *Flame*. Norman Lindsay was going to take me up in *The Australian Mercury*, but there was never a second issue. It didn't faze me. When dear Ron McCuaig thought he'd discovered me again, I only had to reach into my bottom drawer and there were old ones, more recent ones, and new ones as well. There were Hal Porter stories week after week in the *Bulletin*. Slessor was now and again doing a Hal story. It was McCuaig who was important to me as an editor. He knew what I was about because I knew what he had been about in some of his poems. That "Sydney on a Saturday Night" poem — I can't read without breaking down. He knew what I was up to. Editors with the ability to select rather than being an editor crossing out words, they are important.

ML: What about the editors who cross out words, the ones who don't like this or that in your writing?

HP: I've only had two bits of that. Any cuts I've had have been with my permission. One without my permission — the man in *A Handful of Pennies*. I'd put "as he entered her" and Nan McDonald changed it to "as he took her". Fuckin' silly — took her where? Other things are the practicalities of the book, when you are, say, twenty words over and the book therefore needs pruning to avoid another batch of eight pages. I either do it myself, or if I *trust* the editor *completely*, say "Oh well, O.K. mate, chop out some of those, or do you want me to do it for you?" This is only the editing of practical use. I would never let an editor touch what really made a point. Some of them are so silly they'd cut out the one operative sentence, the key.

ML: I'm going to ask the last question and it's just a very general one. Do you see any major changes occurring generally in the Australian literary scene in your time?

HP: Yes, but not terribly major ones. Remember I was only born in 1911. There was pre-Great War stuff. Of War stuff there was none. There was very little World War Two either. In between there was a great deal, almost too much of that Depression stuff. Now, it's boring and terribly sentimental. There haven't been enough influences to make important changes. Australia has never experienced a complete cataclysm. Perhaps the most important thing is that Australians are now able to write more about what is actually going on today than they formerly did. Vance Palmer didn't really write about what was going on. He was writing about what he *thought* was going on. He couldn't quite get to *Australia*. Eve Langley had to scamper about the countryside and live with pea-pickers and feel it intensely to be able to write what was really happening. She made changes. Eleanor Dark got pretty near, and Ken McKenzie in *The Young Desire It*, Tom Hungerford with *The Ridge and the River*. *That* sort of change: the idea that there *is* something here to write about apart from the bloody bush. I don't think it's produced a great deal. When I think of the famous ones now like Thomas Keneally — Christ knows what he's writing about now, he's gone back to Joan of Arc or trains in World War I, which even *I* wouldn't do. And I don't know what Patrick White is up to at the moment. Maybe I've missed some of the big ones coming out, but I haven't read enough of them; I don't know what they are.

Notes

1. This interview is based on two interviews Mary Lord conducted in July 1977, in Melbourne, a published version of which appeared in *Australian Literary Studies* 8 (May 1979). The version printed in this Portable volume is a revision by Mr Porter of the *ALS* publication.
2. "I Wonder Who's Kissing Her Now", in *Summer's Tales II*, ed. Kylie Tennant (Melbourne: Macmillan, 1965).
3. Hal Porter, ed. (Adelaide: Rigby, 1972). An anthology of Australian short stories.
4. "Holiday", *Bulletin*, 5 May 1937, p.4.
5. *Fredo Fuss Love Life* (Sydney: Angus & Robertson, 1974), pp. 19-42.
6. *The Cats of Venice* (Sydney: Angus & Robertson, 1965), pp. 92-106.
7. "The Clairvoyant Goat", *Sun News Pictorial* (Melbourne), 13 January 1976, pp. 20,21.
8. Originally called "And, from Madame's". Winner of the short story section of the Sydney Sesquicentenary Literary Competition, 1938. Twenty years later it was published under the new title "Waterfront" in the *Bulletin*, 13 August 1958, pp. 34-35, 57, and was collected in *A Bachelor's Children* (Sydney: Angus & Robertson, 1962), pp. 21-29.

Select Bibliography

Works of Hal Porter

Novels

A Handful of Pennies. Sydney: Angus & Robertson, 1958.
The Tilted Cross. London: Faber & Faber, 1961. [Another edition, with Introduction by Adrian Mitchell, Adelaide: Rigby, 1971]
The Right Thing. Adelaide: Rigby, 1971.

Volumes of Short Stories

Short Stories. Adelaide: *Advertiser*, [1942].
A Bachelor's Children. Sydney: Angus & Robertson, 1962.
The Cats of Venice. Sydney: Angus & Robertson, 1965.
Mr Butterfry and other Tales of New Japan. Sydney: Angus & Robertson, 1970.
Selected Stories. Edited by Leonie Kramer, Sydney: Angus & Robertson, 1971.
Fredo Fuss Love Life. Sydney: Angus & Robertson, 1974.

Autobiography

The Watcher on the Cast-Iron Balcony. London: Faber & Faber, 1963.
The Paper Chase. Sydney: Angus & Robertson, 1966.
The Extra. Melbourne: Nelson, 1975.

Poetry

The Hexagon. Sydney: Angus & Robertson, 1956.
Elijah's Ravens. Sydney: Angus & Robertson, 1968.
In an Australian Country Graveyard. Melbourne: Nelson, 1974.

Plays

The Tower in *Three Australian Plays*. Introduction by H. G. Kippax, Harmondsworth: Penguin, 1963.
The Professor. London: Faber & Faber, 1966.
Eden House. Sydney: Angus & Robertson, 1969.

General

Stars of Australian Stage and Screen. Adelaide: Rigby, 1965.
The Actors: An Image of the New Japan. Sydney: Angus & Robertson, 1968.
Bairnsdale: Portrait of an Australian Country Town. Sydney: John Ferguson, 1977.

Anthologies

Australian Poetry 1957. Sydney: Angus & Robertson, 1957.
Coast to Coast: Australian Stories 1961-1962. Sydney: Angus & Robertson, 1962.
It Could Be You [short stories]. Adelaide: Rigby, 1972.

Selected Articles

"Reputation's Blowflies: or, Read any Good Books Lately". *Bulletin* (6 January 1962.) pp.21-22.
"Hal Porter's Australia: South Gippsland and its Towns" [written and illustrated by Hal Porter] *Australian Letters* 6 (September 1964) pp.22-50. Reprinted in *The Vital Decade*. Selected by G. Dutton & M. Harris, Melbourne: Sun Books, 1968, pp.162-91.
"Buttercup Country" [written and illustrated by Hal Porter] *Australian* (26 September 1964) p.11.
"Melbourne in the Thirties". *London Magazine* 5 (September 1965) pp.31-47.
"Post-War Japan". *Australians Abroad*. Edited by C. Higham & M. Wilding, Melbourne: Cheshire, 1967, pp.170-79.
"Answers to the Funny, Kind Man". *Southerly* 29 (1969) pp.3-14.
"Martin Boyd", "Thomas Keneally", "Patrick White", [and on his

own work]. *Contemporary Novelists*. Edited by James Vinson, London: St James Press, 1972.

"Gavin's Diary: An Unused Last Chapter of *The Right Thing*". *Southerly* 33 (1973) pp.355-63.

"Interview with Hal Porter". *Australian Literary Studies* 8 (1978) pp.269-79.

Bibliographies

Finch, Janette H. *Bibliography of Hal Porter*. Adelaide: Libraries Board of South Australia, 1966. [See also a review by M. Wilding. *Australian Literary Studies* 3 (1967) pp.142-48.]

Annual Supplement to the Finch bibliography appear under "Bibliographies of Australian Writers: Supplement", in *Index to Australian Book Reviews*, Adelaide, 1966- .

Lord, Mary. "A Contribution to the Bibliography of Hal Porter". *Australian Literary Studies* 4 (1970) pp.405-409.

Selected Criticism

Barnes, J. "New Tracks to Travel: the Stories of White, Porter and Cowan". *Meanjin Quarterly* 25 (1966) pp.154-70.

Burns, R. "A Sort of Triumph over Time: Hal Porter's Prose Narratives". *Meanjin Quarterly* 28 (1969) pp.19-28.

Cantrell, K. "Two Aspects of Hal Porter: 2. *The Professor*". *Southerly* 27 (1967) pp.185-87.

Duncan, R.A. "Hal Porter's Writing and the Impact of the Absurd". *Meanjin Quarterly* 29 (1970) pp.468-73.

Geering, R.G. "Hal Porter, The Watcher". *Southerly* 24 (1964) pp.92-103.

————. "Two Aspects of Hal Porter: 1. *The Paper Chase*". *Southerly* 27 (1967) pp.180-85.

————. "Hal Porter: The Controls of Melodrama". *Southerly* 33 (1973) pp.18-33.

————. "Hal Porter's Autobiography". *Southerly* 36 (1976) pp.123-33.

Kramer, Leonie. *Introduction to Hal Porter Selected Stories*. Sydney: A. & R., 1971.

Lord, M. "Hal Porter's Comic Mode". *Australian Literary Studies* 4 (1970) pp.371-82.

———— *Hal Porter*. Australian Writers and Their Work Series. Melbourne: O.U.P., 1974.

Rolfe, P. "The Middle Age of Innocence". *Bulletin* (14 December 1963) pp.35, 37.